AF257377

Using the Publish or Perish software

Crafting your career in academia

Anne-Wil Harzing

Edition: August 2023

ISBN 978-1-7394538-3-1 (paperback, black & white)

Published by Tarma Software Research Ltd, UK

Author	Harzing, Anne-Wil
Title	Using the Publish or Perish Software. Crafting your career in academia / Anne-Wil Harzing
Edition	1st ed.
ISBN	978-1-7394538-3-1 (paperback, black & white)
Subjects	Academic careers, academic publishing, academic development
Dewey Number	650.14

Table of contents

Detailed table of contents

Introduction

A few years after the Publish or Perish (PoP) software was launched, I wrote the Publish or Perish Book (2010), followed by the Publish or Perish Tutorial in 2016. Many of the use cases and examples in those two books are still valid. However, the Publish or Perish interface has changed a lot and dozens of new features have been added in the past decade. Moreover, these early books didn't discuss any data sources beyond Google Scholar. The current software provides an interface to no less than eight data sources. Hence, I have long felt it was time for an updated guide. However, writing such a guide takes up a huge amount of time, time not easily found in my busy academic life. So, it has taken me a bit longer than I had hoped; I hope the wait was worth it!

This guide provides a very comprehensive overview of all you need to know to make the most effective use of the PoP software. Don't get me wrong, the software is intuitive enough to use without reading its manual, Q&A, or even this guide. However, I still suggest you invest some time in learning more about its features. In this guide, you will get a detailed introduction to its interface, learning how to conduct, manage, import, and export your searches. I will also show how to export full references and abstracts, create a basic or detailed search report and search for free full text versions of the publication results. You will learn all about the metrics that PoP calculates and the eight data sources that the software interfaces with. The two most often used sources – Google Scholar and Google Scholar Profiles – are discussed in detail in separate chapters.

After reading this guide, you will know more about citation analysis than 99% of your academic colleagues. You will learn how to conduct author searches, journal searches, topic and affiliation searches, as well as how to use it for a wide variety of purposes, ranging from preparing tenure and promotion applications, conducting literature reviews and meta-analyses, deciding which journal to submit your paper to, preparing for job interviews, writing laudations/obituaries, finding reviewers, examiners or keynote speakers, preparing for a meeting with your academic hero, finding "citation connections" between scholars, doing bibliometric research and much much more.

A word of caution before we start. This guide provides lay users with an overview of how to use citation analysis in a more effective and responsible way. However, it is important to note that although high quality scholarship might be highly cited, citations are not in and of themselves a measure of quality. When assessing the quality of scholarship, there is no substitute for reading an academic's work. Further, whether using metrics for counting publications or citations, another crucial question that should always be asked is: "Has the scholar asked an important question and investigated it in such a way that it has the potential to advance societal understanding and well-being?" (see e.g., my 2009 article *When Knowledge Wins: Transcending the sense and nonsense of academic rankings* with Nancy Adler).

How Publish or Perish was born

Launched in October 2006, the Publish or Perish software will soon reach adulthood. But how and why did it come to life? As is so often the case with academic services, underlying its creation was a very personal need. Earlier in 2006 my application for promotion to full professor had been rejected because – according to the panel – I had not published enough in high impact Web of Science listed journals.

Working in the field International Business (IB), I found that – at least back in 2006 – very few of the journals I had published in were listed in the Web of Science. Those that *were* listed had low journal impact factors, largely because many of the journals that were citing them were not (yet) included in the Web of Science. This may have been partly caused by the fact that many IB journals were established in Europe. Their editors were not as concerned about rankings as those in the Anglophone world.

As a result, it was very difficult for an International Business scholar to convince a promotion panel that they had achieved just as much impact as academics working in the neighbouring disciplines of Economics and Psychology, or even Management. In these disciplines, a far higher proportion of academic journals was listed in the Web of Science.

When searching for my work in Google Scholar, my case immediately looked much brighter. It turned out my work was actually very highly cited and even my non-traditional publications such as books, book chapters, and a journal ranking list had a strong impact in terms of citations. Unfortunately, the Google Scholar interface didn't make it very easy to aggregate citation metrics in a form that could be compared across academics. Fortunately, I am blessed with an amazing partner – David Adams – who is not only a wonderful husband, but also a brilliant software engineer with a PhD in Operations Research and a good understanding of the world of academia. He offered to create a software programme for me. Thus, in October 2006 Publish or Perish was born.

Using the PoP software allowed me to make a stellar case for impact. I created a bibliometric comparison table with Google Scholar data, including the then very novel h-index (see below). As a compromise I also included the number of citing articles in the Web of Science. It showed my metrics outranked *all* professors in my field in Australia, all recently promoted professors in the Faculty, and many of the long-established professors. I was duly promoted to full professor in 2007. Ironically, the software programme itself is now my most-cited work.

Table 1: Bibliometric comparison with other professors, mean and range are given for each indicator.

Group	h-index	1st authored papers in h-index	Single-authored papers in h-index	Number of ISI citing articles (2006 only)	Number of years as professor
2005/2006 promotions	Mean: 6.3 Range: 4-8	Mean: 4.3 Range: 3-5	Mean: 3.0 Range: 2-4	Mean: 15 Range: 3-34	Recently appointed
IB professors at top Oz unis	Mean: 9.0 Range: 4-16	Mean: 3.3 Range: 1-6	Mean: 1.5 Range: 0-3	Mean: 10 Range: 3-21	15 years (4-28 years)
DoMM established professors	Mean: 14.0 Range: 6-22	Mean: 5.0 Range: 0-11	Mean: 2.0 Range: 0-4	Mean: 46 Range: 8-102	14 years (10-19 years)
Anne-Wil Harzing	13	13	10	63	N/A

The h-indices and citation levels in this table might appear very low by today's standards. That is because - with publications expanding at 10%/year - average citation levels have increased dramatically in the last 15 years.

It was also the start of a new "research hobby" for me, doing research in the field of bibliometrics. Since then, I have published about a dozen articles in journals such as *Scientometrics, Journal of Informetrics,* and *Journal of the Association for Information Science & Technology.* Most of these articles dealt with comparative coverage and the strengths and weaknesses of the different sources for citation data, problematic features of the Web of Science (see Chapter 4), or the introduction of new metrics (see Chapter 3).

Even before I put in my second application for promotion, however, I realised that Publish or Perish might not only be able to help *me*, but also many other academics in a similar situation. I therefore made Publish or Perish freely available on my website, www.harzing.com. Over the years, I have come to realise that PoP can be used for many more purposes than I initially envisaged. This guide documents its many and variable uses and shows you how to get the best out of the software program.

Publish or Perish is widely used

With Publish or Perish everyone with a computer and Internet access can run bibliometric searches. Not surprisingly, the software is used all over the world. It is used by individual academics and librarians in more than 160 countries from Australia to the USA, from Angola to Zimbabwe. It is also used by governments departments (e.g., US Dept of Energy, US Environmental Protection Agency, US Agency for International Development), grant giving agencies (e.g., SSHRC in Canada, CNRS in France) and research laboratories (e.g., Microsoft, Hewlett Packard, IBM).

It is gratifying to know that the software is widely used at highly ranked universities such as Harvard, Stanford, MIT, Oxford, and Cambridge, universities that have access to commercial alternatives. However, it is even more satisfying to see its equally high usage at under-resourced universities in countries like Armenia, Botswana, Mongolia, Paraguay, Tajikistan, Uruguay, and Venezuela. There are over two thousand libraries worldwide that list the software as a free alternative to Scopus and the Web of Science. Publish or Perish clearly fills a need!

> *I live in a very poor country [Venezuela]. It not possible for me to pay WOS or any other bibliographic service. In that sense, PoP has been a huge help and relief. I really thank you for this extraordinary program. You are making our academic lives in economically depressed countries much easier.*

It costs money to keep software free

These days desktop software programmes and apps are often free. However, free software doesn't materialise out of thin air. *Someone* needs to create, maintain, and support it. That costs money. This might not an issue for commercial giants with deep pockets such as Google and Meta, but it is for individuals like me. Therefore, your contribution towards our costs of hosting, bandwidth, and software development is very much appreciated. If you find the Publish or Perish software useful, then this is your chance to say "thank you" to the developers. There are several ways in which you can support us:

1. If you have borrowed this guide from someone else, consider buying your own copy.
2. If you have already bought this guide, consider suggesting it to someone else. Maybe you even want to suggest to your library or Research Dean that they buy multiple copies?
3. Buy other books in my "Crafting your career in academia" series: *Publishing in academic journals*, *Writing successful promotion applications*, *Creating social media profiles*, and *Measuring and improving research impact*. They only cost £5.95 (Kindle) or £9.95 (pbk).
4. Suggest your (Research) Dean they buy a stack of these books to distribute to staff. They make perfect presents to accompany a push for staff to become more effective in any of these areas.
5. Honour us with a (small) donation. For details see: https://harzing.com/resources/publish-or-perish/donation.

Our philosophy

Publish or Perish is software made *for* academics *by* academics. We know the academic world inside out. So, we know what features you want to see. You can even put in feature requests yourself. PoP is a also "commerce-free" zone. We do not feature third-party adds, nor do we track your usage to show you tailored content or sell you things you don't want. Your searches are private, as they should be.

Overview of the book

This guide is composed of four parts. The first part presents the PoP user interface (Chapter 1) and its Multi-searches centre (Chapter 2). The second part explains PoP's metrics (Chapter 3) and data sources (Chapter 4), including two of the most widely used data sources: Google Scholar (Chapter 5) and Google Scholar Profiles (Chapter 6). A third part shows you how to do basic author searches (Chapter 7), journal searches (Chapter 8), and topic searches (Chapter 9).

The fourth part provides guidance for some of the more specialised tasks that PoP users have used the software for: presenting your case for tenure or promotion (Chapter 10), evaluating other academics (Chapter 11), doing a literature review (Chapter 12), deciding where to submit your paper (Chapter 13), and doing bibliometric research (Chapter 14). The final chapter of the book (Chapter 15) reviews how the usage of Publish or Perish has developed over the years.

Screenshots and examples

This guide includes many screenshots of the Publish or Perish software to illustrate how to apply the suggestions in this guide. These screenshots are all of the Mac version of the software, which is the version I use. The Windows version looks slightly different, but the basic layout and all of the software's functions are the identical. Where there are differences, this is pointed out in the text.

In sum

Citations are not just a reflection of the impact that a particular piece of academic work has generated. Citations can be used to tell stories about academics, journals, and research fields, but they can also be used to *distort* stories. This guide is meant to help you create effective stories, but also teaches you how to be a responsible user of research metrics.

—

Stories gain colour through examples and this guide contains many of them. Giving meaningful examples requires a detailed knowledge of the person or field in question. Therefore, examples often involve my own work or the broader field of Business and Management. Wherever possible, however, I have drawn from a broader discipline base, and I would be delighted to hear about your own stories for future editions of the book. Feel free to get in touch with me at anne@harzing.com.

Chapter 1: The Publish or Perish interface

This chapter covers the main Publish or Perish interface. In the next chapter, we will focus on the Multi-searches centre.

New interface

Since version 8, Publish or Perish has a new lay-out. It has a cleaner appearance with a more logical left-to-right flow, and more details visible for the selected paper. Starting on the top left it includes the searches folder tree with the tools pane below, the searches list, search pane and results pane in the middle, and the citation metrics pane and paper details pane on the right.

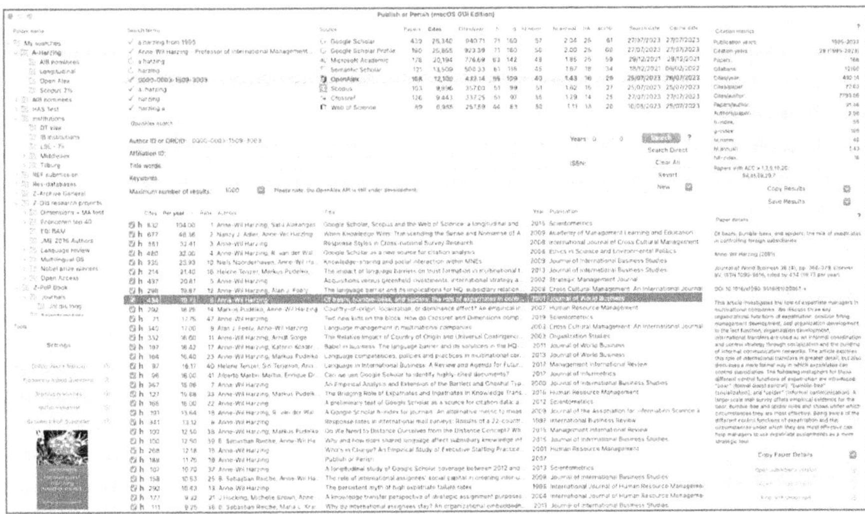

In the next sections, I discuss PoP's main interface including the tools pane, search pane, results pane (including its associated right-click context menu), citation metrics pane, and paper details pane. The folder tree and searches list are part of the Multi-searches centre and will be discussed in Chapter 2.

Tools pane

The tools pane can be found in the lower left-hand side of the interface. It includes links to free resources to help you use the software more effectively. They will take you to the online user's manual, a list of frequently asked questions, an overview of training resources (including multilingual resources), and a link to my YouTube channel which includes various tutorials. Finally, this pane also includes a link to the PoP donations page. Your contribution to the costs of keeping the PoP software free for everyone is much appreciated.

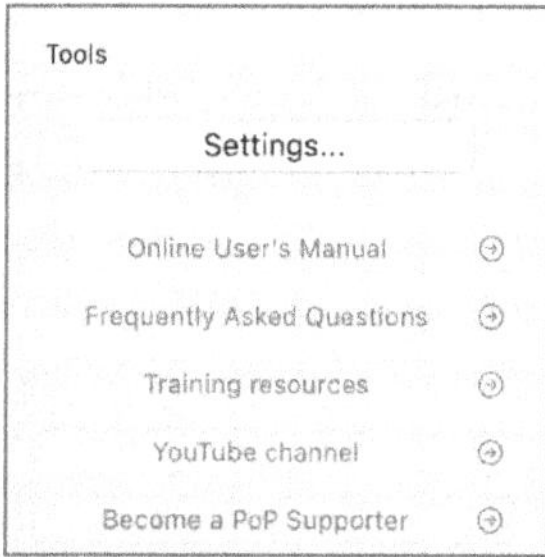

The tools pane also includes a button that takes you to the settings page. Here you can adjust settings for each of the data sources. You should not need to visit this page and I suggest that you keep the settings as default. The main settings that *can* be adjusted are the maximum number of results per search and the number of days that the results are kept in the cache. For data sources that need an API key (e.g., Scopus) or that require its access method be to be specified (e.g., Web of Science), this is where you can do this. Details of this will be discussed with the relevant data sources in Chapter 4.

Please use the available help resources and tips

Many PoP users have been running sub-optimal searches for years, wasting hours of their time. If I got a pound for everyone who said: *Sorry, I didn't know there was a … [fill the blank]*, I would be a very rich woman. Using this guide and the additional help resources will make your searches much more effective.

Search pane

When starting the PoP software, the search pane looks like the screen-shot below. It allows you to select the data source you want to use. It also indicates whether the data source is free (Crossref, Google Scholar, Google Scholar Profiles, OpenAlex, PubMed), requires free registration (Scopus, Semantic Scholar) or only works if the organisation you work for has a paid subscription (Web of Science). You can also import external data. Here we only provide brief information. More details for all data sources can be found in Chapter 4.

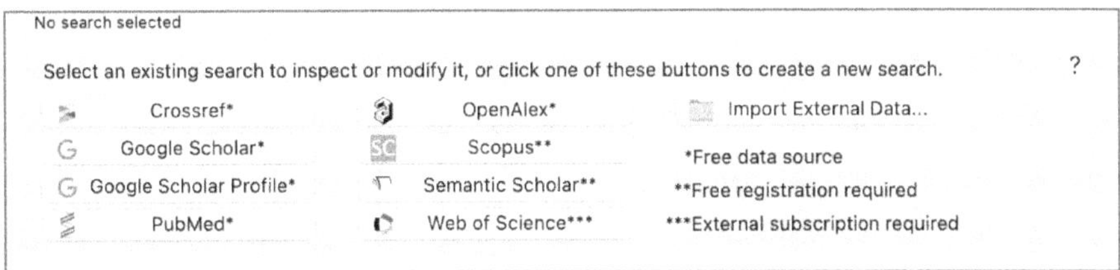

After clicking on the one of the data sources, you will see a search pane that includes all fields for which you are able to search, either on their own or in any combination of fields desired. We have made sure that these search panes look as similar as possible across data sources, whilst at the same time accommodating the essential differences. Most search panes look like the below Crossref pane.

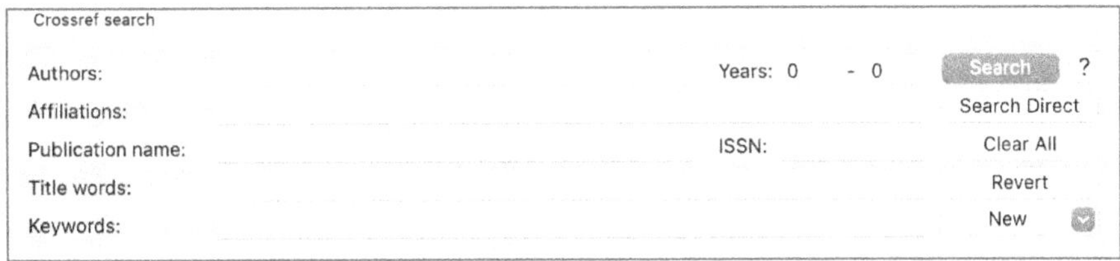

The Scopus search pane is identical to the above Crossref pane. PubMed and the Web of Science are very similar, except that the field Publication name has been replaced with Full journal title to indicate that a full journal title is required in this field.

The Google Scholar search pane is likewise very similar except that Google Scholar does not have an affiliation search and has additional options in terms of limiting the search results and excluding certain type of documents (see later in this section).

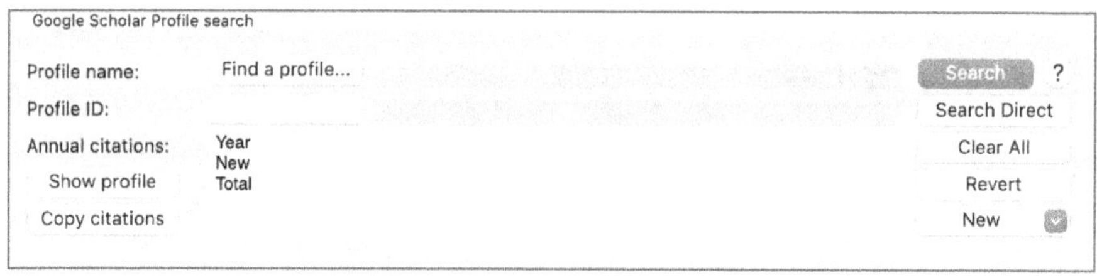

A Google Scholar Profile search looks quite different (see above) as this is a very different type of data source. We discuss searching with Google Scholar Profiles in detail in Chapter 6. Finally, OpenAlex and Semantic Scholar (see below) are different still as their APIs do not match closely with the way Publish or Perish is set up.

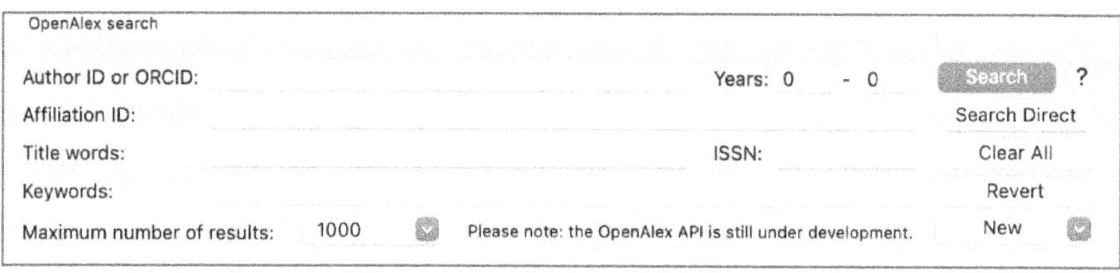

The OpenAlex (OA) search does not allow searches by journal name, though it does support searches by ISSN. For its authors searches it requires an OpenAlex Author ID or ORCID. The Semantic Scholar (SS) search currently only allows simple keywords searches. When entering multiple keywords SS applies an implicit AND, and keywords are matched anywhere in the document, including references.

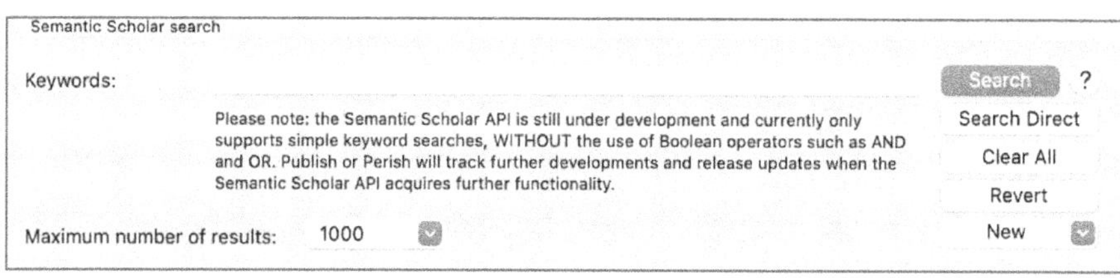

The five remaining buttons on the right-hand of the search pane are as follows:

- **Search** Looks up the current search, using the internal cache if possible. This means that if you have run the search before, the results will come from the cache and the search is not submitted to the data source again. This is quicker and does not create unnecessary strain on the data source.

- **Search Direct** Looks up the current search, bypassing the internal cache and contacting the data source directly. Only use Search Direct if you really want "fresh" data.
- **Clear All** Clears anything you have entered into the search fields. Useful if you want to start with a clean slate.
- **Revert** Restores the search fields to their previous state. This function is only available as long as you have not performed a lookup with the current search fields. Useful if you started changing a search and changed your mind.
- **New** Drop-down button that allows you to select which data source you would like to use.
  - This button also provides the option to duplicate an existing search, which facilitates repeated searching (see later section).

Facilitate repeated searching

The PoP software facilitates search partitioning for searches in all data sources. Many data sources only provide a limited number of results, most typically 200. This means you may not be able to get all results for a particular author, journal, university or set of keywords without partitioning your search by year.

Publish or Perish now makes search partitioning easy: when you click the **New** button and select **Duplicate Current Search**, the new search will be pre-set to the same parameters as the original search, so all you have to do is adjust the year range in the new search (see screenshot below).

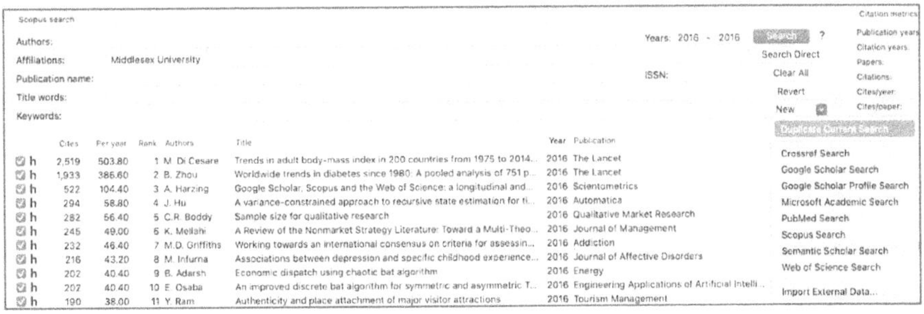

Repeat searches across universities, authors, or journals

This applies if you want to run a large range of searches with broadly the same search parameters and only want to change *one* parameter for each new search. For instance, you may want to:

- do a search for a particular set of keywords for a list of universities. Using this feature, you can duplicate the search and only need to replace the university name.
- do a search for a particular set of journals for a list of authors. Using this feature, you can duplicate the search and only need to replace the author's name (see screenshot below).
- do a search for a particular set of keywords for a list of journals. Using this feature, you can duplicate the search and only need to replace the journal name.

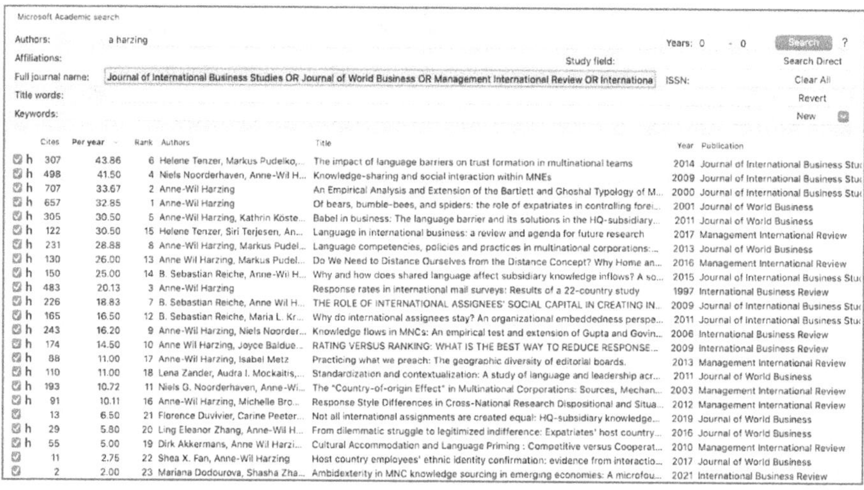

Repeat searches across data sources

This new feature also makes it easier to repeat the same search across a variety of data sources. If for instance you want to repeat an author search done in Scopus in Google Scholar to see whether this results in a larger number of publications and citations, simply click on new and select Google Scholar (see screenshot below).

This will repeat the search with the same search parameters. However, please do note that different data sources might have a slightly different search syntax. In that case you will still need to change the duplicated search. For details on the search syntax in various data sources, see the chapters on author (Chapter 7), journal (Chapter 8), and topic and affiliation searches (Chapter 9).

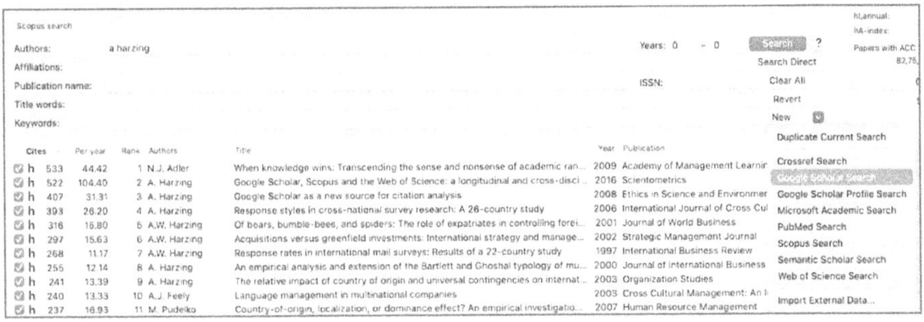

Boolean searches

Boolean searches are a type of structured search process that allows users to combine search terms with operators such as AND, OR, and NOT to limit, broaden, or define their search results. The different data sources vary in the extent to which they allow Boolean searches. The table below is an overview of the currently known options. AND is implicit in most data sources if you combine search terms. So, you do not need to include it in your search. The ISSN field only allows one search term and only accepts NOT in Google Scholar.

Data source	AND	OR	NOT
Crossref	✘	✔	✘
Google Scholar	✔	✔	✔
Google Scholar Profiles	✔	Profile field only	✘
OpenAlex	Keywords field only	✘	✘
PubMed	✔	✔	✘
Scopus	✔	✔	✔ *
Semantic Scholar	✔	✘	✘
Web of Science	✔	✔	✔ *

* Cannot be used as the first operator in the field

Google Scholar: limit the number of search results

Your efforts to find the best possible search string without putting an unnecessary strain on Google Scholar are facilitated by a new PoP feature. First, the default number of results has been limited to 200. We added a drop-down box allowing you to restrict the maximum number of results for Google Scholar searches (see screenshot below). Seven options are pre-set, but you can type any number in the box. As this is a per search limit, the choice does not carry over to other searches except for the "duplicate the current search" option.

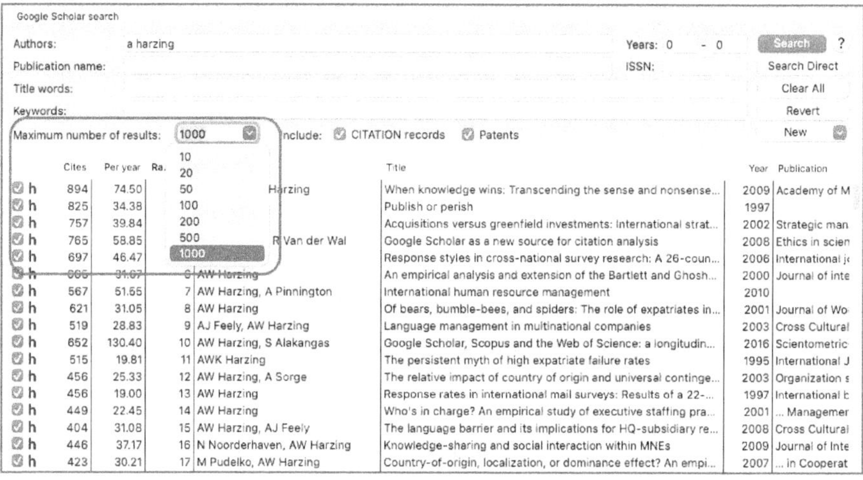

Google Scholar search

| Authors: | a harzing | | Years: 0 - 0 | Search ? |

Publication name: — ISSN: — Search Direct

Title words: — Clear All

Keywords: — Revert

Maximum number of results: 1000 — Include: CITATION records Patents — New

Drop-down options: 10, 20, 50, 100, 200, 500, 1000

	Cites	Per year	Ra.	Authors	Title	Year	Publication
h	894	74.50		Harzing	When knowledge wins: Transcending the sense and nonsense...	2009	Academy of M
h	825	34.38			Publish or perish	1997	
h	757	39.84			Acquisitions versus greenfield investments: International strat...	2002	Strategic man
h	765	58.85		R Van der Wal	Google Scholar as a new source for citation analysis	2008	Ethics in scien
h	697	46.47			Response styles in cross-national survey research: A 26-coun...	2006	International j
h	666	31.07	6	AW Harzing	An empirical analysis and extension of the Bartlett and Ghosh...	2000	Journal of inte
h	567	51.55	7	AW Harzing, A Pinnington	International human resource management	2010	
h	621	31.05	8	AW Harzing	Of bears, bumble-bees, and spiders: The role of expatriates in...	2001	Journal of Wo
h	519	28.83	9	AJ Feely, AW Harzing	Language management in multinational companies	2003	Cross Cultural
h	652	130.40	10	AW Harzing, S Alakangas	Google Scholar, Scopus and the Web of Science: a longitudin...	2016	Scientometric
h	515	19.81	11	AWK Harzing	The persistent myth of high expatriate failure rates	1995	International J
h	456	25.33	12	AW Harzing, A Sorge	The relative impact of country of origin and universal continge...	2003	Organization s
h	456	19.00	13	AW Harzing	Response rates in international mail surveys: Results of a 22-...	1997	International b
h	449	22.45	14	AW Harzing	Who's in charge? An empirical study of executive staffing pra...	2001	... Managemer
h	404	31.08	15	AW Harzing, AJ Feely	The language barrier and its implications for HQ-subsidiary re...	2008	Cross Cultural
h	446	37.17	16	N Noorderhaven, AW Harzing	Knowledge-sharing and social interaction within MNEs	2009	Journal of Inte
h	423	30.21	17	M Pudelko, AW Harzing	Country-of-origin, localization, or dominance effect? An empi...	2007	... in Cooperat

This new option addresses Google Scholar search limitations and makes short searches more convenient. The underlying reason is that Google Scholar only provides 10 results at a time. So, in order to get 1,000 results, Publish or Perish needs to send 100 sub-requests to Google Scholar. This means you will quickly approach the request rate limits set by Google Scholar, which in turn will cause Publish or Perish to limit the request rate by pausing longer and longer between requests. This means searching might become quite slow.

If you only need the top-10/20/50 results, limiting the maximum number of results reduces the load on Google Scholar and speeds up your searches. This new feature is also useful when you are still fine-tuning a complex search and don't need to see all results to establish whether your search is providing the expected output.

Google Scholar: exclude stray citations and patents

The Publish or Perish interface now includes an option to include or exclude CITATION results and patents in Google Scholar searches (see screenshot below).

What are CITATION records?

CITATION results are records where Google Scholar has found *citing* works, but has been unable to find the *cited* work online. Often, these CITATION records are what are commonly called "stray citations", i.e., citations where citing authors have made small mistakes in citing a work. These can be merged into the master record for the work in question, which will potentially increase your h-index. For more details on this see the dedicated chapter on Google Scholar (Chapter 5).

In many cases though these stray citations only clutter your result. If you do an author search it makes the author's publication record look very messy, making it difficult to establish an academic's primary publications, especially if they are recent and not yet highly cited. If you are doing a journal, topic, or affiliation search stray citations are often pure "noise" and do not contribute anything useful to your search. So, excluding them makes a lot of sense in many searches.

Note that you can also exclude CITATION records *after* running the search (see the section on Selection Tools below). However, excluding them *during* the search saves you time waiting for completion of a full Google Scholar search. Some searches might include a lot of these CITATION records.

It is important to realise, however, that Google Scholar assigns the CITATION label to *any* publication where it cannot find the record online, even if the publication in question is very significant and highly cited. This might include many – though not all – non-journal publications [e.g., books, reports]. So, excluding CITATION records might well lead to an underestimation of an author's publications and citation impact, especially in the Social Sciences and Humanities. It might also lead you to miss seminal books if you do a topic search for a literature review.

In my own publication record excluding CITATION records reduces the number of results from 407 to 183. Most of the excluded publications are pure dross and are not missed. However, my citations are reduced by nearly 15% and my h-index is reduced from 71 to 68. This is because a highly cited book, the Publish or Perish software and the Journal Quality List are all excluded. The other metrics are likewise reduced.

So, if you need a complete a complete record for either yourself or an academic you are evaluating, including CITATION records might be essential, especially in the Social Sciences and Humanities. If all you are after is an assessment of someone's journal publications or if you are doing a literature review in disciplines where only journal articles are important, excluding them will dramatically simplify the output and speed up your search at the same time.

Results pane

The results pane can be found below the search pane. The results list displays all results for the current (or first) selected search. If you double-click on an item in the list, Publish or Perish opens your web browser and displays the article's online abstract or full text for the selected item, if any. If an item does not have an online version, its citations or a general search results page is displayed for the item.

The list contains the following columns:

—

- **Cites**. Number of citations. A small blue 'h' icon appears in front of all result items that contribute to the h-index.
- **Per year**. Calculated as the total number of citations divided by the age of the article (i.e., the number of years since publication). If the year of publication is not available, this column shows 0.00.
- **Rank**. Results ranking. This is the order in which the data source returned the results. Typically, earlier ranked entries indicate more relevant results. An irregular rank order when sorted by Cites might indicate that the list contains irrelevant results.
- **Authors**. Author names.
- **Title**. Title of the publication.
- **Year**. Year of publication. This field might be wrong or missing if the data source did not return a recognizable year.
- **Publication**. Journal name or similar. Not always available; sometimes wrong if the data source results are mixed up.
- **Publisher**. Publisher. Not always available; sometimes wrong if the data source results are mixed up.
- **Type**. This column provides an indication of the document type. Further details are below.

What is included in the Type column?

The Type column includes a variety of labels that provide an indication of the kind of publication we are dealing with. However, labels vary by data source, sometimes subtly, sometimes substantially.

- In traditional structured data sources such as Scopus and the Web of Science this will list type labels such as Article, Review, Letter, Editorial Material, Book, Book Chapter, Conference Paper, Correction, and Erratum.
- OpenAlex and Crossref have similar labels with subtly different names such as journal-article and book-chapter, though they typically use fewer of them.
- PubMed also uses a Journal Article label. However, in addition to this it also has labels for Case Report, Clinical Trial, Randomized Controlled Trial, Systematic Review, Review, Preprint, Observational Study, Multicenter study, and Meta-analysis.

- Semantic Scholar doesn't provide type labels.
- Google Scholar Profile uses Book, Book Chapter, Conference Paper, Journal, Thesis, Patent, and Other. Google Scholar will make its best estimate of the type when you import the data. However, you are able change the type yourself by editing the record. If you choose Other and enter a URL in the Source field, your GS Profile will list it as Online Document, which is a very accurate and useful description.
- Google Scholar has a very different set of Type labels. They largely refer to the *medium* of publication, rather than the publication *type*. Most records in Google Scholar do not carry a Type designation. Those that do have one of five types:
  - BOOK, this refers to materials drawn from publishers or Google Books and concerns either books or book chapters. However, this label is sometimes also used for preprints on repositories. Moreover, not all books have a book label. Books that are available in PDF have a PDF label.
  - CITATION, these are results for which Google Scholar was able to find citations, but for which the original work was not found online.
  - DOC, this refers to items that are found in full text online as a Word Document.
  - HTML, this refers to items that are found in full text online in html, i.e., fully visible on the website without any downloads. This usually refers to articles that were published in "Gold Open Access", i.e., published in open access in the original journal format.
  - PDF, this refers to items that are found in full text online as a PDF document.

Resizing and sorting columns

The columns in the results area can be resized to your preference by dragging the lines between them, and will stay that way until you resize them again. Hence, you can decide which fields you want to see in full and which are less important. In the screenshot below, I reduced the width of the author and title column in order to see the publication name in full.

Cites	Per year	Rank	Authors	Title	Year	Publication
h 1,632	102.00	1	AW Harzing	Publish or Perish	2007	
h 1,363	194.71	2	AW Harzin...	Google Scholar,...	2016	Scientometrics
h 1,053	75.21	3	NJ Adler, A...	When knowledge...	2009	The Academy of Management Learning and Education
h 908	60.53	4	AW Harzin...	Google Scholar a...	2008	Ethics in Science and Environmental Politics
h 890	52.35	5	AW Harzing	Response styles...	2006	International Journal of Cross Cultural Management
h 873	41.57	6	AW Harzing	Acquisitions vers...	2002	Strategic Management Journal
h 740	32.17	7	AW Harzing	An empirical anal...	2000	Journal of International Business Studies
h 721	32.77	8	AW Harzing	Of bears, bumble...	2001	Journal of World Business
h 689	53.00	9	AW Harzin...	International Hu...	2010	
h 618	30.90	10	AJ Feely, A...	Language manag...	2003	Cross Cultural Management: An International Journal
h 609	25.38	11	AW Harzing	Managing the mu...	1999	
h 586	45.08	12	AW Harzing	The Publish or P...	2010	Tarma Software Research Pty Ltd, Melbourne Australia
h 579	20.68	13	AW Harzing	The persistent m...	1995	The International Journal of Human Resource Management
h 577	41.21	14	N Noorder...	Knowledge-shari...	2009	Journal of International Business Studies
h 548	34.25	15	M Pudelko...	Country-of-origi...	2007	Human Resource Management
h 519	25.95	16	AW Harzin...	The relative impa...	2003	Organization Studies
h 502	22.82	17	AW Harzing	Who's in charge?...	2001	Human Resource Management

In the Windows version of the software (only), you can also make columns "disappear" by making them really small. So, if you don't need the "rank" column (which indicates the order in which the results were ordered in the data source) between the per year and author column, just make it disappear. If for whatever reason you would like to for instance compare total citations and citations per year directly with the year and journal outlet, just make the author and title field disappear.

Sorting results by clicking on the column heading

You can also sort the results on any column by clicking on the column heading and sort them the other way around by clicking again. As Publish or Perish is a tool for citation analysis, by default the results are sorted by decreasing citations. However, you might want to sort by [citations] per year to see which of your papers have had the biggest impact on a yearly basis.

This is also useful to spot papers that are not currently included in your h-index, but might be in the future if their current annual citation levels are representative of future impact. As you can see in the screenshot below some of my papers (#84, #118, #119, #71, #76 and #99) look like they might become highly cited over the years even though their current citation levels are still modest. You would not be able to spot this as easily when sorting by total citations.

	Cites	Per year	Rank	Authors	Title
h	121	12.10	54	AW Harzing	Document categories in the ISI Web of Knowledge: misunderstanding the Social S...
	48	12.00	84	F Duvivier, C Peeters,...	Not all international assignments are created equal: HQ-subsidiary knowledge tran...
h	190	11.88	42	JB Hocking, M Brown...	Balancing global and local strategic contexts: Expatriate knowledge transfer, appli...
h	188	11.75	43	J Mingers, AW Harzing	Ranking journals in business and management: a statistical analysis of the Harzing...
h	104	11.56	60	AW Harzing, S Alakan...	hla: an individual annual h-index to accommodate disciplinary and career length di...
h	104	11.56	61	AW Harzing, A Giroud	The competitive advantage of nations: An application to academia
h	125	11.36	52	AW Harzing, K Köster,...	Response style differences in cross-national research: dispositional and situationa...
h	100	11.11	64	AW Harzing, M Pudelko	Hablas vielleicht un peu la mia language? A comprehensive overview of the role of...
	11	11.00	118	M Dodourova, S Zhao...	Ambidexterity in MNC knowledge sourcing in emerging economies: A microfounda...
	11	11.00	119	H Kim, BS Reiche, AW...	How does successive inpatriation contribute to subsidiary capability building and...
h	241	10.95	33	AW Harzing	An analysis of the functions of international transfer of managers in MNCs
h	200	10.00	38	NG Noorderhaven, A...	The "country-of-origin effect" in multinational corporations: sources, mechanisms...
	70	10.00	71	LE Zhang, AW Harzing	From dilemmatic struggle to legitimized indifference: expatriates' host country lan...
	57	9.50	76	AW Harzing, S Alakan...	Microsoft Academic is one year old: the Phoenix is ready to leave the nest
h	109	9.08	57	L Zander, AI Mockaiti...	Standardization and contextualization: A study of language and leadership across...
	26	8.67	99	S Zhao, H Tan, M Pap...	The internationalization of innovation towards the South: A historical case study of...

Sorting by author, title, or publication (source) can also be useful when you are trying to merge stray citations as it brings identical publication closer together. Another important use case is when you are devising a strategy to exclude namesakes in another field. Sorting by journal will allow you to easily spot journals in a different field, whereas sorting by author name allows you to spot co-author names that are not co-authors for the author you are searching for.

Right-click popup contextual menu

The context menu is active in the results pane. If you right-click on *any* result in the results list, you will get a popup contextual menu. It is made up of three parts, a first part related to retrieving publications or citations, a second part that allows you to export your data, and a third part that presents various shortcuts to select or unselect results.

Retrieving publications or citations

Open Article in Browser
Open Full Text in Browser
Open Citing Works in Browser
Open Related Works in Browser
Retrieve Citing Works in Publish or Perish
Find Article with Unpaywall

Split Citations

The first part of the contextual menu includes the various options that are available to access the publications that you have found in your search.

- **Open Article in Browser**. Available in all data sources. Opens the currently selected publication in your web browser. This command is only available for some items and may sometimes open the abstract rather than the full article. The same result is achieved by double-clicking on the article.
- **Open Full Text in Browser**. This option is discussed in detail in the next section.
- **Open Citing Works in Browser**. Available only in Google Scholar, Google Scholar Profiles, and Scopus (the first 20 results only). Opens the web page that lists the referencing articles for the current item, if available.
- **Open Related Works in Browser**. Available only in Google Scholar. Opens the web page that lists the articles that Google considers to be related to the current item, if available. For more details see Chapter 5 on Google Scholar.
- **Retrieve citing works in Publish or Perish**. Available only in Google and Google Scholar Profiles. Looks up the citing works for the currently selected results in a separate PoP search. Note that this may take a long time. For more details see Chapter 5 on Google Scholar.
- **Find Article with Unpaywall**. This option is discussed in detail in the next section.
- **Split Citations**: Is only active if you have merged publications. You can use it when you have accidentally merged the wrong publications. See Chapter 5 for details on merging publications.

Search for free full text version

A key new feature in Publish or Perish version 8 is the ability to check for free full-text availability of any of the results. There are two ways to do this, both of which are available through the popup menu in the results list (right-click on a result to access the menu) as well as through the new **Paper details** pane for the selected paper, as shown in the screen shot below.

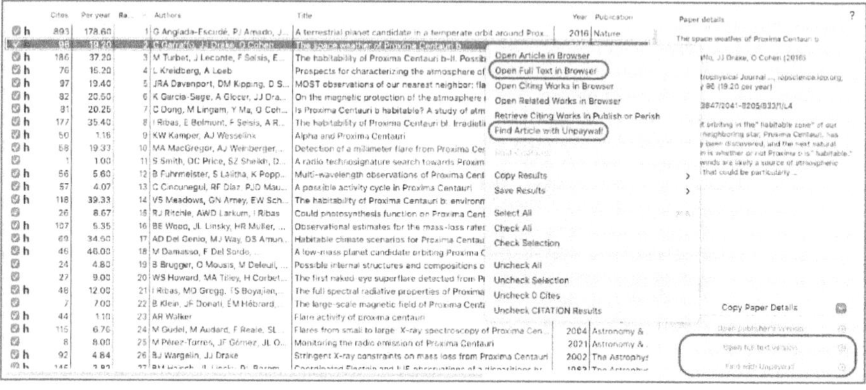

1. Open in full text if available in the data source that you searched
    in, greyed out if no full text can be found in the data source in
    question.

2. Find full-text with Unpaywall, searches the Unpaywall database
    for a full-text option.

Some notes and limitations:

- This feature is not available in Google Scholar Profile and
  OpenAlex searches, but is available in all other data sources.

- Although in most cases the two options provide the same version of the paper, this is not always the case. You might wish to
  try both so as to find the "best" version.

- The free full-text version will often be a pre-publication version. If you prefer the officially formatted journal version and
  your library has access to the journal in question, you might
  wish to login to your university library and use "open article in
  browser" instead.

Exporting your data

Publish or Perish offers two options to export your data: Copy or
Save. When you use the **Copy** command it will be copied to your
computer's clipboard and can be pasted in your programme of choice
(e.g., a word processor or spreadsheet) for further processing. When
you use a **Save** command, you will be asked to provide a file name
which will then be saved in your chosen location.

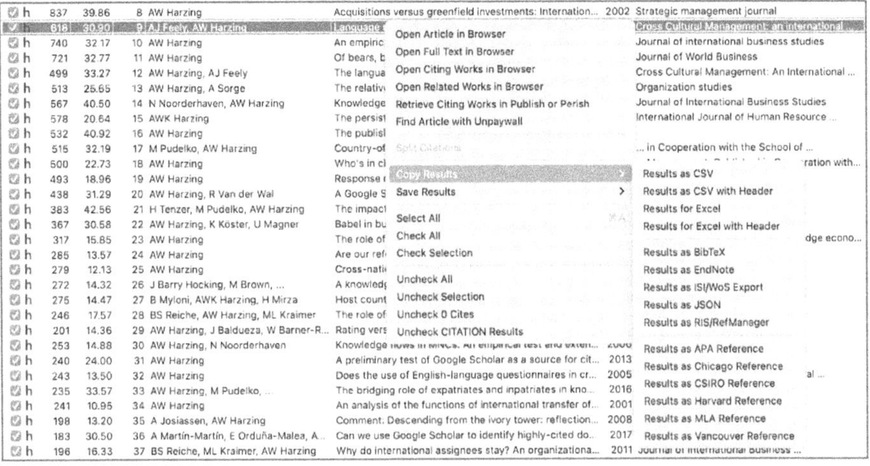

There are three sets of options. The first set of options exports results for further processing in spreadsheets. The second set allows further processing in various reference managers and the Web of Science. The third set copies your results as full references formatted in one of the six most common referencing styles.

The general procedure is as follows:

1. In the **results pane**, check the publications that you want to export. By default, all lines are checked and exported.
2. If desired, click on the column headers to sort the data in the desired order. The sort is stable, which means that you can sort on multiple columns by clicking them in reverse order.
   o For example, to sort primarily by author, secondary by year, and tertiary by publication, click first on **Publication**, then on **Year**, then on **Authors**.

Exporting results for spreadsheet processing

This option is useful if you would like to further analyse citations for a set of publications. The screenshot below for instance shows the resulting export of a selected set of eight publications. Only key details are shown, but the export contains full bibliographic details, as well as additional article-level metrics, such as citations per year, citations per author and the number of authors per paper.

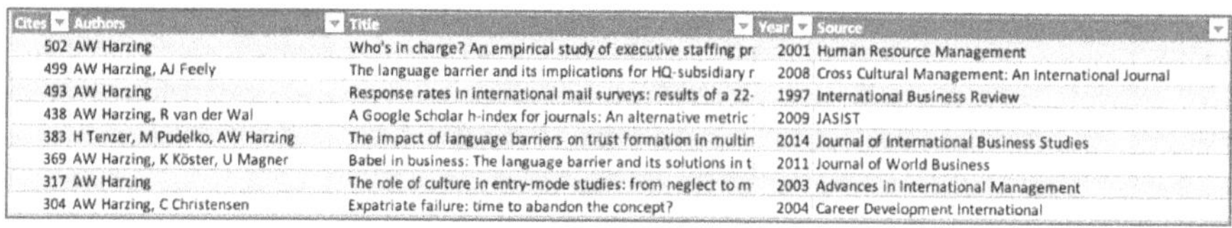

Exporting results for reference managers

You can export the publication data from Publish or Perish to the following formats for import in a variety of reference managers.

- **BibTeX** - a generally used format for bibliographic references, based on the TeX typesetting programme and LaTeX macros.
- **EndNote** - a data exchange format for use with the EndNote programme from Clarivate.
- **JSON** - a generic data format supported by many programs.
- **RefMan/RIS** - a data exchange format used by a variety of reference managers, including Reference Manager.

Exporting full bibliographic references

Publish or Perish can export the full bibliographic details of any of the results, a very handy shortcut if you need the full reference of an article or if you would like to copy all your own publications into a CV. Different data sources have different capabilities in this respect.

- **Crossref**: Exports full bibliographic details of references, including article DOI and journal ISSN.
- **Google Scholar**: References might be incomplete. Author names and journal titles might be truncated
- **Google Scholar Profile**: References are more complete than raw GS data, but might still have occasional missing elements. For your own profile, references can be corrected manually.
- **OpenAlex**: Exports full bibliographic details of references, including article DOI and journal ISSN.
- **PubMed**: Exports full bibliographic details of references, including article DOI and journal ISSN.
- **Scopus**: Exports full bibliographic details of references including article DOI and journal ISSN.

- **Semantic Scholar**: Only exports author, year, title and DOI.
- **Web of Science**: Exports full bibliographic details of references, including article DOI and journal ISSN.

Selection tools

The last section of the popup menu provides you with several options to quickly select or de-select results in the results pane. For all except the first option (Select All), this also results in an automatic recalculation of the citation metrics.

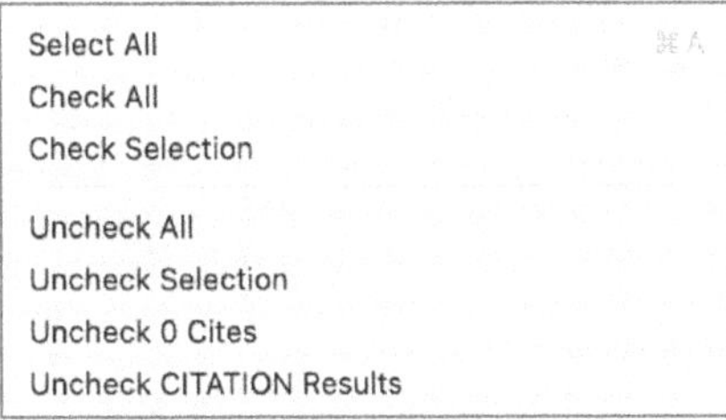

- **Select all**: Selects (i.e., highlights) all items in the results list. Alternatively, press Ctrl+A (Windows) or ⌘+A (Mac).
- **Check all**: Checks all items in the results list, i.e., put a tick in the box in front of the result, which means it is included in any metrics and exporting options.
- **Check selection**: Checks all selected (i.e., highlighted) items in the results list.
- **Uncheck All**: Unchecks all items in the results list. Alternatively, press Ctrl+U (Windows only).
- **Uncheck Selection**: Unchecks all selected (i.e., highlighted) items in the results list.
- **Uncheck 0 Cites**: Unchecks all results that have 0 citations. Alternatively, press Ctrl+0 (that's zero, not Oh) (Windows only).
- **Uncheck CITATION results**: Uncheck all results that have the Type CITATION.

Citation metrics pane

The citation metrics pane is found at the top right-hand corner of the user interface and reports all metrics that Publish or Perish calculates based on the searches that are done by its users. An example of my own metrics, based on a Google Scholar citation profile search, is shown below. The h-index is not only shown in the citation metrics pane, but also by a small blue "h-icon" that appears in front of all result items that contribute to the h-index.

Citation metrics	?
Publication years:	1995-2023
Citation years:	28 (1995-2023)
Papers:	180
Citations:	25907
Cites/year:	925.25
Cites/paper:	143.93
Cites/author:	17593.69
Papers/author:	114.56
Authors/paper:	2.05
h-index:	71
g-index:	160
hI,norm:	56
hI,annual:	2.00
hA-index:	25
Papers with ACC ≥ 1,2,5,10,20:	129,111,84,60,29
Copy Results	
Save Results	

All these metrics are discussed in detail in Chapter 3. In past versions of the software, PoP reported additional, more complicated, metrics. These metrics are still calculated and exported. However, they are no longer shown in the metrics pane as they confused most users.

In the metrics pane you can also find two buttons that can be used to copy or save results on a search level (as opposed to the individual result's level discussed in the next section) in a variety of formats. You can find more information about this in the section on exporting your data in Chapter 2. The option to export a basic or extended search report is discussed next.

Search reports - basic or extended

To simplify record keeping of data searches, Publish or Perish can generate a comprehensive search report in a single command. The easiest way to do this is by using the buttons at the bottom of the Citation metrics pane.

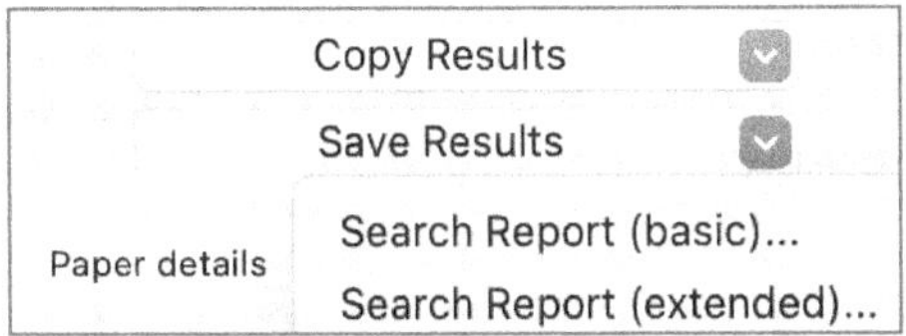

You can either use Copy or Save. When you generate a search report as a **Copy Results [to Clipboard]** command it will be copied to your computer's clipboard as both Rich Text Format (RTF) and as plain text (in Unicode encoding). This makes it suitable for pasting into word processors (which will use the RTF copy, keeping all formatting intact) as well as into plain text editors and other text-based tools (which will see the structured, but unformatted plain text copy).

When you generate a search report as a **Save Results** command it will be written as formatted text in Rich Text Format (RTF), which can be read by most word processors including Microsoft Word, Pages, LibreOffice Writer, SoftMaker TextMaker, and many others.

Content of the report

The search report contains all of the following:

- The search terms and other search parameters

- Data retrieval information: data source, the date of search and of actual data, status of the search request

- **The metrics** that Publish or Perish calculated on the results

- A formatted list of results, *in the order* in which it is shown in the **Results list**

- The abstract of each publication, where available. You must choose the **extended** report format to include abstract. This also formats the publication meta data in a slightly different way for clarity.

Order of the results

You can create a report in *the order in which results are sorted*. This means you can create search reports with commonly used ordering systems such as (reverse) chronological/alphabetical.

If you are interested in citation impact, you can order your report by total number of citations or citations per year (see screenshot below), listing the most cited papers first. However, you can use any other order you see fit such as ordering by journal, publisher or first author.

Two types of reports

Publish or Perish includes a choice between two types of reports:

- Basic: search terms, data retrieval, metrics, and basic results, i.e., full reference for all publications and citations per publication (incl. per year).

- Extended: as above, but results are provided in structured format by title with full bibliographic details, citations, the DOI (formatted as URL), and each paper's abstract, if available.

Below are the first two pages of a **Basic Search Report**, using my own publication record in Google Scholar Profile as an example (see Chapter 6 for details on this).

This option is very convenient if you need a concise overview of this information for performance appraisals, funding applications or simply want to copy a list of your publications and their citations to a CV or website.

Anne-Wil Harzing - Professor of International Management - Middlesex University – Tilburg University

Publish or Perish 8.9.4538.8589 (basic report)
MacOS (x86_64) edition, running on Darwin 22.6.0 (x86_64)

Search terms

Profile ID: vOsDYGsAAAAJ
Profile name: Anne-Wil Harzing - Professor of International Management - Middlesex University - Tilburg University
Profile labels: "International Business" "International HRM" Scientometrics "International Management" Expatriation

Data retrieval

Data source: Google Scholar Profile
Search date: 2023-07-24 16:57:31 +0100
Cache date: 2023-07-24 16:57:33 +0100
Search result: [0] No error

Metrics

Reference date: 2023-07-24 16:57:33 +0100
Publication years: 1995-2023
Citation years: 28 (1995-2023)
Papers: 180
Citations: 25844
Citations/year: 923.00 (acc1=129, acc2=111, acc5=84, acc10=60, acc20=29)
Citations/paper: 143.58
Citations/author: 17557.70
Papers/author: 114.56
Authors/paper: 2.05/2.0/1 (mean/median/mode)
Age-weighted citation rate: 1969.03 (sqrt=44.37), 1217.87/author
Hirsch h-index: 70 (a=5.27, m=2.50, 23982 cites=92.8% coverage)
Egghe g-index: 160 (g/h=2.29, 25840 cites=100.0% coverage)
PoP hI,norm: 56
PoP hI,annual: 2.00
Fassin hA-index: 25
Year New Total citations

Year	New	Total citations
2001	95	721
2002	138	859
2003	156	1015
2004	231	1246
2005	247	1493
2006	360	1853
2007	422	2275
2008	575	2850
2009	724	3574
2010	813	4387
2011	1083	5470
2012	1266	6736
2013	1442	8178
2014	1493	9671
2015	1629	11300
2016	2018	13318
2017	1900	15218
2018	1798	17016
2019	1902	18918
2020	1893	20811
2021	1905	22716
2022	2061	24777
2023	1067	25844

Results

AW Harzing (2007) **Publish or Perish.**, http://www.harzing.com/pop.htm, cited by 1632 (102.00 per year)

AW Harzing, S Alakangas (2016) **Google Scholar, Scopus and the Web of Science: A longitudinal and cross-disciplinary comparison.** *Scientometrics* 106(2), pp. 787-804, cited by 1363 (194.71 per year)

NJ Adler, AW Harzing (2009) **When knowledge wins: Transcending the sense and nonsense of academic rankings.** *The Academy of Management Learning and Education* 8(1), pp. 72-95, cited by 1053 (75.21 per year)

AW Harzing, R van der Wal (2008) **Google Scholar as a new source for citation analysis?.** *Ethics in Science and Environmental Politics* 8(1), pp. 61-73, cited by 908 (60.53 per year)

AW Harzing (2006) **Response styles in cross-national survey research: A 26-country Study.** *International Journal of Cross Cultural Management* 6(2), pp. 243-266, cited by 890 (52.35 per year)

AW Harzing (2002) **Acquisitions versus greenfield investments: International strategy and management of entry modes.** *Strategic Management Journal* 23(3), pp. 211-227, cited by 873 (41.57 per year)

AW Harzing (2000) **An empirical analysis and extension of the Bartlett and Ghoshal typology of multinational companies.** *Journal of International Business Studies* 31(1), pp. 101-120, cited by 740 (32.17 per year)

AW Harzing (2001) **Of bears, bumble-bees, and spiders: The role of expatriates in controlling foreign subsidiaries.** *Journal of World Business* 36(4), pp. 366-379, cited by 721 (32.77 per year)

AW Harzing, A Pinnington (2010) **International Human Resource Management.**, Sage Publications, cited by 689 (53.00 per year)

AJ Feely, AW Harzing (2003) **Language management in multinational companies.** *Cross Cultural Management: An International Journal* 10(2), pp. 37-52, cited by 618 (30.90 per year)

AW Harzing (1999) **Managing the multinationals: An international study of control mechanisms.**, Edward Elgar, cited by 609 (25.38 per year)

AW Harzing (2010) **The Publish or Perish Book: Your guide to Effective and Responsible Citation Analysis.** *Tarma Software Research Pty Ltd, Melbourne Australia*, cited by 586 (45.08 per year)

Using an OpenAlex ORCID search (see Chapter 7 for details on this), the first two pages of an **Extended Search Report** look like this. Note the extensive abstracts and the extended formatting of each paper's bibliographic details.

0000-0003-1509-3003

Publish or Perish 8.9.4538.8589 (extended report)
MacOS (x86_64) edition, running on Darwin 22.6.0 (x86_64)

Search terms

Author ID: 0000-0003-1509-3003
Years: all

Data retrieval

Data source: OpenAlex
Search date: 2023-07-25 15:27:11 +0100
Cache date: 2023-07-25 15:27:21 +0100
Search result: [0] No error

Metrics

Reference date: 2023-07-25 15:27:21 +0100
Publication years: 1995-2023
Citation years: 28 (1995-2023)
Papers: 168
Citations: 12100
Citations/year: 432.14 (acc1=94, acc2=81, acc5=59, acc10=29, acc20=7)
Citations/paper: 72.02
Citations/author: 7793.06
Papers/author: 91.38
Authors/paper: 2.96/2.0/2 (mean/median/mode)
Age-weighted citation rate: 917.81 (sqrt=30.30), 536.80/author
Hirsch h-index: 55 (a=4.00, m=1.96, 10987 cites=90.8% coverage)
Egghe g-index: 109 (g/h=1.98, 12074 cites=99.8% coverage)
PoP hI,norm: 40
PoP hI,annual: 1.43
Fassin hA-index: 16

Results

Google Scholar, Scopus and the Web of Science: a longitudinal and cross-disciplinary comparison
Anne-Wil Harzing, Satu Alakangas (2015)
Scientometrics 106(2), pp. 787-804, Springer Nature (Netherlands), ISSN 0138-9130, cited by 832 (104.00 per year)

https://doi.org/10.1007/s11192-015-1798-9

This article aims to provide a systematic and comprehensive comparison of the coverage of the three major bibliometric databases: Google Scholar, Scopus, and the Web of Science. Based on a sample of 146 senior academics in five broad disciplinary areas, we therefore provide both a longitudinal and a cross-disciplinary comparison of the three databases. Our longitudinal comparison of eight data points between 2013 and 2015 shows a consistent and reasonably stable quarterly growth for both publications and citations across the three databases. This suggests that all three databases provide sufficient stability of coverage to be used for more detailed cross-disciplinary comparisons. Our cross-disciplinary comparison of the three databases includes four key research metrics (publications, citations, h-index, and hI, annual, an annualised individual h-index) and five major disciplines (Humanities, Social Sciences, Engineering, Sciences and Life Sciences). We show that both the data source and the specific metrics used change the conclusions that can be drawn from cross-disciplinary comparisons.

. . . .

When Knowledge Wins: Transcending the Sense and Nonsense of Academic Rankings
Nancy J. Adler, Anne-Wil Harzing (2009)
Academy of Management Learning and Education 8(1), pp. 72-95, Academy of Management, ISSN 1537-260X, cited by 677 (48.36 per year)

https://doi.org/10.5465/amle.2009.37012181

"Not everything that can be counted counts, and not everything that counts can be counted."—Albert Einstein Has university scholarship gone astray? Do our academic assessment systems reward scholarship that addresses the questions that matter most to society? Using international business as an example, we highlight the problematic nature of academic ranking systems and question if such assessments are drawing scholarship away from its fundamental purpose. We call for an immediate examination of existing ranking systems, not only as a legitimate scholarly question vis-à-vis performance—a conceptual lens with deep roots in management research—but also because the very health and vibrancy of the field are at stake. Indeed, in light of the data presented here, which suggest that current systems are dysfunctional and potentially cause more harm than good, a temporary moratorium on rankings may be appropriate until more valid and reliable ways to assess scholarly contributions can be developed. The worldwide community of scholars, along with the global network of institutions interacting with and supporting management scholarship (such as the Academy of Management, AACSB, and Thomson Reuters Scientific) are invited to innovate and design more reliable and valid ways to assess scholarly contributions that truly promote the advancement of relevant 21st century knowledge, and likewise recognize those individuals and institutions that best fulfil the university's fundamental purpose.

. . . .

Response Styles in Cross-national Survey Research
Anne-Wil Harzing (2006)
International Journal of Cross Cultural Management 6(2), pp. 243-266, SAGE Publishing, ISSN 1470-5958, cited by 551 (32.41 per year)

https://doi.org/10.1177/1470595806066332

Studies of attitudes across countries generally rely on a comparison of aggregated mean scores to Likert-scale questions. This presupposes that when people complete a questionnaire, their answers are based on the substantive meaning of the items to which they respond. However, people's responses are also influenced by their response style. Hence, the studies we conduct might simply reflect differences in the way people respond to surveys, rather than picking up real differences in management phenomena across countries. Our 26-country study shows that there are major differences in response styles between countries that both confirm and extend earlier research. Country-level characteristics such as power distance, collectivism, uncertainty avoidance and extraversion all significantly influence response styles such as acquiescence and extreme response styles. Further, English-language questionnaires are shown to elicit a higher level of middle responses, while questionnaires in a respondent's native language result in more extreme response styles. Finally, English-language competence is positively related to extreme response styles and negatively related to middle response styles. We close by discussing implications for cross-national research.

Paper details pane

Publish or Perish version 8 introduced a brand-new paper details pane. The top section of the pane provides details of the (first) paper selected in the results pane. The bottom part of this pane provides the option to copy the paper's details in a variety of outputs and provides three options to get access to the paper itself.

Full paper details

Where available the top section provides:

- bibliographic details of the (first) paper selected in the results pane. For availability, see section above on exporting references.
- the full abstract.

The screenshot below shows what this looks like. For this paper, the full abstract was available, as were most of the paper's meta-data, except for details on volume and page numbers.

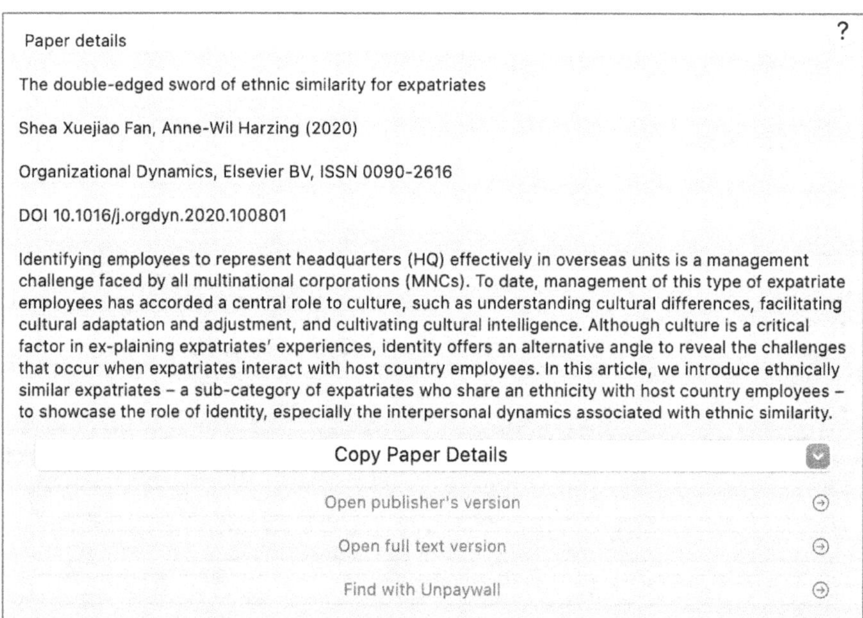

This feature was introduced so that it is easy to "eyeball" the papers by moving down the list of results. This allows you to quickly find the best (set of) papers or to uncheck any papers that are not relevant.

Which data sources provide abstracts?

Note that not all data sources provide (complete sets of) abstracts. Here is a summary:

- CrossRef: provides abstracts for some results only
- Google Scholar: provides the first few lines of the abstract only
- Google Scholar Profile: no abstracts
- OpenAlex: provides abstracts for most, but not all, results
- PubMed: provides abstracts for all results
- Scopus: no abstracts
- Semantic Scholar: no abstracts
- Web of Science: provides abstracts for all results

Copy paper details

The bottom part of this pane provides the option to copy the paper's details (including abstracts) in a variety of outputs. This includes the same output options as discussed in the section on exporting the data. This new feature is ideal for reviewing a set of results in more detail, conducting content analyses in a research project, importing abstracts with other bibliographic details in a reference management program, or even creating word clouds from a set of article abstracts.

Getting access to the paper itself

Next, this part of the pane shows three options to get access to the paper itself. The first refers to the official publisher's version, which may or may not be available to you. This depends on whether the article was published in Open Access, or your library has access to the journal in question.

If you cannot access the official publisher's version, you have two chances of finding a full text version.

1. A full-text available in the data source that you searched in.
2. A full-text in the Unpaywall database.

In most cases the two options provide the same version of the paper, this is not always the case. You might wish to try both so as to find the "best" version.

When trying this for the paper above, the first option indeed led to the publisher's version (see screenshot). However, the article was not published Open Access, so if your university doesn't subscribe to this journal, you may want to try the next two options. Both take you to a pre-publication version in Middlesex University's paper repository.

Organizational Dynamics

Volume 50, Issue 4, October–November 2021, 100801

The double-edged sword of ethnic similarity for expatriates

Even if the article is available in Open Access, you may still want to try the next two options as they will often take you directly to the PDF version of the paper rather than the web version.

In sum

In this chapter we have taken you through the main user interface of the Publish or Perish software, discussing the tools pane, the search pane, the results pane with its pop-up contextual menu, the citation metrics pane, and the paper details pane. The next chapter will focus on the Multi-searches centre, which includes the folder searches tree and the searches list.

Chapter 2: Multi-searches centre

Chapter 1 focused on individual searches. This chapter discusses the PoP features that allow you to keep track of your searches through the Multi-searches centre. The Multi-searches centre is made up of two panes: a searches folder tree view at the top left and a searches list view in the middle (see below). Results for individual searches are shown in a results pane that we discussed in the last chapter. The citation metrics pane of the right was also discussed in Chapter 1.

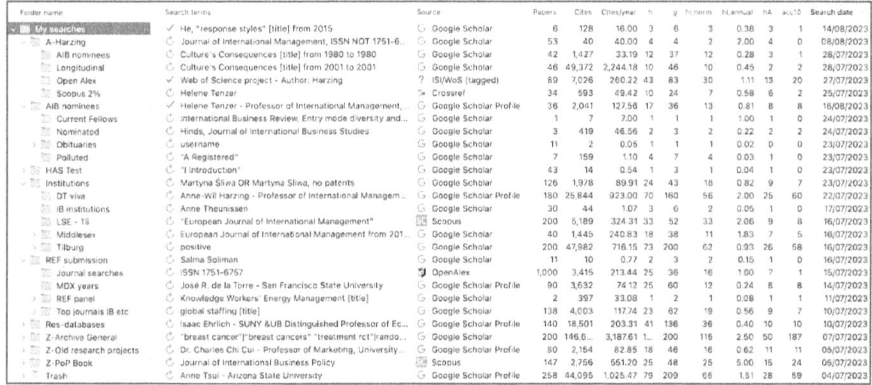

Folder name	Search terms	Source	Papers	Cites	Cites/year	h	g	h.norm	h.annual	hA	acc10	Search date
My searches	He, "response styles" [title] from 2015	Google Scholar	6	128	16.00	3	6	3	0.38	3	1	14/08/2023
A-Harzing	Journal of International Management, ISSN NOT 1751-6...	Google Scholar	53	40	40.00	4	4	2	2.00	4	0	08/08/2023
AIB nominees	Culture's Consequences [title] from 1980 to 1980	Google Scholar	42	1,427	33.19	12	37	12	0.28	3	1	28/07/2023
Longitudinal	Culture's Consequences [title] from 2001 to 2001	Google Scholar	46	49,372	2,244.18	10	46	10	0.45	2	2	28/07/2023
Open Alex	Web of Science project - Author: Harzing	ISI/WoS (tagged)	89	7,026	260.22	43	83	30	1.11	13	20	27/07/2023
Scopus 2%	Helene Tenzer	Crossref	34	593	49.42	10	24	7	0.58	6	2	25/07/2023
AIB nominees	Helene Tenzer - Professor of International Management,...	Google Scholar Profile	36	2,041	127.56	17	36	13	0.81	8	8	16/08/2023
Current Fellows	International Business Review, Entry mode diversity and...	Google Scholar	1	7	7.00	1	1	1	1.00	1	0	24/07/2023
Nominated	Hinds, Journal of International Business Studies	Google Scholar	3	419	46.56	2	3	2	0.22	2	2	24/07/2023
Obituaries	username	Google Scholar	11	2	0.05	1	1	1	0.02	0	0	23/07/2023
Polluted	"A Registered"	Google Scholar	7	159	1.10	4	7	4	0.03	1	0	23/07/2023
HAS Test	"I Introduction"	Google Scholar	43	14	0.54	1	3	1	0.04	1	0	23/07/2023
Institutions	Martyna Śliwa OR Martyna Sliwa, no patents	Google Scholar	126	1,978	89.91	24	43	18	0.82	9	7	23/07/2023
DT viva	Anne-Wil Harzing - Professor of International Managem...	Google Scholar Profile	180	25,844	923.00	70	160	56	2.00	25	60	22/07/2023
IB institutions	Anne Theunissen	Google Scholar	30	44	1.07	3	6	2	0.05	1	0	17/07/2023
LSE - Tß	"European Journal of International Management"	Scopus	200	5,189	324.31	33	52	33	2.06	9	8	16/07/2023
Middlesex	European Journal of International Management from 201...	Google Scholar	40	1,445	240.83	18	38	11	1.83	7	5	16/07/2023
Tilburg	positive	Google Scholar	200	47,982	716.15	73	200	62	0.93	26	58	16/07/2023
REF submission	Salma Soliman	Google Scholar	11	10	0.77	2	3	2	0.15	1	0	16/07/2023
Journal searches	ISSN 1751-6757	OpenAlex	1,000	3,415	213.44	25	36	16	1.00	7	1	15/07/2023
MDX years	José R. de la Torre - San Francisco State University	Google Scholar Profile	90	3,632	74.12	25	60	12	0.24	8	8	14/07/2023
REF panel	Knowledge Workers' Energy Management [title]	Google Scholar	2	397	33.08	1	2	1	0.08	1	1	11/07/2023
Top journals IB etc	global staffing [title]	Google Scholar	138	4,003	117.74	23	62	19	0.56	9	7	10/07/2023
Res-databases	Isaac Ehrlich - SUNY &UB Distinguished Professor of Ec...	Google Scholar Profile	140	18,501	203.31	41	136	36	0.40	10	10	10/07/2023
Z-Archive General	"breast cancer"|"breast cancers" "treatment rct"|rando...	Google Scholar	200	146,6...	3,187.61	1...	200	115	2.50	50	187	07/07/2023
Z-Old research projects	Dr. Charles Chi Cui - Professor of Marketing, University...	Google Scholar Profile	80	2,154	82.85	18	46	16	0.62	11	11	05/07/2023
Z-PoP Book	Journal of International Business Policy	Scopus	147	2,756	551.20	25	48	25	5.00	15	24	05/07/2023
Trash	Anne Tsui - Arizona State University	Google Scholar Profile	258	44,095	1,025.47	79	209	66	1.51	28	59	04/07/2023

In this chapter, we will discuss the tree view and the searches view, and show you how to export and import your data. This includes import from Scopus and the Web of Science, re-importing PoP data after corrections and exporting and importing Publish or Perish archives to transfer data between computers or between users. We will also discuss three key use cases that are facilitated by the Multi-searches centre: comparing metrics across data sources, conducting longitudinal comparisons, and aggregating searches.

Searches folder tree view

The tree on the left-hand side of the Publish or Perish Multi-searches centre displays all the available searches folders. The folders are containers that help you organise your searches.

When you start using PoP the searches folder tree only contains one folder called "My searches". This folder automatically stores the searches that you perform. You cannot delete this folder or change its name. However, you can create as many folders as you like. Searches folders can be nested, and they can be rearranged by dragging and dropping with the mouse, just like you would do in File Explorer on Windows or Finder on Mac. Folders can also be copied (**Ctrl+C** or ⌘+C), cut (**Ctrl+X** or ⌘+X), and pasted (**Ctrl+V** or ⌘+V).

Nested folders for effective search management

The screenshot below illustrates how folders can be nested to create logical containers for your searches. I recommend you organise your searches if you are planning to run them on a regular basis. It is very easy to get lost in a long list of recent searches.

The screenshot below shows my own current folder structure. As I do a lot of bibliometric research, it includes lots of folders and sub-folders. Your folder structure may not be as extensive, but it is still helpful to brings some structure in your searches.

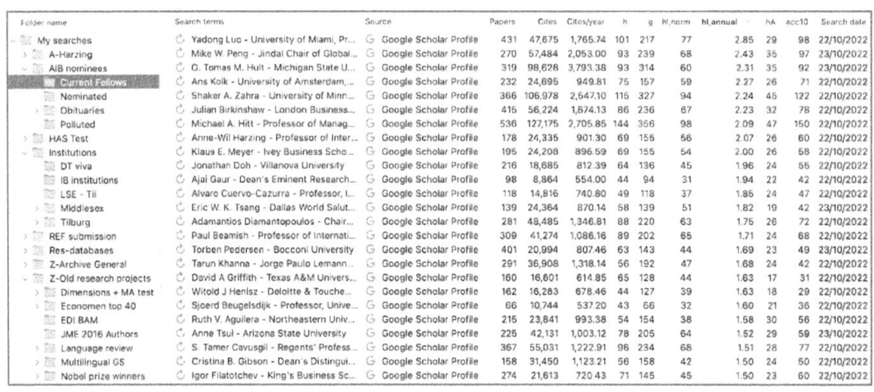

Folder name	Search terms	Source	Papers	Cites	Cites/year	h	g	hI,norm	hI,annual	hA	acc10	Search date
My searches	Yadong Luo - University of Miami, Pr...	Google Scholar Profile	431	47,675	1,765.74	101	217	77	2.85	29	98	22/10/2022
A-Harzing	Mike W. Peng - Jindal Chair of Global...	Google Scholar Profile	270	57,484	2,053.00	93	239	68	2.43	35	97	23/10/2022
AIB nominees	G. Tomas M. Hult - Michigan State U...	Google Scholar Profile	319	98,628	3,793.38	93	314	60	2.31	35	92	23/10/2022
Current Fellows	Ans Kolk - University of Amsterdam,...	Google Scholar Profile	232	24,695	949.81	75	157	59	2.27	26	71	22/10/2022
Nominated	Shaker A. Zahra - University of Minn...	Google Scholar Profile	366	106,978	2,547.10	116	327	94	2.24	45	122	22/10/2022
Obituaries	Julian Birkinshaw - London Business...	Google Scholar Profile	415	56,224	1,874.13	86	236	67	2.23	32	78	22/10/2022
Polluted	Michael A. Hitt - Professor of Manag...	Google Scholar Profile	536	127,175	2,705.85	144	356	98	2.09	47	150	22/10/2022
HAS Test	Anne-Wil Harzing - Professor of Inter...	Google Scholar Profile	178	24,335	901.30	69	155	56	2.07	26	60	22/10/2022
Institutions	Klaus E. Meyer - Ivey Business Scho...	Google Scholar Profile	195	24,208	896.59	69	155	54	2.00	26	68	22/10/2022
DT viva	Jonathan Doh - Villanova University	Google Scholar Profile	216	18,685	812.39	64	136	45	1.96	24	55	22/10/2022
IB institutions	Ajai Gaur - Dean's Eminent Research...	Google Scholar Profile	98	8,864	554.00	44	94	31	1.94	22	42	22/10/2022
LSE - Tii	Alvaro Cuervo-Cazurra - Professor, I...	Google Scholar Profile	118	14,816	740.80	49	118	37	1.85	24	47	22/10/2022
Middlesex	Eric W. K. Tsang - Dallas World Salut...	Google Scholar Profile	139	24,364	870.14	58	139	51	1.82	19	42	23/10/2022
Tilburg	Adamantios Diamantopoulos - Chair...	Google Scholar Profile	281	48,485	1,346.81	88	220	63	1.75	26	72	22/10/2022
REF submission	Paul Beamish - Professor of Internati...	Google Scholar Profile	309	41,274	1,086.16	89	202	65	1.71	24	68	22/10/2022
Res-databases	Torben Pedersen - Bocconi University	Google Scholar Profile	401	20,994	807.46	63	143	44	1.69	23	49	23/10/2022
Z-Archive General	Tarun Khanna - Jorge Paulo Lemann...	Google Scholar Profile	291	36,908	1,318.14	56	192	47	1.68	24	42	22/10/2022
Z-Old research projects	David A Griffith - Texas A&M Univers...	Google Scholar Profile	160	16,601	614.85	65	128	44	1.63	17	31	22/10/2022
Dimensions + MA test	Witold J Henisz - Deloitte & Touche...	Google Scholar Profile	162	16,283	678.46	44	127	39	1.63	18	29	22/10/2022
Economen top 40	Sjoerd Beugelsdijk - Professor, Unive...	Google Scholar Profile	66	10,744	537.20	43	66	32	1.60	21	36	22/10/2022
EDI BAM	Ruth V. Aguilera - Northeastern Univ...	Google Scholar Profile	215	23,841	993.38	54	154	38	1.58	30	56	22/10/2022
JME 2016 Authors	Anne Tsui - Arizona State University	Google Scholar Profile	225	42,131	1,003.12	78	205	64	1.52	29	59	23/10/2022
Language review	S. Tamer Cavusgil - Regents' Profess...	Google Scholar Profile	367	55,031	1,222.91	96	234	68	1.51	28	77	22/10/2022
Multilingual GS	Cristina B. Gibson - Dean's Distingui...	Google Scholar Profile	158	31,450	1,123.21	56	158	42	1.50	24	50	22/10/2022
Nobel prize winners	Igor Filatotchev - King's Business Sc...	Google Scholar Profile	274	21,613	720.43	71	145	45	1.50	23	60	22/10/2022

It is also a good idea to clean out your "My searches" folder periodically, so that even if you do not want to make the effort to organise your searches into folders, you can keep some order in your searches. Simply select the searches you want to discard and delete them using your keyboard or right-click context menu.

Searches list view

The list in the middle of the top half of the PoP user interface shows the searches that you have conducted. These searches can be moved between folders by dragging and dropping them with the mouse, just like you would do in File Explorer on Windows or Finder on Mac. Searches can also be copied (**Ctrl+C** or ⌘+C), cut (**Ctrl+X** or ⌘+X), and pasted (**Ctrl+V** or ⌘+V).

If you are looking for a specific search and can remember the search you did, you can find it by rapidly typing the first couple of letters. This will take you to the first occurrence of this sequence of letters.

Results list in the Multi-searches centre

The screenshot below shows the full results of the searches shown in the folder "Economen top 40", subfolder publications between "2012-2016" only. This was part of a research project I did on the use of new metrics and data sources for the Dutch Economics top-40. The results can be sorted on any column, simply click on the column heading. By default, the searches are sorted in the order in which they were executed. The list below has been sorted by hI,annual.

Search terms	Source	Papers	Cites	Cites/year	h	g	hI.norm	hI,annual	hA	acc10	Search date
Arnold B. Bakker - Professor of Work and Orga...	Google Scholar Profile	215	7,841	1,568.20	48	84	28	5.60	26	73	21/12/2017
Daan van Knippenberg - Drexel University	Google Scholar Profile	71	2,532	506.40	23	50	16	3.20	16	24	21/12/2017
Ron Boschma - Professor in Regional Economic...	Google Scholar Profile	85	2,078	415.60	24	45	16	3.20	14	17	21/12/2017
Jakob de Haan - Hoogleraar University of Groni...	Google Scholar Profile	175	1,854	370.80	22	40	15	3.00	14	20	21/12/2017
Jan van Ours - Erasmus School of Economics,...	Google Scholar Profile	66	1,284	256.80	18	35	14	2.80	12	15	21/12/2017
Marcel Timmer - Professor Economic Growth a...	Google Scholar Profile	49	4,836	967.20	20	49	13	2.60	16	18	21/12/2017
Anne-Wil Harzing - Professor of International M...	Google Scholar Profile	36	1,034	206.80	16	32	13	2.60	11	13	21/12/2017
Albert J. Menkveld - VU University Amsterdam	Google Scholar Profile	34	1,225	245.00	13	34	11	2.20	9	9	21/12/2017
Siem Jan Koopman - Professor of Econometrics...	Google Scholar Profile	82	1,043	208.60	19	31	11	2.20	11	11	21/12/2017
Caspar Chorus - Delft University of Technology	Google Scholar Profile	95	925	185.00	18	28	11	2.20	10	8	21/12/2017
PC Verhoef	Google Scholar	51	1,525	305.00	17	39	10	2.00	11	13	21/12/2017
Rik Pieters - Tilburg University	Google Scholar Profile	39	941	188.20	15	30	10	2.00	9	7	21/12/2017
Wolf Wagner - Professor of Finance, Rotterdam...	Google Scholar Profile	38	400	80.00	14	19	10	2.00	6	4	21/12/2017
Werner BF Brouwer - Professor of Health Econo...	Google Scholar Profile	105	1,407	281.40	23	33	9	1.80	11	16	21/12/2017
Erwin Bulte - Professor of development econo...	Google Scholar Profile	65	1,071	214.20	15	32	9	1.80	9	6	21/12/2017
Andre Lucas - VU University Amsterdam and Ti...	Google Scholar Profile	54	864	172.80	13	29	9	1.80	10	10	21/12/2017
Luc Renneboog - Tilburg University	Google Scholar Profile	61	750	150.00	13	26	9	1.80	8	8	21/12/2017
Cees Withagen	Google Scholar	47	700	140.00	13	26	9	1.80	8	7	21/12/2017
Robert Inklaar - Professor of Economics, Univer...	Google Scholar Profile	33	1,773	354.60	9	33	8	1.60	8	4	21/12/2017
Harry Huizinga, NOT "HW Huizinga"	Google Scholar	40	1,033	206.60	11	32	8	1.60	8	8	21/12/2017
Jos Van Ommeren -	Google Scholar Profile	63	642	128.40	14	23	8	1.60	8	6	21/12/2017
Marius van Dijke - Professor in behavioural ethi...	Google Scholar Profile	45	634	126.80	14	24	8	1.60	9	7	21/12/2017

You may notice I sneaked myself in the list. I wasn't listed in the Economics top-40 as I do not work in the Netherlands, but was curious to see how my record compared with this list.

List view columns

The list view displays the following columns. It is not possible to
change the columns that are displayed, but this might change in a
future version of Publish or Perish. For more details on the various
citation metrics, please refer to Chapter 3 on citations metrics.

Column	Description
Search terms	An abbreviated rendering of the search parameters, intended as a reminder about the search. To see all search parameters, simply click on the search. This will also allow you edit the search.
Source	The source of data (e.g., Google Scholar, WoS, Scopus, Google Scholar Profile, OpenAlex)
Papers	The number of results (~papers) returned by the search.
Cites	The total number of citations returned by the search.
Cites/year	The total number of citations in the search divided by the number of years spanned by the results.
h	Hirsch's h-index calculated for the search results.
g	Egge's g-index calculated for the search results.
hI,norm	Normalised individual h-index for the search results.
hI,annual	Annualised individual h-index for the search results.
hA	Annualised h-index for the search results.
Search Date	The date on which this search was last performed.
Cache Date	The date on which the search data were last retrieved from the date source in question.

Search terms are prefaced by one of three symbols.

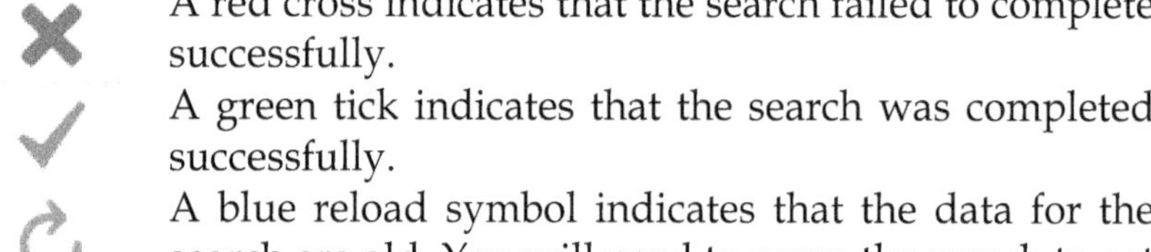

A red cross indicates that the search failed to complete
successfully.

A green tick indicates that the search was completed
successfully.

A blue reload symbol indicates that the data for the
search are old. You will need to rerun the search to get
more recent data.

Exporting your results

The Publish or Perish Multi-searches centre not only makes it easy to organise your searches, but also to export all your search results for further processing. This is particularly useful if you want to do bibliometric research with the PoP results.

The easiest way to export is to select the searches you want to export and right-click to access the pop-up menu. You can also use the **Copy Results** or **Save results** buttons below the Citations pane (for details see Chapter 1). You can export both the results, i.e., the actual list of publications, and the metrics for the search(es) in question. Whether you use Copy or Save as is a matter of preference.

Export the results

Let's assume we are working with a set of Dutch Economists as I did for the project in the paper below. The screenshot shows the top of the list of searches that I conducted in 2014 with nine names selected.

- Harzing, A.W.; Mijnhardt, W. (2015) **Proof over promise: Towards a more inclusive ranking of Dutch academics in Economics & Business**, *Scientometrics*, vol. 102, no. 1, pp. 727-749.

Search terms	Source	Papers	Cites	Cites/year	h	g	hl,norm	hl,annual	hA	acc10	Search date
"Alessie R" from 1988	Google Scholar	192	2,431	86.82	23	46	15	0.54	7	5	20/01/2014
"Anufriev M" from 2004	Google Scholar	57	300	25.00	10	16	7	0.58	4	0	20/01/2014
"Baillon A", NOT "AF Baillon" AND N...	Google Scholar	29	312	34.67	8	17	5	0.56	4	1	20/01/2014
"Baltussen R" from 1996	Google Scholar	170	3,331	166.55	31	54	18	0.90	9	7	20/01/2014
"Barkema Harry" OR "Barkema HG"...	Google Scholar	54	6,693	304.23	19	54	17	0.77	13	13	20/01/2014
"Beck Thorsten", NOT "WO Patent"...	Google Scholar	426	24,753	1,456.06	60	155	43	2.53	23	43	20/01/2014
"Beetsma R" from 1994	Google Scholar	272	3,538	160.82	31	57	23	1.05	9	7	20/01/2014
"Belderbos R" from 1992	Google Scholar	213	3,594	149.75	25	59	20	0.83	9	8	20/01/2014
"Benschop Y" from 1996	Google Scholar	92	1,435	71.75	19	37	14	0.70	6	3	20/01/2014
"Beugelsdijk S" from 2001	Google Scholar	121	2,391	159.40	27	48	19	1.27	9	7	20/01/2014
"Bijmolt T" from 1994	Google Scholar	147	2,059	93.59	25	44	16	0.73	7	3	20/01/2014
"Blazevic V", NOT cancer AND NOT...	Google Scholar	54	372	28.62	7	19	6	0.46	4	1	20/01/2014
"Bleichrodt H" from 1995	Google Scholar	162	3,845	183.10	33	61	22	1.05	7	5	20/01/2014
"Bloemen Hans" OR "HG Bloemen",...	Google Scholar	72	614	32.32	14	24	13	0.68	4	0	20/01/2014
"Bloemer J", NOT "JW Bloemer" AN...	Google Scholar	176	4,673	173.07	23	68	16	0.59	9	7	20/01/2014
"Boone Jan", NOT "J* Boone" AND...	Google Scholar	146	1,900	118.75	20	42	14	0.88	7	4	20/01/2014
"Boot A", NOT "AM Boot" AND NOT...	Google Scholar	400	7,478	257.86	24	85	21	0.72	10	10	20/01/2014
"Borghans L" from 1996	Google Scholar	292	2,564	128.20	23	46	18	0.90	7	3	20/01/2014
"Borm Peter" OR "Borm PEM", NOT...	Google Scholar	290	2,346	93.84	26	42	14	0.56	6	0	22/01/2014
"Boswijk P" OR "Boswijk HP" from 1...	Google Scholar	129	1,298	54.08	17	35	14	0.58	4	1	20/01/2014
"Bovenberg A", NOT genetics from 1...	Google Scholar	712	8,826	294.20	40	89	33	1.10	11	11	20/01/2014
"Bronnenberg B" from 1996	Google Scholar	99	2,958	147.90	23	54	15	0.75	7	3	20/01/2014

If you would like to export the *results*, i.e., the articles published by these nine Economist(s) to Excel for further analysis, simply select any searches you want to export (as many as you want), right-click and select **Copy Results as CSV**, **Copy Results for Excel** or **Save as CSV**.

Copy [...] for Excel with Header most useful

I normally find the **Excel with Header** option most useful. After you paste to Excel, it shows you the data in a nice column format that you can then convert to a sortable table with just one click [Use **Insert Table** in Excel]. The current table is sorted by citations, but obviously you can sort it in any way you want.

Cites	Authors	Title	Year	Source	Publisher
1380	HG Barkema, JHJ Bell, JME Pennings	Foreign entry, cultural barriers and learning	1996	Strategic management journal	repub.eur.nl
1164	HG Barkema, F Vermeulen	International expansion through start-up or acquis	1998	Academy of Management journal	amj.aom.org
813	JMM Bloemer, HDP Kasper	The complex relationship between consumer satis	1995	Journal of economic psychology	Elsevier
761	J Bloemer, K De Ruyter	On the relationship between store image, store sa	1998	European Journal of Marketing	emeraldinsight.com
678	F Vermeulen, H Barkema	Learning through acquisitions	2001	Academy of Management Journal	amj.aom.org
575	L Borghans, AL Duckworth, JJ Heckman, ...	The economics and psychology of personality trait	2008	Journal of Human ...	jhr.uwpress.org
564	HG Barkema, F Vermeulen	What differences in the cultural backgrounds of pa	1997	Journal of international business studies	JSTOR
528	HG Barkema, O Shenkar, F Vermeulen, ...	Working abroad, working with others: How firms l	1997	Academy of Management ...	amj.aom.org
493	J Bloemer, KO De Ruyter, ...	Linking perceived service quality and service loyalt	1999	European Journal of ...	emeraldinsight.com
450	J Bloemer, K De Ruyter, ...	Investigating drivers of bank loyalty: the complex r	1998	International Journal of ...	emeraldinsight.com
426	HG Barkema, LR Gomez-Mejia	Managerial Gompensation and Firm Performance	1998	Academy of Management Journal	amj.aom.org
416	K De Ruyter, M Wetzels, ...	On the relationship between perceived service qua	1998	International Journal of ...	emeraldinsight.com
340	JM Pennings, H Barkema, S Douma	Organizational learning and diversification	1994	Academy of Management journal	amj.aom.org
312	F Vermeulen, H Barkema	Pace, rhythm, and scope: Process dependence in b	2002	Strategic Management Journal	Wiley Online Library
265	S Beugelsdijk, HLF De Groot, ...	Trust and economic growth: a robustness analysis	2004	Oxford Economic ...	Oxford Univ Press
265	K De Ruyter, J Bloemer, P Peeters	Merging service quality and service satisfaction. A	1997	Journal of Economic Psychology	Elsevier
254	J Bloemer, G Odekerken-Schroder	Store satisfaction and store loyalty explained by cu	2002	Journal of Consumer Satisfaction ...	lilt.ilstu.edu
227	M Van Rooij, A Lusardi, R Alessie	Financial literacy and stock market participation	2011	Journal of Financial Economics	Elsevier
224	HG Barkema, JAC Baum, EA Mannix	Management challenges in a new time	2002	Academy of Management ...	amj.aom.org
223	Y Benschop, H Doorewaard	Covered by equality: the gender subtext of organiz	1998	Organization Studies	oss.sagepub.com

Export the metrics

Exporting the actual papers is useful if you are interested analysing the most cited papers by a particular set of authors, or if you would like to analyse the journals they publish or even do a thematic analysis of their publications.

However, in a bibliometrics project like this you would normally be more interested in the citation metrics, that is the number of papers, citations, h-index etc., for the individual authors, journals or topics covered in the searches (see Chapters 7-9 for more information on author, journal, and topical searches).

If you have organised all searches in a dedicated folder all you need to do to export metrics is click anywhere in the results list, click **Ctr+A** or ⌘**+A** to select all results, right-click and select one of the **Copy Metrics…** commands. This allows you to copy all the metrics to the Windows/Mac clipboard for pasting them into a variety of other programs.

Again, for most users the best option is to use the **Copy Metrics for Excel** command. To ensure you copy the headers with the names of the metrics into your file, use **Copy Metrics for Excel with Header**. Then paste the results into an Excel worksheet. With one click you insert a table, and your data are ready for further processing.

Query	Papers	Citations	Years	Cites_Year	Cites_Paper	Cites_Author	Papers_Author	Authors_Paper
Alessie R from 1988: all	192	2431	26	93.5	12.66	913.15	70.95	3.01
Anufriev M from 2004: all	57	300	10	30	5.26	146.5	26.1	2.51
Baillon A, NOT "AF Baillon" in:	29	312	7	44.57	10.76	113	12.62	2.79
Baltussen R from 1996: all	170	3331	18	185.06	19.59	993.28	50.25	3.79
Barkema Harry OR "Barkema I	54	6693	20	334.65	123.94	2924.03	23.69	2.72
Beck Thorsten, NOT "WO Pate	426	24753	15	1650.2	58.11	9735.52	206.32	2.67
Beetsma R from 1994: all	272	3538	20	176.9	13.01	1749.43	128.88	2.52
Belderbos R from 1992: all	213	3594	22	163.36	16.87	1724.77	95.7	2.84
Benschop Y from 1996: all	92	1435	18	79.72	15.6	761.29	43.87	2.63
Beugelsdijk S from 2001: all	121	2391	13	183.92	19.76	1258.61	59.72	2.53
Bijmolt T from 1994: all	147	2059	20	102.95	14.01	754.63	57.48	3.06
Blazevic V, NOT cancer norovi	54	372	11	33.82	6.89	153.16	29.12	2.59
Bleichrodt H from 1995: all	162	3845	19	202.37	23.73	1726.09	72.61	2.75
Bloemen Hans OR "HG Bloem	72	614	17	36.12	8.53	446.46	43.39	2.28

Importing Scopus data

Publish or Perish supports direct searches in Scopus. However, as this is the free version of Scopus, it is limited to 200 results and only lists the first author of any paper. So, if your university has a Scopus subscription, you can also conduct your searches in the Scopus web interface and import the data into Publish or Perish.

Note: Unfortunately, I currently do not have access to Scopus at my university. Hence the screenshots in the instructions below date back to 2015. The current web interface might look a little different, but the key steps should be very similar. If you find they are not, please do contact me at anne@harzing.com and I will investigate further.

Five easy steps

1. Conduct a search in Scopus. [If you don't know how to do this, contact your librarian].

2. Once you have the correct set of results, click on the drop-down field next to the check-box and click **Select all** to select all records.

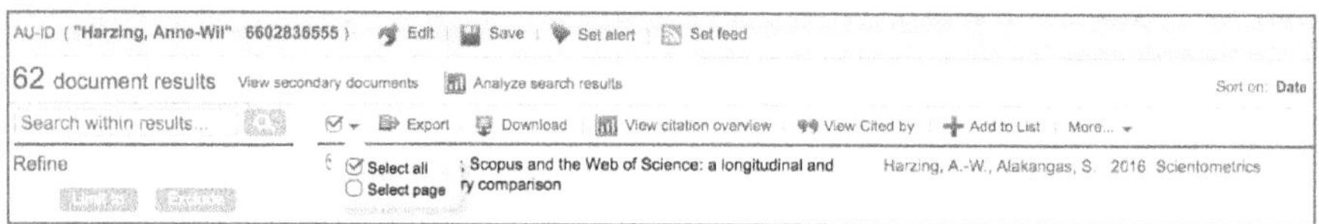

3. Click on the drop-down field next to export. You will get a pop-up menu. On that menu, select CSV export and save the file with a meaningful name. Do *not* change anything under "Choose the information to be exported". Doing so will make the file unreadable for Publish or Perish.

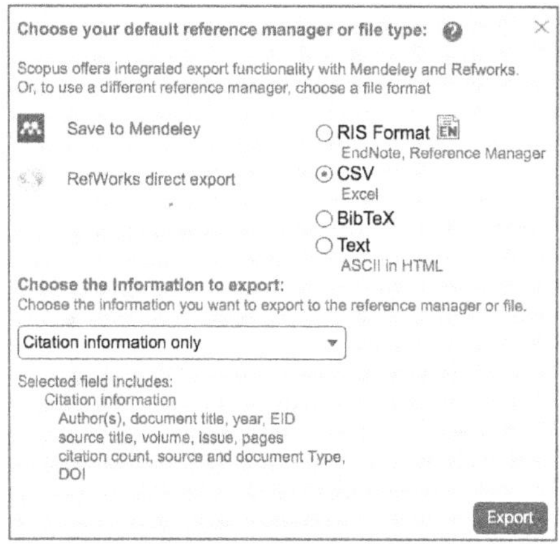

4. This provides you with a .csv file that you can then import into Publish or Perish. Simply click anywhere in the folder where you would like to store the imported results, right-click and then click on **Import External Data**.

5. Publish or Perish will now import the Scopus data into the Multi-searches centre. The results will appear in the folder that you are in when you import the data.

Compact list ready for further analysis

The result is a compact list of publications that can then be sorted in any way you want. Metrics and results can be exported for further analyses just like the results of searches in Google Scholar or any of the other data source that can be accessed directly from the Publish or Perish interface.

Importing Web of Science data

Publish or Perish supports direct searches in the Web of Science. However, this option is only available if your university has a Web of Science subscription with appropriate API support. If this is not the case and you still want to use PoP to conduct research with Web of Science data, you can conduct your search in the Web of Science web interface (if you have access) and import the data into PoP.

Five easy steps

1. Conduct a search in the Web of Science. [If you don't know how to do this, contact your librarian].

2. Once you have the correct set of results, click on the drop-down field **Export** (see screenshot below). Click on **Plain text file**.

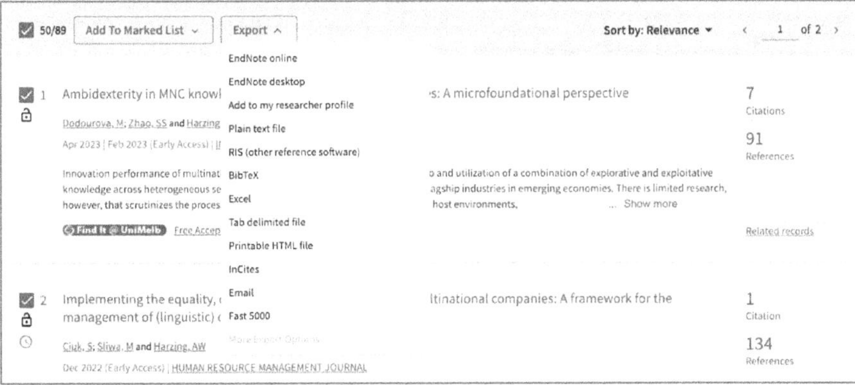

3. On the resulting pop-up box (see screenshot below), you can leave the Record Options to default, unless you have more than 50 results. In that case, specify the number of records you want to export (third radio button). In addition, you need to select the "Full Record and Cited References" under record content. Web of Science has changed their record format and citation information is no longer provided in the default Author, Title, Source record.

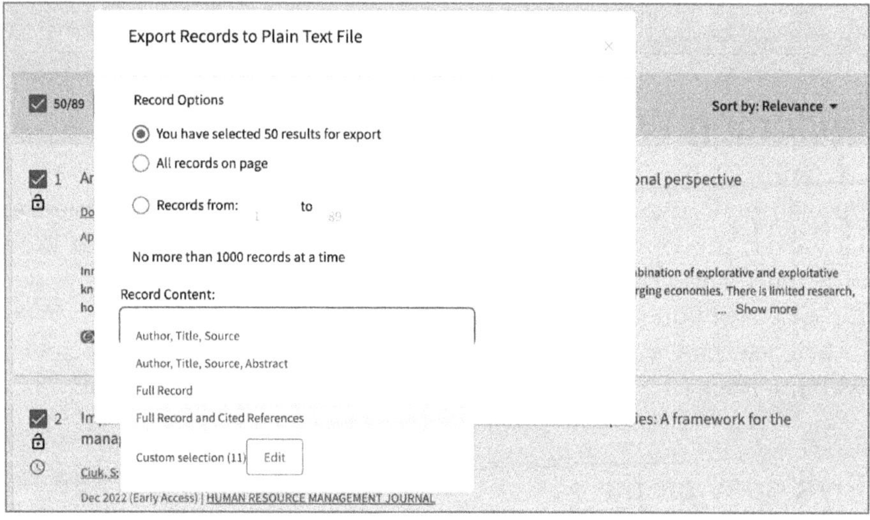

4. This provides you with a .txt file that you can then import into Publish or Perish. Simply click anywhere in the folder where you would like to store the imported results, right-click and then click on **Import External Data**.

5. Publish or Perish will now import the Web of Science data into the Multi-searches centre (see screenshot below). The results will appear in the folder that you are in when you import the data.

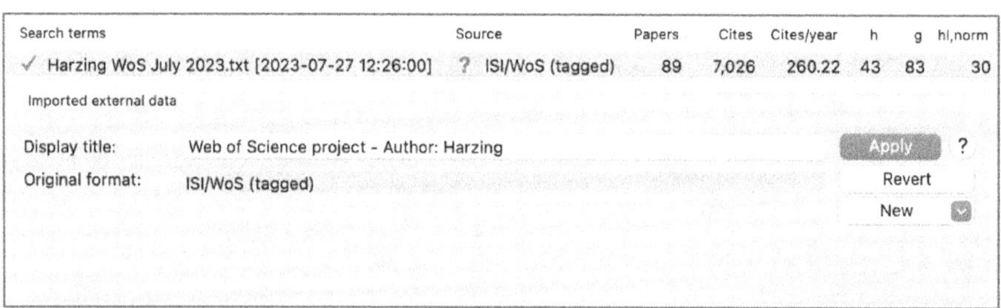

If you forgot to use descriptive filename when exporting the file from the Web of Science, you can still change it by changing the Display title and clicking **Apply**. Note that the above screenshot was taken before I clicked on Apply.

Compact list ready for further analysis

The result is a compact list of publications that can then be sorted in any way you want (see screenshot below). Metrics and results can be exported for further analyses just like the results of searches in Google Scholar or any other data source that can be accessed directly from the Publish or Perish interface.

Re-Importing exported PoP data

As described in the section on exporting, you can export the results of a search to for instance Excel. Subsequently you can *re-import* this same file back into Publish or Perish. Why would you want to do this? One reason would be to aggregate searches (as described in the last section of this chapter). Another would be to make corrections.

Making corrections and recalculate metrics

This can be very useful if you want to make (minor) corrections to the results and then have Publish or Perish recalculate the metrics. For example, you might want to:

- Adjust any years that Google Scholar parsed wrongly.

- Complete truncated titles or author lists.

- Correct titles for any records where Google Scholar parsed the wrong version of the paper as a master record.

- Remove irrelevant publications altogether, rather than simply of un-ticking them in PoP. This will make it much easier to subsequently clean up the results further by merging as you will have fewer records to work with.

In order to do this, follow these steps:

1. Right-click on the search you wish to export.

2. Chose **Save as CSV** and give the file a meaningful name.

3. Open the file in Excel. [**Note**: Don't worry if you see strange squiggly letters; this is just Excel not coping well with accented letters. They will be fine once you reimport the data into PoP].

4. Make the required changes.

5. Save the file again in CSV format.

6. Reimport the file into Publish or Perish by clicking on **Import External data**.

Worked example: corrected data

Google Scholar parsing is much better now than it was in the early years, and I could not find a good example for a recent search. Hence, I am using an old example from the 2016 Publish or Perish Tutorial. The two screenshots under old and new results below show my six most highly cited publications on a citations per year basis. The first screenshot shows the original data. The second screenshot shows the corrected data. Changes made were:

- Changed the year for the third publication from 2007 to 2008, the correct publication year.
- Changed the year for a publication (not visible in the first screenshot) parsed as 2013 (as its online first publication date) to 2014 (as its print publication date).
- Changed the title for the third publication into its correct title (the reported title is the title of an earlier working paper).

Old results

Cites		Per year	Authors	Title	Year
✓	h 436	72.67	NJ Adler, AW H...	When knowledge wins: Transcending the sense and nonsense of academic rankings	2009
✓	h 342	68.40	AW Harzing, A ...	International human resource management	2010
✓	h 372	46.50	AW Harzing, R ...	Google Scholar: the democratization of citation analysis	2007
✓	h 305	55.88	AW Harzing	Publish or perish	2007
✓	h 450	36.31	AW Harzing	Acquisitions versus greenfield investments: International strategy and management of entry modes	2002
✓	h 164	32.80	AW Harzing	The publish or perish book	2010

New results

Cites		Per year	Authors	Title	Year
✓	h 436	72.67	NJ Adler, AW Harzing	When knowledge wins: Transcending the sense and nonsense of academic rankings	2009
✓	h 342	68.40	AW Harzing, A Pinnin...	International human resource management	2010
✓	h 372	53.14	AW Harzing, R Van d...	Google Scholar: a new source for citation analysis	2008
✓	h 305	38.13	AW Harzing	Publish or perish	2007
✓	h 450	34.62	AW Harzing	Acquisitions versus greenfield investments: International strategy and management of entry modes	2002
✓	34	34.00	H Tenzer, M Pudelko	The impact of language barriers on trust formation in multinational teams	2014

Effect of the corrections

As a result, the citations per year for the third paper increased from 46.50 per year to 53.14 per year. Changes for the language barrier and trust formation paper were more dramatic as its citations per year increased from 17 to 34, making it my 6th most highly cited paper per year instead of my 27th most highly cited.

Conclusion

Obviously, one would not go through the effort of manually correcting the results for every single search. However, the ability to make corrections and re-import the data might be a lifesaver for one-off important occasions such as an application for tenure or promotion.

Exporting and Importing Archives

Having spent a lot of time on creating searches and logical folder structures in the Multi-searches centre, you obviously do not want to go through this entire process a second or even third time. This might be necessary in the following situations:

- Transferring your work after buying a new computer.

- Reinstating your work after a computer hard-disk crash.

- Sharing your searches with a research collaborator or research assistant.

Whatever the reason, Publish or Perish has a sophisticated system for archiving your data, and exporting or importing them.

Archiving your data

To save your Publish or Perish searches and the associated results data to an archive, use the **Export to Archive** command. You can then reload these data into Publish or Perish on the same computer or on a different computer through the **Import from Archive** command.

Publish or Perish data archives store the following information:

- The selected searches and their parameters,

- The search results,

- The metrics for the search results,

- The folder structure that contains the searches that are being exported.

Exporting the data archive

To export the Publish or Perish data archive, please use the following procedure.

1. Go to the Multi-searches centre.

2. Select the searches or the folder to export, or the **My searches** root to export the entire searches tree.

3. Right-click on the selected item and choose **Export to Archive**, or choose **File > Export to Archive** from the main menu.

4. When prompted, enter a file name for the data archive and click **Save**.

Publish or Perish will then save the searches with all their parameters and their metrics, plus the complete results for each search. The resulting archive file has a .pxa file extension and can be used to import the same searches and their data into Publish or Perish on the same or a different computer.

Importing the data archive

To import a Publish or Perish data archive that you or someone else previously exported, use the following procedure.

1. Choose **File > Import from Archive** from the main menu.

2. When prompted, select the archive that you want to import and click **Open**.

Publish or Perish will then load the searches and their data from the archive and merge them into your existing searches tree in the Multi-searches centre. Unless the file is very large, this typically takes only a few seconds. So, if you think nothing happened you probably just blinked ☺.

Rules applied when merging searches

While merging, Publish or Perish applies the following rules:

- If an incoming search is the same as an existing search, the existing search is overwritten if the incoming data are newer. If the incoming data are older than the existing data, no change is made.

- If an incoming search has no counterpart in the existing tree, it is simply added to the tree.

- If an incoming folder is already present in the existing tree, its contents are merged with the existing folder's contents.

- If an incoming folder is not yet present in the existing tree, it is added to the tree and its contents are then processed further.

The nitty gritty details….

During the merge process, Publish or Perish uses internal IDs to track individual searches and folders. The purpose of these IDs is to locate the correct searches and folders even if they have been moved to a new location in the existing tree after the data archive was originally exported. On occasion, this might cause imported searches or folders to show up in a different location than they were in when originally exported, but that is by design and avoids duplicating the information in the old and the new tree locations.

Comparing metrics across data-sources

Even if you are not doing any real bibliometric research, the Multi-searches centre allows you to instantly compare citation metrics from different data-sources. The screenshot below shows that in my case there is quite a big difference between the data-sources. As discussed in Chapter 5, this is quite typical for a Social Sciences scholar.

Search terms	Source	Papers	Cites	Cites/year	h	g	hI,norm	hI,annual	hA	acc10
✓ a harzing from 1995	Google Scholar	439	26,340	940.71	71	160	57	2.04	25	61
✓ Anne-Wil Harzing - Prof...	Google Scholar Profile	180	25,855	923.39	71	160	56	2.00	25	60
✓ 0000-0003-1509-3003	OpenAlex	168	12,100	432.14	55	109	40	1.43	16	29
✓ a. harzing	Scopus	103	9,996	357.00	51	99	51	1.82	15	27
✓ harzing	Crossref	126	9,443	337.25	51	97	36	1.29	14	25
✓ harzing a	Web of Science	89	6,955	257.59	44	83	30	1.11	13	20

Google Scholar and Google Scholar Profiles report by far the highest citation counts, with the Web of Science presenting the lowest count. The four other data sources are in between these two extremes, but none of them get close to Google Scholar (Profiles). PubMed is not shown as I am a Social Sciences scholar, and this data source only includes articles in the Bio-medical Sciences. Semantic Scholar isn't show as you are only able to do keywords searches in Publish or Perish for this data source.

Longitudinal comparisons

The Publish or Perish Multi-searches centre is also very useful if you want to run the same search periodically to compare metrics over time. To ensure you keep the results of older searches intact, you need to copy the search and run the copied search again. If you run the original search again, the old results will be replaced by the new data.

Longitudinal results for individuals might be important to establish progress for a tenure, promotion, or grant application. However, they can also serve many other purposes, such as the growth of publications in a particular research area, or the development of impact of particular journals over time.

Longitudinal data also allow us to illustrate the features of different research metrics. For the Publish or Perish tutorial (2016), I kept monthly searches for my own name between May 2013 and December 2015. You can see that the number of citations is increasing quite rapidly. In contrast, the h-index, and the hI,norm increase at a much slower rate. The number of citations per year also increases, but dips every January when the year is increased by 1.

Finally, the hI,annual was quite stable over time, dipping in January when the year is increased by 1, gradually rising again over the year as the hI,norm increases and then dipping again the next January. This shows that it is very hard to substantially increase the hI,annual. Even maintaining it needs a steady increase in the hI,norm to counteract the natural decline over the years.

Query	Papers	Cites	Cites/year	h	g	hI,norm	hI,annual	Query date
"A Harzing"...	198	5344	296.89	36	70	32	1.78	02/05/2013
"A Harzing"...	199	5459	303.28	37	71	32	1.78	02/06/2013
"A Harzing"...	200	5714	317.44	38	73	32	1.78	01/07/2013
"A Harzing"...	201	5730	318.33	37	73	32	1.78	12/08/2013
"A Harzing"...	202	5815	323.06	37	74	32	1.78	01/09/2013
"A Harzing"...	202	5927	329.28	37	74	32	1.78	04/10/2013
"A Harzing"...	205	6041	335.61	37	75	32	1.78	02/11/2013
"A Harzing"...	204	6154	341.89	39	76	32	1.78	01/12/2013
"A Harzing"...	207	6322	332.74	39	77	32	1.68	03/01/2014
"A Harzing"...	207	6451	339.53	40	78	33	1.74	31/01/2014
"A Harzing"...	223	6636	349.26	39	79	32	1.68	28/02/2014
"A Harzing"...	223	6727	354.05	39	79	33	1.74	01/04/2014
"A Harzing"...	224	6825	359.21	39	80	33	1.74	03/05/2014
"A Harzing"...	225	6915	363.95	40	80	33	1.74	02/06/2014
"A Harzing"...	234	7113	374.37	40	82	34	1.79	02/07/2014
"A Harzing"...	236	7191	378.47	40	82	34	1.79	01/08/2014
"A Harzing"...	235	7330	385.79	40	83	34	1.79	03/09/2014
"A Harzing"...	234	7395	389.21	40	83	34	1.79	03/10/2014
"A Harzing"...	243	7506	395.05	41	84	34	1.79	01/11/2014
"A Harzing"...	248	7641	402.16	41	85	35	1.84	30/11/2014
"A Harzing"...	249	7742	387.10	41	85	35	1.75	01/01/2015
"A Harzing"...	253	8103	405.15	42	87	35	1.75	01/02/2015
"A Harzing"...	253	8230	411.50	42	88	35	1.75	04/03/2015
"A Harzing"...	253	8356	417.80	42	89	35	1.75	01/04/2015
"A Harzing"...	255	8467	423.35	42	89	35	1.75	30/04/2015
"A Harzing"...	259	8638	431.90	42	90	35	1.75	01/06/2015
"A Harzing"...	244	8913	445.65	44	92	35	1.75	02/07/2015
"A Harzing"...	245	9041	452.05	44	93	36	1.80	01/08/2015
"A Harzing"...	248	9117	455.85	44	93	36	1.80	03/09/2015
"A Harzing"...	250	9203	460.15	44	94	36	1.80	03/10/2015
"A Harzing"...	251	9309	465.45	44	94	36	1.80	03/11/2015
"A Harzing"...	250	9430	471.50	44	95	36	1.80	04/12/2015

In the past year, I have resumed my monthly snapshots and the same pattern reappears. However, the rate of increase in my h-index has slowed down further. This is only logical, as once the h-index reaches a high level, it becomes progressively harder to increase it. Every new publication entering the h-index will need to reach a larger number of citations.

Search terms	Source	Papers	Cites	Cites/year	h	g	hI,norm	hI,annual	hA	acc10	Search date
Anne-Wil Harzing -...	Google Scholar Profile	178	24,113	893.07	69	155	56	2.07	25	60	13/09/2022
Anne-Wil Harzing -...	Google Scholar Profile	178	24,306	900.22	69	155	56	2.07	26	60	13/10/2022
Anne-Wil Harzing -...	Google Scholar Profile	179	24,458	905.85	70	156	56	2.07	26	60	12/11/2022
Anne-Wil Harzing -...	Google Scholar Profile	179	24,675	913.89	70	157	56	2.07	26	61	13/12/2022
Anne-Wil Harzing -...	Google Scholar Profile	180	24,829	886.75	70	157	56	2.00	24	57	12/01/2023
Anne-Wil Harzing -...	Google Scholar Profile	180	24,949	891.04	70	157	56	2.00	24	56	16/02/2023
Anne-Wil Harzing -...	Google Scholar Profile	180	25,169	898.89	70	158	56	2.00	24	56	15/03/2023
Anne-Wil Harzing -...	Google Scholar Profile	180	25,337	904.89	70	159	56	2.00	24	56	12/04/2023
Anne-Wil Harzing -...	Google Scholar Profile	180	25,529	911.75	70	159	56	2.00	24	58	15/05/2023
Anne-Wil Harzing -...	Google Scholar Profile	180	25,742	919.36	70	160	56	2.00	24	58	13/06/2023
Anne-Wil Harzing -...	Google Scholar Profile	180	25,776	920.57	70	160	56	2.00	25	59	13/07/2023
Anne-Wil Harzing -...	Google Scholar Profile	180	25,953	926.89	71	161	56	2.00	25	60	13/08/2023

You will also notice that my hI,annual (hI,norm divided by academic age) is only marginally higher than it was 10 years ago. This is despite a doubling of the h-index and a 75% increase in the hI,norm. As a time-sensitive metric the hI,annual declines with every new calendar year. Thus, it needs a steady increase in the hI,norm to counteract its natural decline over the years.

Likewise, new age-corrected metrics such as the hA, the largest number of papers in the dataset that have obtained at least hA citations per year on average, and the acc10, the number of articles with at least 10 citations per year take a hit every January and only slowly crawl back to their original level if citations increase sufficiently.

Aggregating searches

The Publish or Perish Multi-searches centre also makes it possible to aggregate searches at a higher level of aggregation in just two simple steps and less than 20 seconds. There might be several scenarios in which you might want to aggregate searches, especially for Google Scholar searches.

- **Academic metrics across a research group/department.** Calculating metrics at the level of a research group, department, or school after searching for individual **academics** in that entity. As Google Scholar does not have a reliable affiliation search, this is the only way to assess the collective performance of a group of researchers in Google Scholar.
- **Article metrics across a research group/department.** Calculating metrics at the level of a research group, department, or school after searching for individual **articles** published by that entity.
- **Metrics for a collection of articles**. Calculating the metrics for **any collection of articles** of interest. For instance, one might want to assess the collective impact of a specific set of articles in a particular field of research.
- **Combine results of split-year searches for one journal**. Combining the results of several **identical** journal searches split up by year to address the Google Scholar 1,000 results limit. This

would allow you to get a comprehensive record of publications in most journals as few have more than 1,000 publications a year.

- **Combine results of different journal searches**. Combining the results of several **different** searches that could not be combined into a single search because of Google Scholar limitations in field size. For instance, you might want to search for articles on a specific topic in a range of say a dozen journals, but Google Scholar's journal field only allows a certain number of characters.

Example: Institutional aggregation

Let's assume we want to assess the performance of the Department of Management & Marketing at the University of Melbourne (my previous employer). As the bulk of the output may have been published by its professors, we searched for each of the fifteen full professors in the department. We then select all searches and right-click to get the pop-up menu. Select **Save Results as CSV…** and give the file a meaningful name.

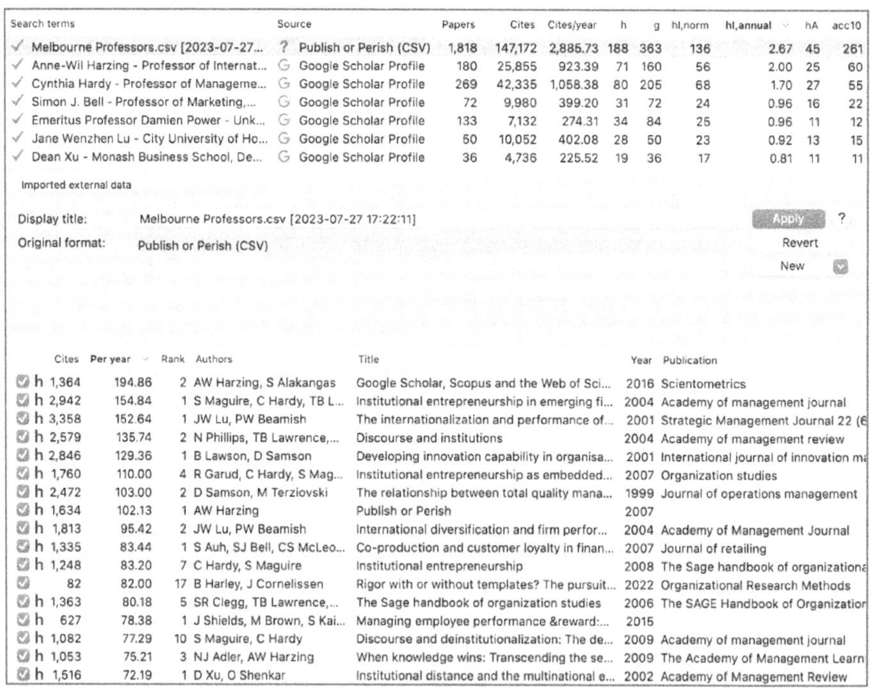

Search terms	Source	Papers	Cites	Cites/year	h	g	hI,norm	hI,annual	hA	acc10
✓ Melbourne Professors.csv [2023-07-27…	? Publish or Perish (CSV)	1,818	147,172	2,885.73	188	363	136	2.67	45	261
✓ Anne-Wil Harzing - Professor of Internat…	G Google Scholar Profile	180	25,855	923.39	71	160	56	2.00	25	60
✓ Cynthia Hardy - Professor of Manageme…	G Google Scholar Profile	269	42,335	1,058.38	80	205	68	1.70	27	55
✓ Simon J. Bell - Professor of Marketing,…	G Google Scholar Profile	72	9,980	399.20	31	72	24	0.96	16	22
✓ Emeritus Professor Damien Power - Unk…	G Google Scholar Profile	133	7,132	274.31	34	84	25	0.96	11	12
✓ Jane Wenzhen Lu - City University of Ho…	G Google Scholar Profile	50	10,052	402.08	28	50	23	0.92	13	15
✓ Dean Xu - Monash Business School, De…	G Google Scholar Profile	36	4,736	225.52	19	36	17	0.81	11	11

Imported external data

Display title: Melbourne Professors.csv [2023-07-27 17:22:11]   Apply   ?

Original format: Publish or Perish (CSV)   Revert

New

	Cites	Per year	Rank	Authors	Title	Year	Publication
✓ h	1,364	194.86	2	AW Harzing, S Alakangas	Google Scholar, Scopus and the Web of Sci…	2016	Scientometrics
✓ h	2,942	154.84	1	S Maguire, C Hardy, TB L…	Institutional entrepreneurship in emerging fi…	2004	Academy of management journal
✓ h	3,358	152.64	1	JW Lu, PW Beamish	The internationalization and performance of…	2001	Strategic Management Journal 22 (6
✓ h	2,579	135.74	2	N Phillips, TB Lawrence,…	Discourse and institutions	2004	Academy of management review
✓ h	2,846	129.36	1	B Lawson, D Samson	Developing innovation capability in organisa…	2001	International journal of innovation ma
✓ h	1,760	110.00	4	R Garud, C Hardy, S Mag…	Institutional entrepreneurship as embedded…	2007	Organization studies
✓ h	2,472	103.00	2	D Samson, M Terziovski	The relationship between total quality mana…	1999	Journal of operations management
✓ h	1,634	102.13	1	AW Harzing	Publish or Perish	2007	
✓ h	1,813	95.42	2	JW Lu, PW Beamish	International diversification and firm perfor…	2004	Academy of Management Journal
✓ h	1,335	83.44	1	S Auh, SJ Bell, CS McLeo…	Co-production and customer loyalty in finan…	2007	Journal of retailing
✓ h	1,248	83.20	7	C Hardy, S Maguire	Institutional entrepreneurship	2008	The Sage handbook of organizationa
✓	82	82.00	17	B Harley, J Cornelissen	Rigor with or without templates? The pursuit…	2022	Organizational Research Methods
✓ h	1,363	80.18	5	SR Clegg, TB Lawrence,…	The Sage handbook of organization studies	2006	The SAGE Handbook of Organizatior
✓ h	627	78.38	1	J Shields, M Brown, S Kai…	Managing employee performance &reward:…	2015	
✓ h	1,082	77.29	10	S Maguire, C Hardy	Discourse and deinstitutionalization: The de…	2009	Academy of management journal
✓ h	1,053	75.21	3	NJ Adler, AW Harzing	When knowledge wins: Transcending the se…	2009	The Academy of Management Learn
✓ h	1,516	72.19	1	D Xu, O Shenkar	Institutional distance and the multinational e…	2002	Academy of Management Review

Subsequently, we re-import this file into PoP. The screenshot above shows part of the resulting data, sorted by hI,annual. Combined, the Department's professors have an h-index of 188, published no less than 1818 papers and have nearly 150,000 citations. Having the complete list of the articles published by professors in the also allows one to assess which are the Department's most highly cited articles, both overall and per year, which journals its academics publish in etc. etc.

Example: Aggregation of collection of articles

The next screenshot shows the results of an aggregation of 230 articles related to the role of language in international business. We used this for a review article on this topic that we wrote in 2015. It allowed us to assess the collective impact of this relatively new field of study. With nearly 10,000 citations and more than 40 citations per article, the field was starting to have an impact.

Search terms	Source	Papers	Cites	Cites/year	h	g	hI,norm	hI,annual	hA	acc10
Language Review Articles.csv [2015-12-...	Publish or Perish (CSV)	230	9,526	244.26	55	90	42	1.08	16	44
Host country language ability and expat...	Google Scholar	1	11	11.00	1	1	1	1.00	1	1
Corporate language-based communicati...	Google Scholar	1	7	7.00	1	1	1	1.00	1	0
Does mother tongue make for women's...	Google Scholar	1	4	4.00	1	1	1	1.00	1	0
Employee commitment to corporate glo...	Google Scholar	1	4	4.00	1	1	1	1.00	1	0
The silent board: How language diversit...	Google Scholar	1	4	4.00	1	1	1	1.00	1	0
"Corporate Language Proficiency and R...	Google Scholar	1	2	2.00	1	1	1	1.00	1	0

Imported external data

Display title: Language Review Articles.csv [2015-12-17 15:10:37]

Original format: Publish or Perish (CSV)

	Cites	Per year	Rank	Authors	Title	Year	Publication
h	340	20.00	1	R Marschan-Piekkari, D W...	In the shadow: The impact of language on st...	1999	International Business Review
h	292	36.50	1	J Melitz	Language and foreign trade	2008	European Economic Review
h	261	13.74	1	R Marschan, D Welch, L...	Language: The forgotten factor in multinatio...	1997	European Management Journal
h	239	21.73	1	L Louhiala-Salminen, M C...	English as a lingua franca in Nordic corporat...	2005	English for Specific ...
h	237	18.23	1	AJ Feely, AW Harzing	Language management in multinational com...	2003	Cross Cultural Management: An ...
h	209	9.50	1	BH Schmitt, Y Pan, NT Ta...	Language and consumer memory: The impa...	1994	Journal of Consumer Research
h	199	18.09	1	C Nickerson	English as a lingua franca in international bu...	2005	English for specific purposes
h	199	18.09	1	E Vaara, J Tienari, R Piekk...	Language and the circuits of power in a mer...	2005	Journal of management ...
h	181	12.93	1	C Welch, R Marschan-Pie...	Corporate elites as informants in qualitative...	2002	International Business ...

Rerunning this search nearly eight years later allowed me to establish that the field is going very strong indeed. The combined 230 articles are now garnering more than 38,000 citations for an average of 165 citations per article. Half of the articles had at least 10 citations per year, indicating a strong and enduring impact.

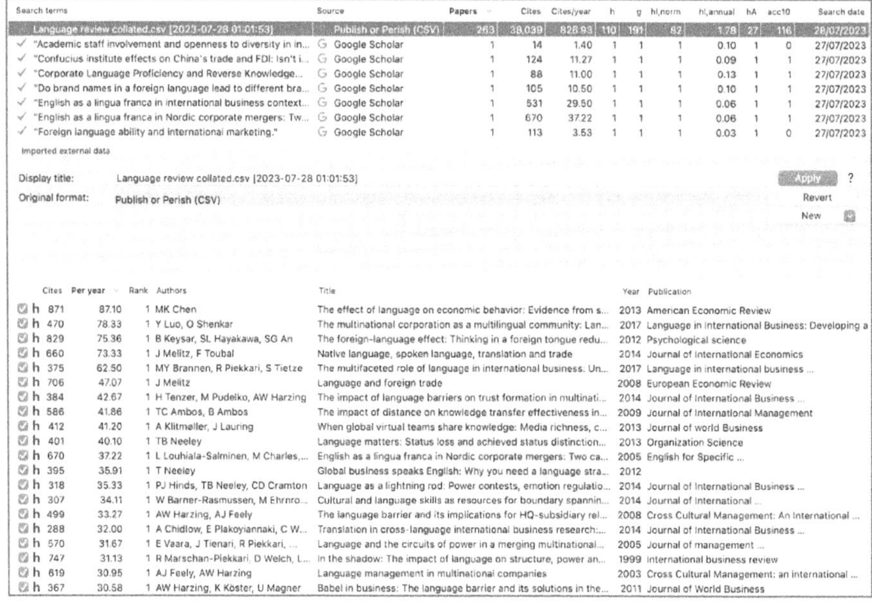

Search terms	Source	Papers	Cites	Cites/year	h	g	hi,norm	hi,annual	hA	acc10	Search date
Language review collated.csv [2023-07-28 01:01:53]	Publish or Perish (CSV)	263	38,039	826.93	110	191	82	1.78	27	116	28/07/2023
✓ "Academic staff involvement and openness to diversity in in... G Google Scholar		1	14	1.40	1	1	1	0.10	1	0	27/07/2023
✓ "Confucius institute effects on China's trade and FDI: Isn't i... G Google Scholar		1	124	11.27	1	1	1	0.09	1	1	27/07/2023
✓ "Corporate Language Proficiency and Reverse Knowledge... G Google Scholar		1	88	11.00	1	1	1	0.13	1	1	27/07/2023
✓ "Do brand names in a foreign language lead to different bra... G Google Scholar		1	105	10.50	1	1	1	0.10	1	1	27/07/2023
✓ "English as a lingua franca in international business context... G Google Scholar		1	531	29.50	1	1	1	0.06	1	1	27/07/2023
✓ "English as a lingua franca in Nordic corporate mergers: Tw... G Google Scholar		1	670	37.22	1	1	1	0.06	1	1	27/07/2023
✓ "Foreign language ability and international marketing." G Google Scholar		1	113	3.53	1	1	1	0.03	1	0	27/07/2023

Imported external data

Display title: Language review collated.csv [2023-07-28 01:01:53] Apply ?

Original format: Publish or Perish (CSV) Revert

New

	Cites	Per year	Rank	Authors	Title	Year	Publication
h	871	87.10	1	MK Chen	The effect of language on economic behavior: Evidence from s...	2013	American Economic Review
h	470	78.33	1	Y Luo, O Shenkar	The multinational corporation as a multilingual community: Lan...	2017	Language in International Business: Developing a
h	829	75.36	1	B Keysar, SL Hayakawa, SG An	The foreign-language effect: Thinking in a foreign tongue redu...	2012	Psychological science
h	660	73.33	1	J Melitz, F Toubal	Native language, spoken language, translation and trade	2014	Journal of International Economics
h	375	62.50	1	MY Brannen, R Piekkari, S Tietze	The multifaceted role of language in international business: Un...	2017	Language in international business ...
h	706	47.07	1	J Melitz	Language and foreign trade	2008	European Economic Review
h	384	42.67	1	H Tenzer, M Pudelko, AW Harzing	The impact of language barriers on trust formation in multinati...	2014	Journal of International Business ...
h	586	41.86	1	TC Ambos, B Ambos	The impact of distance on knowledge transfer effectiveness in...	2009	Journal of International Management
h	412	41.20	1	A Klitmøller, J Lauring	When global virtual teams share knowledge: Media richness, c...	2013	Journal of world Business
h	401	40.10	1	TB Neeley	Language matters: Status loss and achieved status distinction...	2013	Organization Science
h	670	37.22	1	L Louhiala-Salminen, M Charles,...	English as a lingua franca in Nordic corporate mergers: Two ca...	2005	English for Specific ...
h	395	35.91	1	T Neeley	Global business speaks English: Why you need a language stra...	2012	
h	318	35.33	1	PJ Hinds, TB Neeley, CD Cramton	Language as a lightning rod: Power contests, emotion regulatio...	2014	Journal of International Business ...
h	307	34.11	1	W Barner-Rasmussen, M Ehrnro...	Cultural and language skills as resources for boundary spannin...	2014	Journal of International ...
h	499	33.27	1	AW Harzing, AJ Feely	The language barrier and its implications for HQ-subsidiary rel...	2008	Cross Cultural Management: An International ...
h	288	32.00	1	A Chidlow, E Plakoyiannaki, C W...	Translation in cross-language international business research:...	2014	Journal of International Business ...
h	570	31.67	1	E Vaara, J Tienari, R Piekkari, ...	Language and the circuits of power in a merging multinational...	2005	Journal of management ...
h	747	31.13	1	R Marschan-Piekkari, D Welch, L...	In the shadow: The impact of language on structure, power an...	1999	International business review
h	619	30.95	1	AJ Feely, AW Harzing	Language management in multinational companies	2003	Cross Cultural Management: an international ...
h	367	30.58	1	AW Harzing, K Köster, U Magner	Babel in business: The language barrier and its solutions in the...	2011	Journal of World Business

Example: Journal aggregation

A journal like *Scientometrics* publishes a very large number of articles per year. Hence a search without year limitations will always run into the Google Scholar limitation of 1,000 results. Thus, low cited articles will not show up in your searches.

So, if you wanted to have a complete record of articles published in *Scientometrics* for the last 10 years, you could run five searches for 2013-2014, 2015-2016, 2017-2018, 2019-2020 and 2021-2022 and then combine them into one file (see screenshot below). I conducted this search in OpenAlex, which – though showing lower levels of citations than Google Scholar – is much quicker in its searches.

This allows you to compare the 3,665 papers published in the journal in the last decade, rather than focusing only on the 1,000 most cited ones. This is especially important for more recent articles, as these are likely to fall outside the top 1,000 if one conducts an aggregate search for 2006-2015.

Search terms	Source	Papers	Cites	Cites/year	h	g	hI,norm	hI,annual	hA	acc10
✓ ISSN 0138-9130 from 2013 to 2014	OpenAlex	588	16,279	1,527.90	58	84	34	3.40	12	21
✓ ISSN 0138-9130 from 2015 to 2016	OpenAlex	692	19,024	2,378.00	57	107	35	4.38	16	38
✓ ISSN 0138-9130 from 2017 to 2018	OpenAlex	771	15,241	2,540.17	50	79	31	5.17	15	40
✓ ISSN 0138-9130 from 2019 to 2020	OpenAlex	805	9,502	2,375.50	37	56	23	5.75	16	43
✓ ISSN 0138-9130 from 2021 to 2022	OpenAlex	809	3,371	1,685.50	19	32	12	6.00	13	28
✓ OA Scientometrics.csv [2023-07-27 19:34:30]	Publish or Perish (CSV)	3,665	62,417	6,241.70	84	138	54	5.40	26	170

Imported external data

Display title: OA Scientometrics.csv [2023-07-27 19:34:30] [Apply] ?

Original format: Publish or Perish (CSV) Revert

New

	Cites	Per year	Rank	Authors	Title	Year	Publication
h	1,667	208.38	1	Philippe Mongeon, Adèle Paul-Hus	The journal coverage of Web of Science and Scopus: a comparat...	2015	Scientometrics
h	846	141.00	1	Nees Jan van Eck, Ludo Waltman	Citation-based clustering of publications using CitNetExplorer an...	2017	Scientometrics
h	266	133.00	1	Vivek Kumar Singh, Prashasti Sin...	The journal coverage of Web of Science, Scopus and Dimensions...	2021	Scientometrics
h	971	121.38	2	Ole Ellegaard, Johan Albert Wallin	The bibliometric analysis of scholarly production: How great is th...	2015	Scientometrics
h	833	104.13	3	Anne-Wil Harzing, Satu Alakangas	Google Scholar, Scopus and the Web of Science: a longitudinal a...	2015	Scientometrics
h	273	91.00	1	Junwen Zhu, Weishu Liu	A tale of two databases: the use of Web of Science and Scopus i...	2020	Scientometrics
h	268	89.33	2	Alberto Martín-Martín, Mike Thel...	Google Scholar, Microsoft Academic, Scopus, Dimensions, Web...	2020	Scientometrics
h	421	60.14	4	Iman Tahamtan, Askar Safipour Af...	Factors affecting number of citations: a comprehensive review of...	2016	Scientometrics
h	296	59.20	2	Michael Gusenbauer	Google Scholar to overshadow them all? Comparing the sizes of...	2018	Scientometrics
h	272	45.33	3	Kai Li, Jason Rollins, Erjia Yan	Web of Science use in published research and review papers 199...	2017	Scientometrics

I sorted the result by citations per year. As is immediately apparent, articles dealing with comparative coverage of data sources are highly cited. No less than six of the top-10 most cited articles deal with this topic! If you are wondering why the rank column has duplicates, this is because articles were ranked within their separate searches.

In sum

In this chapter, we discussed the Multi-searches centre, which includes the searches folder tree and the searches list. We also showed you how you can export and import your data. This included import from Scopus and the Web of Science, re-importing Publish or Perish data after corrections, and exporting and importing PoP archives to transfer data between computers or users. Finally, we discussed three use cases that are facilitated by the Multi-searches centre: comparing metrics across data sources, conducting longitudinal comparisons, and aggregating searches.

In this chapter we have repeatedly referred to citation metrics and have assumed an intuitive understanding of most of these metrics. In the next chapter, however, we take a deep dive into the landscape of citation metrics, discussing both the traditional simple and the newer more sophisticated metrics.

Chapter 3: Citation Metrics

Publish or Perish can be used simply to search for publication titles and/or outlets in the context of literature reviews (see Chapter 12), assessment of an academic's or institution's publication profile (see Chapters 7 and 9), or the assessment of journal content (see Chapter 8). However, its main purpose is to provide users with publication and citation metrics. Citations are typically seen as an approximation of research quality. Although by no means synonymous, the two concepts are undoubtedly related. On average shoddy work attracts few citations and high-quality, meaningful work is more likely to be cited.

In fact, the journal impact factor (JIF) – one of the best-known citation metrics – is based on this assumption. Devised by Eugene Garfield it was originally intended to help librarians make decisions about journal subscriptions. Available since 1975 for journals included in the Web of Science (see Chapter 4), it was published by the Institute for Scientific Information (ISI) in yearly Journal Citation Reports (JCR). The metric reflects the yearly mean number of citations in a focal year to the articles published in the last two years in a given journal. The idea is that journals in which articles are on average highly cited are of higher quality. The JIF is copyrighted by Clarivate, the current owner of ISI, prohibiting its reproduction.

Over the years, the JIF has been subject to very considerable criticism. First, it doesn't address disciplinary differences in publication and citation patterns. It also has a whole range of technical problems and has been shown to be open to manipulation by unscrupulous editors. However, the JIF's most significant drawback lies in its predominant usage, which reflects a conflation of levels of analysis. The JIF is a *journal* level metric, but JIFs are often used to evaluate the individual *articles* published in the journal. It is even used to evaluate individual *academics*, looking at the average JIF of the journals they publish in. However, citations are highly skewed. Not every publication in a journal with a high JIF will be highly cited, some publications published in journals with a low JIF have a lot of citations. Hence, using the JIF to evaluate individual articles – let alone individual academics – is ill-advised.

Publish or Perish therefore focuses its citation analyses on individual articles and academics instead. In this chapter we will discuss all metrics that are included in the software. We will not only explain the metrics, but also discuss their advantages and disadvantages. For detail on the problems of using of metrics in research evaluation, see my book *Measuring and improving research Impact* (2023).

Note: PoP's metrics pane was simplified in 2019 as most users were confused by the many unfamiliar and often complex metrics. However, all metrics that were ever included in Publish or Perish remain available in the exported results. This means you can continue any longitudinal research projects that use these metrics.

Traditional simple metrics

This section focuses on two traditional simple metrics – publications and citations – and their direct derivatives, such as citations per year, citations per paper, papers and citations by author, and authors per paper. These metrics are shown at the top of the metrics pane in the Publish or Perish software (see below for my own metrics).

Citation metrics	?
Publication years:	1995-2023
Citation years:	28 (1995-2023)
Papers:	180
Citations:	25844
Cites/year:	923.00
Cites/paper:	143.58
Cites/author:	17557.70
Papers/author:	114.56
Authors/paper:	2.05

Publication and citation years

Publish or Perish calculates both the number of publication years and the number of citation years for the entity that the user has searched for (e.g., the author, journal, institution, or topic). These two metrics only measure *full* years starting from the first year of publication and exclude the current (incomplete) year. However, the software does *show* the current year, both for publications (unless the academic the academic has not published in that year) and for citations.

If you are conducting a search in which you have limited the number of years (see Chapter 1), the *publication* year metric will be adjusted to these years. Again, the last year is not included in the count. This means that if you search for publications between 2011 and 2016, the *recorded* number of publication years is five.

The *actual* number of publication years might lie anywhere between almost six years (Jan 2011 until Dec 2016) to just over four years (Dec 2011 until Jan 2016). However, as the data sources do not provide the exact publication date of individual articles, Publish or Perish cannot calculate publication years with this level of granularity. We therefore take the middle way and calculate any range of publication years as follows: [last year]-[first year]-[1 year]

Citation years, however, follow a different logic. The starting year is either the first year of publication for an author/journal/topic or the first year in a specific year range that the user has entered in the software. The end year for citations, however, is always the current year. The year range in the software only limits publications, *not* citations. Unfortunately, there is no easy way to limit citations by year in the PoP software. If you really need citations per year, use the Google Scholar Profile Search, which provides a distribution of citations over the years (see screenshot below). If you click on **Copy citations** this information will be copied to the clipboard. You can then past it to Excel or another programme to do further analyses.

Year	2001	2002	2003	2004	2005	2006	2007	2008	2009	2010	2011	2012	2013	2014	2015	2016	2017	2018	2019	2020	2021	2022	2023
New	90	136	158	239	246	361	429	558	733	813	1080	1285	1442	1499	1655	2019	1937	1788	1906	1876	1924	2086	653
Total	675	811	969	1208	1454	1815	2244	2802	3535	4348	5428	6713	8155	9654	11309	13328	15265	17053	18959	20835	22759	24845	25498

Publications

The Publication metric counts the *number* of publications. This simple metric is quite useful for searches by journal or topic. It provides you with a clear indication of the *volume* of output in a specific journal or on a specific topic. However, using this metric to *evaluate* research quality for individual academics or even universities is problematic for two reasons.

First, counting publications ignores vast quality differences *between* publications, such as articles, books, book chapters, and conference papers. Depending on the level of the conference and the discipline, a conference paper might take a few days to write, a serious research monograph might well take a year or even several years. Even *within* the same category, such as journal publications, there can be vast quality differences. A publication in a low-level journal with a light touch peer review might only take a few weeks to write and a few months to get published. In contrast, publications in top journals might take many months to write and polish, and 1-3 years to get through several rounds of very demanding peer review.

The second problem is that a publication metric is heavily dependent on publication practices within a discipline. In the Life Sciences and some of the Natural Sciences high performing academics might well publish several articles every month. But these articles are short and might be the product of lab research in which individuals only have a minor input in every paper. In these disciplines, it is not unusual for publications to have dozens – or in some cases even hundreds – of co-authors, with only one or two of them playing a significant role in writing up the paper. The review process is generally quite quick, with manuscripts often published within months of submission.

In the Humanities, academics might be working for many years on a single book. In the Social Sciences co-authorships are more common, but they rarely exceed five, with two or three authors being most common. Papers are often 20-40 pages long and go through three or four rounds of revisions with 5-10 pages of reviewer comments not unusual for some journals. They can take many years to publish. Hence, in most of the Humanities and Social Sciences academics would be very happy to publish one or two good papers a year.

Citations

After publications, the number of citations to an academic's body of work is probably the second most used research metric. However, it comes with its own caveats. As discussed in more detail in Chapter 4, the number of recorded citations differs dramatically between data sources. Even when using a comprehensive data source – such as Google Scholar – disciplinary differences in the number of citations are not "erased" entirely.

Beyond disciplinary differences, there are three additional problems in using citations as a measurement of research impact. First, just like publications, citations can differ in "quality". Second, in many of the disciplines – and especially in the Social Sciences and Humanities – publications only start gathering citations after a few years. Third, citations can be very skewed. This is true not only for universities and journals, but also for an individual academic's record.

Citation "quality": not all citations are alike

Some citations are very superficial and only refer to someone's work in a tokenistic way; other citations engage deeply with a publication. Yet other publications might be *refuting* the work they are referring to. For those categorically opposed to metrics, the latter is often used as an argument against the use of citations, although as we will see below refuting – also called contrasting – citations are very rare.

In recent years, services have sprung up that try to "rate" citations. Scite_ for instance divides citations into three categories: supporting, mentioning, and contrasting, based on *"rhetorical function"*. Semantic Scholar reports highly influential citations (see screenshot below; the lightbulb indicates influential citations), based on *"a number of factors including the number of citations to a publication, and the surrounding context for each"*. These services clearly have a lot of potential. However, their classification methods are not yet very transparent. Moreover, the percentage of citations in the "default" category – i.e., mentioning or not being highly influential – typically lies between 94% and 98% of total citations, indicating low discriminatory power.

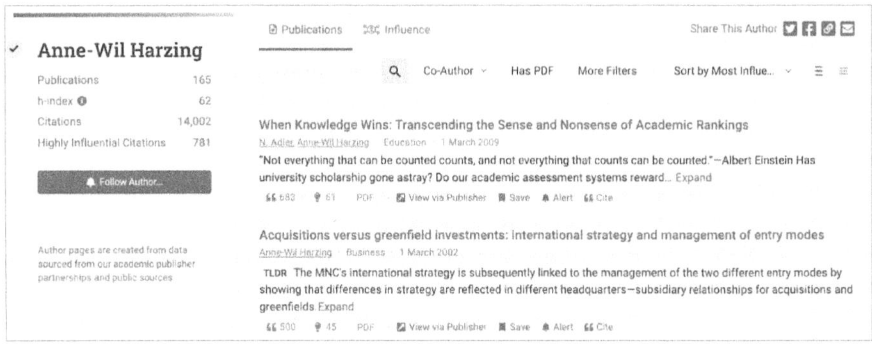

A review of two dozen academics in the Social Sciences showed these proportions do not differ much between academics in the same field. Semantic Scholar's highly influential citations were generally in the range of 5-6% of an academic's total citations. In the same discipline, Scite_'s supporting citations are typically in the 1.5-2.5% range and contrasting citations in the 0.1-0.3% range (see below). Although these services might thus be useful for doing literature reviews, they do not seem to add much value beyond "raw citations" in terms of measuring research impact. Moreover, their web services are often very slow, making repeated searches frustrating.

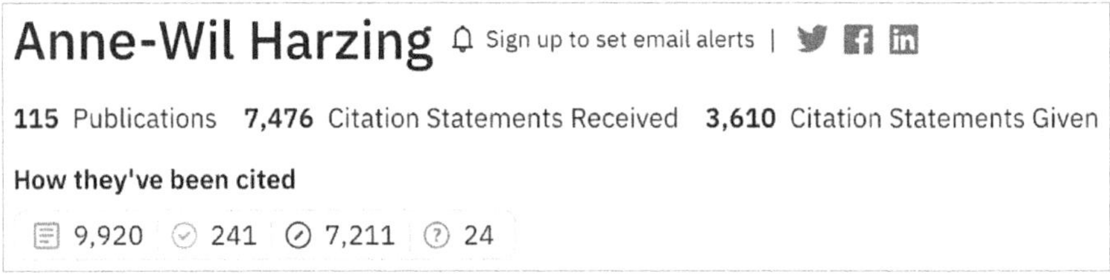

Citations are slow to pick up

In most disciplines citations only start picking up after a few years. This is especially true for the Social Sciences and Humanities, where the publication process is more drawn-out with multiple rounds of revisions. Accepted publications can also take a long time to appear in print. Thus, if someone is writing a paper in 2019 and cites a paper published in 2018, it might well take until 2022, 2023 or even 2024 before the citing paper appears in print. This means that in these fields it is hard to evidence impact for recently published papers.

In contrast, in disciplines such as Molecular Biology & Genetics or Astrophysics the time lapse between research and publication and publication and citation is generally much shorter. Papers are often published within a year of writing. Thus, citations to another paper will be visible within a year too. Hence, a PhD student or postdoc in these fields can be expected to have citations, but this is not usually true in the Social Sciences and Humanities.

As a corollary, citations obviously increase over time. This means comparing raw citations for academics at different career stages is inadvisable. Below we discuss some newer h-index based metrics that correct for career stage. However, simple metrics such as citations per year can also help (see "Derived metrics"). Time-adjusted metrics like this provide a fairer comparison between academics with different lengths of publication history.

Citations are highly skewed

Citations are highly skewed. This is true at the level of institutions, or departments, in that – depending on the size of the grouping – it is often a small group of highly-cited academics that account for most of the institution's citations. This is also true at the journal level. Some studies found a mere 15% of the articles to make up 50% of the citations in a journal and the most cited 50% of the articles to be cited, on average, ten times as often as the least cited half. The percentages will differ across journals, time, and disciplines, but the general principle still holds. In fact, the discovery of the general law of skewness in *any* bibliometric measure is one of the fundamental laws of bibliometrics. It is called Lotka's law (1926) after its author.

However, skewness can also occur within an individual academic's record. A high citation count might be due to one or a few papers, even papers that an individual has only been tangentially involved in as one of many authors. This is particularly significant in the Life Sciences, where for instance guidelines for doing research in an area typically become very highly cited. A Middlesex colleague in the Life Sciences was one of over 2,000 academics to co-author guidelines for research on autophagy. The article's more than 12,000 citations to date make up more than 90% of her citation count.

However, this might also occur in the Social Sciences with articles that are particularly timely. Another one of my Middlesex colleagues was one of more than 40 academics co-authoring a timely article on using social and behavioural science to support COVID-19 research. Despite having been published recently, the article has more than 5,000 citations and makes up well over half of his citation record.

Although no doubt both articles are of considerable significance, the non-lead authors in these articles have made only a very small contribution to them. As such these academics' citation count should be seen in a different light from those of academics who have achieved the same citation counts with articles that they single-authored, lead authored, or co-authored with a small group of colleagues. If you are using raw citations as a metric, it is therefore important to have a look at co-authorship patterns. Although this is hard to automate, even a quick glance at someone's publication record in Publish or Perish will easily identify these outliers, as well as other authorship patterns, such as the extent of single-authorship and lead authorship.

Derived metrics

Derived metrics are calculated based on two other metrics through simple division. Publish or Perish provides five derived metrics.

- **Citations per paper** = total citations/total papers. This metric is useful to assess the average impact of publications by an academic, a journal or an institution. Like all citation averages this can be influenced by highly cited outliers.
- **Citations per year** = total citations/years elapsed since first paper. This metric is useful to compare academics, journals, or institutions with different publication histories.
- **Citations per author** = divides citations for each publication by the number of authors and sums the resulting citations; this is the single-authored equivalent number of citations for the author in question.
- **Papers per author** = divides each publication by the number of authors and sums the fractional author counts; this is the single-authored equivalent number of papers for the author in question.

- **Authors per paper** = adds up the total number of authors that are involved in the publications for the author in question and divides this by the number of papers. *[Please note: One or two publications with many authors can increase this metric substantially. Hence, it is not as good a reflection of an author's individual productivity as the number of papers per author.]*

Newer – more sophisticated – metrics

Until the mid-2000s, publications, citations, and the JIF were the only metrics widely known in the academic community. This changed with the introduction of the h-index in 2005by physicist Jorge Hirsch, an index combining publications and citations. It took the academic world by storm, largely because it appears to have struck the right balance between sophistication and simplicity. As a sign of its wide acceptance, it is prominently displayed in nearly all citation databases, including the Web of Science, Scopus, and Google Scholar.

Just like for the JIF, there is a cottage industry of publications listing its drawbacks, but most of these relate to the metrics it is composed of (publications and citations). Some drawbacks, e.g., its inability to compare across career stages and disciplines, have been (partially) resolved by the h-index variants we will discuss below. We also discuss a second new metric that has captured the public imagination, the g-index, as well as an individual paper metric, ACC. These newer metrics are all displayed in the bottom part of the PoP metrics pane (see below for my own record).

h–index:	71
g–index:	160
hl,norm:	56
hl,annual:	2.00
hA-index:	25
Papers with ACC ≥ 1,2,5,10,20:	
129,111,84,60,29	

h-index

The h-index is a statistic that tries to capture both publications and citations in one metric, but addresses some of the disadvantages of relying on *one* of these metrics only. It is defined as follows:

A scientist has index h if h of his/her Np papers have at least h citations each, and the other (Np-h) papers have no more than h citations each.

If you have a h-index of 10 this means that you have 10 papers with at least 10 citations each. The h-index can run from 0 if you have no citations at all to over 100. However, most fields will have relatively few academics with h-indices over 40. The h-index thus combines an assessment of quantity (the number of publications) with an approximation of quality (impact, or citations to these papers).

An academic cannot achieve a high h-index without publishing a large number of papers. However, this is not enough. These papers will need to be cited to be incorporated in the h-index. The h-index is therefore preferable over the number of papers, which might be boosted by many low-level papers. Unless these papers are impactful and highly cited, they will not count for the h-index. Hence, the h-index favours academics who publish a continuous stream of papers with lasting and above-average impact.

The h-index is *also* preferably over the total number of citations as it corrects for "one hit wonders", i.e., academics who have authored (or co-authored) one or a limited number of highly cited papers but have not shown a sustained academic performance. As such the h-index addresses two key problems that we identified previously in our discussion of publications and citations: low-level publications and the very skewed nature of citations for some academics. However, it does not address incomparability across disciplines and career stages. This led to the introduction of various h-index alternatives, which will be discussed next.

In Publish or Perish the h-index is not only shown as one of the metrics in the citation metrics pane, but also by a small blue "h-icon" that appears in front of all result items that contribute to the h-index.

h-index alternatives

The popularity of the h-index led to a barrage of attempts to improve on this metric, with well over fifty h-index variants or alternatives proposed to date. Most attempts are missing the point of the h-index as a "sophisticated, but simple metric". They are trying to make the metric more "accurate" or incorporate more of the academic's total citations.

However, calculating the h-index with several decimal points only serves to create an illusion of precision that is not warranted by the underlying metrics. Devising metrics that incorporate "excess citations" over and beyond those needed for inclusion in the h-index is an equally futile endeavour. You can simply use citations as a metric. Metrics addressing the fact that the h-index doesn't include all papers or citations negate the very purpose of the h-index.

However, there are a few h-index alternatives attempting to address the two core problems of the h-index: its inability to compare across disciplines and its inability to compare across time and career stages. We will discuss the three most important alternatives: the hI,norm, the hI,annual and the hA-index.

hI,norm

The hI,norm is an individual h-index which corrects for disciplinary differences in publication and citation patterns. One of the most important reasons for higher (lower) publication and citation levels is a larger (smaller) number of co-authors. A larger number of co-authors means each author needs to spend less time on a paper and can thus publish more papers. A larger number of co-authors also generally leads to a larger number of citations.

Therefore, individual h-indices adjust the h-index for the number of co-authors, acknowledging the larger authorship contributions in the Humanities, Social Sciences and Engineering when compared to the Natural and Life Sciences. This follows a similar principle to the calculation of single-author equivalent publications where the number of publications is divided by the number of co-authors.

The first individual h-index was proposed by Batista *et al.* in 2006, shortly after the original h-index. It divides the standard h-index by the *average* number of authors in the articles that contribute to the h-index; the resulting index is called hI. However, in the PoP software we have implemented another individual h-index, the hI,norm, that takes a different approach: instead of dividing the total h-index by the average number of co-authors, the hI,norm first normalises the number of citations for *each* paper by dividing the number of citations by the number of authors for that paper. Then it calculates hI,norm as the h-index of the *normalised* citation counts.

This approach is more fine-grained and more accurately accounts for any co-authorship effects that might be present. It is a better approximation of the per-author impact, which is what the original h-index set out to provide. We kept the hI available in the PoP software for continuity, but it is no longer shown as one of the key metrics.

Note that someone who co-publishes with others will not need to *publish* more articles to achieve the same hI,norm as an academic who publishes single-authored articles. However, the co-authored articles will need to gather more *citations* to become part of the hI,norm, as the article's citations will be divided by the number of co-authors. The example below, created in 2015, shows that academics with the same or very similar h-indices can have very different individual h-indices and visa versa.

h-index:	45	h-index:	44	h-index:	23	h-index:	18
g-index:	97	g-index:	79	g-index:	67	g-index:	53
hI,norm:	37	hI,norm:	20	hI,norm:	20	hI,norm:	18
hI,annual:	1.85	hI,annual:	0.91	hI,annual:	0.67	hI,annual:	0.45

The first box shows my own metrics in 2015. I am an academic in the Social Sciences with a substantial number of single-authored articles. The second screenshot presents a Physics Professor at the University of Melbourne with a similar h-index, but a much lower hI,norm. Most of his articles were co-authored with at least three other academics. The third and fourth screenshot show two other Professors at the same University (in the Social Sciences and Humanities) with a similar hI,norm as the Physics Professor, but with much lower h-indices. Their work was largely (or solely) single-authored.

hI,annual

The hI,annual (hIa for short) was introduced by Harzing, Alakangas and Adams in 2014 (*hIa: An individual annual h-index to accommodate disciplinary and career length differences*, published in *Scientometrics*). It was designed to address two key problems of the h-index: its inability to compare academics both in different disciplines and at different career stages.

It is calculated by dividing the hI,norm, discussed in the previous section, by an individual's academic age, i.e., the number of years elapsed since their first publication. The hIa-index thus measures the average number of single-author equivalent h-index "points" that an academic has accumulated in each year of their academic career to date.

A hIa of 1.0 means that an academic has consistently published one article per year that, when corrected for the number of co-authors, has accumulated enough citations to be included in the h-index. The last three last academics in the hI,norm example we discussed above have very different hI,annual indices (0.45-0.91), despite having very similar hI,norm indices (18-20). This is because their academic age runs from 22 to 40 years.

To show how the hIa develops over different career stages, I have reproduced the metrics of four high-performing individuals at very different career stages. They have been publishing for 9, 20, 29, and 40 years respectively. As is immediately obvious, the h-index and hI,norm indices for these four academics differ substantially. However, their hI,annual indices are very similar indeed. Using the hIa might thus be useful to "spot" high performers early in their career.

9 years		20 years		29 years		40 years	
h-index:	24	h-index:	45	h-index:	69	h-index:	82
g-index:	49	g-index:	97	g-index:	167	g-index:	212
hI,norm:	17	hI,norm:	37	hI,norm:	53	hI,norm:	69
hI,annual:	1.89	hI,annual:	1.85	hI,annual:	1.83	hI,annual:	1.73

Obviously, there is no guarantee that the younger academics will continue to grow their h-index (and thus hI,norm) over the next 10, 20 or 30 years. Unless academics keep publishing high-impact work and their current publications continue to acquire more citations, their hIa will decline naturally with age. Hence, maintaining a high hIa for more than 20 years is indicative of academics who are both very productive and impactful.

hA-index

The hA-index is a relatively recent index and was proposed by Yves Fassin in the ISSI Newsletter in 2020. The calculation of the hA-index follows a similar pattern as the h-index, but divides the citation count of each paper by the age of the paper before ranking them and calculating the index as follows:

> the h_a-index of a given dataset is the largest number of papers in the dataset that have obtained at least h_a citations per year on average.

In doing so, the hA-index gives a measure of the *sustained* citation *rate* of the data set, rather than only the total number of citations. This means that the hA-index provides a fairer comparison for academics at different career stages. Older academics see their hA-index decline if their papers do not continue to accumulate citations at the same rate. Younger academics will see recent papers with a decent yearly citation rate, but a relatively low number of total citations, properly recognised in the hA-index.

In contrast to the hIa index, which divides the (individual) h-index by the total number of years in the data-set, the hA index divides the citation count of *each* paper by the age of that paper. The hA index can be verified by sorting the results in Publish or Perish on the citations per year column. Simply "travel down" until the citations per year metric is equal to the number of articles. Note that at the request of Yves Fassin the citations per year metric is rounded up if it is >.5.

	Cites	Per year	Rank	Authors	Title	Year	Publication
h	1,376	196.57	2	AW Harzing, S Alakangas	Google Scholar, Scopus and the Web of Science: A longitudinal a...	2016	Scientometrics
h	1,636	102.25	1	AW Harzing	Publish or Perish	2007	
h	1,053	75.21	3	NJ Adler, AW Harzing	When knowledge wins: Transcending the sense and nonsense of...	2009	The Academy of Management Learning and Education
h	909	60.60	4	AW Harzing, R van der Wal	Google Scholar as a new source for citation analysis?	2008	Ethics in Science and Environmental Politics
h	689	53.00	9	AW Harzing, A Pinnington	International Human Resource Management	2010	
h	891	52.41	5	AW Harzing	Response styles in cross-national survey research: A 26-country...	2006	International Journal of Cross Cultural Management
h	587	45.15	12	AW Harzing	The Publish or Perish Book: Your guide to Effective and Responsi...	2010	Tarma Software Research Pty Ltd, Melbourne Australia
h	387	43.00	21	H Tenzer, M Pudelko, AW Har...	The impact of language barriers on trust formation in multinationa...	2014	Journal of International Business Studies
h	872	41.52	6	AW Harzing	Acquisitions versus greenfield investments: International strategy...	2002	Strategic Management Journal
h	579	41.36	13	N Noorderhaven, AW Harzing	Knowledge-sharing and social interaction within MNEs	2009	Journal of International Business Studies
h	152	38.00	50	AW Harzing	Two new kids on the block: How do Crossref and Dimensions com...	2019	Scientometrics
h	224	37.33	36	H Tenzer, S Terjesen, AW Har...	Language in International Business: A Review and Agenda for Fut...	2017	Management International Review
h	548	34.25	15	M Pudelko, AW Harzing	Country-of-origin, localization, or dominance effect? An empirical...	2007	Human Resource Management
h	236	33.71	35	AW Harzing, M Pudelko, B Se...	The bridging role of expatriates and inpatriates in knowledge tran...	2016	Human Resource Management
h	499	33.27	18	AW Harzing, AJ Feely	The language barrier and its implications for HQ-subsidiary relati...	2008	Cross Cultural Management: An International Journal
h	722	32.82	8	AW Harzing	Of bears, bumble-bees, and spiders: The role of expatriates in co...	2001	Journal of World Business
h	742	32.26	7	AW Harzing	An empirical analysis and extension of the Bartlett and Ghoshal ty...	2000	Journal of International Business Studies
h	438	31.29	20	AW Harzing, R van der Wal	A Google Scholar h-index for journals: An alternative metric to me...	2009	JASIST
h	619	30.95	10	AJ Feely, AW Harzing	Language management in multinational companies	2003	Cross Cultural Management: An International Journal
h	370	30.83	22	AW Harzing, K Köster, U Mag...	Babel in business: The language barrier and its solutions in the H...	2011	Journal of World Business
h	185	30.83	45	A Martin-Martin, E Orduna-M...	Can we use Google Scholar to identify highly-cited documents?	2017	Journal of Informetrics
h	268	26.80	29	AW Harzing, M Pudelko	Language competencies, policies and practices in multinational c...	2013	Journal of World Business
h	520	26.00	16	AW Harzing, A Sorge	The relative impact of country of origin and universal contingenci...	2003	Organization Studies
h	609	25.38	11	AW Harzing	Managing the multinationals: An international study of control me...	1999	
h	173	24.71	48	AW Harzing, M Pudelko	Do we need to distance ourselves from the distance concept? Wh...	2016	Management International Review
h	240	24.00	34	AW Harzing	A preliminary test of Google Scholar as a source for citation data:...	2013	Scientometrics

In the above example, the count for the number of articles hits 25 as the number of citations per year is 25.38. The next article has 24.71 citations per year. Even though this is rounded up to 25, it isn't high enough to take the hA to 26.

g-index

I do not believe that attempts to capture "excess citations" beyond the h-index are very useful, whether conceptually or practically. However, there is one index based on this principle, the g-index, that has received a considerable amount of attention. Hence, by popular demand it is included in the key metrics set in Publish or Perish. It is similar to the h-index in that it combines publications and citations, but it is weighed a bit more heavily towards citations. The g-index is calculated based on the distribution of citations received by a given researcher's publications, such that:

> *given a set of articles ranked in decreasing order of the number of citations that they received, the g-index is the unique largest number such that the top g articles received together at least g2 citations.*

A g-index of 20 denotes that an academic has published at least 20 articles that *combined* have received at least 400 citations. However, unlike the h-index these citations *could* be generated by only a small number of articles. For instance, an academic with 20 papers, 15 of which have no citations with the remaining five having respectively 350, 35, 10, 3 and 2 citations would have a g-index of 20, but a h-index of 3 (three papers with at least three citations each).

Roughly, h is the number of papers of a certain "quality" [citations] threshold, a threshold that rises as h rises; g allows citations from higher-cited papers to be used to bolster lower-cited papers in meeting this threshold. Therefore, in all cases g is at least h, and is in most cases higher. However, unlike the h-index, the g-index "saturates" whenever the average number of citations for all published papers exceeds the total number of published papers; the way it is defined, the g-index is not adapted to this situation.

By definition, the maximum level of an academic's h-index and g-index is limited by the number of their papers. However, whereas in the case of the h-index this is not a *practical* limitation as papers still need to be cited to be included in the h-index; it is in the case of the g-index. This leads to the counterintuitive result that, once saturated, the g-index – a citation-based metric – will increase when publishing an additional paper, even if this paper never gets cited.

ACC: Annual citation count

The ACC metric focuses on individual publications. For each paper it calculates the number of citations per year by dividing a paper's total citations by its years since publication. Publish or Perish then displays the number of papers with at least 1, 2, 5, 10, and 20 citations per year. Note that the various ACC levels are subsets of each other; all articles in acc10 are also part of acc5, acc2, and acc1; etc.

Illustration of metrics in Publish or Perish

Below we provide an illustration of how these metrics can be used to assess an academic's publication and citation record, starting with the traditional metrics before moving on to the newer, composite metrics.

Traditional simple metrics

Publish or Perish provides access to all the metrics that I discussed above, apart from the journal impact factor, which is copyrighted by Clarivate. The screenshot below shows my own metrics for July 2023, based on my Google Scholar Profile. The left-hand side displays the traditional simple metrics, such as the number of years an academic has been publishing, their total number of publications and citations. It also shows the average number of citations per year and per paper, the average number of citations and citations per author, as well as the average number of authors per paper.

Citation metrics	?	Papers/author:	114.56
Publication years:	1995-2023	Authors/paper:	2.05
Citation years:	28 (1995-2023)	h-index:	71
Papers:	180	g-index:	160
Citations:	25864	hI,norm:	56
Cites/year:	923.71	hI,annual:	2.00
Cites/paper:	143.69	hA-index:	25
Cites/author:	17568.19	Papers with ACC ≥ 1,2,5,10,20: 129,111,84,60,29	

It is important, however, to realise the limitations of metrics using averages. Although my average number of citations per year is around 900, this varies from 100-200 per year in the early 2000s to closer to 2,000 per year since 2015. Likewise, the average number of citations per paper of just over 140 includes seventeen publications with more than 500 citations and three with more than 1,000 citations, but also some 20 publications without any citations. Most of the latter are recent publications, conference papers or book reviews.

My authors/paper metrics shows that *on average* I published with only one co-author. However, my academic record is a combination of largely single-authored publications in the early phase of my academic career, publications with one co-author in the middle phase of my career and publications with two or three co-authors in recent years. So, it is always important to look behind the averages and to compare different career stages for the same academic.

Composite metrics

The right-hand side of the screenshot above shows all the metrics we have discussed in some detail in the previous section. My h-index is 71; this means that I have published 71 articles that have at least 71 citations each. In a publication set comprised of 180 publications, ranging from publications in top journals and research monographs to book reviews, short conference papers and some blogposts, the h-index provides a useful first cut assessment of the number of *impactful* publications.

My g-index is 160; this means I have published 160 articles that combined have at least 25,600 citations. Like the h-index, this metric does incorporate publications as well as citations. However, in practice it is very highly correlated with the total number of citations. For academics with a substantial number of publications and an average number of cites/per paper that doesn't exceed the number of papers, the g-index is simply the square root of the number of citations. Hence, in many cases the g-index provides very little information over and beyond the number of publications and citations. We only maintain it in the PoP output because of popular demand.

The next three metrics show the various h-index alternatives that correct for disciplinary and career stage differences. At 56 my hI,norm is relatively high in comparison to my h-index of 71. This is due to the large number of single-authored papers in my h-index. My hIa is also quite high at 2.00. In a study I conducted of some 150 professors at the University of Melbourne, a university that ranks in the top-50 worldwide, only a dozen academics had a hI,annual above 1.0. Hence, most academics are likely to have a hIa that is *substantially* below 1.0.

At 25 my hA-index shows that I have published 25 papers that have at least 25 citations *per year*. As explained above, the h-index and the hA-index can easily be "eyeballed" in Publish or Perish by sorting your publications by the number of citations or the number of citations per year respectively and simply "traveling down" the list until the rank in the list matches the number of citations (per year). You can see below how this works for the hA index.

	Cites	Per year	Rank	Authors	Title	Year	Publication
☑ h	1,376	196.57	2	AW Harzing, S Alakangas	Google Scholar, Scopus and the Web of Science: A longitudinal a...	2016	Scientometrics
☑ h	1,636	102.25	1	AW Harzing	Publish or Perish	2007	
☑ h	1,053	75.21	3	NJ Adler, AW Harzing	When knowledge wins: Transcending the sense and nonsense of...	2009	The Academy of Management Learning and Education
☑ h	909	60.60	4	AW Harzing, R van der Wal	Google Scholar as a new source for citation analysis?	2008	Ethics in Science and Environmental Politics
☑ h	689	53.00	9	AW Harzing, A Pinnington	International Human Resource Management	2010	
☑ h	891	62.41	6	AW Harzing	Response styles in cross-national survey research: A 26-country...	2006	International Journal of Cross Cultural Management
☑ h	587	45.15	12	AW Harzing	The Publish or Perish Book: Your guide to Effective and Responsi...	2010	Tarma Software Research Pty Ltd, Melbourne Australia
☑ h	387	43.00	21	H Tenzer, M Pudelko, AW Har...	The impact of language barriers on trust formation in multinationa...	2014	Journal of International Business Studies
☑ h	872	41.52	6	AW Harzing	Acquisitions versus greenfield investments: International strategy...	2002	Strategic Management Journal
☑ h	579	41.36	13	N Noorderhaven, AW Harzing	Knowledge-sharing and social interaction within MNEs	2009	Journal of International Business Studies
☑ h	152	38.00	50	AW Harzing	Two new kids on the block: How do Crossref and Dimensions com...	2019	Scientometrics
☑ h	224	37.33	36	H Tenzer, S Terjesen, AW Har...	Language in International Business: A Review and Agenda for Fut...	2017	Management International Review
☑ h	548	34.25	15	M Pudelko, AW Harzing	Country-of-origin, localization, or dominance effect? An empirical...	2007	Human Resource Management
☑ h	236	33.71	35	AW Harzing, M Pudelko, B Se...	The bridging role of expatriates and inpatriates in knowledge tran...	2016	Human Resource Management
☑ h	499	33.27	18	AW Harzing, AJ Feely	The language barrier and its implications for HQ-subsidiary relati...	2008	Cross Cultural Management: An International Journal
☑ h	722	32.82	8	AW Harzing	Of bears, bumble-bees, and spiders: The role of expatriates in co...	2001	Journal of World Business
☑ h	742	32.26	7	AW Harzing	An empirical analysis and extension of the Bartlett and Ghoshal ty...	2000	Journal of International Business Studies
☑ h	438	31.29	20	AW Harzing, R van der Wal	A Google Scholar h-index for journals: An alternative metric to me...	2009	JASIST
☑ h	619	30.95	10	AJ Feely, AW Harzing	Language management in multinational companies	2003	Cross Cultural Management: An International Journal
☑ h	370	30.83	22	AW Harzing, K Köster, U Mag...	Babel in business: The language barrier and its solutions in the H...	2011	Journal of World Business
☑ h	185	30.83	45	A Martin-Martin, E Orduna-M...	Can we use Google Scholar to identify highly-cited documents?	2017	Journal of Informetrics
☑ h	268	26.80	29	AW Harzing, M Pudelko	Language competencies, policies and practices in multinational c...	2013	Journal of World Business
☑ h	520	26.00	16	AW Harzing, A Sorge	The relative impact of country of origin and universal contingenci...	2003	Organization Studies
☑ h	609	25.38	11	AW Harzing	Managing the multinationals: An international study of control me...	1999	
☑ h	173	24.71	48	AW Harzing, M Pudelko	Do we need to distance ourselves from the distance concept? Wh...	2016	Management International Review
☑ h	240	24.00	34	AW Harzing	A preliminary test of Google Scholar as a source for citation data:...	2013	Scientometrics

For the next article in the list to enter the hA-index and increase it to 26, it would need to gain 9 citations to make up the necessary 7 (the number of years since publication) times 26 citations. However, at the same time the last article currently captured in the hA-index (the book *Managing the multinationals*) would need to gather 15 additional citations to make up 24x26 (624) citations. For the hA to increase to 27, the next article not yet in the hA would need to gain 30 citations (10x27-240). Moreover, the three articles that currently have between 24.71 and 26.00 citations per year would also need to increase their citations.

This shows how difficult it is for an individual's hA index to increase beyond a certain level. Because of its recency, there hasn't been much research on the hA to date. However, in the University of Melbourne sample I mentioned earlier, there are only six academics with a hA above 20, with half of the sample having a hA of 10 or lower. And remember, this is a group of professors at one of the world's top universities. So don't be disappointed if your hA is quite low.

Given the "strictness" of the hA, we have therefore also implemented a more flexible annual citation metric in Publish or Perish, the ACC. This simply lists the number of papers that have at least 1, 2, 5, 10, or 20 citations per year. This allows academics to pick a metric that puts their record in the best possible light.

In my case the ACCs are 129, 111, 84, 60 and 29. So mentioning the first three ACC metrics is probably not very useful. Most likely, I would use the number of papers cited at least 10 times a year, which is 60. For more details on how to use of metrics to make your case for impact, see Chapters 7 and 10 and another one of my books in the *Crafting your career in academia* series: *Measuring and improving research impact* (2023).

In sum

Publish or Perish calculates a wide variety of metrics that focus on both productivity (volume of publications) and impact (citations) or a combination thereof. It also provides various metrics that adjust publications or citations by year or by author. The variety of metrics provided by Publish or Perish allows you to select the metrics most appropriate to your purpose.

In addition to the choice of metrics, the second important choice in doing any type of bibliographic analyses is the source of publication and citation data. This is what we will turn to in the next chapter.

Chapter 4: Data sources

Publish or Perish is a software programme that retrieves and analyses academic citations from external data sources; it does not include a database of its own. This chapter provides an overview of the nine data sources that the Publish or Perish software interfaces with.

We discuss their key features and provide an assessment of their strengths and weaknesses. More detail on how to conduct effective author, journal, topic and affiliation searches in these data sources can be found in Chapters 7-9.

In this chapter, we also provide an analysis of the limitations of the most commonly used commercial data source: the Web of Science. The most commonly used free data source is Google Scholar. Therefore, Chapter 5 will provide a detailed introduction into the strengths and weaknesses of Google Scholar, whereas Chapter 6 does the same for Google Scholar Profiles.

Quick overview of the available data sources

Currently available data sources in Publish or Perish are listed below (in alphabetical order). Note that we cannot guarantee the continued availability of any of these data sources. The Publish or Perish software has been continuously maintained and updated since 2006, and during that time we have seen many changes to data sources and their content.

Although we have been able to keep Publish or Perish compatible with whatever data sources and information were available at any time, unforeseen circumstances may force us to (reluctantly) abandon one or more data sources. Your continued support and advocacy of both the Publish or Perish software and the external data sources that we use will help to ensure that you and we can keep using Publish or Perish in the future.

- **Crossref**, available since 2017
- **Google Scholar** (GS), available since 2006
- **Google Scholar Profile** (GSP), available since 2012
- **Microsoft Academic** (MA), available since 2009
- **OpenAlex** (OA), available since 2022
- **PubMed**, available since 2021
- **Scopus**, available since 2017, external import available since 2013
- **Semantic Scholar**, available since 2021
- **Web of Science** (WoS), available since 2017, external import available since 2013
- **External data import**: Available since 2013. Allows importing of externally obtained data from the following: Scopus, Web of Science, RefMan, EndNote, and many others. External data import was discussed in detail in Chapter 2.

Crossref

Crossref launched early 2000 as a cooperative effort among the main publishers. It has been freely available in PoP since 2017. Crossref provides 1,000 results per search and returns its results in batches of 100. As such its searches are quick.

Unfortunately, its search syntax is idiosyncratic. Crossref implements every search as if it is an OR search. This means that adding search terms only *expands* the number of results, rather than *restricting* it. Hence, unlike in other data sources, it is not possible to narrow down results by including multiple search terms. This makes accurate author and journal title searches very difficult. In Chapters 7 and 8, we will provide some workarounds for this.

However, Crossref *can* be useful for ISSN and topic searches. In this context it should be noted that Crossref:

- can only search for one ISSN at a time, so it is not possible to search for multiple journals at the same time.

- implements every search as an OR search; hence, adding additional search terms expands rather than contracts the search.
- parses the year of online first for articles as publication year; thus, it is not possible to get a full and accurate list of articles published in a journal for a particular year.

Crossref coverage is more comprehensive than that of Scopus and the Web of Science. In addition to covering most journals, it covers more conference proceedings and book chapters than the two commercial databases do. In Chapter 14 we provide a detailed example of how its coverage of conference proceedings can be used to research the history of a discipline. Crossref makes citation data available under the Initiative for Open Citations. Its citation levels are quite similar to Scopus, but higher than the Web of Science.

Google Scholar (Profiles)

PoP's first data source, available since the launch of Publish or Perish in 2006. It is still most users' favourite because of its comprehensive and free coverage. However, because of the need to limit request rates and delivery of results in batches of 10, searches can be slow for single searches to *very* slow for repeated searches with 1,000 results.

Google Scholar Profiles were introduced by Google in 2012. Google Scholar Profile searches were made available in PoP shortly afterwards based on a (known) profile ID search. Since 2016, PoP offers a more natural author name search. GS Profile searches are an excellent alternative to Google Scholar for those authors who have a GS profile as it combines Google Scholar's comprehensive and free coverage with easy disambiguation of authors.

Google Scholar remains the most popular data source amongst our users. It is used more than all other data sources combined. Nearly 95% of the respondents to our user survey use Google Scholar as *one* of their sources. Two thirds use it as their *only* data source. Google Scholar Profiles is very popular for author searches. We will therefore provide a detailed discussion of the strengths and weaknesses of Google Scholar in Chapter 5 with Chapter 6 covering GS Profiles.

Microsoft Academic

Microsoft Academic (MA) was the first data source to be added to Publish or Perish after Google Scholar. Its first incarnation (Microsoft Academic Search) was launched in 2009 and was included in PoP shortly afterwards. However, it attracted very little attention from the bibliometric community. In comparison to its competitor Google Scholar, MAS coverage was not impressive; it stopped being updated entirely after 2012.

Its successor, Microsoft Academic (MA), launched in 2016, was a huge step-up. The first of my trilogy of published studies (see below) on its coverage showed that it had much improved on its earlier incarnation. For the most important type of academic publications – journal articles and books – its publication and citation coverage were quite similar to Google Scholar, leaving both Scopus and WoS very far behind, especially in terms of citation counts.

- Harzing, A.W. (2016) **Microsoft Academic (Search): a Phoenix arisen from the ashes?**, *Scientometrics*, vol. 108, no. 3, 1637-1647.
- Harzing, A.W.; Alakangas, S. (2017) **Microsoft Academic: Is the Phoenix getting wings?**, *Scientometrics*, vol. 110, no. 1, pp. 371-383.
- Harzing, A.W.; Alakangas, S. (2017) **Microsoft Academic is one year old: the Phoenix is ready to leave the nest**, *Scientometrics*, vol. 112, no. 3, pp. 1887-1894.

A second, large scale, comparison for 145 academics across the five main disciplinary areas confirmed that citation coverage for Google Scholar and MA was similar for four of the five disciplines. For the fifth discipline, the Humanities, MA citation coverage was substantially lower than Google Scholar, reflecting MA's lower coverage of non-journal publications. However, MA coverage for the Humanities still dwarfed coverage for this discipline in Scopus and WoS.

A third article, a year after the launch of MA, updated both earlier analyses. It found that some of the early teething problems had been resolved and that citation counts for the Humanities had improved.

In 2017, I also conducted a very large-scale analysis of citation levels in Microsoft Academic for articles published between 2008 and 2013 by UK universities. This study is discussed in Chapter 14 as an example of bibliometric research at the institutional level.

Only one year after its re-launch, MA was rapidly become the data source of choice; as it appeared to be combining the comprehensive coverage across disciplines, displayed by GS, with the more structured approach to data presentation, typical of Scopus and WoS.

Unfortunately, its offering was discontinued in December 2021 by Microsoft. Past MA searches remain visible in PoP and their results can be exported, but no new searches can be conducted. Non-profit OurResearch has worked with MA to continue its offerings. This partnership resulted in OpenAlex (discussed in the next section).

OpenAlex

Launched in 2022 by non-profit OurResearch (which was formerly known as ImpactStory), it provides an alternative to the discontinued Microsoft Academic data. OpenAlex has been available in PoP since early 2022. OpenAlex provides 1,000 results per search and returns results in batches of 50. As such its searches are quick.

Searches in OA are currently less flexible than those in most other data sources covered by PoP. This is because of the more restricted structure of its API. This means that:

- Author searches are *only* possible using either an ORCID or an OpenAlex ID, which you will need to look up on its web interface. You cannot use an author's name.
- Journal searches are *only* possible using ISSNs. You cannot use a journal's name.
- Affiliation searches are only possible using an OpenAlex ID, which you will need to look up on its web interface. You cannot use a university's name.
- Title words and keywords searches are possible using natural word search terms, but Title words only allows one search term.

OpenAlex "inherited" Microsoft Academic's data and made further efforts to clean up the data. As such its coverage is much better than most other data sources. Both publication and citation counts are higher than all other data sources except Google Scholar (Profiles).

However, its citation coverage is substantially lower than citation counts reported for MA in Publish or Perish. We do not know the exact reason for this. However, most likely it is because OpenAlex uses MA *linked* citation counts, rather than its more liberal *estimated* citation counts. MA estimated citation counts were on average 66% higher than MA linked citation counts.

[Technical detour] MA only included citations if it could validate both citing and cited papers as credible. Credibility was established through a sophisticated machine learning based system and citations that were not credible were dropped. The number of dropped citations, however, is used to estimate "true" citation counts. Estimated citation counts are using a technique statisticians have developed to estimate the true size of a population if one can only observe a small portion, but can afford to sample multiple times. The math allows taking a portion of the data, counting how many "new" items are not seen before, and inferring how small a portion was sampled. MA's "linked" citations are a statistical sample of the true citations that each paper receives. MA can also find other samples from the web, including GS, other publishers' websites, etc. MA combines all these as multiple samples and applies the size estimation formula on them.

PubMed

A longstanding and well-respected free data source in the Biomedical disciplines. Out of principle, Publish or Perish only includes data sources that cover the entire spectrum of disciplines, that is the Life Sciences, Natural Sciences, Engineering, Social Sciences, and Arts & Humanities. In 2020, however, we added the subject-specific data source PubMed in order to facilitate research related to COVID-19. It only covers biomedical research.

PubMed provides 1,000 results per search and returns its results in batches of 200. As such its searches are very quick. However, PubMed doesn't provide citations. Hence, no metrics can be calculated beyond those related to authors and papers.

Publish or Perish uses the PubMed advanced search to allow users to search for authors, journals, ISSNs, affiliations, title words, and keywords, as well as use year limitations. This mirrors all the options available in the other data sources. However, the results of this search will be different from the results of the general PubMed search field on the website. This searches in all (40) available PubMed fields and thus provides very broad results that need to be filtered manually.

Scopus

Scopus was launched in 2004 as Elsevier's alternative to Thomson Reuter's Web of Science, which until then had been the only available bibliographic data source. Just like the Web of Science, Scopus is a curated, subscription-based data source that has a selective approach to coverage in that journals need to apply for inclusion and need to meet certain quality criteria.

Subscription costs for these two data sources cost vary depending on the exact package and the size of the university and are not publicly available. However, informal data gathering suggests they are in the order of $40,000 to $150,000 per year. A free (but limited) version of Scopus has been available in Publish or Perish since 2017 for direct search, with external import available since 2013. The free Scopus direct search provides 200 results per search and returns its results in batches of 20. As such searches are not as quick as other data sources.

It also requires requesting a free API key from Elsevier. The Scopus API key dialog box will appear automatically when you perform a Scopus search without an API key. It will direct you to the Elsevier Developers web site to obtain an API key from Elsevier, then lets you enter the API key for Publish or Perish to use. Publish or Perish then presents this API key to the Scopus server each time it performs a search.

Scopus has a high level of accuracy, but – especially in Engineering, the Social Sciences and Humanities – lower coverage and citation counts than Google Scholar or OpenAlex. Its coverage is usually, though not always, slightly better than the Web of Science, especially in Engineering, the Social Sciences and Humanities.

Semantic Scholar

Semantic Scholar (SS) is an AI powered search tool developed by the Allen Institute. Introduced in PoP in 2021 with a default API key kindly provided by SS. SS provides 1,000 results per search and it returns its results in batches of 100. As such its searches are quick. In terms of citation coverage, Semantic Scholar is second only to Google Scholar (Profiles). Because of the current structure of its API, however, we are only able to implement basic keyword searches.

Web of Science

The Web of Science, also known as the Web of Knowledge, is by far the oldest bibliographic data source. It was originally produced by the Institute of Scientific Information, which was set up by Eugene Garfield, the "father of citation indexing". It is currently owned by Clarivate, but for a long time it was offered by Thomson (later Thomson Reuters). Thus, many academics still refer to it as Thomson ISI.

A direct Web of Science search has been available in PoP since 2017, with external import available since 2013. The Web of Science API provides 200 results per search and returns its results in batches of 100. As such its searches are quick. Just like the Scopus, the Web of Science, is a curated, subscription-based data source that has a selective approach to coverage in that journals need to apply for inclusion and need to meet certain quality criteria. It has a very high level of accuracy, but – especially in Engineering, the Social Sciences and Humanities – lower coverage and citation counts than Google Scholar or OpenAlex.

Clarivate does not offer a free version. To use Web of Science from Publish or Perish, you or the organization that you work for must have a Web of Science Web Services (APIs) subscription and then sign in to Web of Science from within the Publish or Perish software. The Web of Science sign in dialog box (see below) appears automatically when you perform a Web of Science search but are not currently signed in to a Web of Science session.

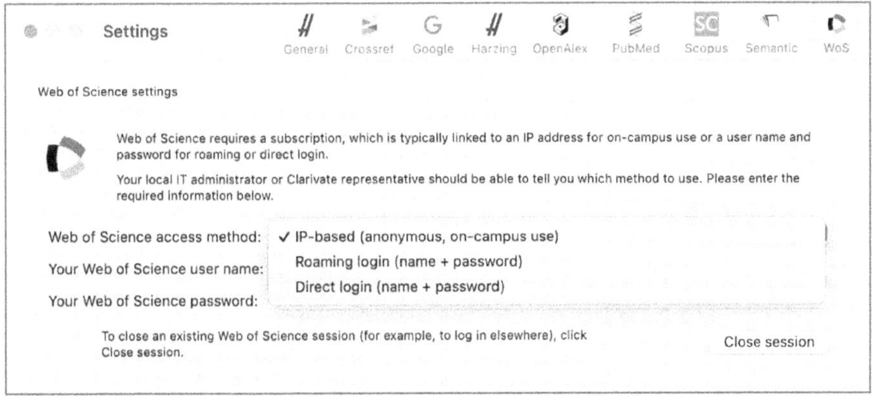

IMPORTANT: The Web of Science Web Services (APIs) subscription is different from a standard web browser-based Web of Science subscription and is not included in all organizational subscriptions. With a subscription, you can use Web of Science in one of two ways:

- Anonymously, if your computer is currently connected to the network of an organization that subscribes to Web of Science. This requires no special action on your part.

- With a registered username and password. This requires that you register for your own WoS account while (at the time of registration only) your computer was connected to your organization's network. This option allows roaming (off-campus) access to Web of Science. You will, however, need to periodically login within your organization's network to keep your roaming access active.

Maximum number of results

Publish or Perish does *not* by itself limit the number of results that you will receive for searches in Publish or Perish. Any limits are imposed by the original data source. Remember that Publish or Perish is only an *interface* to these data sources! Below is a list of the current limitations. Publish or Perish only has access to limited APIs for the two commercial data sources, which limits the total number of results to 200. The free data sources provide a much larger number of results, but even they are limited to 1000. Full details for each source are as follows:

- Crossref: 1000
- Google Scholar: 1000
- Google Scholar Profile: 1000
- OpenAlex: 1000
- PubMed: 1000 (for unknown reasons *some* author/affiliation searches and *some* title/keyword searches are restricted to 199 or 398 results)
- Scopus: 200
- Semantic Scholar: 1000
- Web of Science: 200

Whilst these limitations are annoying, consider whether you *really* need more results? Will you really use all 200 or 1000 results, or even more? Would it not be better to make your search more specific, so you will only get the results that are really relevant to you?

What if you really, positively, absolutely, need more than the number of results that the data source allows for any given search, and you cannot make your search more specific? Then partition your search by using non-overlapping year ranges. Publish or Perish makes this easy: when you click the **New** button, the new search will be pre-set to the same parameters as the original search, so all you have to do is adjust the year range in the new search. In the next section we show you how to do this.

Partitioning searches to address results limitations

Let's assume you are interested in a complete overview of *all* articles published in Scientometrics in the last decade, because you would like to do a thematic analysis using the content of its abstracts over the years. Given that the journal publishes 400-500 articles a year, it would be impossible to request all articles in one search.

Instead, you would simply start with 2013 and then either copy this search or use the **New** button and adapt the year. This way you would end up with 10 searches, one for each year (see below screenshot). The ten years' worth of results of these searches (including the abstracts) can then be exported to Excel or another programme and you are ready to start your analysis.

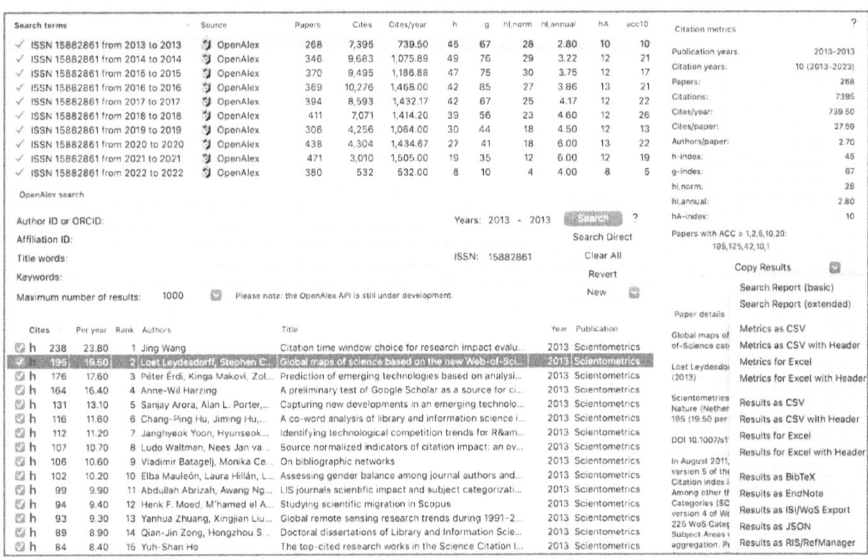

There is a lot more you can do with these results. If for instance you are interested in the most cited articles in the last decade, you can re-import the resulting file into PoP. The screenshot below shows the results: a decade of *Scientometrics* with nearly 4,000 articles sorted on citations per year. I am very proud that one of my own articles is in the top-5 most cited articles in the journal in the last decade.

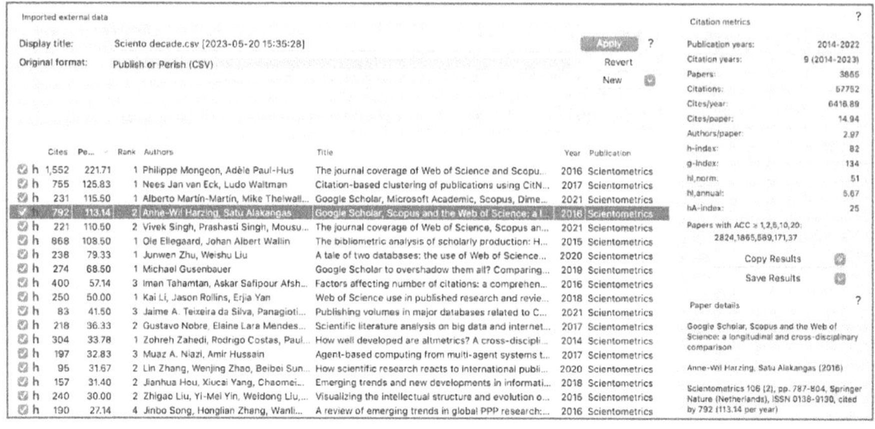

	Cites	Pe...	Rank	Authors	Title	Year	Publication
h	1,552	221.71	1	Philippe Mongeon, Adèle Paul-Hus	The journal coverage of Web of Science and Scopu...	2016	Scientometrics
h	755	125.83	1	Nees Jan van Eck, Ludo Waltman	Citation-based clustering of publications using CitN...	2017	Scientometrics
h	231	115.50	1	Alberto Martín-Martín, Mike Thelwall...	Google Scholar, Microsoft Academic, Scopus, Dime...	2021	Scientometrics
h	792	113.14	2	Anne-Wil Harzing, Satu Alakangas	Google Scholar, Scopus and the Web of Science: a l...	2016	Scientometrics
h	221	110.50	2	Vivek Singh, Prashasti Singh, Mousu...	The journal coverage of Web of Science, Scopus an...	2021	Scientometrics
h	868	108.50	1	Ole Ellegaard, Johan Albert Wallin	The bibliometric analysis of scholarly production: H...	2015	Scientometrics
h	238	79.33	1	Junwen Zhu, Weishu Liu	A tale of two databases: the use of Web of Science...	2020	Scientometrics
h	274	68.50	1	Michael Gusenbauer	Google Scholar to overshadow them all? Comparing...	2019	Scientometrics
h	400	57.14	3	Iman Tahamtan, Askar Safipour Afsh...	Factors affecting number of citations: a comprehen...	2016	Scientometrics
h	250	50.00	1	Kai Li, Jason Rollins, Erjia Yan	Web of Science use in published research and revie...	2018	Scientometrics
h	83	41.50	3	Jaime A. Teixeira da Silva, Panagioti...	Publishing volumes in major databases related to C...	2021	Scientometrics
h	218	36.33	2	Gustavo Nobre, Elaine Lara Mendes...	Scientific literature analysis on big data and internet...	2017	Scientometrics
h	304	33.78	1	Zohreh Zahedi, Rodrigo Costas, Paul...	How well developed are altmetrics? A cross-discipli...	2014	Scientometrics
h	197	32.83	3	Muaz A. Niazi, Amir Hussain	Agent-based computing from multi-agent systems t...	2017	Scientometrics
h	95	31.67	2	Lin Zhang, Wenjing Zhao, Beibei Sun...	How scientific research reacts to international publi...	2020	Scientometrics
h	157	31.40	2	Jianhua Hou, Xiucai Yang, Chaomei...	Emerging trends and new developments in informati...	2018	Scientometrics
h	240	30.00	2	Zhigao Liu, Yi-Mei Yin, Weidong Liu,...	Visualizing the intellectual structure and evolution o...	2016	Scientometrics
h	190	27.14	4	Jinbo Song, Honglian Zhang, Wanli...	A review of emerging trends in global PPP research:...	2016	Scientometrics

Web of Science (and Scopus) limitations

As the oldest bibliographic data base, the Web of Science is held in very high esteem by many academics. Whereas there is no doubt that that WoS is a high-quality data source, I would caution against a blanket assumption that its data are always fully accurate.

Below I discuss four key limitations of the Web of Science: its high level of stray citations for non-journal publications, inaccurate matching of publications in the Cited Reference search, a serious lack of author disambiguation in the Essential Science Indicators, and misclassification of journal articles in the Social Sciences in particular as proceedings papers or reviews. At the end of this section, I will also briefly discuss limitations of the Scopus database.

WoS stray citations

Many Publish or Perish users see the existence of "stray citations" in Google Scholar (for details see Chapter 5) as an indication of its low-quality data. This is because they compare it with a complete absence of stray citations in the Web of Science. But that is only true when you use the Web of Science general search.

Web of Science also offers a "Cited Reference" search. This search is used to search for citations to publications that are *not* included in the Web of Science. This covers nearly all books and other non-journal publications, but also journals not covered in the Web of Science. In this search references with small inaccuracies are listed separately and non-journal publications are referenced in many different ways.

One of the most-cited academics in the Social Sciences – Geert Hofstede –published a book called *"Culture's Consequences"*. This book was first published in 1980, with a second revised edition in 2001. These two versions respectively have more than 21,000 and nearly 11,000 citations under the title *"Cultures Consequences"*.

However, there are also more than 200 stray citation records in the Web of Science Cited Reference search, all referring to the same two books (see screenshot below for the 2001 book). This even excludes another 50+ records that refer inaccurately to different publication years, as well as another 50+ that refer to an inaccurate title. All in all, the Web of Science easily lists 300+ stray citations for these titles.

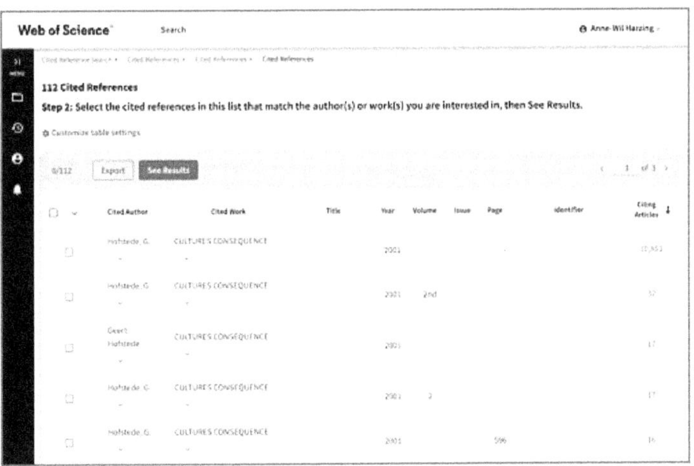

Some of these stray citation entries refer to specific page numbers in the book and hence have been entered as separate entries. Moreover, the author's name has been mangled among others as Hoefstede, Hofsteder, Hofestde, Hofesteade, Hoffsteade, Hofstade, Hofstadler, Hofsteds, Hofstee, Hofstefe, Hofstrde, Hoftede, Hoftsedc, Hoftsede, Hofstede, Holstede, Hosfede, Hosfstede, Hufstede, Ilofstede and even Infstede and fstede.

Many stray entries in Web of Science are simple misspellings of the title, with four of the strangest misspellings "Cultures Cionsequenc", "Cultues Ucultures Co", "Cultural Conseauence" and "Cultures Ocnsequence". No, I am not joking, see screenshots below for evidence. In many of these cases, the references were actually correctly listed in the referring works; the spelling errors appear to have been made by Web of Science data entry staff.

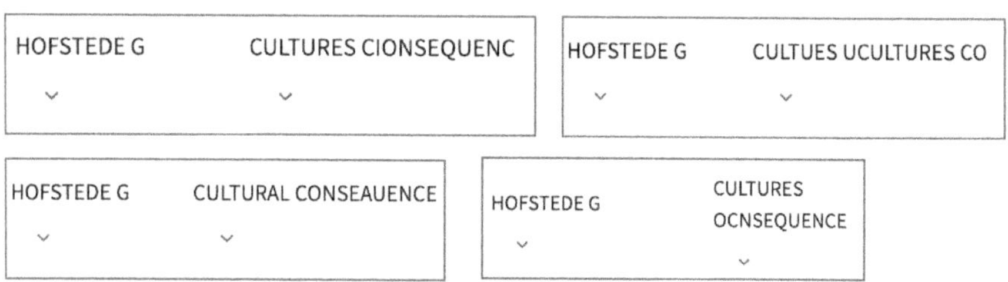

In contrast, Google Scholar shows less than 60 variations of the two editions of this title (see screenshot below). Hence Google Scholar's aggregation mechanism might in fact be better – rather than worse – than the Web of Science!

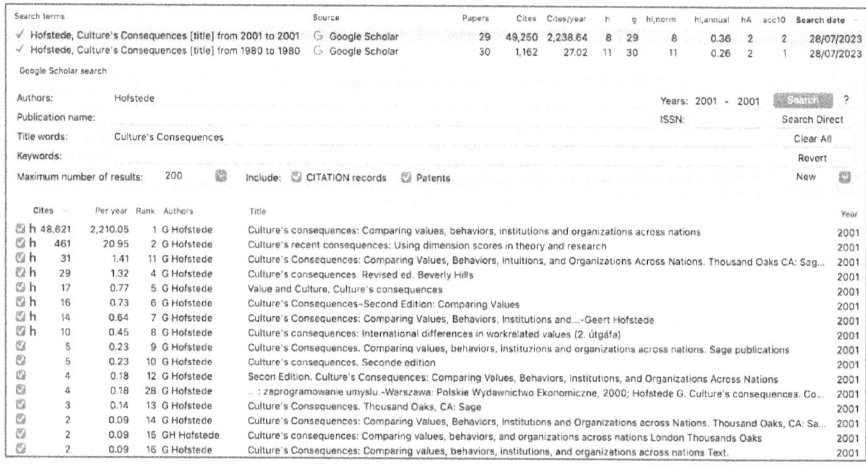

Search terms	Source	Papers	Cites	Cites/year	h	g	hI,norm	hI,annual	hA	acc10	Search date
✓ Hofstede, Culture's Consequences [title] from 2001 to 2001	G Google Scholar	29	49,250	2,238.64	8	29	8	0.36	2	2	28/07/2023
✓ Hofstede, Culture's Consequences [title] from 1980 to 1980	G Google Scholar	30	1,162	27.02	11	30	11	0.26	2	1	28/07/2023

Google Scholar search

Authors:	Hofstede		Years: 2001 – 2001	Search	?
Publication name:			ISSN:		Search Direct
Title words:	Culture's Consequences				Clear All
Keywords:					Revert
Maximum number of results:	200	Include: ☑ CITATION records ☑ Patents		New	

Cites	Per year	Rank	Authors	Title	Year
☑ h 48,621	2,210.05	1	G Hofstede	Culture's consequences: Comparing values, behaviors, institutions and organizations across nations	2001
☑ h 461	20.95	2	G Hofstede	Culture's recent consequences: Using dimension scores in theory and research	2001
☑ h 31	1.41	11	G Hofstede	Culture's Consequences: Comparing Values, Behaviors, Intuitions, and Organizations Across Nations. Thousand Oaks CA: Sag...	2001
☑ h 29	1.32	4	G Hofstede	Culture's consequences. Revised ed. Beverly Hills	2001
☑ h 17	0.77	5	G Hofstede	Value and Culture, Culture's consequences	2001
☑ h 16	0.73	6	G Hofstede	Culture's Consequences–Second Edition: Comparing Values	2001
☑ h 14	0.64	7	G Hofstede	Culture's Consequences: Comparing Values, Behaviors, Institutions and...-Geert Hofstede	2001
☑ h 10	0.45	8	G Hofstede	Culture's consequences: International differences in workrelated values (2. útgáfa)	2001
☑ 5	0.23	9	G Hofstede	Culture's Consequences. Comparing values, behaviors, instituzions and organizations across nations. Sage publications	2001
☑ 5	0.23	10	G Hofstede	Culture's consequences. Seconde edition	2001
☑ 4	0.18	12	G Hofstede	Secon Edition. Culture's Consequences: Comparing Values, Behaviors, Institutions, and Organizations Across Nations	2001
☑ 4	0.18	28	G Hofstede	... : zaprogramowanie umyslu.-Warszawa: Polskie Wydawnictwo Ekonomiczne, 2000; Hofstede G. Culture's consequences. Co...	2001
☑ 3	0.14	13	G Hofstede	Culture's Consequences. Thousand Oaks, CA: Sage	2001
☑ 2	0.09	14	G Hofstede	Culture's Consequences: Comparing Values, Behaviors, Institutions and Organizations across Nations. Thousand Oaks, CA: Sa...	2001
☑ 2	0.09	15	GH Hofstede	Culture's consequences: Comparing values, behaviors, and organizations across nations London Thousands Oaks	2001
☑ 2	0.09	16	G Hofstede	Culture's Consequences: Comparing values, behaviors, institutions, and organizations across nations Text.	2001

A separate search without the author's name showed that in Google Scholar there are less than a handful misspellings of Hofstede's name, lending credence to my assumption that the inaccurate names in the Web of Science may have been data entry errors rather than errors of referring authors.

Publication matching in Cited Reference search

Publication matching in the Cited Reference database can be fraught, especially for non-traditional publications. For example, in 2017 I was suddenly robbed of *all* citations to the Publish or Perish software after they were inaccurately attributed to Peter Jacso's article about Google Scholar (for details see my blogpost: *Web of Science: How to be robbed of 10 years of citations in one week!*).

This was fixed after I alerted Clarivate. However, in the following weeks the PoP citations were variously attributed to my white paper Reflections on the h-index and to the Publish or Perish book. In 2018, Clarivate ascribed them all to an article by Emilio Delgado Lopez-Cozar in the Spanish journal Relieve (*Revista ELectrónica de Investigación y EValuación Educativa*).

The same year, I experienced one of those rarest of Monopoly events: a bank error in my favour. My citation level was suddenly boosted with nearly 3,000 citations by inaccurately crediting me with one of the most highly cited articles in bibliometrics: Hirsch's 2005 h-index article (for details see my blogpost: *Bank error in your favour? How to gain 3,000 citations in a week*).

And if you don't believe me, the screenshot below shows that week's partial result for my normal "Harzing A" search in the WoS Cited Reference search function. Sandwiched in between a list of some of my first-authored articles and articles where I am the last author, you can find Hirsh's 2005 PNAS article with 2996 citations.

Harzing, Anne-Wil	INT BUSINESS REV	1997	6		641	10.1016/S0969-5931(97)00040-1	172	
Harzing, A. W. K. + [Show all authors]	INT HRM CONT ISSUES	1999			67		12	
Harzing, A.W. + [Show all authors]	INT HUMAN RESOURCE M	2004					72	
Harzing, AWK + [Show all authors]	NEW PERSPECTIVES RES	2008	3		13		7	
Hirsch, JE	P NATL ACAD SCI USA	2005	102	46	16569	10.1073/pnas.0507655102	2996	View Record in Web of Science Core Collection
Hocking, J. Barry; Brown, Michelle; Harzing, Anne-Wil – [Hide all authors]	HUM RESOUR MANAGE	2007	46	4	513	10.1002/hrm.20180	49	View Record in Web of Science Core Collection
Hocking, JB; Brown, M; Harzing, AW – [Hide all authors]	INT J HUM RESOUR MAN	2004	16	3	565	10.1080/0958519042000181269	79	View Record in Web of Science Core Collection
Joslassen, Alexander; Harzing, Anne-Wil	EUR MANAG REV	2008	5	4	264	10.1057/emr.2008.19	42	View Record in Web of Science Core Collection

A search in the Web of Science general search did confirm that Hirsh's article had somehow been linked with my name (see screen-shot below). This gremlin returned twice in 2020.

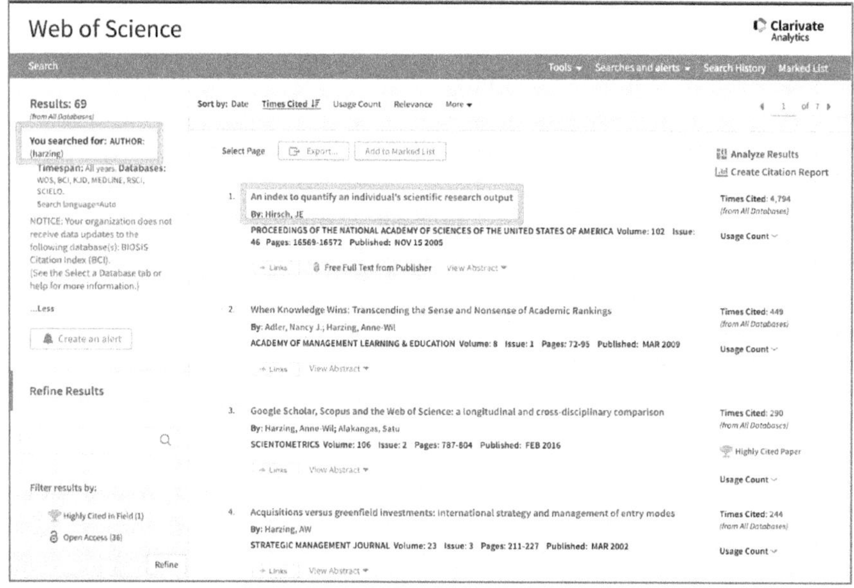

Ultimately all these errors were fixed. I even received an extensive and much appreciated official apology by a Clarivate representative for the disappearing citations. However, the main problem remains: the (semi) manual process used to update Cited Reference records in the Web of Science is rather fragile.

Lack of author disambiguation

In doing some bibliometric research in 2015 I noticed that nearly the entire top 1,000 most cited academics in Thomson Reuters' Essential Science Indicators seemed to be composed of Asian academics, most of them Chinese.

Although I was familiar with the fact that Chinese academics had been catching up rapidly in the "publication game" I couldn't quite believe that they had left scholars from all other countries behind. So, I started to investigate. For details, see the following paper.

- Harzing, A.W. (2015) **Health warning: Might contain multiple personalities. The problem of homonyms in Thomson Reuters Essential Science Indicators**, *Scientometrics*, 105(3): 2259-2270.

The table below shows the extreme discrepancy between the overall distribution of papers across different countries/name origins and the representation of these name origins in the top 1,000 academics in Thomson Reuters' Essential Science indicators.

Name origin	% of WoS papers at country level	% of top 1,000 ESI academics
Anglo	35.30%	1.10%
Chinese	11.60%	62.80%
European	33.50%	0.80%
Indian	2.70%	5.20%
Japanese	5.00%	15.40%
Korean	2.60%	14.70%
Others	9.50%	0.00%

Academics in Anglo or European countries make up a very large share, nearly 70% in fact, of the papers published in the WoS. However, Anglo and European names make up less than 2% of the top 1,000 most productive academics. In contrast, academics in Asian countries, who contribute only 22% of the number of papers published in the WoS, make up more than 98% of the top 1,000 most productive academics. Furthermore, for any country, academics with common names and fewer initials also *appear* to be more productive than their more uniquely named counterparts.

Y Wang: the world's most productive academic

This appearance of high productivity is indeed nothing more than an appearance, caused purely by the fact that these "academic superstars" are in fact composites of many individual academics with the same name. Looking at the most productive academic in the Essential Science Indicators ranking – Y Wang – clearly shows how the namesake problem distorts the underlying reality.

Y Wang makes every other academic look like a slacker, having published around 30,000 papers in just 10 years, for an average of nearly 9 papers a day. Our most productive academic is also a true *homo universalis*; they published more than 100 papers in *each* of 73 distinct research areas, ranging from Business to Computer Science, Biochemistry to Astronomy, Oncology to Materials Science, and Toxicology to Mathematics. Moreover, Y Wang is affiliated with more than 500 different universities in nearly 100 different countries.

" Y Wang, Y Zhang and Y Li make every other academic look like a slacker. Each has published around 30,000 papers in just 10 years, for an average of nearly 9 papers a day. **"**

From a recent paper in *Scientometrics* showing how ambiguity in author names has compromised Thomson Reuters's ranking of the most cited researchers.

However, when we look at the actual list of publications, we discover the secret behind this incredible productivity. Y Wang suffers from a serious case of multiple personalities. It is impossible to establish how many academics called Y Wang were amalgamated to create this one academic superstar.

However, based on our investigation of on one of the more common Y Wangs - Yang Wang - alone, we estimate Y Wang is likely to be a composite of thousands of academics. The Chinese expression 张三李四 ("three Zhang, four Li", which means "anyone" or "just everybody") seems to be particularly appropriate here. Not surprisingly this astonishing story elicited some interest from the general media (see above).

The problem persists even in 2023

However, what surprised me is that nothing appears to have been done to resolve this issue. When checking the Essential Science Indicators in July 2023, I discovered Y Wang had been dethroned by Y Zhang. However, the overall pattern had remained very similar indeed. The top-100 was nearly entirely composed of Chinese scholars, with a sprinkling of Indian and Korean scholars thrown in. The names Zhang, Wang, Li and Liu alone made up 60% of the results.

Total: 104045	Authors	Web of Science Documents	Cites ▾	Cites/Paper	Top Papers
1	ZHANG, Y	107,509	1,939,085	18.04	
2	WANG, Y	109,405	1,868,656	17.08	
3	LIU, Y	93,552	1,679,518	17.95	
4	WANG, J	86,236	1,665,416	19.31	
5	LI, Y	91,348	1,544,468	16.91	
6	LI, J	81,266	1,437,371	17.69	1,210
7	ZHANG, J	74,700	1,365,025	18.27	1,116
8	ZHANG, L	70,994	1,332,328	18.77	1,162
9	WANG, L	73,078	1,285,399	17.59	1,124
10	WANG, H	58,567	1,141,238	19.49	997
11	LIU, J	56,886	1,118,569	19.66	982
12	ZHANG, H	56,017	1,075,435	19.20	1,009
13	CHEN, Y	53,224	1,026,736	19.29	934

In fact, it appears the problem may have even become worse. Above is a screenshot of the first page of the ESI web interface. It shows that the two most prolific scholars have now published more than 100,000 papers each in just 10 years. Y Wang now makes even their former selves seem like a slacker. Rather than nearly 9 papers a day, Y Wang has upped their productivity to 30 papers a day!

This lack of author disambiguation in the Web of Science Essential Science Indicators makes the problem of disambiguating authors in Google Scholar (see Chapter 5) pale in insignificance.

Document misclassification

In January 2010, I documented a limitation of the Web of Knowledge that disproportionally affects the Social Sciences: its misclassification of journal articles containing original research into the "proceedings paper" or the "review" category. For details see this paper.

- Harzing, A.W. (2013) **Document categories in the ISI Web of Knowledge: Misunderstanding the Social Sciences?**, *Scientometrics*, 93(1): 23-34.

Journal articles classified as proceedings papers

In short, the Web of Knowledge classified journal articles as proceedings papers if they included *any* indication that the work had been presented at a conference or workshop. This was true even if the conference or workshop in question didn't even publish proceedings.

This misclassification of papers shows a very limited understanding of the research process, the review process, as well as the publication process in the Social Sciences. Any research paper worth its salt will have been presented at multiple conferences. However, the paper that is subsequently submitted to a journal will normally be vastly different from the paper that was earlier presented at a conference.

Moreover, an even longer and more extensive process of revision is likely for the many papers that are not accepted by the first journal approached. As acceptance rates of top journals in the Management field are well below 10%, papers are often submitted to several journals before they get their first revise & resubmit. Maturation of the author(s)' ideas, reorientation toward different journals, as well as the review process itself means that virtually every paper published has been substantially revised.

Hence, the end-product that is published by a journal often bears very little resemblance to the paper that was originally presented at a conference, many years before publication. A conference proceedings classification for these papers is thus wholly inaccurate.

So, were all papers presented at conferences categorised as proceedings papers? No, this happened only to those papers whose authors explicitly acknowledged in the paper that early versions of the paper had been presented at a conference, or to papers whose authors were kind enough to simply thank participants of a particular workshop for their input. A nice reward for being professional and collegial!

Clarivate now appears to be double-badging proceedings papers as articles. Even though I would argue that the proceedings label is as incorrect as ever, at least filtering results by the article category no longer leads to ignoring mature pieces of academic scholarship.

Original research classified as review papers

Some papers in Business & Management that clearly present original research, published in the top journals in the field, were categorised as review papers, i.e., derivative work that synthesises work of other academics.

The reason? They had more than 100 references! No, I am not joking. Thomson Reuters said:

> *In the JCR system any article containing more than 100 references is coded as a review. [...] also coded as reviews [...] are articles whose titles contain the word "review" or "overview."*

For instance, Michael Lounsbury's 2001 *Administrative Science Quarterly* article had 95 references and was categorised with the "article" document type. In contrast, his 2004 article in *Social Forces* with 101 references was categorised in the "review" document type, even though the article contained sections titled "Theory and Hypotheses" and "Data and Methods". In addition, the abstract and even the title clearly refer to empirical work.

It is absolutely true that a "real" review article will tend to have many references. However, the reverse certainly does not hold true, there are many papers with more than 100 references that are not review articles. One cannot presume a direct relationship between the number of references in a paper and its level of originality.

Thomson Reuters appears to have remedied this erroneous practice in February 2010, shortly after I published my white paper on this topic. This was just in time as, because of the increasing reference lists over the years, we were on the brink of having the majority of articles published in Management journals classified as derivative work.

For instance, between 2006 and 2009 only half of all articles published in two of the top journals in Management, the *Academy of Management Review* (which despite its title publishes originally theory-building articles) and *Administrative Science Quarterly* were classified as articles. The others were inappropriately designated as reviews.

Between February 2010 and July 2023 only nine articles in AMR and five articles in ASQ have been classified as reviews. Nine of these were essays and classification as review thus makes some sense. However, one article in AMR and four articles in ASQ (all appearing in the same June issue in 2015) are regular articles with novel conceptual or empirical contributions. They all have more than 100 references though. Hence, it appears occasional errors still occur.

Scopus limitations

During my career I have never had reliable access to Scopus. Thus, I have not been able to conduct similar forensic analyses for Scopus. However, cursory studies that I have done illustrate that Scopus has similar problems with stray citations in its equivalent of the WoS Cited references search. I have been unable to investigate whether Scopus has similar problems with publication matching, but given its much more modern processing systems, I would expect these problems to be less frequent.

Author disambiguation in Scopus tends to be good. Although occasional mistakes do occur, I have found most of their author profiles to be very clean. Scopus also reacts promptly to requests to merge problems. However, Scopus does seem to have suffered from similar problems as the Web of Science in terms of document classification. More than half of the articles in AMR between 2006 and 2009 were classified as review papers. This problem has gradually declined since then and currently only editorials are classified as review articles. Although this is not correct, it doesn't do as much harm as classifying original work as reviews.

Conclusion

Although the document category misclassifications have now been mostly resolved, the problem with stray citations in the Cited Reference search and with author disambiguation in the Essential Science indicators are still as present as ever. My specific problems in terms of publication matching have also been resolved, but I do not know how many other problems of this type go unnoticed.

In virtually all cases, data correction only happened *after* I reported them, having spent weeks to research the problems. I enjoy detective work and I feel responsible to ensure that these errors do not disadvantage researchers. In some cases, I even published the results of my investigation in peer reviewed journals. However, I do not think it is appropriate to act as an unpaid quality control officer for a company that is making substantial profits based on their "high-quality" data.

Clarivate does appear to be more proactive in maintaining data quality than Thomson Reuters ever was, and Scopus seems to have fewer problems than WoS. However, I haven't had the time in recent years to engage in these forensic investigations, so I do not know what problems might still be out there. Google Scholar has received a lot of flak over the years about the problems with its data, but it is clear that Web of Science and Scopus data are not squeaky clean either. So, if you are a senior academic administrator who is wedded to the Web of Science/Scopus and are discarding Google Scholar out of hand, think again.

Which data source to use?

See below for an overview of the advantages and disadvantages of the various data sources. Please note that any restrictions and constraints in these data-sources are *inherent* to these sources. Publish or Perish doesn't restrict or otherwise change results, it is simply an *interface* to these data sources.

Every data source has its own unique syntax that – oftentimes – is not fully documented. In the Chapters 7-9 on Author searches, Journal searches, Topic and Affiliation searches you will find detailed descriptions and examples of effective use. Below is a brief summary of the main advantages and disadvantages of each data source.

However, to get the best out of the different data sources you need to be prepared to experiment with different search strategies. If you find that some things are not working as you expect, please share your findings by sending me an email at anne@harzing.com, so that, collectively, we can improve these instructions.

Data source	Advantages	Disadvantages
Crossref	No need for a subscription key Provides cleaner data and smaller number of irrelevant results than Google Scholar Good data source for topic searches and journal searches by ISSN Search speed fast	Reports fewer citations than Google Scholar and OpenAlex because it has more limited coverage The use of NOT or AND in keyword searches results is ignored; Crossref reverts to OR searches Author search is problematic; it is very difficult to disambiguate authors Year of publication is year of online-first, which may be different from year of print publication Provides abstracts for some results only
Google Scholar (GS)	No need for a subscription key "Forgiving" search syntax Usually provides the largest number of publications and citations Search speed medium for single search with limited number of results	Usually provides a larger number of irrelevant results than other data sources Author disambiguation more difficult than in GSP, OpenAlex and WoS Because of necessary search rate limitation, speed slows down considerably when doing multiple searches in quick succession or running searches with many results Year of publication can be year of online first for up to a year after print publication Provides the first few lines of abstracts only
Google Scholar Profile (GSP)	No need for a subscription key Most "forgiving" search syntax Search speed **very** fast, 1-5 seconds for most authors Manual curation by the academic **usually** means cleaner results than GS	Only available if academic in question has set up a profile Can contain "dirty data" if academic has not curated their profile Can be consciously manipulated by unscrupulous academics by adding papers not written by the academic themselves Does not provide abstracts

OpenAlex	No need for a subscription key	Author search requires ORCID of OA ID. Cannot conduct an author search by name
	Provides cleaner data and smaller number of irrelevant results than Google Scholar	Journal search requires OA ID. Cannot conduct a journal search by name
	Search speed fast even for repeated searches and searches with many results	Affiliation search requires OA ID. Cannot search by university name
	Coverage second only to Google Scholar and SS	Matches year of publication as online first rather than print publication
	Provides full abstracts for most results	
PubMed	No need for a subscription key	Specialised data source for biomedical subjects only
	Provides cleaner data and smaller number of irrelevant results than Google Scholar	For unknown reasons results are restricted to 398/199 for some authors and affiliations and some combinations of title and keywords only
	Search speed **very** fast, even for repeated searches and searches with many results	Does NOT include citations; hence citation metrics cannot be calculated
	Provides full abstracts for all results	
Scopus	Provides cleaner data and smaller number of irrelevant results than Google Scholar	Full results require (non-free) subscription
	Typically reports more citations than Web of Science	Search speed slow, but still acceptable
		Typically reports fewer citations than all other sources except the Web of Science, because it includes fewer journals in some fields and has a limited coverage of books, book chapters and conference papers
		Does not provide abstracts

	Very good data source for key word searches and journal searches by ISSN	
Semantic Scholar	Access courtesy of S2. You do not need a subscription key. Provides cleaner data and smaller number of irrelevant results than Google Scholar Useful source for topic searches Search speed fast even for repeated searches and searches with many results Second only to GS(P) in terms of coverage and citation rates	Due to current structure of its API, you are only able to do topic searches Search terms are matched anywhere in the document. No ability to restrict searches to the title only. Does not provide full bibliographic details, only author title and year, no publication source, or other details. Does not provide abstracts
Web of Science	Provides cleaner data and smaller number of irrelevant results than Google Scholar Search speed **very** fast for nearly any kind of searches Allows wildcards (e.g., global*) for easier searches Provides full abstracts for all results	Requires (non-free) subscription Typically reports fewer citations than all other sources because it includes fewer journals in many fields (esp. Social Sciences and Humanities) and has a very limited coverage of books, book chapters and conference papers. Typically, is last data source to include recent publications as it doesn't include "in press" papers.

In sum

This chapter provided an overview of the nine data sources that the Publish or Perish software interfaces with. In this chapter we only listed their key features. A more detailed discussion on how to conduct effective author, journal, topic, and affiliation searches in these data sources can be found in Chapters 7-9.

We also provided a detailed analysis of the limitations of the most commonly used commercial data source: the Web of Science. As the most commonly used free data source is Google Scholar, the next chapter will provide a detailed introduction to the strengths and weaknesses of Google Scholar, whereas Chapter 6 does the same for Google Scholar Profiles.

Chapter 5: Google Scholar: strengths and weaknesses

As we have learned in the last chapter, Publish or Perish provides an interface to no less than eight different data sources: Crossref, Google Scholar, Google Scholar Profile, Pudmed, OpenAlex, Scopus, Semantic Scholar, and the Web of Science. Until December 2021 Microsoft Academic was included in this list; unfortunately, Microsoft decided to discontinue its offering.

Of these eight data sources, Google Scholar typically provides better coverage than the traditional data sources – Scopus and the Web of Science – as well as any of the newer data sources. Moreover, Google Scholar is free to use and has a very "forgiving" search syntax, which means that it is easy to get results. It is thus not surprising that Google Scholar remains the most popular data source amongst our users. It is used more than all other data sources combined. Nearly 95% of the more than 10,000 users to our user survey use Google Scholar as one of their sources and nearly two thirds use it as their only data source.

There are now many bibliometric studies that rely on Google Scholar (with Publish or Perish) to do their research. As of July 2023, a search for the words: *Harzing "Publish or Perish"* results in around 7,500 hits, with significant increases over the past three years (2023 estimated).

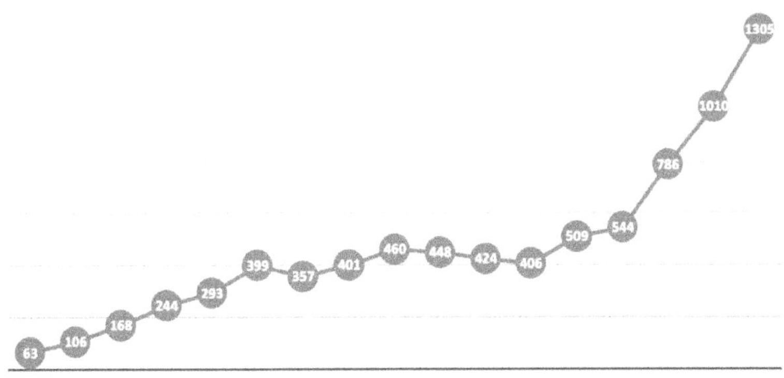

This chapter therefore provides a detailed discussion of the strengths of Google Scholar, with the next chapter covering Google Scholar Profiles. We will discuss its more comprehensive coverage of non-traditional publications, as well as its multilingual coverage and will address some of the common misconceptions about Google Scholar that have led some academics to discard it out of hand.

However, despite its considerable advantages, Google also has its drawbacks, many of which derive from the fact that Google Scholar is not a bibliometric database. Instead, it simply crawls the scholarly literature on the Web. Therefore, this chapter also covers the main limitations of Google Scholar and – where possible – shows you how to work around these.

Google Scholar strengths

There are four very simple, but important, advantages of using Google Scholar:

1. It is free.
2. It is easy to use.
3. It is comprehensive in its coverage.
4. It includes a much larger number of publications in languages other than English.

Google Scholar is free

An important practical reason for using Google Scholar is that it is freely available to anyone with an Internet connection. Clarivate's Web of Science and Elsevier's Scopus are only available to academics whose institutions are able and willing to bear the (very substantial) subscription costs. As Pauly & Stergiou (2005:34) indicate:

"free access to [...] data provided by Google Scholar provides an avenue for more transparency in tenure reviews, funding and other science policy issues, as it allows citation counts, and analyses based thereon, to be performed and duplicated by anyone".

Google Scholar is easy to use

Searches in Google Scholar are intuitive and can be conducted without much knowledge of the underlying database. Publish or Perish has been carefully designed to enable use by academics with limited knowledge of bibliometrics or even software. It presents the Google Scholar interface in an even more accessible format.

Initially, Google Scholar searches in Publish or Perish were also very quick. This advantage has unfortunately eroded over the years. In 2013, Google Scholar reduced the maximum number of results per request from 100 to 20. Later it reduced this further to 10 results per request. This means that Publish or Perish now has to perform up to 10 times as many requests per search in order to show the full results.

More data requests mean that Publish or Perish hits the maximum number of requests that Google Scholar allows per hour sooner. If the number of requests in your search exceeds the maximum that Google Scholar allows, your IP address will be temporarily blocked by Google Scholar. To avoid hitting the maximum allowable request limit, Publish or Perish uses an adaptive request rate limiter. This limits the number of requests that are sent to Google Scholar within a given period, both in the short-term (during the last 60 seconds) and in the medium term (during the last hour).

Google Scholar is comprehensive

In addition to free access and ease of use, a very important advantage of Google Scholar is the comprehensiveness of its coverage. This is because it covers not just citations in journals that are listed in the Web of Science or Scopus database, but also citations to and in:

1. Books and book chapters.
2. Conference proceedings.
3. Working papers and government reports.
4. Journals not listed in Web of Science or Scopus, including journals in languages other than English.

This makes a very significant difference. First, Google Scholar covers citations **IN** all academic journals. This not only includes academic journals that *are* listed in the Web of Science or Scopus, but also those that are *not* listed in these databases, but are available on the Internet on web pages that Google Scholar classifies as scholarly. Moreover, provided they are available on the Internet, Google Scholar *also* includes citations in books, book chapters, conference proceedings, white papers, and government reports.

In addition, Google Scholar also covers citations **TO** all of these publications, including not only academic journals that are, and are not, listed in the Web of Science or Scopus, but *also* books, book chapters, conference proceedings, white papers, government reports, and even databases and software.

Discipline	Scopus citations as % of GS citations	WoS citations as % of GS citations
Humanities	11.5%	7.0%
Social Sciences	30.0%	22.7%
Engineering	57.6%	45.7%
Sciences	64.2%	65.6%
Life Sciences	70.5%	66.8%

The table above summarises part of the results of a 2016 study of 146 academics in the Life Sciences, Sciences, Engineering, Social Sciences and Humanities. It compares average citations levels in Scopus and the Web of Science with those in Google Scholar for each of the five disciplines. As is immediately apparent, both Scopus and the Web of Science miss a huge number of citations in the Humanities and Social Sciences. This is mostly because they do not include book publications, and in some disciplines cover only a fraction of the journals. However, even in Engineering, the Sciences and the Life Sciences, Google Scholar reports between one-and-a-half and twice as many citations as the Web of Science and Scopus.

Google Scholar is multilingual

For a 2016 symposium at the *European Academy of Management* on the role of language in academia, I investigated how non-Anglophone academics – publishing mainly in their own language – performed in Google Scholar, Scopus, and the Web of Science. I looked at a small sample of academics: two French academics, two German academics, and two Brazilian academics. In my choice I focused on academics in the field of Business Administration or Organisational Sociology. To maximise my chances of finding a significant number of citations, I purposefully selected professors that had a strong reputation in their country and a significant number of publications. Data were originally collected in May 2016 and updated in July 2023.

I had expected the mainly non-English language publications of these academics to be underrepresented in the Web of Science and Scopus. However, the actual results (see below) surprised and even shocked me. In Google Scholar, the total citations for these academics ran from 3664 to 4837, with h-indices running from 23 to 29.

To put these citation records into perspective: in the same month, the Social Science Full Professors included in the study discussed above – employed at a university ranked in the top-30 in the world for the Social Sciences – on average had 4661 Google Scholar citations and a h-index of 30.

Name	Citations GS	Citations WoS	Citations Scopus	H-index GS	H-index WoS	H-index Scopus	English pubs in GS H-index
Chanlat, Jean-Francois (F)	3937	9	16	26	1	2	2
Charreaux, Gerard (F)	3664	10	86	28	1	5	1
Hax, Herbert (G)	3992	13	0	24	2	0	1
Laux, Helmut (G)	4370	8	24	29	2	3	0
Motta, Fernando (B)	4837	5	0	28	1	0	0
Ramos, Guerreiro (B)	4379	32	0	23	3	0	3
Overall mean	4197	13	21	26.3	1.7	1.7	1.2

So, in comparison with professors working at a world leading Anglophone university, these six French, German and Brazilian academics thus all had a *very* respectable citation record. In Google Scholar that is! However, these same academics were almost completely *invisible* in both the Web of Science and Scopus.

In the WoS, only half of the French, German, and Brazilian academics even reached double digit citations. In Scopus, half of the academics had no citations at all, most likely because their significant work was published before 1996. Scopus coverage before 1996 is not comprehensive. For these six academics the average number of citations in the Web of Science was only 0.25% [yes that is a quarter of 1%!] of their citations in Google Scholar, whereas for Scopus it reached the grand total of 0.55%.

In terms of the h-index, the average for both the Web of Science and Scopus was 1.7, a far cry from the average of 26.3 in Google Scholar. The figure below compares the h-index for the six non-Anglophone scholars with University of Melbourne Social Science professors across the three databases. For both groups the h-index for Google Scholar exceeds that of both Scopus and the Web of Science. However, whereas for Google Scholar the h-indices of the two groups are fairly similar, for Scopus and the Web of Science they are miles apart.

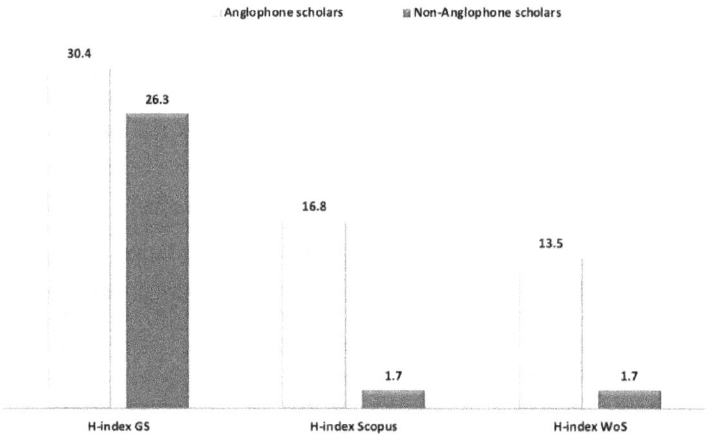

Finally, I looked at the number of English-language publications that made it to these six scholars' Google Scholar h-index and found this to be none for two of them, one for another two, and two or three for the remaining two. Virtually all their most-cited publications had been published in their own language. This small-scale comparison shows that whereas Google Scholar is decidedly multi-lingual, "speaking" French, German, and Portuguese (as well as many other languages), both the Web of Science and Scopus are much more mono-lingual English with only a sprinkling of the other languages.

When I repeated the same analysis in 2023, the results were largely similar. Google Scholar citations for most of the non-Anglophone scholars had nearly doubled and their average h-index was now 32.3. Web of Science and especially Scopus citations and h-index had likewise increased; considerably so for the two French-speaking scholars. Since 2016 they had published several articles in English or saw their earlier English-language publications attract more citations. However, the average proportion of Web of Science and Scopus citations remained below 1% of Google Scholar citations; even for those who increased their Scopus citations it didn't get much over 2%.

I do acknowledge that the large differences in citations and h-index between Google Scholar on the one hand, and the Web of Science and Scopus on the other hand, are not *only* related to the latter data sources' monolingualism. The non-Anglophone scholars differed from the comparison group of University of Melbourne scholars in their choice of publication outlets too, i.e., they are regularly publishing books and book chapters as well as journal articles.

However, even here language does play a role, given that the recent expansions of the Web of Science and Scopus with book indices tend to focus on English-language books only. Moreover, this does not negate the basic argument that non-Anglophone scholars are invisible in the Web of Science and Scopus, whereas they are well-represented in Google Scholar. So, if you publish in languages other than English, only Google Scholar speaks your language proficiently!

In sum

I would be the first to acknowledge that Google Scholar does have some important drawbacks, the most important of which are summarised later in this chapter. There is also the non-negligible danger that – with easy access to bibliometric tools – comes a certain level of inexpert or plain ignorant use. However, with the traditional databases ignoring a large part of academics' research output, it is not surprising that academics have turned to Google scholar in mass. In the remainder of this chapter, we therefore discuss three new Google Scholar features implemented in PoP, address key misconceptions about Google Scholar and discuss Google Scholar drawbacks.

New Google Scholar features

Google Scholar's key features are discussed in the chapters on author, journal, topic and affiliation searches. The features below are relevant for all these search types and add to Google Scholar's strengths.

Open related works

The PoP interface now includes an "open related works in browser" option. This is visible when you right-click on any result (see screenshot). It links to works that Google Scholar judges to be related to the result in question. This is useful if you have identified a core article for a set of search parameters and would like to find similar articles.

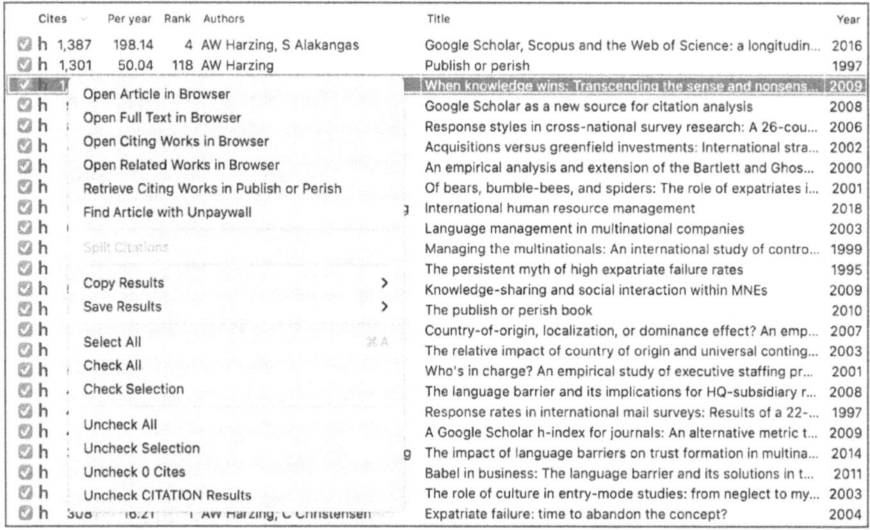

DOI extraction

DOIs were already available for most non-Google data sources but Publish or Perish now also extracts the DOI for Google Scholar results (if present). DOIs are visible in the new Paper details pane and are included in all export options, including the exporting of references.

Cites		Per year	Rank	Authors	Title
h	1,387	198.14	4	AW Harzing, S Alakangas	Google Scholar, Scopus and the Web of Science: a longitudin...
h	1,301	50.04	118	AW Harzing	Publish or perish
h	1,051	75.07	5	NJ Adler, AW Harzing	When knowledge wins: Transcending the sense and nonsens...
h	905	60.33	7	AWK Harzing, R Van der Wal	Google Scholar as a new source for citation analysis
h	892	52.47	6	AW Harzing	Response styles in cross-national survey research: A 26-cou...
h	837	39.86	8	AW Harzing	Acquisitions versus greenfield investments: International stra...
h	743	32.30	10	AW Harzing	An empirical analysis and extension of the Bartlett and Ghos...
h	723	32.86	11	AW Harzing	Of bears, bumble-bees, and spiders: The role of expatriates i...
h	670	134.00	94	BS Reiche, H Tenzer, AW Harzing	International human resource management
h	620	31.00	9	AJ Feely, AW Harzing	Language management in multinational companies
h	610	25.42	122	AW Harzing	Managing the multinationals: An international study of contro...
h	579	20.68	15	AWK Harzing	The persistent myth of high expatriate failure rates
h	568	40.57	14	N Noorderhaven, AW Harzing	Knowledge-sharing and social interaction within MNEs

Paper details

Language management in multinational companies

AJ Feely, AW Harzing (2003)

Cross Cultural Management: an international ..., emerald.com, cited by 620 (31.00 per year)

DOI 10.1108/13527600310797586

The importance of language management in multinational companies has never been greater than today. Multinationals are becoming ever more conscious of the importance of ...

Retrieval of citing works

You can retrieve citing works of any publication in Publish or Perish by right-clicking on it and selecting the relevant option. You can do this for a single publication, for all results of a search, or for a sub-set of the results (see next section).

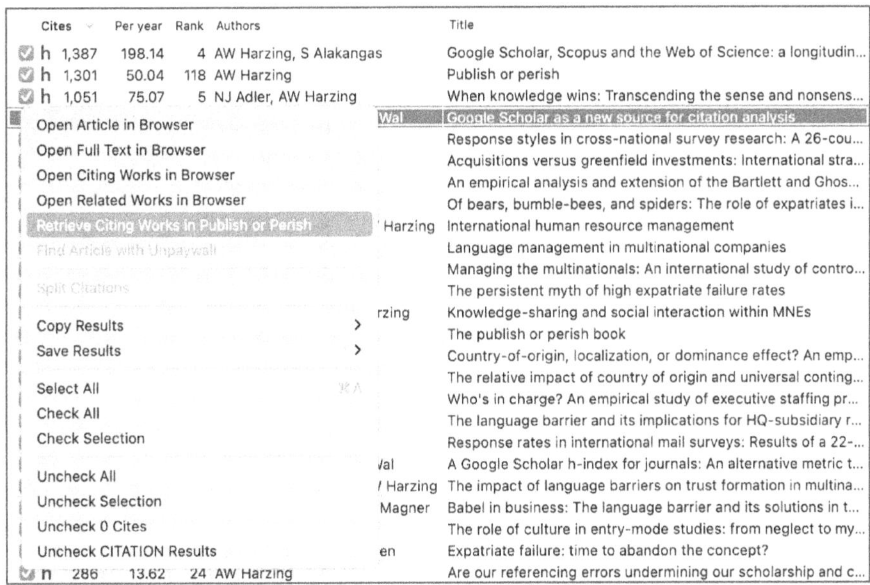

Retrieve citing works for a sub-set of the results

If you would like to retrieve citing works for a sub-set of the results, simply select the relevant results and right-click. This may be useful if you would like to establish citing works for a set of articles on a particular research topic.

For example, I have written quite a few articles on international mail surveys, focusing on their challenges, response rates, response styles and language effects. To retrieve all publications citing these articles I first need to select these articles. There are two ways to do this. The easiest way is to first uncheck all results (right-click anywhere in the results panel and select uncheck all) and then simply check only the publications you are interest in (see below).

Cites	Per year	Rank	Authors	Title	Year
☑ h 892	52.47	6	AW Harzing	Response styles in cross-national survey research: A 26-cou...	2006
☑ h 494	19.00	19	AW Harzing	Response rates in international mail surveys: Results of a 22-...	1997
☑ h 279	12.13	25	AW Harzing	Cross-national industrial mail surveys: why do response rate...	2000
☑ h 245	13.61	32	AW Harzing	Does the use of English-language questionnaires in cross-na...	2005
☑ h 201	14.36	29	AW Harzing, J Baldueza, W Bar...	Rating versus ranking: What is the best way to reduce respo...	2009
☑ h 181	18.10	42	AW Harzing, BS Reiche...	Challenges in international survey research: A review with illu...	2013
☑ h 126	11.45	48	AW Harzing, M Brown, K Köster,...	Response style differences in cross-national research: dispo...	2012
☑ h 117	7.80	52	M Pudelko, AW Harzing	The golden triangle for MNCs: Standardization towards head...	2008
☑ h 109	9.08	50	L Zander, AI Mockaitis, AW Har...	Standardization and contextualization: A study of language a...	2011

Another way to do this would be to select each of the nine articles without first unchecking all results. This might be quicker if you are only interested in a few articles. Once the articles are selected, right-click and click "Retrieve Citing Works in Publish or Perish". PoP then retrieves all publications citing one or more of the articles in this set.

Publish or Perish automatically de-duplicates citing publications. So, if a particular publication cites more than one publication in you set, it will only be shown once. The screenshot below shows the most highly cited citing works of the set of publications. Once you have retrieved all cited works, you can then export them in any format for further analysis if so desired.

Google Scholar citing references

Display title: [Citing works]   Years: 0 - 0   Retrieve   ?

Cited works:
Response styles in cross-national survey research: A 26-country study   Retrieve Direct
Response rates in international mail surveys: Results of a 22-country study   Apply
Cross-national industrial mail surveys: why do response rates differ between countries?
Does the use of English-language questionnaires in cross-national research obscure national differences?   Revert
Rating versus ranking: What is the best way to reduce response and language bias in cross-national research?   New

Cites	Per year	Rank	Authors	Title	Year
☑ h 35,273	881.83	12	G Yukl	Leadership in Organizations, 9/e	1981
☑ h 6,706	352.95	1	JW Berry, JW Berry, YH Poor...	Cross-cultural psychology: Research and applications	2002
☑ h 3,675	3,675.00	2	FJR Van de Vijver, K Leung	Methods and data analysis for cross-cultural research	2021
☑ h 1,169	106.27	3	V Taras, BL Kirkman, P Steel	Examining the impact of Culture's consequences: a three-decade, multilevel, meta...	2010
☑ h 969	138.43	4	KG Grunert, S Hieke, J Wills	Sustainability labels on food products: Consumer motivation, understanding and use	2014
☑ h 663	55.25	5	V Taras, J Rowney, P Steel	Half a century of measuring culture: Review of approaches, challenges, and limitati...	2009
☑ h 553	61.44	6	DH Weaver, L Willnat	The global journalist in the 21st century	2012
☑ h 508	46.18	7	L Håkanson, B Ambos	The antecedents of psychic distance	2010
☑ h 498	55.33	8	T Rockstuhl, JH Dulebohn, S...	Leader–member exchange (LMX) and culture: A meta-analysis of correlates of LM...	2012
☑ h 477	34.07	9	M Pudelko, AW Harzing	Country-of-origin, localization, or dominance effect? An empirical investigation of...	2007

What if there are more than 1,000 citations?

Google Scholar never provides more than 1,000 results. This can be a problem if you want a complete set of citing works for highly cited publications. We therefore added year ranges to retrieve citing works in Publish or Perish. To use this feature, you will need to cancel the search after it has started and include the year ranges at that stage.

This allows you to "partition" your search when there are more than 1,000 citing works. This is very useful if you are doing an analysis of all works citing a seminal contribution in a particular field. Simply copy the search as many times as you need and adapt the year ranges. After that you can aggregate these results again to a single record in Publish or Perish. For details on how to do this see the section in Chapter 2 on aggregation.

Obviously, you can also use this if you are interested only in citations in a specific year or for instance citations in the last 3 or 5 years. The screenshot below shows the results for a citing works search for the seven articles I have published in the *Journal of International Business Studies*. I limited the search to citations from 2016 onwards to retrieve only recent citations. The screenshot below shows the first seven of some 1,100 citing works.

Google Scholar citing references

Display title: [Citing works]   Years: 2016 - 0   Retrieve   ?

Cited works:
Why and how does shared language affect subsidiary knowledge inflows? A social identity perspective
Why do international assignees stay? An organizational embeddedness perspective
The role of international assignees' social capital in creating inter-unit intellectual capital: A cross-level m
The impact of language barriers on trust formation in multinational teams
Knowledge-sharing and social interaction within MNEs

Retrieve Direct / Apply / Revert / New

	Cites	Per year	Rank	Authors	Title	Year
h	1,353	270.60	2	MEM Barak	Managing diversity: Toward a globally inclusive workplace	2016
h	605	151.25	2	PW Hom, TW Lee, JD Shaw...	One hundred years of employee turnover theory and research.	2017
h	513	102.60	1	DC Thomas, MF Peterson	Cross-cultural management: Essential concepts	2016
h	237	59.25	1	APJ Schotter, R Mudambi, YL Doz...	Boundary spanning in global organizations	2017
h	220	55.00	2	ID Apriliyanti, I Alon	Bibliometric analysis of absorptive capacity	2017
h	200	50.00	4	Y McNulty, C Brewster	Theorizing the meaning (s) of 'expatriate': establishing boundary co...	2017
h	194	38.80	3	RL Tung	New perspectives on human resource management in a global conte...	2016

Misconceptions about Google Scholar

Many bibliometricians and university administrators are fairly conservative in their approach to citation analysis. It is not unusual to see them prefer either the Web of Science or Scopus as "the gold standard" and discard Google Scholar out of hand, simply because they have heard some wild-west stories about its "overly generous" coverage. These stories are typically based one or more of the following misconceptions.

- First, the impression that everything "on the web" citing an academic's work counts as a citation.
- Second, the assumption that any publication that is not listed in the Web of Science or Scopus is not worth considering at all.
- Third, a generalised impression that citation counts in Google Scholar are completely unreliable.

Myth 1: Everything on the Internet counts

Some academics are under the impression that *anything* posted on the web is counted in Google Scholar. However, Google Scholar only indexes *scholarly* publications. As their website indicates *"We work with publishers of scholarly information to index peer-reviewed papers, theses, preprints, abstracts, and technical reports from all disciplines of research."*

Some non-scholarly citations, such as student handbooks, library guides or editorial notes slip through. However, incidental problems like this are unlikely to distort citation metrics, especially robust ones such as the h-index. Moreover, even these types of citations could still be argued to represent impact.

Although there might thus be some overestimation of the number of scholarly citations in Google Scholar, for many disciplines this is preferable to the significant and systematic under-estimation of scholarly citations in Web of Science or Scopus. Moreover, provided that you compare like with like, i.e., compare citation records for the *same* data source, this should not be a problem.

Myth 2: GS contains low-quality publications

There is also a frequent assumption that Web of Science or Scopus listing is a stamp of quality and that one should ignore publications and citations outside these databases. There are two problems with this assumption. First, the Web of Science and Scopus are skewed towards the (Life) Sciences, English-language, and North American journals. Second, the Web of Science and Scopus ignore the majority of publications in the Social Sciences and Humanities and Engineering that are not journal publications.

As a result, a large number of publications and citations in the Social Sciences & Humanities, as well as Engineering & Computer Science, are ignored. In the Social Sciences & Humanities this is mainly caused by an almost complete neglect of books, chapters, publications in languages other than English, and publications in non-listed journals. In Engineering & Computer Science, this is caused by a very selective coverage of conference proceedings. Ignoring these publication types means ignoring a large part of scholarship in these disciplines. Both the Web of Science and Scopus have started to expand their coverage of "non-traditional" publications in recent years. However, it is still very selective and is mostly focused on recent publications.

Myth 3: Google Scholar is completely unreliable

Peter Jacsó, a prominent academic in Information & Library Science, published several highly critical articles about Google Scholar. When confronted with titles such as *"Dubious hit counts and cuckoo's eggs"* *"Deflated, inflated and phantom citation counts"*, Deans, administrators and tenure/promotion committees could be excused for assuming Google Scholar provides completely unreliable data. Some of Jacsó's critique may have been justified, but I was unable to reproduce most of the Google Scholar failures in his paper. This suggests that Google Scholar has rectified these failures. More generally, Google Scholar has significantly improved its parsing since the early years. However, many academics and academic administrators are still using Jacsó's 2006 articles as arguments against *any* use of Google Scholar.

Google Scholar parsing has improved significantly

Initially, searching for author names that included diacritics, apostrophes or ligatures was problematic in Google Scholar. The latter two problems have been resolved. The former problem, however, is still present. Here are some examples for a few of my co-authors:

- A search for MR Olivas-Lujan provides nearly twice as many publications and citations as a search for MR Olivas-Luján.

- A search for Martyna Sliwa provides 40% more publications and 60% more citations than a search for Martyna Śliwa.

- A search for Axele Giroud provides 50% more publications and twice as many citations than a search for Axèle Giroud.

In Google Scholar's defence though, in virtually all cases the missing publications are due to the fact that the author's name did *not* include these diacritics in the actual online publication. We do not know whether the missing diacritics are caused by authors using an inconsistent spelling for their name or by publishers stripping names of diacritics. However, Google Scholar's parsing was arguably correct.

Note that the results for the searches with names stripped of diacritics *also* include all publications *with* diacritics. Hence, when searching for an author whose name includes diacritics it is wise to use the version of their name without diacritics. To be doubly sure one could also decide to search for both name variants, e.g., Martyna Śliwa OR Martyna Sliwa.

Another problem that Peter Jacsó identified was the appearance of "phantom authors" such as "username", "password", "I Introduction", "Introduction", "A Registered", "P Login", and "SD Access". Recent searches show that this problem has been largely resolved. Any remaining cases are of the CITATION document type, which means that Google Scholar was unable to find the original document online. In any case, virtually none of these results have any citations, which means that they do not impact citation metrics.

Citation metrics are robust

Most of the metrics used in Publish or Perish are fairly robust and insensitive to occasional errors as they will not generally change the h-index or g-index and will only have a minor impact on the number of citations per paper. There is no doubt that Google Scholar's automatic parsing occasionally provides us with nonsensical results. However, these errors do not appear to be as frequent or as important as implied by Jacsó's articles. They also do not generally impact the results of author or journal searches much, if at all.

Google Scholar errors are random

What is most important is that I have no reason to believe that the Google Scholar errors identified in Jacsó's articles are anything else than *random*. Hence, they will not normally advantage or disadvantage individual academics, journals, or disciplines.

In contrast, commercial databases such as the Web of Science and Scopus have *systematic* errors. They do not include many of the journals in the Social Sciences and Humanities, nor have good coverage of conferences proceedings, books, or book chapters.

Thus, even though using multiple data-sources is always a good idea, rejecting Google Scholar out of hand because of presumed parsing errors is not rational. Nor is presuming Web of Science and Scopus are error-free simply because they charge high subscription fees.

Is Google Scholar perfect? Of course not!

Of course, this doesn't mean that Google Scholar doesn't have its own problems. Google Scholar's disadvantages are mostly related to it not being structured as a bibliographic database in the same way that e.g. the Web of Science and Scopus are. This means that its data are not always processed with 100% accuracy. Hence the main drawback in Google Scholar lies in its lower data quality. In this section I will discuss its main drawbacks and any workarounds where available.

Wrong master record

Many publications have multiple occurrences on the Web. For instance, my 2009 article with Nancy Adler occurs no less than 17 times (see below). In nearly all cases, Google Scholar correctly identifies the most appropriate record – usually on the official publisher's website – as the "master record" to which all citations are ascribed. Double-clicking on a publication in Publish or Perish leads you to that record.

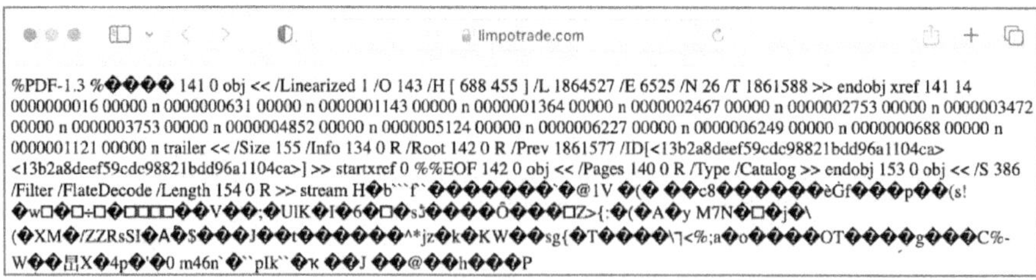

However, in an estimated 1-3% of the publications, Google Scholar – for unknown reasons – "picks" the wrong record as master record, even if a more appropriate one is available. Fortunately, these problems are rare. It typically occurs with non-journal publications, such as conference papers or book chapters. I verified the top-100 most cited publications in my own record and only in *one case* was the wrong master record selected (see below).

The above publication had eight occurrences on the Web, including six instances that linked to a pre-publication version on my website. However, instead Google Scholar picked a record that linked to an online version with complete gibberish (see screenshot below).

Is there a work-around?

There isn't anything you can do about this beyond writing to Google Scholar. They might not respond to individual support requests. However, they may investigate the issue to see whether it represents a more general problem. In the past, several of my publications that referred to the wrong master record were resolved in the end.

Truncating author and journal names

In the early days, Google Scholar provided complete records for both authors and the publication source. However, since about 2012 both fields are regularly truncated, with part of the field replaced by dots […].

We do not know why Google Scholar decided to do this. It might be related to the "space" available in these fields. Unfortunately, it can make finding the right publication frustrating, both in the Google Scholar web interface and in Publish or Perish:

- Sometimes the name of the author one is searching for does not seem to appear in the record at all. This is because it is replaced by dots.
- With common journal names, it becomes almost impossible to distinguish in which journal an article is published. *European journal of….* and *International journal of….* could be one of many hundreds of titles.

Author truncation

There does not seem to any logic to author truncation. Sometimes four or more authors are shown in full (see one but last result in the screenshot below). In other cases, the third of only three authors is truncated. That said, if you normally co-author with only one or two others, author truncation is generally not very problematic. Out of the 47 co-authored publications in my h-index, only eight were truncated, and the 23 single-authored ones are also shown in full.

Authors
J Barry Hocking, M Brown, ...
B Myloni, AWK Harzing, H Mirza
BS Reiche, AW Harzing, ML Kraimer
AW Harzing, J Baldueza, W Barner-Rasmussen, ...
AW Harzing, N Noorderhaven
AW Harzing
AW Harzing
AW Harzing, M Pudelko, ...
AW Harzing
A Josiassen, AW Harzing
A Martín-Martín, E Orduña-Malea, AW Harzing, ...
BS Reiche, ML Kraimer, AW Harzing

NG Noorderhaven, AW Harzing
BS Reiche, AW Harzing, M Pudelko
A Harzing, G Hofstede
JB Hocking, M Brown, ...
AW Harzing, BS Reiche, ...
AW Harzing, M Pudelko
AW Harzing
J Mingers, AW Harzing
AW Harzing
BS Reiche, AW Harzing
AW Harzing, M Brown, K Köster, S Zhao
AW Harzing, A Giroud

Truncation is mainly a problem for disciplines where a large number of co-authors are very common such as the Life Sciences and some of the Sciences. Below is a list of the 20 most cited articles by Shyamali Chandrika Dharmage, a Professor of Epidemiology. Only for two of the twenty articles (the third and fourth) is the complete author list shown. Note that in publications with many authors, Google Scholar will normally attempt to show the author you are searching for. This often results in suppression of authors that occur earlier in the author list as can be seen in 14 of the records below.

Authors
..., MC Matheson, GS Hamilton, SC Dharmage
..., M Wake, MLK Tang, SC Dharmage, ...
SC Dharmage, JL Perret, A Custovic
CM Bennett, M Guo, SC Dharmage
..., AJ Lowe, G Bowatte, KJ Allen, SC Dharmage
..., AL Ponsonby, MLK Tang, SC Dharmage, ...
..., J Perret, MJ Abramson, M Matheson, SC Dharmage
SC Dharmage, AJ Lowe, MC Matheson, JA Burgess, ...
..., G Jones, MJ Abramson, CF Robertson, SC Dharmage, ...
..., JA Revez, J Beesley, MC Matheson, SC Dharmage, ...

..., EH Walters, MC Matheson, SC Dharmage
R Tham, G Bowatte, SC Dharmage, DJ Tan, ...
..., T Dwyer, MLK Tang, D Hill, SC Dharmage
..., AJ Lowe, LC Gurrin, SC Dharmage, ...
..., MJ Abramson, JL Hopper, SC Dharmage
RL Peters, JJ Koplin, LC Gurrin, SC Dharmage, ...
..., GW Montgomery, AL Hartikainen, SC Dharmage, ...
..., D Tey, M Robinson, SC Dharmage, ...
..., AJ Henderson, JY Tung, SC Dharmage, ...
RL Peters, KJ Allen, SC Dharmage, MLK Tang, ...

Journal truncation

The logic to journal truncation seems even more obscure. Similar to authors, some journals with long names are written in full, whereas some shorter ones are truncated. However, as the screenshot below, which lists the seven most highly cited articles in *International Journal of Cross Cultural Management*, shows, the same journal can also be truncated in many different ways.

Year	Publication	Publisher
2007	... journal of cross cultural ...	journals.sagepub.com
2003	International journal of cross cultural management	journals.sagepub.com
2006	... journal of cross cultural management	journals.sagepub.com
2008	International journal ...	journals.sagepub.com
2002	... of Cross Cultural Management	journals.sagepub.com
2001	... Journal of cross cultural management	journals.sagepub.com
2003	International journal of cross cultural ...	journals.sagepub.com

Journal titles appear to be more likely to be truncated when there are more authors or authors with longer names, so it seems likely that Google Scholar applies a limit to the maximum number of characters to the two fields combined.

Is there a work-around?

Alex Harrison at the European Society of Endocrinology shared a work-around that allows you to correct truncated results via Mendeley. Use Publish or Perish to generate a list of articles (including truncated entries) and save the results as BibTeX, EndNote, or RIS/Reference Manager (Select the Query, Right-click and click **Save to File**). Import this file into a new folder in Mendeley, right click and select "update details". This completes most of the truncated entries. Please note that this is limited to entries where Mendeley can find the full entry and is thus more likely to work for traditional publications such as journal articles.

Unfortunately, we are currently not aware of any workarounds that do not require a roundtrip through Mendeley. However, if it is more important to you to have the lead authors of the article shown, you might want to use a Google Scholar Profile search (see next chapter) instead. The results for Google Scholar Profile searches always truncate at the *end* of the author list. Moreover, a Google Scholar Profile search will generally show a larger number of authors than a regular Google Scholar search, usually at least six. For my own record a Google Scholar Profile truncates only six of my 180 articles, those that reported on large multi-country studies and had 25+ co-authors.

Online listing as year of publication

The majority of publishers will make accepted articles available on their website well before they are published in print, using terms such as "online first", "early view" or "advance online publication". Unfortunately, this leads to some inconsistency in the reporting of the year of publication in Google Scholar and thus Publish or Perish.

Especially in the Social Sciences journals often have long publication backlogs. Articles can be available in online first for 6-24 months before they appear in print. Google Scholar parses articles as soon as they are available online (typically within a week of the article being listed) and can thus record both the publication and its citations to them *well* before they appear in print.

The advantage of this is that Google Scholar presents a much more up to date record of an academic's research output than for instance the Web of Science, which usually only enters publications after they have been published in print (and sometimes with substantive delays even then). Unfortunately, this creates some confusion when searching in Google Scholar as to *when* articles are published, as even *after* they have appeared in print, the publisher's website will normally list the online publication date as well (see screenshot below).

International Business Review

Volume 32, Issue 2, April 2023, 101854

Ambidexterity in MNC knowledge sourcing in emerging economies: A microfoundational perspective

Mariana Dodourova [a] ✉ , Shasha Zhao [b] ☐ ✉ , Anne-Wil Harzing [a] ✉

^a Middlesex University, The Burroughs, London, NW4 4BT, United Kingdom
^b University of Surrey, Stag Hill, Guildford, GU2 7XH, United Kingdom

Received 27 August 2020, Revised 22 March 2021, Accepted 10 April 2021, Available online 17 April 2021, Version of Record 13 February 2023.

The discrepancy between online first and official publication year can be quite large for some journals or for individual articles. The article above was available in online first in April 2021 and was finally published in April 2023, i.e., a delay of two years. Currently (July 2023) Google Scholar still lists the article as being published in 2021.

A problem arises with the calculation of citation metrics when Google Scholar parses the online publication date as the publication year for *some* articles, but not for others. This means that one cannot get an accurate record of what is published in a journal in a particular year. It also means that any time-sensitive paper and author metrics such as citations per year and the hA will be incorrect for the articles that are shown with their online publication date.

For the journal above, we verified all 93 articles listed in Google Scholar as being published in 2021. Out of these articles, most (84) were published *in print* in 2021 and had been published in online first between 2019 and 2021. However, nine articles were published *in print* in 2023, but were first available *online* in 2021 and listed this as their publication year. All these nine articles had been published in the April 2023 issue. In contrast, articles published in the February 2023 issue were accurately listed as published in 2023, even if they had been available in online first in 2022 or 2021 [as many had].

The discrepancy between publication year and Google Scholar listing thus appears to be a transient problem. It is likely to be caused by the fact that Google Scholar only recrawls already parsed articles a few times a year.

Is there a work-around?

Ideally, we would want Google Scholar to parse a publication with its online publication year as soon as it is published but revert to the in-print publication year as soon as this is available. This seems to be what Google Scholar does as a matter of principle. In practice, however, there appears to be a delay for some articles and/or publishers. Hence, it is wise to use the following rule of thumb in interpreting year of publication.

- For articles that are not yet published in print, Google Scholar will show the "online first" year of publication.
- For articles published in print more than 6-12 months ago, the year of publication listed in Google Scholar is likely to be the year of in print publication.
- For articles published in print within the last 6-12 months, it is wise to manually verify the year of publication.

Stray citations

Google Scholar results (and thus Publish or Perish) often report multiple occurrences of the same publication. Please note that this is not the same as multiple web versions of the same paper as these are normally aggregated under one master record.

What we refer here are "stray citations", versions of the document that have not been aggregated under the master record. These second (and sometimes third and further) versions typically only have a small number of citations each. Stray citations are generally the result of misspelling of an author's name, the title of the publication or the journal, or listing of the wrong volume, issue, or page numbers. They can also occur through Google Scholar parsing errors.

The effect on the citation analysis is that:

- The total number of articles may come out higher than the actual number, because duplicates are counted separately.
- The citations per paper may come out lower, for the same reason.
- The h-index and g-index may come out differently because citations are spread over the duplicates.

It is important to note that stray citation records are not unique to Google Scholar. As we discussed in the previous chapter, they are very prevalent in the Web of Science as well if you use the "Cited Reference" search [which includes citations to books and non-WoS listed journals] rather than the general search function.

Stray citations are more frequent for publications that are of a "non-standard" format, such as books, book chapters, conference papers, and software as – unlike journal articles – there is no universally agreed way to reference them. The Publish or Perish software itself for instance is referenced in more than fifty different ways. Below are some examples.

Publish or perish	Publish or Perish Website.(2016)
Publish or perish (4.6)	Publish or Perish, Available
Publish or Perish (Version 2.8), software program	Publish or Perish, revisado 27 de noviembre 2011
Publish or perish (Version 3.6)[Computer software]	Publish or Perish, version 2.5. 3171
Publish or perish (Version 3.6)[Software]	Publish or Perish, version 2.8
Publish or Perish (Version 4.17. 0)	Publish or Perish, version 2.8. 3644
Publish or Perish (Version: 4.25. 1)[Software]	Publish or Perish, version 3
Publish or Perish 2.0	Publish or Perish, version 3.0. 1813; 2010
Publish or Perish 3.1	Publish or perish, version 3.0. 3869
Publish or Perish 4 user's manual. 2007	Publish or perish, version 3.0. 3883 (18 August 2010)
Publish or Perish [computer program]	Publish or perish, version 3.0. 4084
Publish or perish [computer software]	Publish or Perish, version 3.1. 4004
Publish or Perish [computer software](8.1. 3625)	Publish or Perish, version 3.2. 4150
Publish or Perish [Computer software](Version 6)	Publish or Perish, version 4.4. 8

Most stray citations are of the CITATION document type

Most stray citations are of the Google Scholar document type called "CITATION". These are results for which Google Scholar was able to find citations, but for which the original work was not found online. However, the reverse is not necessarily true: not all results with a "CITATION" document type are stray citations.

Most books and book chapters, and non-print works such as software programs will have a "CITATION" document type. Two of my own more highly cited works – a research monograph, and the Publish or Perish software - carry the CITATION document type.

[CITATION] Managing the multinationals: An international study of control mechanisms

AW Harzing - 1999 - research.tilburguniversity.edu

Managing the multinationals: An international study of control mechanisms — Tilburg University Research Portal Skip to main navigation Skip to search Skip to main content Tilburg University …

☆ Save   🙶 Cite   Cited by 609   Related articles   »

[CITATION] Publish or perish

AW Harzing

☆ Save   🙶 Cite   Cited by 1296   Related articles   »

Is there a work-around?

Yes, Publish or Perish offers two important features that allow you to deal effectively with stray citations.

First, you can uncheck the CITATION records box [see screenshot below]. This ensures that your search results *exclude* these records. Obviously, this is not a good idea if you are doing an author search and expect your search to include non-traditional publications. However, it may be helpful when getting a clean record for all articles in a particular journal.

Google Scholar search

Authors:

Publication name:

Title words:

Keywords:

Maximum number of results: Include: ☑ CITATION records ☑ Patents

Second, if you consider the stray citations to be valid, you can merge them simply by dragging them onto the master record. We will discuss this in some detail below.

How to merge "stray citation" records?

So, what to do if one of your Publish or Perish searches shows up a lot of stray citation records? If these stray citation records have no citations and if you are only interested in total citation counts or the h-index, I suggest you simply ignore them. They will no impact on these metrics.

If instead, you are interested in an accurate count of *publications*, I suggest you deselect them, either one-by-one or by selecting all of them and right-clicking to access the context menu, which will allow you to "uncheck" them all on one go. If, however, one or more of these stray citation records have a non-negligible number of citations (as in the screenshot below), you can merge them into their master record.

532	40.92	16	AW Harzing	The publish or perish book	2010
53	4.42	79	AW Harzing	The publish or perish book	2011
18	1.50	160	AW Harzing	The Publish or Perish Book, Part 2: Citation analysis for a...	2011
2	0.15	343	AW Harzing	The publish or perish book. Melbourne, Australia: Tarma...	2010
3	0.23	301	AW Harzing	The publish or perish book. Tarma Software Research	2010
10	0.77	210	AW Harzing	The publish or perish book: Tarma software research Mel...	2010
2	0.15	384	AWK Harzing	The publish or perish book: Tarma software research Mel...	2010
2	0.15	352	AW Harzing	The publish or perish book: Tarma Software Research Pt...	2010
3	0.23	279	AW Harzing	The publish or perish book: Tarma Software Research Pt...	2010
3	0.23	288	AW Harzing	The Publish or Perish book: Your guide to effective and r...	2010
2	0.20	372	AW Harzing	The publish or perish book: Your guide to effective and r...	2013
2	0.50	336	AW Harzing	The Publish or Perish Book: Your guide to Effective and R...	2019
2	0.17	391	AW Harzing	The publish or perish book: Your guide to effective and r...	2011

Duplicates can be merged into the master record by dragging the stray citation(s) onto the master record. The merged record will have a symbol with stacked documents in front of it. Note that I have used another example as the little blue h symbol partly obscures the stacked document symbol.

	52	2.17	162	AWK Harzing	MNC Staffing policies for the CEO-position in foreign sub...

Create a Google Scholar Citation Profile for persistent merging

Merging records in Publish or Perish is NOT persistent. As soon as you conduct a new search, Publish or Perish will need to "refresh" the data coming from Google Scholar (or another source).

If the records are still separate in the underlying data sources, they will appear as separate records again in Publish or Perish. I would therefore not encourage you to spend a significant amount of time on merging records, unless you are doing so for an important occasion such as a performance appraisal, tenure, or promotion application.

If you would like persistently merged records, the best solution is to set up a Google Scholar Citation Profile, which is easy and very quick to do and merge the relevant records there. Publish or Perish allows you to do Google Scholar Profile searches (see Chapter 6 for details). Thus, any work you put into cleaning up your Google Scholar Profile is well worth the effort.

All citations attributed to the last edition of a book

Many books, especially textbooks, go through several editions. Below is the 5th edition of my IHRM textbook, which was in fact published in 2019. The first edition was published in 1995, the 2nd in 2004, the 3rd in 2011, and the 4th in 2014. Google Scholar does not seem to have picked up the 6th edition (2022) yet.

> **International human resource management**
>
> BS Reiche, H Tenzer, AW Harzing - International Human Resource …, 2018 - torrossa.com
>
> International human resource management (IHRM) is a rapidly changing area of specialist and generalist practice. It is also a lively and growing academic subject having links with …
>
> ☆ Save 💬 Cite   Cited by 668   Related articles ≫

668 citations is a very respectable number of citations for such a young book, but if we look at the citing works, we understand why. As is shown in the image below, many of the citing works date from *well* before 2019, going back to the mid-nineties. In fact, only about 130 citations dated from 2019 onwards.

☑ h	578	20.64	9	AWK Harzing	The persistent myth of high expatriate failure rates	1995
☑ h	107	3.96	70	N Forster, M Johnsen	Expatriate management policies in UK companies new to…	1996
☑ h	77	2.85	113	R Verburg	Developing HRM in foreign-Chinese joint ventures	1996
☑	29	1.07	150	ED Honeycutt Jr, JB Ford	Potential problems and solutions when hiring and trainin…	1996
☑	40	1.54	140	C Brewster	International HRM: beyond expatriation	1997
☑	14	0.54	197	AH Mcpherson, WK Roche	Peripheral location equals localized labour? Multinational…	1997
☑ h	271	10.42	481	C Brewster, H Scullion	A review and agenda for expatriate HRM	1997
☑ h	156	6.24	42	G Martin, P Beaumont	Diffusing'best practice'in multinational firms: prospects,…	1998
☑ h	67	2.68	90	W Stewart Howe, G Martin	Internationalisation strategies for management education	1998

Google Scholar simply aggregates all citations to a book to its latest edition. So, if a book has multiple editions with the same title, all its citations will be attributed to its latest edition. This may make sense from the perspective of Google Scholar's function of presenting users with an indication of books that have had a lasting impact. However, it doesn't really make sense from a bibliometric perspective as it:

- Severely overestimates the number of citations per year that the book has received.
- Typically results in these books being listed at the top of an academic's publication ranking when sorting results on the [cites] per year column.

- May count citations to content that is not even included in the latest edition.
- Overvalues the contribution of authors/editors that have only been involved in recent editions. Sebastian Reiche and Helene Tenzer have been involved since the 5th edition, but in their Google Scholar records are credited with nearly 550 citations to earlier editions.
- Erases the contribution of authors/editors that have only been involved in earlier editions. Ashly Pinnington was involved in the 3rd and 4th edition and Joris van Ruysseveldt was involved in the 1st and 2nd edition, but a search for their names doesn't show the textbook.

Is there a work-around?

Unfortunately, there is currently no work-around for this. Therefore, vigilance is required when noticing a book that is unusually highly cited for its age.

You cannot restrict citation years

Many Publish or Perish users would like to know how many citations they have received in the last year or the last five years and expect the year limitations in Publish or Perish to achieve this.

- For instance: You have just done a search with specific start and end years, for example from 2000 to 2005. However, the results do not show 6 citation years as you expected, but 23 citation years (if the search is done in 2023). What's going on?
- Answer: The search period (2000 to 2005 in this specific example) restricts the original *publications*. It does not restrict the *citations*.

Regardless of the start and end years in your search, the results will *always* show the citations until the present day, give-or-take a few weeks. And because Publish or Perish shows *citation* metrics, we must count all years from the start year until the present day.

Is there a work-around?

Theoretically, you could use "Retrieve citations to your work in Publish or Perish" to get all citations to your work and classify them by year. However, this would require PoP to send many queries to Google Scholar, which will likely lead to very slow searches and CAPTCHAs. If you have created a GS Citations profile, however, you do get a breakdown of citations per year from 2001 onwards.

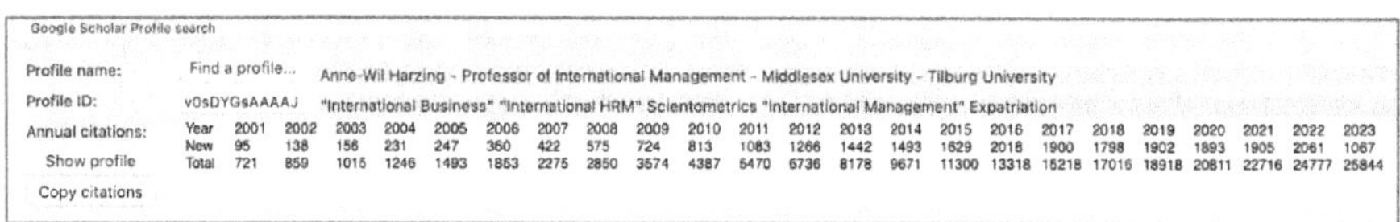

Google Scholar Profile search																							
Profile name:	Find a profile…	Anne-Wil Harzing - Professor of International Management - Middlesex University - Tilburg University																					
Profile ID:	vOsDYGsAAAAJ	"International Business" "International HRM" Scientometrics "International Management" Expatriation																					
Annual citations:	Year	2001	2002	2003	2004	2005	2006	2007	2008	2009	2010	2011	2012	2013	2014	2015	2016	2017	2018	2019	2020	2021	2022	2023
	New	95	138	156	231	247	360	422	575	724	813	1083	1266	1442	1493	1629	2018	1900	1798	1902	1893	1905	2061	1067
Show profile	Total	721	859	1015	1246	1493	1853	2275	2850	3574	4387	5470	6736	8178	9671	11300	13318	15218	17016	18918	20811	22716	24777	25844
Copy citations																								

After clicking on "Copy citations", and pasting them in Excel, I was able to create the graph below with just a few mouse clicks.

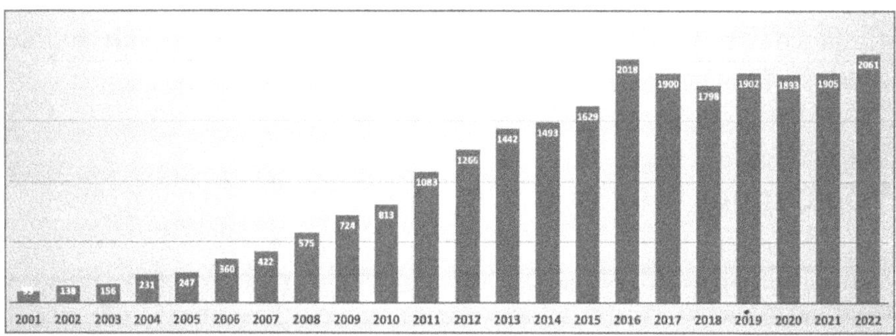

Alternatively, you can also go to your (or someone else's) Google Scholar Citations profile online where you will see a small graph with your citations in the last eight years, as well as the total number of citations and your h-index in the last five years (see screenshot).

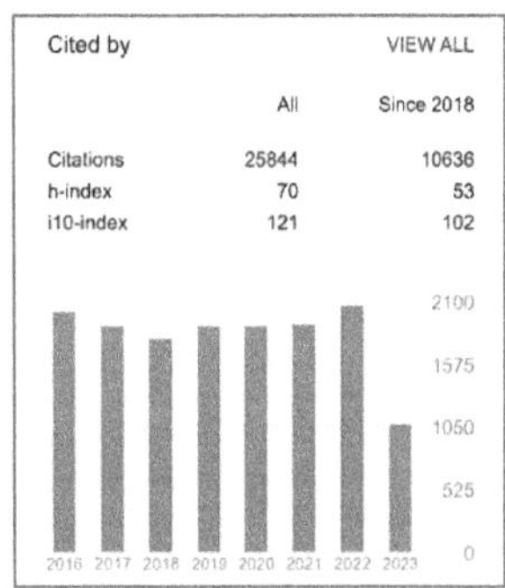

CAPTCHAS

Publish or Perish is doing everything it can to limit burdening Google Scholar with too many queries.

- We keep results in the cache, so there is no need to search Google Scholar if you run the same search repeatedly within a short period.
- We limit the request rate so that if you perform searches that yield many results (several hundred or more) or issue several searches in short succession, the request rate limiter will insert progressively longer delays, keeping the overall request rate within acceptable limits.
- We alert you if your request rate is running too high.

However, you may still find that if you conduct many searches in a short space of time, especially if these are searches with many results, you will get a notice from Google Scholar asking you to verify that you are not a robot.

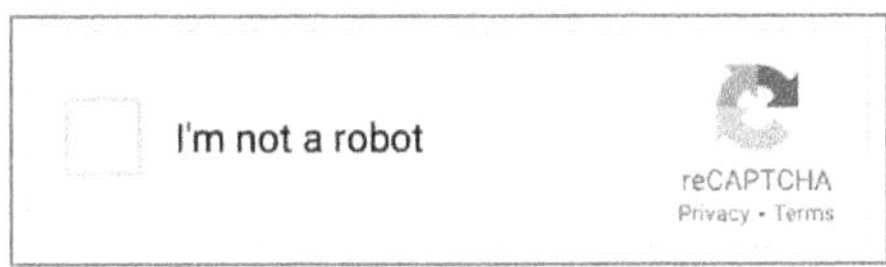

After clicking the box, you will be presented with either a range of images from which you need to select a specific type of image or a squiggly word that you need to type into a box. Once you have identified the correct images (usually traffic lights, oceans, bridges, cars, mountains, stairs, etc.), you will often get a second set of images. If you identify both sets correctly, your search will proceed as normal.

Is there a work-around?

We realise this is very annoying, but there is really nothing we can do about this. You can try to avoid this by not running too many searches in a short space of time and being smart in your searches so that you do not get hundreds of irrelevant results. You can also use the new option to limit the number of results in Google Scholar (see below). This is particularly helpful if you are still refining your search and just want to see what kind of results you get.

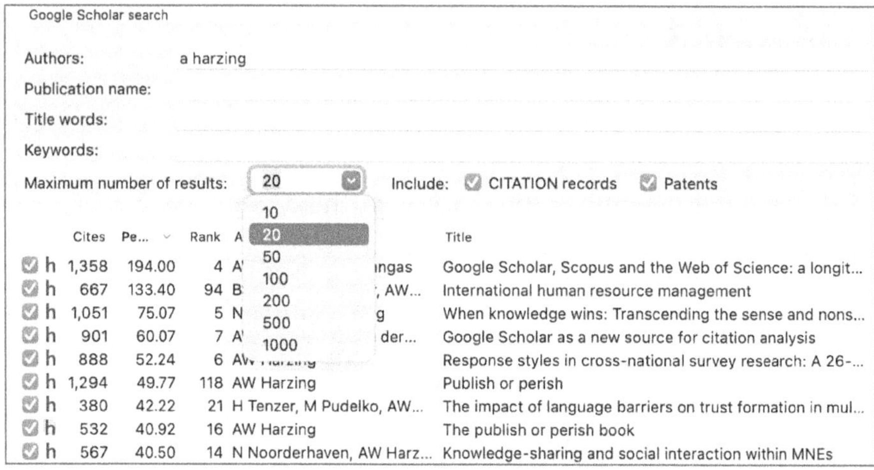

PoP and Google Scholar do not match?

PoP does *not* give results that are different from Google Scholar! It is as accurate or as inaccurate as Google Scholar itself. If you conduct the *same* search in Publish or Perish as in Google Scholar, you will get the *same* result. We do not perform any magic or adjust your record!

If the Publish or Perish results differ from the ones you get by using Google Scholar directly, this is typically caused by the fact that in Publish or Perish we use the Advanced Scholar Search capabilities of Google Scholar, whereas your manual search probably used the standard Google Scholar search. The latter is equivalent to a **Keywords** search, which matches the search terms *anywhere* in the searched documents (author, title, source, abstract, references etc.) and usually provides far too many irrelevant results for an effective citation analysis.

Worked example: standard search vs. author search

If you would for instance search for my name using the standard Google Scholar search rather than the author search, you would get more than 1,000 papers (with only the first 1,000 shown by Google Scholar) and nearly 75,000 citations (see screenshot).

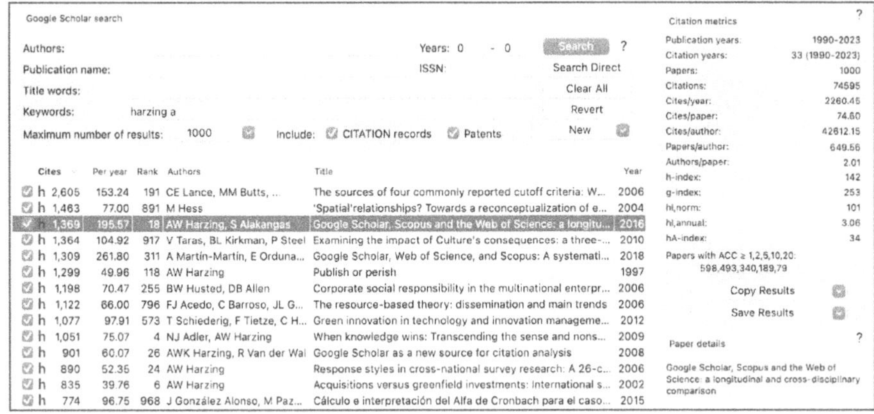

	Cites	Per year	Rank	Authors	Title	Year
h	2,605	153.24	191	CE Lance, MM Butts, ...	The sources of four commonly reported cutoff criteria: W...	2006
h	1,463	77.00	891	M Hess	'Spatial'relationships? Towards a reconceptualization of e...	2004
h	1,369	195.57	18	AW Harzing, S Alakangas	Google Scholar, Scopus and the Web of Science: a longitu...	2016
h	1,364	104.92	917	V Taras, BL Kirkman, P Steel	Examining the impact of Culture's consequences: a three-...	2010
h	1,309	261.80	311	A Martín-Martín, E Orduna...	Google Scholar, Web of Science, and Scopus: A systemati...	2018
h	1,299	49.96	118	AW Harzing	Publish or perish	1997
h	1,198	70.47	255	BW Husted, DB Allen	Corporate social responsibility in the multinational enterpr...	2006
h	1,122	66.00	796	FJ Acedo, C Barroso, JL G...	The resource-based theory: dissemination and main trends	2006
h	1,077	97.91	573	T Schiederig, F Tietze, C H...	Green innovation in technology and innovation manageme...	2012
h	1,051	75.07	4	NJ Adler, AW Harzing	When knowledge wins: Transcending the sense and nons...	2009
h	901	60.07	26	AWK Harzing, R Van der Wal	Google Scholar as a new source for citation analysis	2008
h	890	52.35	24	AW Harzing	Response styles in cross-national survey research: A 26-c...	2006
h	835	39.76	6	AW Harzing	Acquisitions versus greenfield investments: International s...	2002
h	774	96.75	968	J González Alonso, M Paz...	Cálculo e interpretación del Alfa de Cronbach para el caso...	2015

Instead, an *author* search for "harzing a" results in "just" 513 papers and some 26,320 citations. The keyword search matches "harzing a" *anywhere* in the document, including all articles citing my work that appear in full text in Google Scholar and where "harzing a" appears in the reference list.

In the above screenshot the resulting papers are ordered by number of citations, not by Google Scholar rank, which is the standard ranking for a general search. As you can see in the rank column, highly cited articles that are less relevant (i.e., that do not have my name in a prominent field, such as the author field) have a low Google Scholar rank (191, 891, and 917), whereas the first paper that is authored by me has a relatively high Google Scholar rank (#18).

Is there a work-around?

In virtually all cases a Google Scholar advanced search will give you a much better result than a standard search. However, if you absolutely *do* need to get the same results in Publish or Perish as with a standard Google Scholar search, do the following.

1. Empty all text fields except **Keywords**.
2. Enter your search terms in the **Keywords** field.
3. Click on Search.

When the results appear, click on the Rank column header to sort the results in the order in which Google Scholar returned them.

In sum

This chapter has provided an extensive overview of the strengths and weaknesses of using Google Scholar as a source of publication and citation data. Using Google Scholar means sacrificing a certain level of accuracy. In the majority of bibliometric analyses, especially those at higher levels of aggregation and those focusing on robust metrics such as the h-index, Google Scholar's inevitable slip-ups will not significantly influence the results.

If 99+% accuracy is required, Google Scholar will always need to be triangulated with other data sources. However, as a scholar in the Social Sciences, I am more than happy to accept the occasional Google Scholar lapse in return for a coverage that is vastly superior to Scopus and the Web of Science and does not discriminate against scientific publication practices outside the (Life) Sciences.

One way to ensure that Google Scholar data are more reliable is to manually curate them in a Google Scholar Profile. The next chapter therefore provides more details on the why and how of this option.

Chapter 6: Google Scholar Citations Profile

In 2012 – 8 years after the introduction of Google Scholar – Google introduced the option of creating a Google Scholar Citations Profile. The screenshot below shows the top part of my profile. A few months later, we introduced a Google Scholar Citations Profile search option in the Publish or Perish software.

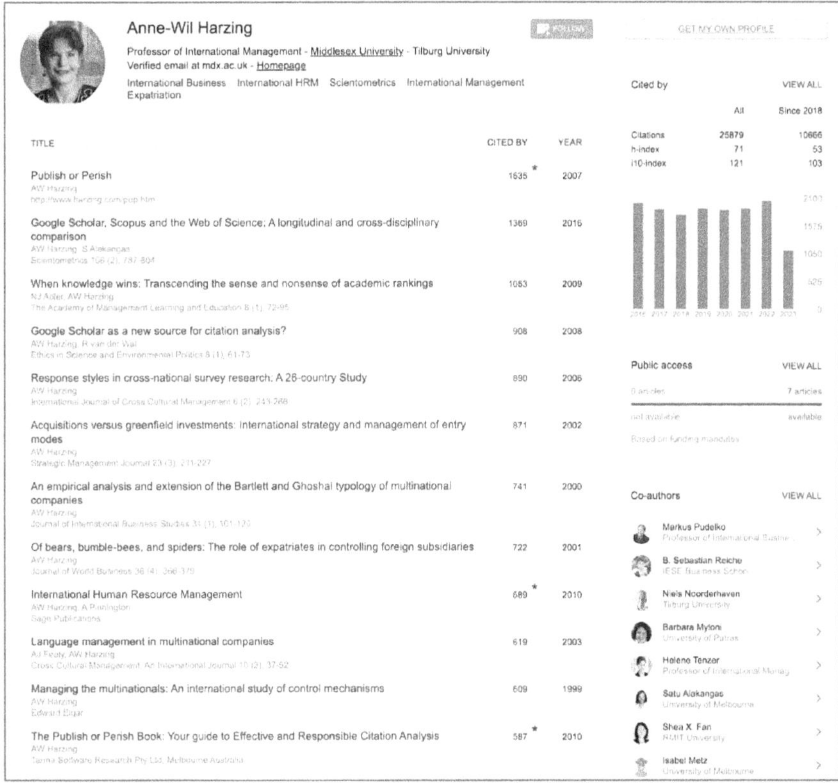

The effectiveness of PoP GS Profile searches depends on the accuracy of your profile. Hence, in this chapter I'll first explain why you need a GS profile, how to create it, keep it up to date and clean, and enrich it. I'll also show you how to get information from your profile through alerts and exports.

Subsequently, I'll explain how you can use Publish or Perish to search in GS profiles, not just for authors, but also for labels and institutions. This allows you to calculate a wide variety of metrics and use the PoP software's superior features for sorting andexporting based on the cleaner and more accurate Google Scholar Profile data.

Why do I need a Google Scholar Profile?

Google Scholar Profiles are increasingly used by academics, Deans, and research administrators to get a quick overview of an academic's publications, citations, and research interests. Google Scholar is the most comprehensive source of publication and citation data for the Social Sciences, Humanities, and Engineering. It normally includes more publications and citations than the Web of Science and Scopus, which favour the Life and Natural Sciences. An academic working in the Social Sciences will on average have 3 to 6 times as many citations in Google Scholar than in the Web of Science.

This is because rather than working with a list of approved journals, Google Scholar simply parses academic publications from what it can find on the web. Hence, any journal publications that can be found on websites with an academic focus will be covered in Google Scholar. Moreover, Google Scholar also includes non-journal type publications, such as books, book chapters, conference papers, white papers, and even – as you can see in my profile above – software.

A great solution for "stray" citations

Creating a GS profile is also a great solution for one of the biggest annoyances in citation analysis: the presence of "stray" citations. Note that with the term stray citations I don't mean the existence of multiple versions of the same paper online; Google Scholar normally aggregates those under one master record. Stray citations are records that have not been aggregated under their master record. They typically have only a few citations, and are often the result of misspelling of an author's name, the title of the publication or the journal.

Stray citations tend to be particularly common for "non-traditional" publications, such as software, books, book chapters, and conference papers as there is generally no standardised way to reference them. It is therefore much harder for Google Scholar to figure out whether they do refer to the same publication.

For instance, although Google Scholar does a much better job than the Web of Science to accurately capture citations to my Publish or Perish software programme, there are still many stray citations (see the screenshot below), which – in my GS Profile – I have all merged into the master record.

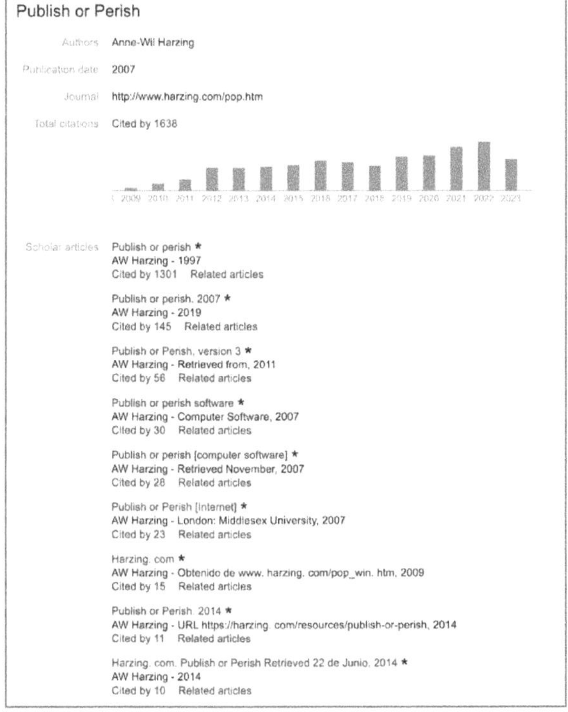

You can merge stray citations by logging into your profile, checking the box in front of the records you want to merge, and clicking merge (see screenshot below). Sorting by publication title will make it easier to find duplicates. Note that the two publications below are separate publications, the first one being a conference paper that preceded the official journal publication. Hence, I have not actually merged them on my profile.

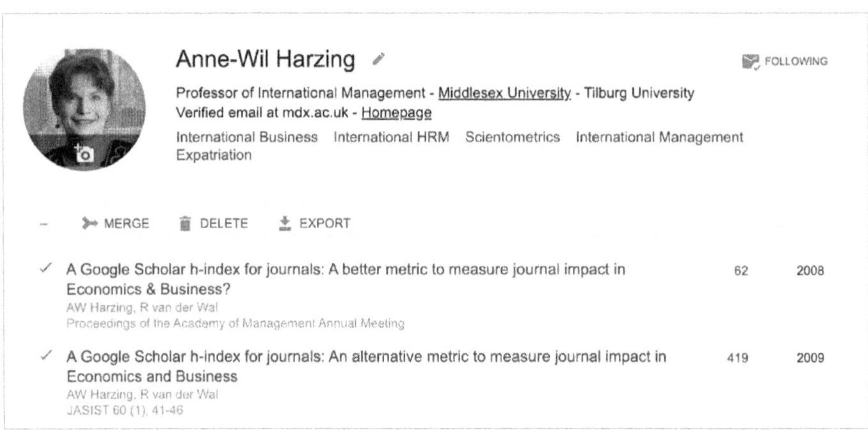

If you have many publications, it is a lot easier to spot stray citations by using a Google Scholar Profile search in Publish or Perish. You will get a compact overview of your publications and the ability to sort on *all* fields, not just title and year. Below you can see my Google Scholar profile in Publish or Perish, with all publications starting with an "A" being visible.

Google Scholar Profile search

Profile name: Find a profile... Anne-Wil Harzing - Professor of International Management - Mi   Search   ?

Profile ID: v0sDYGsAAAAJ   "International Business" "International HRM" Scientometrics "In   Search Direct

Annual citations:	2012	2013	2014	2015	2016	2017	2018	2019	2020	2021	2022	2023	Clear All
	1268	1443	1494	1632	2020	1905	1799	1906	1892	1904	2052	1183	
Show profile	6743	8186	9680	11312	13332	15237	17036	18942	20834	22738	24790	25973	Revert

Copy citations   New

	Cites	Per year	Rank	Authors	Title	Year
✓	60	4.00	74	AW Harzing, R van der Wal	A Google Scholar h-index for journals: A better metric to m...	2008
✓ h	439	31.36	20	AW Harzing, R van der Wal	A Google Scholar h-index for journals: An alternative metric...	2009
✓ h	272	14.32	28	JB Hocking, M Brown, AW...	A knowledge transfer perspective of strategic assignment...	2004
✓ h	160	17.78	49	AW Harzing	A longitudinal study of Google Scholar coverage between 2...	2014
✓ h	241	24.10	34	AW Harzing	A preliminary test of Google Scholar as a source for citatio...	2013
✓	5	0.33	139	BS Reiche, ML Kraimer, A...	A social capital perspective of knowledge sharing and care...	2008
✓	15	0.56	113	AW Harzing	About the paucity of empirical research in SIHRM: A test of...	1996
✓ h	873	41.57	6	AW Harzing	Acquisitions versus greenfield investments: International st...	2002
✓	3	1.00	143	L Zander, A Mockaitis, AW...	Action Intent: Getting closer to leadership behavior in 22 c...	2020
✓	13	13.00	116	M Dodourova, S Zhao, AW...	Ambidexterity in MNC knowledge sourcing in emerging eco...	2023
✓ h	242	11.00	33	AW Harzing	An analysis of the functions of international transfer of man...	2001
✓ h	743	32.30	7	AW Harzing	An empirical analysis and extension of the Bartlett and Gho...	2000
✓	55	5.00	77	I Metz, AW Harzing	An update of gender diversity in editorial boards: a longitud...	2012
✓	1	0.11	157	H Beddi, M Valax	Anne-Wil Harzing: les modes de contrôle dans les relations...	2014
✓	13	0.87	118	AW Harzing	Arbitrary decisions in ranking studies: A commentary on Xu...	2008
✓ h	286	13.62	25	AW Harzing	Are our referencing errors undermining our scholarship and...	2002
✓	0	0.00	179	AW Harzing, N Noorderha...	Australian and New Zealand subsidiaries: victims of geogra...	2007
✓	70	3.89	72	AW Harzing	Australian research output in economics and business: hig...	2005

How to create a Google Scholar Profile?

Creating a profile is very quick and simple. Unless you have a very common name, you should be able to do this in less than 5 minutes.

1. You'll need a Google account before you can begin – use your existing account or create one.

2. Go to https://scholar.google.co.uk and click on 'My profile'

3. Follow the instructions, adding your affiliation information and your University email address. (Remember to validate the email address – you'll receive an email asking you to do this).

4. Add a link to your University home page or your favourite online profile.

5. Add a photo if you want to personalise your profile, which is highly recommended.

6. Click on 'Next step' to create your basic profile.

7. Add your publications – Google will suggest a list and ask you to confirm that they are yours. Look through these carefully and don't import them wholesale because:

   o Publications by other authors may be included in the suggestions if you have a common name.

   o There may be some types of articles that you don't want to include. Google Scholar also indexes content such as newsletters, book reviews, and sometimes even editorial board membership lists.

8. Make your profile public – this means that others will be able to find it and discover your body of work. Otherwise, you will be the only one who is able to see it, which defeats the whole purpose of creating a profile in the first place.

How do I keep my profile clean?

There are two ways to keep your profile up to date. The easiest way to do this is to use the default settings when setting up your profile. This means Google Scholar automatically adds any publications that its algorithm thinks are yours. So, whenever you have a new publication, Google Scholar will automatically add it. Whilst this may seem a tempting option, it creates two problems: inclusion of rubbish publications and profile pollution.

Automatic profiles may include rubbish

The Google Scholar algorithm will add anything that carries your name. This includes not only legitimate journal publications, books, chapters, and conference papers, but also "rubbish". Google Scholar draws its information from the web without human intervention. Therefore, it sometimes finds "publications" that are not real. Here are some publications Google Scholar found for me:

> **Presentation Outline**
> AW Harzing - 2008
>
> **ACOUISITIONS VERSUS GREENFIELD LLLLLL GGGGG LSGGGG LGGGGGGGGS LGGGGG LG GGGLS GGGGGGGLG GGGGGGGGG GG GGGGGLG GGGLLL**
> AW Harzing - 2002
>
> **Rare earth elements (REE) are needed to produce many cutting-edge products, and their depletion is a major concern. In this paper, we identify unique characteristics ...**
> AW Harzing, W Mijnhardt, Y Ju, SY Sohn - Scientometrics, 2015

The first two are clearly nonsense. The third is a data parsing error. I was accidentally added as an author on a paper in the same issue of a journal in which I *had* published a paper.

For most academics these errors are rare and "rubbish" publications typically don't have any citations. Hence, they don't appear at the top of your profile. However, they still pollute your profile. And if you sort your profile by year some of these rubbish publications might obscure your real academic contributions.

Automatic profiles lack author disambiguation

Second, the Google Scholar algorithm will add anything it *thinks* you have published. This algorithm works well if – like me – you are the only academic publishing under your last name, or the only one with a specific combination of initial/first name and last name.

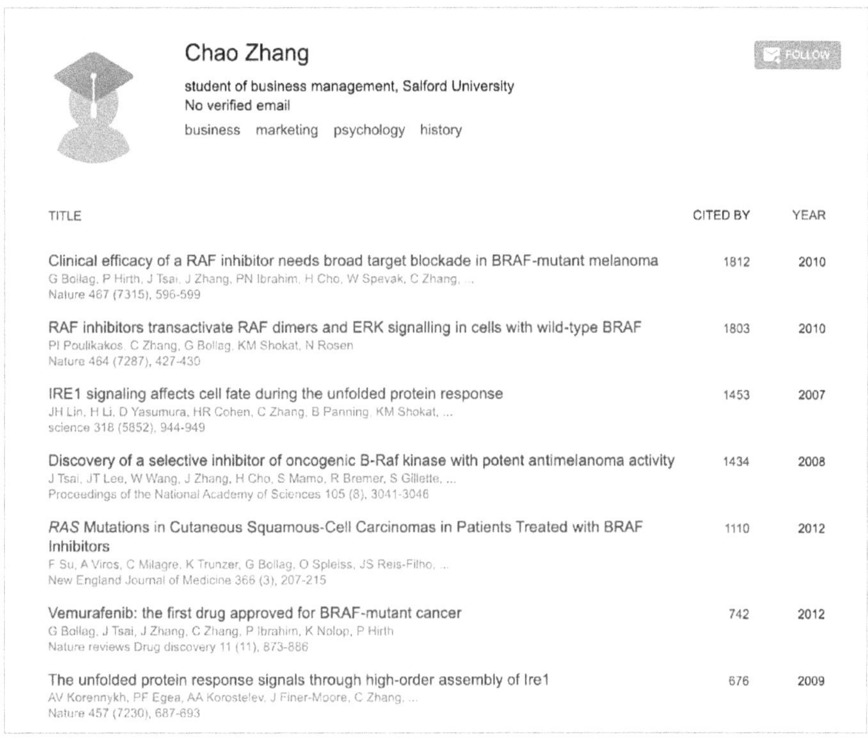

However, this algorithm falls down if you have "namesakes", that is academics with a name that is identical to yours. If you are called Garcia, Johnson, Kim, Lee, Li, Martin, Müller, Patel, Rossi, Sato, Silva, Smith, or Zhang, you are likely to have many academic namesakes.

If you have such a common name, your profile might very quickly look like the above profile by a "student of business management" featuring lots of Science and Life Science articles. This will make it impossible to even find your own publications, let alone get a fully accurate list of your publications.

Please note that this problem of namesakes is by no means limited to Google Scholar. Scopus and the Web of Science perform a bit better in author disambiguation as they are using additional criteria such as disciplinary area. However, even their disambiguation is by no means perfect either. For a hilarious illustration of the lack of author disambiguation in the Web of Science, see the discussion of Web of Science limitations in Chapter 4 and my blogpost: *"Health Warning: Might Contain Multiple Personalities"*, which found the most highly cited academics to be amalgamations of thousands of individuals.

Avoiding profile pollution

It can be hard to keep your online profiles up-to-date and errorfree. At the same time, doing so can be considered an ethical obligation for researchers. Although there might be valid (and not so valid) reasons for *not* creating the various online profiles, once you have created such a profile it is your responsibility to ensure it is accurate and free of errors.

For Google Scholar profiles this means ensuring that the publications listed on your profile are both complete *and* accurate. Just like you wouldn't list non-existent degrees or job experiences on your LinkedIn profile, it is an ethical obligation to ensure that your Google Scholar Profile only lists publications and citations that are yours.

Fortunately, this is trivially easy to do. Simply change Google Scholar's default *automatic* addition of publications to *manual*. This means that you can quickly verify any publications before they are added. It thus prevents profile pollution. Rest assured that this is not a time-consuming chore either. Adding new publications is as simply as clicking on a link in an update email alert from Google Scholar.

To put your profile updates on manual, log in to your Google Scholar profile and Click on the + sign next to TITLE and chose "Configure article updates". Click *"Don't automatically update my profile. Send me email to review and confirm updates"* (see the two screenshots below).

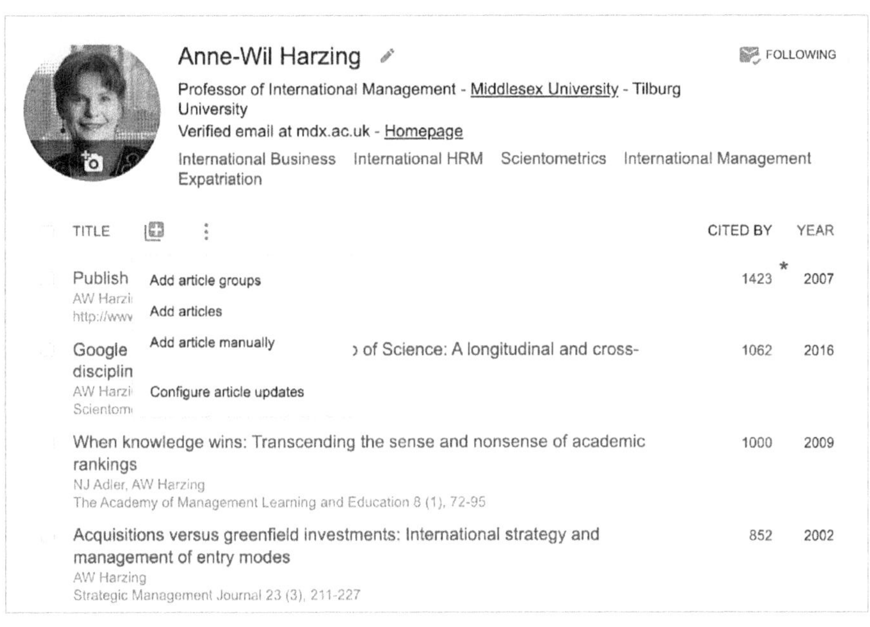

What if I no longer have access to my GS Profile?

Some academics find that they no longer have access to their Google Scholar Profile. This could happen if a research assistant or research administrator had originally created the account for you and has now disappeared without a trace. Or maybe you created a Google account by using an email address you no longer have access to. In that case, you can write to Google to delete your profile. However, from what I have heard from colleagues in this situation, you do not always get a satisfactory answer to your request.

The next best option seems to be to create an entirely new profile and ensure you keep this profile up-to-date and clean. This obviously runs the risk of profile confusion. However, if your other profile is out-of-date and/or includes several papers from another discipline, most academics will understand what your correct GS profile is. To make it easier to find your correct profile, you could consider using one of the five allowed discipline labels (see the next section) to say something like "correct profile".

Enriching your profile

Beyond the addition of a professional picture, there are two ways in which you can enrich your Google Scholar profile: adding co-authors and adding meaningful keywords.

Adding co-authors

Adding co-authors allows academics to better understand where your research is positioned. You will find an alert to add co-authors in the top-left corner. You can only add co-authors who have created GS Profiles themselves, but it is up to you to decide whether to add all your co-authors or just the ones you really want to feature.

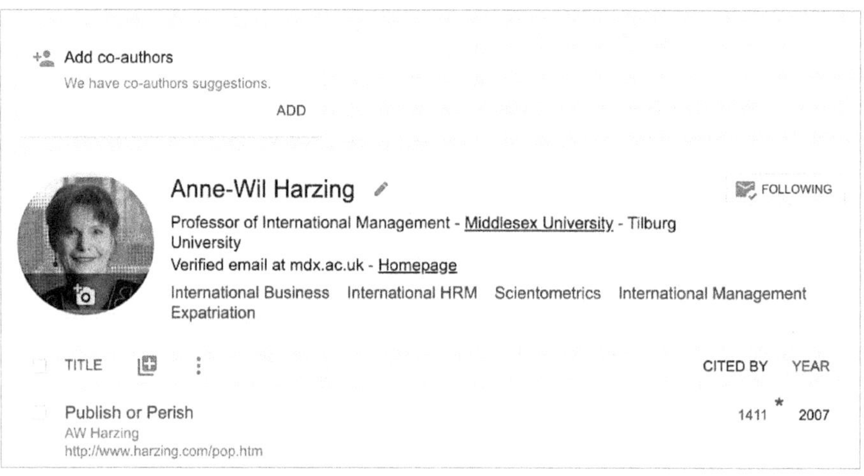

Adding labels/keywords

You can add up to five labels to your profile. Think of these labels as keywords describing your disciplinary area(s) and research topic(s). Each label can contain multiple words. It is crucial to ensure these labels are meaningful. Labels are meaningful if they represent a *clearly defined* academic community. This means they should neither be too broad (e.g., don't use Social Sciences or Humanities) nor too narrow (e.g., expatriate adjustment, expatriate spouses). Usually, a combination of 2-3 relatively broad keywords and 2-3 more specialised keywords works well.

If you choose labels that are too broad, you will find that there are tens of thousands of academics listed in this area, making it hard for you to stand out. If you choose labels that are too narrow, you might find that you are the only one listed in that area. Whereas this might sound great, most likely it means that nobody will be searching for these keywords. Other academics might also wonder whether your research is too specialised to be of interest to them.

Good labels in the broader field of Business & Management could be sub-disciplines such as: leadership, human resource management, organisation theory, strategic management, entrepreneurship, and international business. Finding the right keywords is likely to be an iterative process. First, define some keywords and check whether people with similar keywords include academics who are leaders in your research area. Alternatively, look up some key authors in your field and check which keywords they use.

In my case, I used two relatively broad labels to position myself in my core disciplinary area: International Business and the narrower International Management. As I have conducted research on data sources and metrics to measure research performance, I also added the label Scientometrics. I considered using Bibliometrics, which captures a similar field, but found most key academics in the field used Scientometrics. Finally, I also added two narrower keywords for the sub-discipline of International Management in which I have done most of my work: International HRM and Expatriation.

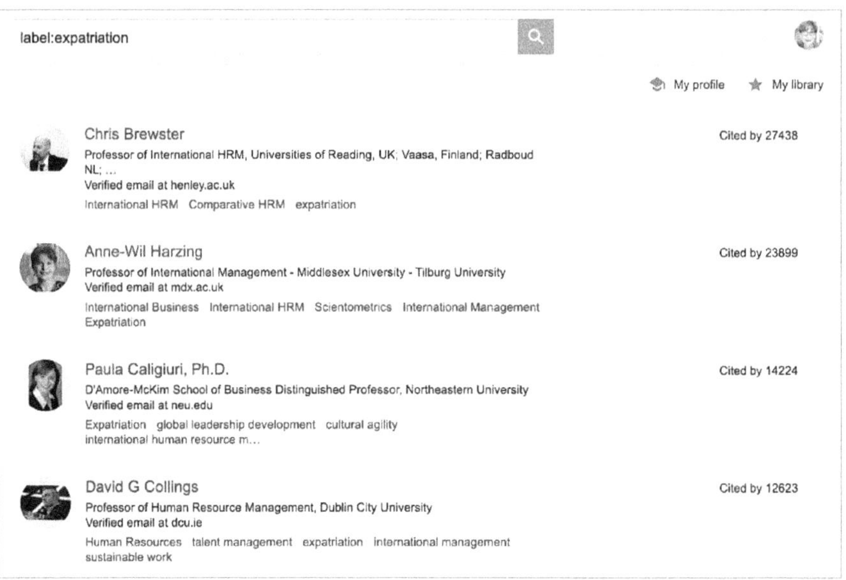

As shown in the screenshot above you will get a list of academics ranked by citations when you click on the label. You will normally be ranked higher within a narrower subdiscipline. For instance, I am ranked second in expatriation and International HRM and seventh in International Management, but only 24th in International Business.

Getting information from your profile

Once your profile is set up and you have ensured it is complete and error-free, you can start deriving information from it. The two most important information retrieval functions are publication/citation alerts and exporting lists of publication.

Getting publication and citation alerts

You can use your Google Scholar Profile to keep up to date with citations to your own work as well new publications and citations for key academics in your field. You will get an email a few times a week if your work or that of the academics you are following is cited. You can cancel these alerts any time you want.

To activate citation alerts to your own work, click on the blue Follow button on top right-hand side of your profile (see screenshot below). You can activate email alerts for new articles/citations to your work. The former is useful if you have kept Google Scholar profile updates on automatic. With new article alerts you can easily spot it if Google Scholar has added an inappropriate article to your profile.

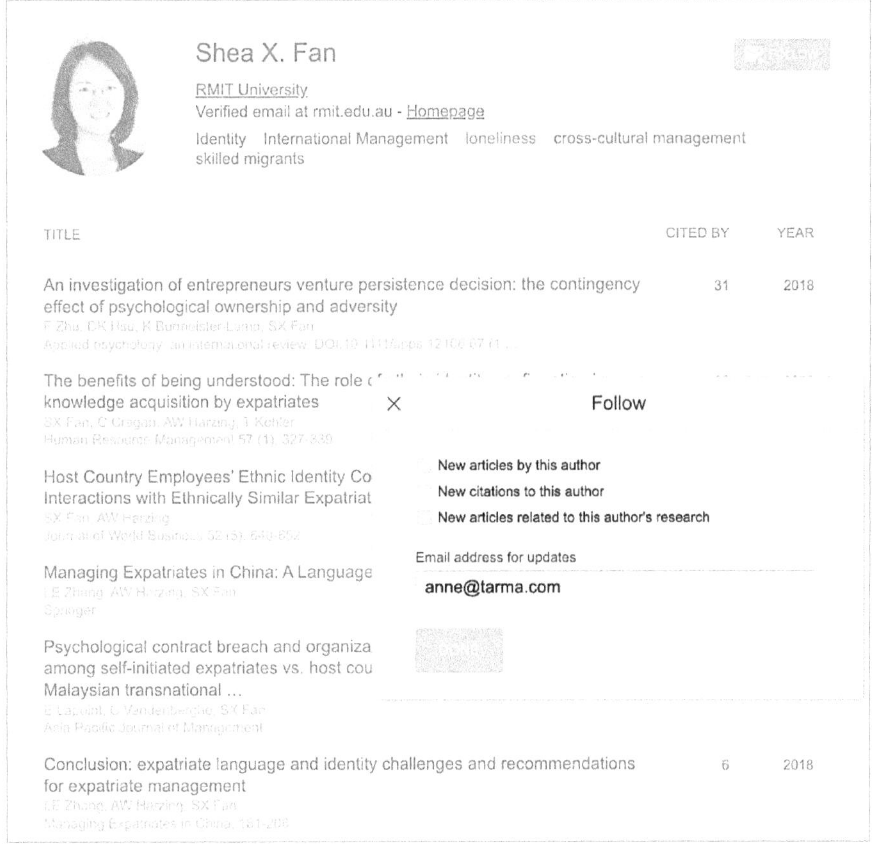

Citation alerts serve a few functions. First, they show you how other academics are building on your work. As such, they also allow easy identification of academics that you may want to approach for collaborative projects. Second, articles citing your own work generally deal with topics you are interested in. Hence, they are a useful way to keep up to date with the literature in your field. Third, seeing other academics cite your work might be a nice ego boost ☺.

You can use the same Follow button to get alerts for *other* academics. This can be useful if you want to keep up to date with publications from a particular author or citations to their work. These could be key authors in your research field, academics you admire, or even your own mentees or colleagues.

Exporting your publications

If you'd like to have a comprehensive list of your own publications, e.g., for copying into your CV, a website, or a funding application, you can export your publications by clicking on the box to the left of title. This makes the export option visible (see screenshot below).

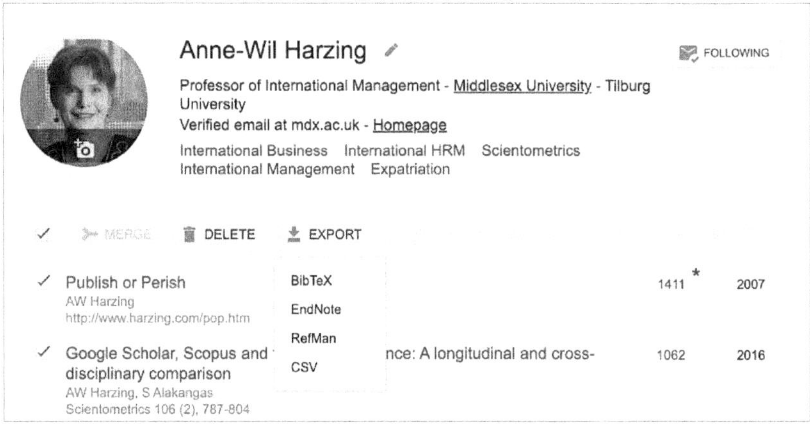

If you export your publications to BibTex you can also import your full list of publications into your ORCID profile within seconds (you will need to create an ORCID profile first). The screenshot below shows you how to do this. Please note, however, that Google Scholar is not a bibliographic database. This means that it doesn't have complete "meta-data", such as DOI, abstract etc.

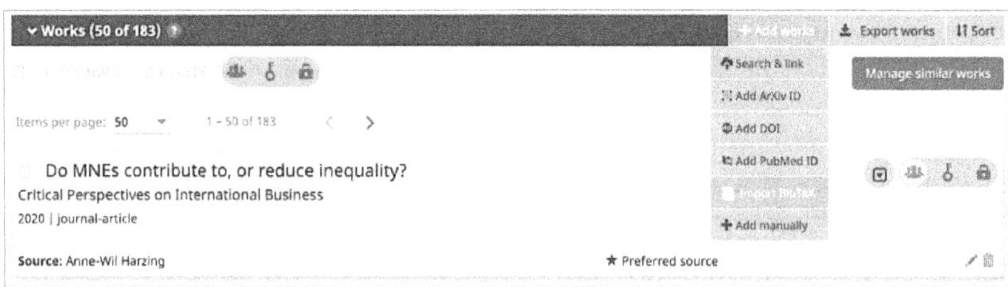

Hence, if (most) of your publications are included in Scopus, linking to your Scopus profile is a better option. You don't need to have a Scopus subscription for this and – unless your name is very common – the profile that Scopus has created automatically for you will usually be correct. Linking to Scopus can be done through the "Search & link" option in the screenshot above. After linking to Scopus, you can always add the remaining publications through Google Scholar.

GS Profiles and Publish or Perish

Since 2012, the Publish or Perish software allows you to do Google Scholar Profile searches. Thus, any work you put into cleaning up your Google Scholar Profile is well worth the effort as you will be able to display your complete profile with a neat list of publications in Publish or Perish and sort it any way you like.

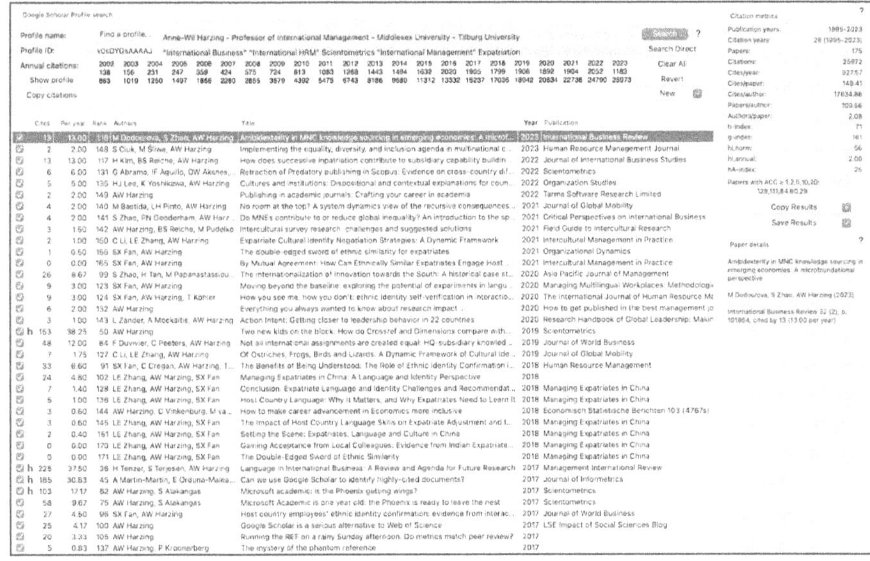

The latter is more difficult in the web interface, which only allows sorting by title and year and by default only provides you with 20 results. Publish or Perish also provides you with a wealth of citation metrics based on your accurate and complete profile (see top right-hand of the screenshot above).

Searching for authors

The most common reason why academics use a Publish or Perish Google Scholar Profile search is to find their own or someone else's GS Profile. To search for an academic's Google Scholar profile just enter any part of their first or last name and/or their affiliation. Note that a Google Scholar Profile search is very "forgiving", unlike most structured databases which have a restrictive syntax.

For instance, if you can't recall someone's last name, a search with their first name and university might provide a good result. The screenshot below shows a search for anyone with the first name Paul at Middlesex University. However, note that Google Scholar does not place any limitations on what you include and do *not* include in your profile name. Hence, some profiles might not have given names or universities included.

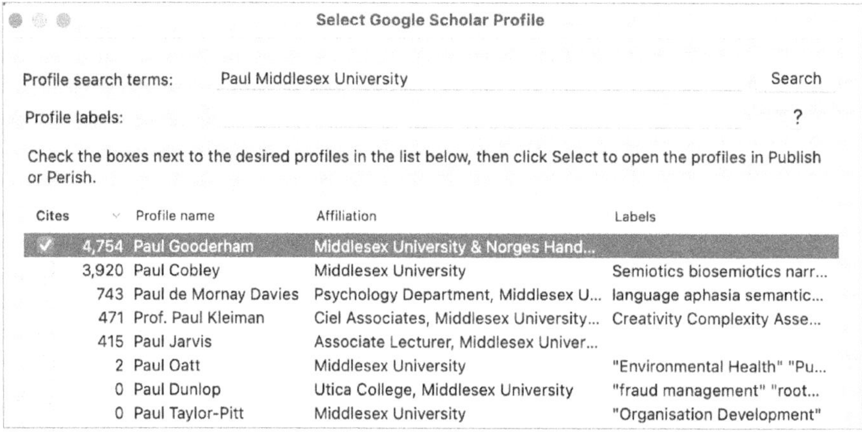

After you have found the Paul you were looking for (in my case Paul Gooderham who works in my School), tick the box in front of their name and click on search. This will show the academic's full citation profile in the Publish or Perish software (see screenshot below). This will provide a full list of publications that can be filtered and sorted in any way, as well as all relevant citation metrics. Moreover, using the "Copy citations" button will copy your yearly citations to the clipboard for pasting into for instance Excel for further analysis.

		2007	2008	2009	2010	2011	2012	2013	2014	2015	2016	2017	2018	2019	2020	2021	2022
		104	129	148	210	249	299	298	342	328	357	326	351	322	303	295	187
		610	739	887	1097	1346	1645	1943	2285	2613	2970	3296	3647	3969	4272	4567	4754

Cites	Per ye...	Rank	Authors	Title	Year	Publication
✓ h 844	36.70	1	PN Gooderham, O Nordhaug, K...	Institutional and rational determinants of org...	1999	Administrative Science Quarterly
✓ h 426	30.43	2	E Døving, PN Gooderham	Dynamic capabilities as antecedents of the s...	2008	strategic management journal
✓ h 344	19.11	3	PN Gooderham, A Tobiassen, E...	Accountants as sources of business advice f...	2004	International small business journal
✓ h 259	18.50	4	P Gooderham, E Parry, K Ringdal	The impact of bundles of strategic human re...	2008	The International Journal of Human F
✓ h 257	13.53	5	PN Gooderham, O Nordhaug	International management: cross-boundary...	2003	
✓ h 250	22.73	6	P Gooderham, DB Minbaeva, T...	Governance mechanisms for the promotion...	2011	Journal of Management Studies

Searching for labels (key words)

Publish or Perish can also search for labels. This makes it very easy to get an overview of the most cited academics in a particular field. It can be particularly helpful when looking for collaborators, reviewers, keynote speakers etc. The screenshot below shows a search for one of my own labels "International Management". Note that you will need to join words with an underscore. If you don't, Google Scholar will interpret this as two different labels.

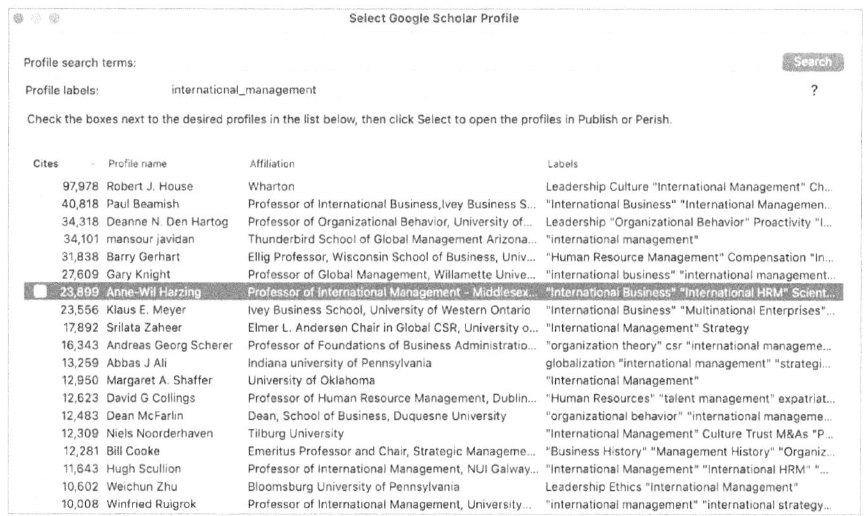

Cites	Profile name	Affiliation	Labels
97,978	Robert J. House	Wharton	Leadership Culture "International Management" Ch...
40,818	Paul Beamish	Professor of International Business,Ivey Business S...	"International Business" "International Managemen...
34,318	Deanne N. Den Hartog	Professor of Organizational Behavior, University of...	Leadership "Organizational Behavior" Proactivity "I...
34,101	mansour javidan	Thunderbird School of Global Management Arizona...	"international management"
31,838	Barry Gerhart	Ellig Professor, Wisconsin School of Business, Univ...	"Human Resource Management" Compensation "In...
27,609	Gary Knight	Professor of Global Management, Willamette Unive...	"international business" "international management...
23,899	Anne-Wil Harzing	Professor of International Management - Middlesex...	"International Business" "International HRM" Scient...
23,556	Klaus E. Meyer	Ivey Business School, University of Western Ontario	"International Business" "Multinational Enterprises"...
17,892	Srilata Zaheer	Elmer L. Andersen Chair in Global CSR, University o...	"International Management" Strategy
16,343	Andreas Georg Scherer	Professor of Foundations of Business Administratio...	"organization theory" csr "international manageme...
13,259	Abbas J Ali	Indiana university of Pennsylvania	globalization "international management" "strategi...
12,950	Margaret A. Shaffer	University of Oklahoma	"International Management"
12,623	David G Collings	Professor of Human Resource Management, Dublin...	"Human Resources" "talent management" expatriat...
12,483	Dean McFarlin	Dean, School of Business, Duquesne University	"organizational behavior" "international manageme...
12,309	Niels Noorderhaven	Tilburg University	"International Management" Culture Trust M&As "P...
12,281	Bill Cooke	Emeritus Professor and Chair, Strategic Manageme...	"Business History" "Management History" "Organiz...
11,643	Hugh Scullion	Professor of International Management, NUI Galway...	"International Management" "International HRM" "...
10,602	Weichun Zhu	Bloomsburg University of Pennsylvania	Leadership Ethics "International Management"
10,008	Winfried Ruigrok	Professor of International Management, University...	"international management" "international strategy...

Please note that fields in Google Scholar are self-selected and not standardised. For one of my other areas of expertise, I have seen four different variants in use: "International HRM", "International HR" "IHRM", and "International Human Resource Management".

Searching for institutions

Publish or Perish can also search for institutions. To do so you need to use the "profile search terms" field. This provides an overview of the most cited academics in a particular institution. It might be helpful if you are looking for a collaborator in a specific institution or if you are a PhD student looking for a supervisor in that institution.

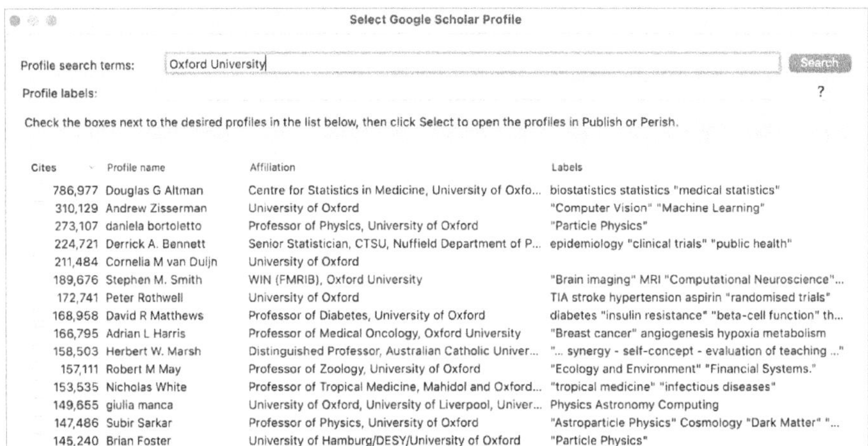

Unlike for the profile labels field, Google Scholar is very liberal in its matching in this field. Hence, if you search for Oxford University it will also match University of Oxford (see screenshot above). You can combine institutional and label searches to narrow down your search (see screenshot below).

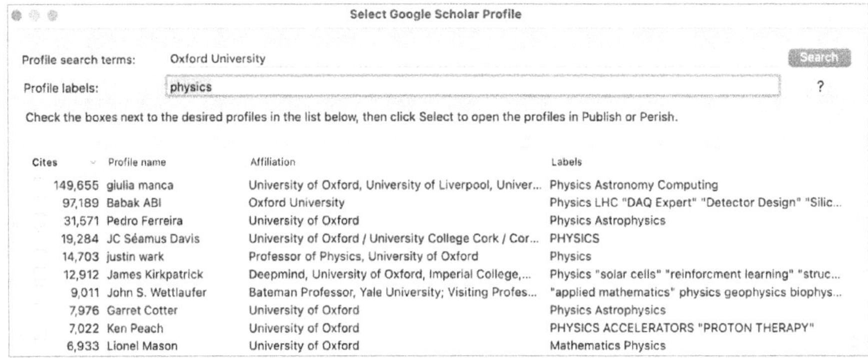

Again, note that these profile labels are self-defined. Hence, there is no guarantee that this search will provide you with *all* academics in Physics working at the University of Oxford. However, it is useful as a first "quick and dirty" approximation.

In sum

Creating a basic Google Scholar Profile only takes 5-10 minutes. By spending another 20-50 minutes, you can create a "model profile" that includes a clean and complete overview of all your publications, lists your co-authors, and has effective labels that position you in your preferred research area.

You can also use your Google Scholar Profile to get alerts for new publications and citations that are of interest to you and use the export function if you need a complete list of your publications quickly. Finally, using by Publish or Perish software you can get more out of the Google Scholar Profiles by calculating key citation metrics and searching for authors, labels, and institutions.

Note that after setting up a Google Scholar profile, it requires very little maintenance, especially if you put your publication updates to manual. Hence, it is well worth the effort to ensure your Google Scholar Profile is as good as possible.

Chapter 7: Author searches

This chapter explains how to conduct effective author searches in the PoP software. Most PoP users are primarily using Google Scholar for their searches. If the author that you are searching for does have a Google Scholar Profile, I *strongly* suggest you use a PoP Google Scholar Profile search (see Chapter 6). This is a better option than Google Scholar as it presents a disambiguated and complete record of an academic's publications.

However, if this is not the case, the instructions in this chapter will help. I provide a large range of options to ensure your Google Scholar author searches result in a clean set of results. In the last section, I will also discuss author searches in the other data sources.

Author search: the basics

Finding your own or someone else's publications, citations, h-index, and many other metrics by using Google Scholar data is easy. Just type the author's name and initial in the **Authors** field. You do not need to use quotes around the name, PoP automatically quotes it for you, but you may want to get in the habit of doing this as it helps for other types of searches. Google Scholar search syntax is very flexible.

- It doesn't matter whether you use caps ("A Harzing" or "A HARZING") or lower case letters ("a harzing").
- The order of the search terms doesn't matter either, you can use "a harzing" or "harzing a".

If you have many publications, you might need to wait for quite a while before PoP can retrieve all of them from Google Scholar. In the past, Google Scholar searches in Publish or Perish were much quicker. However, in 2013 Google Scholar reduced the maximum number of results per request from 100 to 20. Later it reduced this further to 10 results per request. This means that Publish or Perish now has to perform up to 10 times as many requests per search in order to show the full results.

More data requests mean that Publish or Perish hits the maximum number of requests that Google Scholar allows per hour sooner. If the number of requests exceeds the maximum that Google Scholar allows, your IP address will be temporarily blocked by Google Scholar.

To avoid hitting the maximum allowable request limit, Publish or Perish uses an adaptive request rate limiter. This limits the number of requests that are sent to Google Scholar within a given period, both short-term (during the last 60 seconds) and medium term (during the last hour). A search for my name resulted in more than 500 publications (see below screenshot) and took more than 10 minutes.

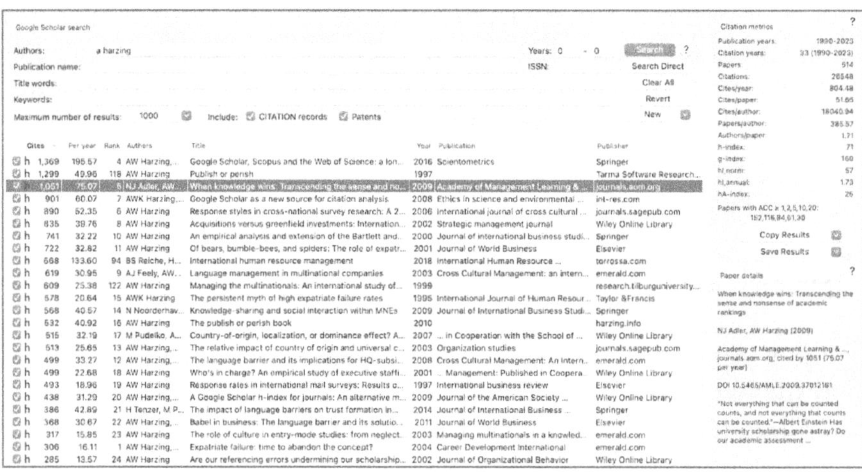

This is caused largely by the very large number of stray citations (for more details see later in this chapter) for non-journal publications in my record, such as the Publish or Perish software, the journal quality list, several books, and many book chapters. There are nearly 100 stray citations for the Publish or Perish software alone. In case you are wondering…. those funny blue "h's" in front of the cites indicate that this publication is part of the set of publications that contributes to the h-index, i.e., the h-core set.

However, for scholars with a more limited number of publications, or a much cleaner publication record with fewer non-journal publications, the complete results will show up much quicker. As a rule of thumb, an author search with less than 150 results will take less than a minute (unless you have conducted any other searches before running the search).

Limit the number of search results

Your efforts to find the best possible search string without putting an unnecessary strain on Google Scholar are facilitated by a new PoP feature. First, the default number of results has been limited to 200. Second, we added a drop-down box allowing you to restrict the maximum number of results for Google Scholar searches (see screenshot below). Seven options are pre-set, but you can type any number in the box. As this is a per search limit, the choice does not carry over to other searches except for the "duplicate the current search" option.

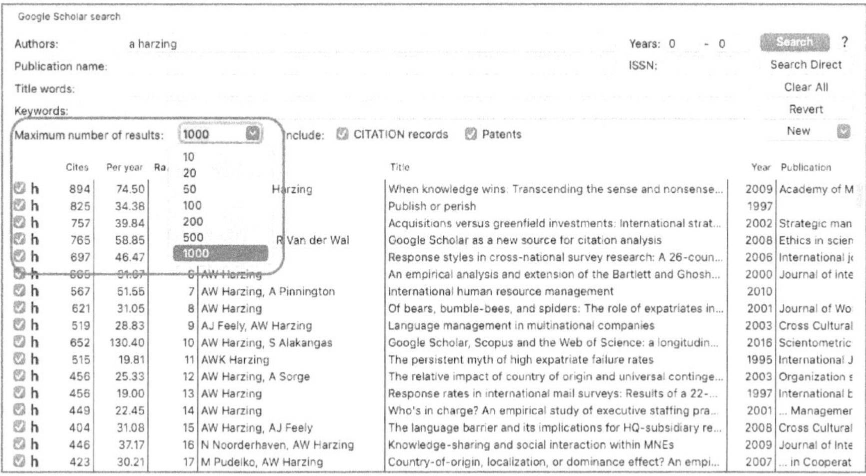

This feature is very useful if you are still fine-tuning a complex author search and don't need to see all results to establish whether your search is providing the expected output. Once you have found the best search string, you can then relax this restriction to get all results.

In the remainder of this chapter, I discuss a wide range of options to reduce irrelevant results as well as results for namesakes of the focal author. In doing so I am using several of my former University of Melbourne colleagues as examples. There are three reasons for this:

1. Each of these academics has a Google Scholar Profile. This gives me a canonical publication record that I can use to compare the effectiveness of my searches with.

2. These academics all have good publication records and a varied set of publications, giving me ample material to work with.

3. As a former Research Dean of the Faculty, I am familiar with their research and can identify their publications easily.

Please note that not all of the options discussed below were able to provide a fully complete publication record for the focal academics. However, remember that in other data sources you may find only a subset of their publications in the first place!

Option 1: Use selective exclusion/inclusion

If the list of results in Publish or Perish is fairly limited, the quickest way to remove stray citations or to disambiguate your focal author's publications from those of a namesake is selective exclusion. You can manually exclude irrelevant publications from the analysis by checking or clearing the boxes in the Results list. Here are some shortcuts:

- Use the right-click menu **Uncheck All** option to exclude all records and then only include relevant results.

- Use the right-click menu **Uncheck Selection** button to exclude only the selected results.

- If you made a mistake in excluding results, simply use the right-click menu to **Check all** or subset of results.

- [Windows version only] When you use the keyboard to travel up and down in the Results list, pressing the space bar toggles the check mark on and off on the selected record.

Selecting relevant publications can be made easier by sorting results by **Cites**, **Authors**, **Title**, **Year**, **Publication**, or **Publisher**. Sorting is done simply by clicking on the corresponding column heading. Click twice to reverse the sort order. Sorting by author is often an effective way to exclude many publications in one go as one can easily identify authors with inappropriate initials or recognise irrelevant co-authors.

In contrast to the refinements described in the other options, changes in the Results pane take effect immediately and are reflected in the Citation metrics pane. You do not have to resubmit your search.

The disadvantage is that these exclusions are not persistent. The next time you do the search in Google Scholar, you will need to do them all over again. All other search options in this chapter are persistent. So, investing some time into fine-tuning your search is worthwhile.

Option 2: Exclude stray citations and patents

By far the quickest way to reduce the number of irrelevant results in a Google Scholar author search is to exclude CITATION records. The Publish or Perish interface includes an option to include or exclude both CITATION results and patents in Google Scholar searches (see screenshot below). Excluding patents is not necessary for academics in most disciplines as patent results are rare. However, the exclusion CITATION results often makes a big difference.

Google Scholar search				
Authors:	a harzing		Years: 0 - 0	Search ?
Publication name:			ISSN:	Search Direct
Title words:				Clear All
Keywords:				Revert
Maximum number of results: 1000	Include:	CITATION records ✓ Patents		New

What are CITATION records?

CITATION results are records where Google Scholar has found citing works, but has been unable to find the cited work online. Often, these CITATION records are what are commonly called "stray citations", i.e., citations where citing authors have made small mistakes in citing a work. In most cases these stray citations only clutter your result.

If you do an author search it makes the author's publication record look messy, making it difficult to establish an academic's primary publications, especially if they are recent and not yet highly cited. So, excluding them makes a lot of sense in many searches. However, it is important to note that Google Scholar assigns the CITATION label to *any* publication where it cannot find the record online, even if the publication in question is very significant and highly cited.

This might include many – though not all – non-journal publications [e.g., books, reports]. This might easily lead to an underestimation of an author's impact, especially in the Social Sciences and Humanities.

In my own publication record excluding CITATION records reduces the number of results from over 500 to less than 200. The majority of the excluded publications are pure dross and will not be missed. However, my citations are reduced by nearly 15% and my h-index is reduced from 71 to 68 because one highly cited book, the Publish or Perish software and the Journal Quality List are excluded. The other metrics are likewise reduced.

So, if you need a fully complete record for yourself or an academic you are evaluating, including CITATION records might be essential. This is especially true in the Social Sciences and Humanities, where book publications are common and in Engineering where software and conference publications might be common publication outputs. If all you are after is an assessment of someone's journal publications, then excluding them will dramatically simplify the output and speed up your search at the same time.

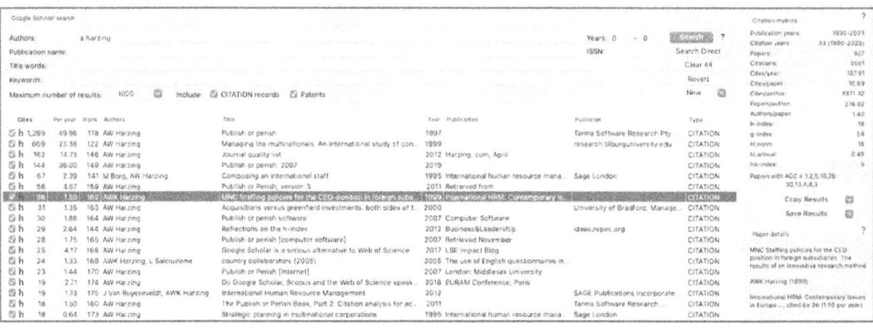

Note that if you are concerned about missing important publications can also exclude CITATION records *after* conducting a search. To do so you can sort results on the **Type** column and review which CITATION records you want to keep. The screenshot below shows the more than 300 CITATION records in my own publication record. Combined they have more than 3,500 citations. However, the vast majority of the citation records – 270 of them – have five or fewer citations.

Most of than 2,600 of the 3,500 citations can be attributed to the three publications I listed above, but there are also some book chapters with a significant number of citations. Hence, for my own record I would probably conduct a search with CITATION records included, and first merge all stray citations for the PoP software, the Publish or Perish book and the Journal Quality List. I would then review the remaining CITATION records with more than 10 citations and ignore the remainder of the results as reviewing all of them would be very time-consuming. Ignoring them would not impact on my h-index or related metrics and does not impact my total citations levels much as it reduces them by less than 2%.

Option 3: Use multiple initials

One way to disambiguate authors in Publish or Perish, i.e., to ensure you do not include publications by an academic's namesake is to use multiple initials in your search. Many academics, including nearly all US academics, have a "middle" name. Hence, you might want to use multiple initials when searching.

Until 2023 when my niece Tessa Harzing started publishing in cell biology, my last name was unique in academia. But imagine that this was not the case, and you needed to include more than one initial to limit the search. My full name is Anne-Wil Käthe Harzing. So, how would you search for me if you wanted to get a clean author record?

Logically, AK might seem the most appropriate option, Anne-Wil as my first and Käthe my second name. However, searching for AK Harzing does not result in *any* records. This is because Anne-Wil is interpreted by Google Scholar as two names. I have compounded this problem myself by using AW as my initials in official settings. Moreover, I don't like Käthe much and have not used it in most of my publications, though I did do so in the early years of my career.

As a result, these three searches offer very different results.

- "AK Harzing" (resulting in 0 records and 0 citations)
- "AW Harzing" (resulting in 429 records with 24,341 citations)

- "AWK Harzing" (resulting in 36 records with 1,904 citations)

Moreover, each of the three searches with multiple initial results in lower total citation count than the original 26,548 citations for "A Harzing" and thus underestimates my citation impact. So, I suggest you use this option with caution.

Useful for Anglophone North Americans

However, I have found this search strategy to be quite effective for Anglophone North Americans who:

a. tend to have a middle initial, and

b. tend to use it systematically when publishing

For instance, if you are looking for a complete publication record for one of my former Melbourne colleagues Carol Kulik, searching for "C Kulik" will also match "CLC Kulik", "CL Kulik", "CC Kulik", "CJ Kulik", "CM Kulik", and even "AC Kulik". It provides 735 results.

Hence, you could search for "CT Kulik" instead. This provides only 235 results with 14,118 citations. Triangulation with Carol Kulik's Google Scholar Profile shows that this restricted Google Scholar search correctly identifies nearly all of Carol's publications.

The only exception is an article where – for unknown reasons – her name is (incorrectly) listed as "T Carol Kulik" on the publisher's web record (though not on the print version of the article). Obviously, Carol added this article to her Google Scholar Profile, but it is not found in a Google Scholar search for "CT Kulik". It *is* found with a search for C Kulik.

Overall, this strategy can thus be a bit hit-and-miss. It will only work if you are certain that the academic in question has used their initials consistently over the years. Many academics are not consistent in the initials that they use in their publications. Even if they are, references by other authors to their articles may use other combinations or formats. So, it is usually safer to start your search with only one initial.

Option 4: Exclude multiple initials

When searching for an author who only publishes with *one* initial, you could exclude other academics with the same last name and first initial, but with *multiple* initials rather than one initial.

For instance, Graham Sewell, another one of my former Melbourne colleagues, has only published as "G Sewell". So, you could exclude other academics with the *same* last name and first initial, but multiple initials by using wildcards, i.e., the symbol * which means any letter. To do so you need to put "-G* Sewell", "-G** Sewell", "-G*** Sewell" in the **Keywords** field.

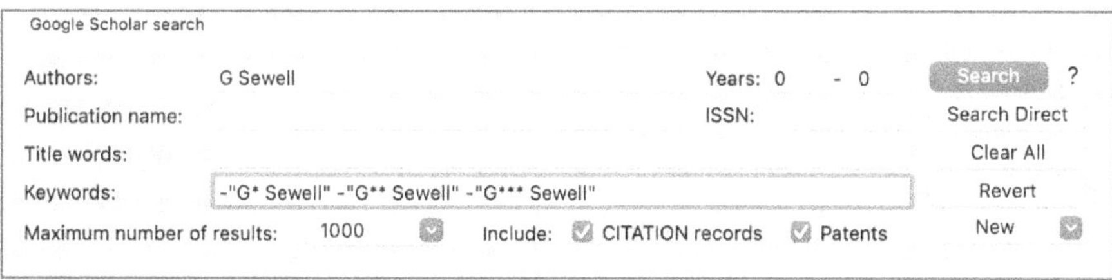

You will need to use the **Keywords** field for this as Google Scholar strips away any * in author searches and thus you would have the identical inclusion and exclusion terms, leaving you with no results. Also note that you will need to use quotes around the search terms. If you exclude G* Sewell (without quotes), GS will interpret this as excluding both G and Sewell, again leaving you with no results at all.

This search would exclude "GJ Sewell", "GW Sewell", "GWF Sewell" "GJTP Sewell" as well as dozens of other combinations in one go. This reduced the number of results from more than 1,400 to around 700 results. [Note that Google Scholar only ever show 1,000 results, but the web interface estimated there to be 1,400 results.]

Unfortunately, you cannot use "*G Sewell" to exclude "EG Sewell" or "RG Sewell" as this excludes all names with a "G" in them, including "G Sewell", our target academic. Hence, these need to be excluded one by one (see screenshot below). However, in contrast to the wildcard exclusions, they can be excluded in the author field for a more intuitive search.

Cites		Per year	Rank	Authors	Title	Year	Publication
h	1,196	299.00	1	G Sewell, B Wilkinson	'Someone to Watch over Me': surveillance, discipline and t...	2019	Postmodern Management Theory
h	1,132	45.28	2	G Sewell	The discipline of teams: The control of team-based indust...	1998	Administrative science quarterly
h	501	23.86	3	P Fleming, G Sewell	Looking for the good soldier, Švejk: Alternative modalities...	2002	Sociology
h	419	52.38	4	G Sewell, L Taskin	Out of sight, out of mind in a new world of work? Autonom...	2015	Organization studies
h	304	17.88	5	G Sewell, JR Barker	Coercion versus care: Using irony to make sense of organi...	2006	Academy of Management review
h	277	13.19	7	G Sewell	Quantum mechanics and its emergent macrophysics	2002	
h	269	17.93	6	N Phillips, G Sewell, S Jaynes	Applying critical discourse analysis in strategic manageme...	2008	Organizational research ...
h	250	8.06	9	G Sewell, B Wilkinson	Empowerment or emasculation? Shopfloor surveillance in...	1992	Reassessing human resource ...
h	190	15.83	8	C Bardin, A Astier, A Vulto, G Se...	Guidelines for the practical stability studies of anticancer...	2011	Annales ...
h	146	8.11	11	G Sewell	Nice work? Rethinking managerial control in an era of kno...	2005	Organization
h	133	12.09	10	G Sewell, JR Barker, D Nyberg	Working under intensive surveillance: When does 'measuri...	2012	Human Relations
h	121	4.48	16	CF Chen, G Sewell	Strategies for technological development in South Korea a...	1996	Research Policy
h	120	9.23	12	A Spicer, G Sewell	From national service to global player: Transforming the or...	2010	Journal of management Studies

This leaves us with other academics who have published with only one initial, but with different given names such as Gary Sewell, Gavin Sewell, Granville Sewell, Guy Sewell. Excluding these as well (see screenshot above) reduces the results to around 200 records. Unfortunately, this is as far as we can get by excluding homonyms as there are at least three other academics called Graham Sewell, including a Physicist (see result #8) and a medical researcher (see result #7).

Hence, further disambiguation will need to be done by the other strategies discussed in the remainder of the chapter, such as using the author's full given name, year restrictions, inclusion or exclusion of affiliation, and inclusion or exclusion of research topics. Alternatively, if – rather than needing a complete author record – you were only interested in finding Graham Sewell's h-index you could simply review the remaining records and exclude false hits. Given that his namesakes haven't generally published highly cited work, this took me only 30 seconds.

Option 5: Use full given name

A good option to limit the number of false hits, is to search with the author's full given name, for instance "Carol Kulik" or "Graham Sewell". For Carol Kulik this results in a clean set of results, including all of Carol's own publications without those of any namesakes. For Graham Sewell this results in 157 publications (see below), including all of his own publications and 60-70 publications of namesakes.

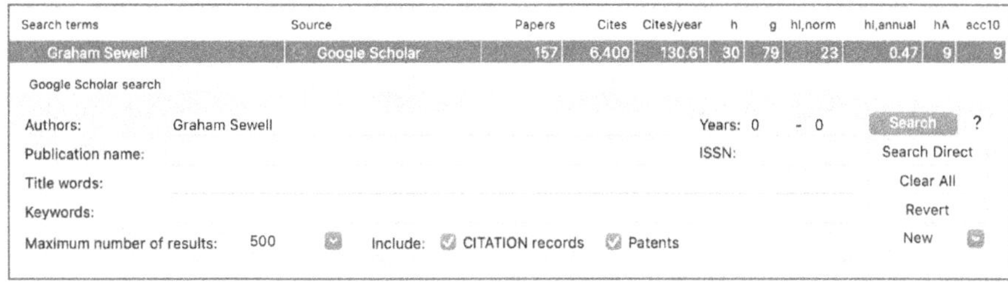

This is a further improvement on the 200-odd records we were left with in the previous section after doing a search with his initials only. It also makes it much easier to further disambiguate this record.

Does not work if authors use initials only

However, this will exclude any publications in which the author's given names are not spelled out in full. Although most journals use full given names case, *some* journals in *some* fields (e.g., Operations Research) use initials only. This means that for some academics you might miss many publications. Thus, in disciplines where publication outputs feature both full given names and, I would recommend only relying on the use of the author's given name:

- as a last resort for authors with very common names,
- as a very "quick-and-dirty" check to see whether a particular academic has published something.

Option 6: Use year restrictions

If you know that a certain author has only published after (or before) a certain year, you can enter the start or end years in the **Year** fields in Publish or Perish. Doing so for Graham Sewell reduces the number of publications by namesakes with another dozen.

You can also use the year fields if you want to analyse the author's publications from a specific period *only*. For instance, you could look at someone's publications, and their associated citations, and h-index for the last five years alone.

Below is an example of my own record, with stray citations removed and duplicates merged. Note that not all publications will have the correct year attributed. For instance, the official launch of the Publish or Perish software was 2007. Most academics refer to that year, but there were enough stray citations with a "publication" year between 2018 and 2023 for the software to make it to the h-index. The top line shows the key metrics. The citation metrics pane shows all metrics, including the number of citation years. This is four rather than five as Publish or Perish doesn't count the current year.

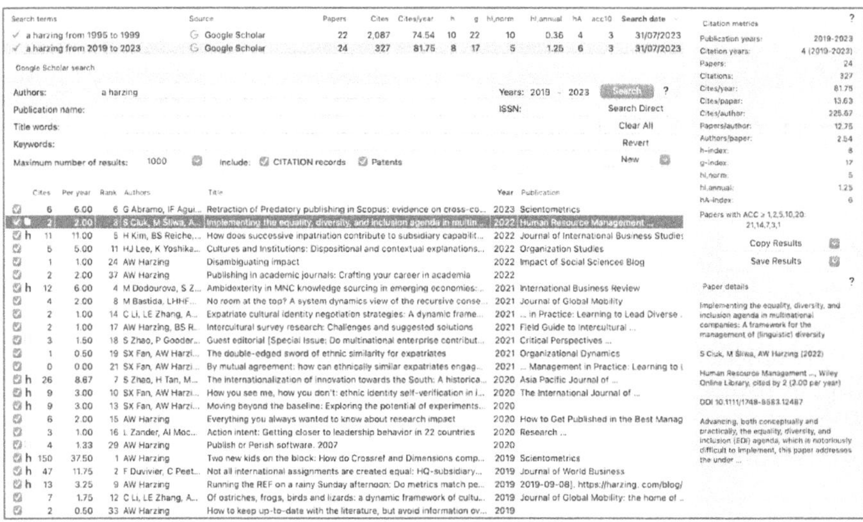

Note that these results are not the same as what is shown on your Google Scholar profile for the last five years. Your Google Scholar Profile shows citations in the last five years to **all** your publications, not to publications in the last five years only. Obviously, you do not need to stick to searching for the last five years, you can use any time period you want, including single years.

The screenshot below shows the first five years of my academic publishing career. Note that in this case citations are for the *entire* time span between the first year in the dataset and the current period as can be seen in the citation metrics pane. Time-sensitive metrics are also calculated using the entire timespan. This means that whilst the hA-index – which is based on individual papers – is still meaningful, the hI,annual – which is based on someone's entire career – is not.

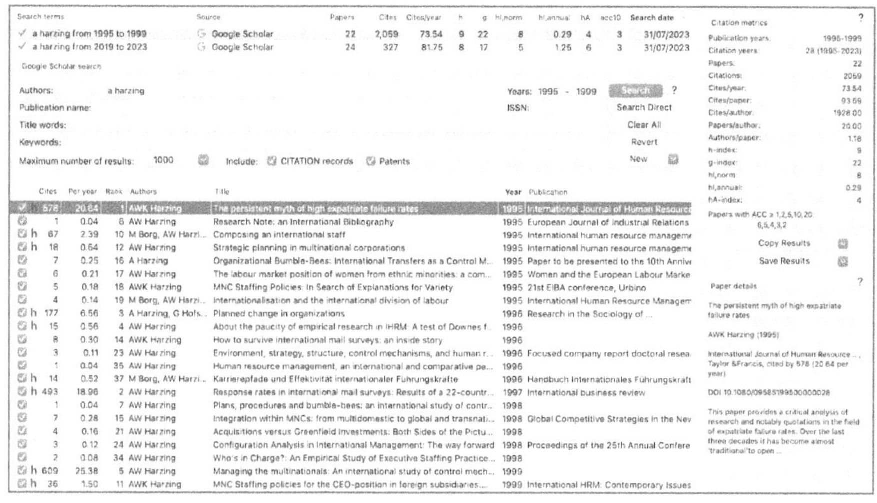

Option 7: Exclude/include research fields

How do you disambiguate your author record in Publish or Perish if you are unlucky enough to have a namesake with *exactly* the same family name and given name and no second initial to differentiate? There are many Peter Smiths or Michelle Browns! In that case, you can use research fields to restrict the search. You will probably need to combine this with other search strategies described above.

Let's take Michelle Brown, another former colleague of mine at the University of Melbourne working in industrial relations and human resource management, as an example. Looking for "M Brown" alone gets us nowhere. The Google web interface reports more than one million results, of which Google Scholar only shows the first 1,000.

These 1,000 results do not even include all of Michelle's own papers. Google Scholar limits the results to the 1,000 most cited papers and even the least cited result still had some 150 citations. Hence any of Michelle's papers with fewer citations are not reported. Using Michelle Brown instead of "M Brown" already limits the number of results to some 6,000 papers, but this is still way too many.

Hence, we embarked on a number of additional techniques.

- Excluding "M* Brown" and "M** Brown" brings the results down to a more manageable 705.
- Excluding "JM Brown" "KM Brown" "LM Brown", limiting the starting year to 1997, and unticking the patents box brings the results further down to 547.

Fortunately, most of the "offending" publications are not highly cited. So, if you are only interested in her h-index, you could simply untick the publications that are not hers. These are clearly identifiable as they are in very different fields, such as animal behaviour, medicine, and criminology. Traveling down the list of h-index publications took me less than a minute and resulted in the correct h-index.

But what if you really want to ensure you have her complete record. Then you could consider excluding her namesakes by using words that appear in the title of their publications such as dogs, crime, prison, criminology, blood, cancer, and infection. I suggest you put them in the keywords field, so that they are matched anywhere in the article for maximum impact.

With half a dozen manual exclusions in the h-core set that belonged to namesakes in a different discipline, this reduced the total number of results 256 and the results were close to Michelle's Google Scholar Profile (see below). However, a strategy like this quickly runs up against the 256-character limit that Google Scholar imposes across fields, so it only works if you can find really good exclusion terms. It also risks inadvertently excluding legitimate publications if the terms have alternative meaning, e.g., excluding healthcare would exclude Michelle's publications in that industry.

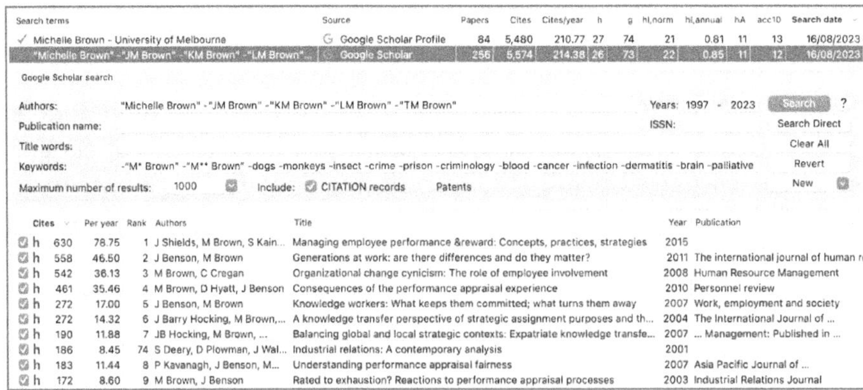

Search terms	Source	Papers	Cites	Cites/year	h	g	hi,norm	hi,annual	hA	acc10	Search date
✓ Michelle Brown – University of Melbourne	G Google Scholar Profile	84	5,480	210.77	27	74	21	0.81	11	13	16/08/2023
"Michelle Brown" -"JM Brown" -"KM Brown" -"LM Brown"...	Google Scholar	256	5,574	214.38	26	73	22	0.85	11	12	16/08/2023

Google Scholar search

Authors:	"Michelle Brown" -"JM Brown" -"KM Brown" -"LM Brown" -"TM Brown"	Years: 1997 - 2023 Search ?
Publication name:		ISSN: Search Direct
Title words:		Clear All
Keywords:	-"M* Brown" -"M** Brown" -dogs -monkeys -insect -crime -prison -criminology -blood -cancer -infection -dermatitis -brain -palliative	Revert
Maximum number of results: 1000 Include: ☑ CITATION records Patents		New

Cites	Per year	Rank	Authors	Title	Year	Publication
☑ h 630	78.75	1	J Shields, M Brown, S Kain...	Managing employee performance &reward: Concepts, practices, strategies	2015	
☑ h 558	46.50	2	J Benson, M Brown	Generations at work: are there differences and do they matter?	2011	The international journal of human r(
☑ h 542	36.13	3	M Brown, C Cregan	Organizational change cynicism: The role of employee involvement	2008	Human Resource Management
☑ h 461	35.46	4	M Brown, D Hyatt, J Benson	Consequences of the performance appraisal experience	2010	Personnel review
☑ h 272	17.00	5	J Benson, M Brown	Knowledge workers: What keeps them committed; what turns them away	2007	Work, employment and society
☑ h 272	14.32	6	J Barry Hocking, M Brown,...	A knowledge transfer perspective of strategic assignment purposes and th...	2004	The International Journal of ...
☑ h 190	11.88	7	JB Hocking, M Brown, ...	Balancing global and local strategic contexts: Expatriate knowledge transfe...	2007	... Management: Published in ...
☑ h 186	8.45	74	S Deery, D Plowman, J Wal...	Industrial relations: A contemporary analysis	2001	
☑ h 183	11.44	8	P Kavanagh, J Benson, M...	Understanding performance appraisal fairness	2007	Asia Pacific Journal of ...
☑ h 172	8.60	9	M Brown, J Benson	Rated to exhaustion? Reactions to performance appraisal processes	2003	Industrial Relations Journal

Hence another strategy would be to start at the other end and work with *inclusions* rather than exclusions. Michelle works in industrial relations and human resource management, with a special interest in performance pay. So, what happens if we simply *include* these three research fields in the keywords field? Remember that in Google Scholar keyword searches are conducted in the full document, so if these words are mentioned anywhere in the article, the record will be selected. You will need to use OR between the terms, otherwise only records with all three terms will be shown.

Hey presto, this provides us with more than 97% of Michelle's actual citations (as verified in her GS profile). The additional publications in her GS Profile are all stray references either without citations or with one or two citations. However, the h-index for the Google Scholar search is 26 instead of the 27 in her Google Scholar Profiles. This is because Michelle published one article with me on a *completely* different topic: response styles in mail surveys. If we include my name in the keywords, Michelle's h-index increases by one and citations are virtually identical with her Google Scholar Profile.

Search terms	Source	Papers	Cites	Cites/year	h	g	hI,norm	hI,annual	hA	acc10	Search date
✓ Michelle Brown - University of Melbourne	Google Scholar Profile	97	5,461	143.71	27	73	21	0.55	11	13	31/07/2023
"Michelle Brown", "industrial relations" OR "human resource management" O...	Google Scholar	78	5,319	204.58	26	72	20	0.77	11	12	31/07/2023

Google Scholar search

Authors: "Michelle Brown" — Years: 1997 - 2023 [Search] ?
Publication name: — ISSN: — Search Direct
Title words: — Clear All
Keywords: "industrial relations" OR "human resource management" OR "performance pay" — Revert
Maximum number of results: 1000 Include: ☑ CITATION records Patents — New

Cites	Per year	Rank	Authors	Title	Year	Publication
h 627	78.38	7	J Shields, M Brown, S Kaine, C Dolle-Samuel..	Managing employee performance &reward: Concepts, practices, str...	2015	
h 556	46.33	5	J Benson, M Brown	Generations at work: are there differences and do they matter?	2011	...journal of human resource management
h 541	36.07	2	M Brown, C Cregan	Organizational change cynicism: The role of employee involvement	2008	Human Resource Management
h 457	35.15	14	M Brown, D Hyatt, J Benson	Consequences of the performance appraisal experience	2010	Personnel review
h 330	18.33	3	M Brown, JS Heywood	Performance appraisal systems: determinants and change	2005	British journal of industrial relations
h 272	14.32	12	J Barry Hocking, M Brown, ...	A knowledge transfer perspective of strategic assignment purposes...	2004	.. Resource Management
h 270	16.88	31	J Benson, M Brown	Knowledge workers: What keeps them committed; what turns them...	2007	Work, employment and society
h 190	11.88	10	JB Hocking, M Brown, ...	Balancing global and local strategic contexts: Expatriate knowledge..	2007	...Resource Management ..
h 186	8.45	19	S Deery, D Plowman, J Walsh, M Brown	Industrial relations: A contemporary analysis	2001	
h 183	11.44	36	P Kavanagh, J Benson, M Brown	Understanding performance appraisal fairness	2007	Asia Pacific Journal of ...
h 172	8.60	4	M Brown, J Benson	Rated to exhaustion? Reactions to performance appraisal processes	2003	Industrial Relations Journal
h 162	14.73	11	M Brown	Responses to work intensification: does generation matter?	2012	... International Journal of Human Resource Manage..
h 149	8.28	23	M Brown, J Benson	Managing to overload? Work overload and performance appraisal pr...	2005	Group &Organization Management
h 138	6.27	30	M Brown	Unequal pay, unequal responses? Pay referents and their implicatio...	2001	Journal of Management Studies
h 100	7.14	1	M Brown, I Metz, C Cregan, . .	Irreconcilable differences? Strategic human resource management...	2009	Asia pacific Journal of ...
h 96	16.00	6	M Brown, CT Kulik, C Cregan, ...	Understanding the change–cynicism cycle: the role of HR	2017	...Resource Management
h 80	6.15	8	J Benson, M Brown	Employee voice: does union membership matter?	2010	Human Resource Management Journal
h 79	3.76	16	M Brown, JS Heywood	Paying for performance: An international comparison	2002	
h 73	5.21	9	CT Kulik, C Cregan, I Metz, .	HR managers as toxin handlers: The buffering effect of formalizing...	2009	... Resource Management
h 57	8.14	39	M Brown, CT Kulik, V Lim	Managerial tactics for communicating negative performance feedba...	2016	Personnel Review
h 45	9.00	13	J Benson, M Brown, M Glennie, ...	The generational "exchange" rate: How generations convert career...	2018	Human Resource ...
h 43	1.95	17	M Brown	Merit pay preferences among public sector employees	2001	Human resource management journal
h 43	3.91	21	I Metz, CT Kulik, M Brown, C Cregan	Changes in psychological contracts during the global financial crisi...	2012	... Resource Management
h 40	2.50	26	M Brown, LA Geddes, ...	The determinants of employee-involvement schemes: Private secto...	2007	Economic and Industrial ...
h 37	2.47	22	K Wilson, M Brown, C Cregan	Job quality and flexible practices: An investigation of employee per...	2008	... of Human Resource Management
h 27	3.38	33	D Scott, M Brown, J Shields, RJ Long, ...	A global study of pay preferences and employee characteristics	2015	... & Benefits Review

Obviously, this strategy only works if an author has worked in a well-defined field, but if this is the case and you cannot refine your search in other ways, it can be a good option.

Remember though that Google Scholar is **not** a bibliometric database like the Web of Science or Scopus. Google Scholar only has fields for authors, title, source, and year. It does not have dedicated fields for research area. Hence, if you do a keyword search with research areas Google Scholar will match those *anywhere* in the document. This means that you might still get inaccurate results, if for instance the research area occurs in one of the references, even though the article itself is in another field. However, this will be rare.

Option 8: Use affiliation

As an alternative to research fields, you can also try using university affiliations to disambiguate the publication record of your focal author from their namesakes in Publish or Perish. This is particularly effective if this author has only worked in a limited number of places.

For instance, another of my former colleagues at the University of Melbourne – Prakash Singh – is also very difficult to search for as both Prakash and Singh are very common names for ethnic Indians. According to the Google Scholar web interface "P Singh" provides more than 300,000 results. Even "Prakash Singh" provides more than 4,000 results, of which Googles Scholar only shows 1,000. My former colleague only has about 90 publications, and not all of them are even shown in the first 1,000 results of these searches.

Fortunately, Prakash had published most of his work as "PJ Singh", but even that search provided more than 600 results and missed a number of his publications as "Prakash Singh". So, the solution was to search for "PJ Singh" OR "Prakash Singh", but restrict the search by university affiliation, as I knew Prakash had only published with two affiliations: "University of Melbourne" and "Monash University". This provided a reasonably good result.

However, it did pull in two publications from namesakes in other disciplines that worked at Monash or Melbourne University (see screenshot below). Excluding these, the search provides about 85% of Prakash's citations and a h-index of 27 instead of 30. Thus, whilst the results give us a rough indication, they appear to be incomplete.

Search terms	Source	Papers	Cites	Cites/year	h	g	hI,norm	hI,annual	hA	acc10	Search date
✓ "PJ Singh" OR "Prakash Singh", "University of Melbourne" OR "Monash University"	Google Scholar	87	4,980	226.36	29	70	18	0.82	13	15	01/08/2023
✓ Prakash Singh - University of Melbourne	Google Scholar Profile	103	5,658	257.18	30	75	21	0.95	13	16	01/08/2023

Google Scholar search

Authors: "PJ Singh" OR "Prakash Singh" — Years: 0 – 0 [Search] ?
Publication name: — ISSN: — Search Direct
Title words: — Clear All
Keywords: "University of Melbourne" OR "Monash University" — Revert
Maximum number of results: 1000 — Include: ☑ CITATION records ☑ Patents — New

Cites	Per year	Rank	Authors	Title	Year	Publication
h 1,214	71.41	46	K Burgess, PJ Singh, R Koroglu	Supply chain management: a structured literature review and implications for future research	2006	International journal of operations & ...
h 375	19.74	20	PJ Singh, AJR Smith	Relationship between TQM and innovation: an empirical study	2004	Journal of Manufacturing Technology ...
h 353	50.43	62	K Dembek, P Singh, V Bhakoo	Literature review of shared value: A theoretical concept or a management buzzword?	2016	Journal of Business Ethics
h 345	38.33	29	S Al-Balushi, AS Sohal, PJ Sing...	Readiness factors for lean implementation in healthcare settings–a literature review	2014	Journal of health ...
h 341	24.36	30	PJ Singh, D Power	The nature and effectiveness of collaboration between firms, their customers and suppliers: a su...	2009	Supply Chain Management: An Internatior
h 221	13.00	28	B Bernstein, PJ Singh	An integrated innovation process model based on practices of Australian biotechnology firms	2006	Technovation
h 209	12.29	48	PJ Singh, M Feng, A Smith	ISO 9000 series of standards: comparison of manufacturing and service organisations	2006	International Journal of Quality & ...
h 166	15.09	18	V Bhakoo, P Singh, A Sohal	Collaborative management of inventory in Australian hospital supply chains: practices and issues	2012	Supply Chain Management: An ...
✓ 146	24.33	35	... P Marks, CL Smith, MS Arms...	A prospective randomized clinical trial in total hip arthroplasty—comparing early results between...	2017	The Journal of ...
h 125	7.35	13	PJ Singh, A Smith	An empirically validated quality management measurement instrument	2006	Benchmarking: An International Journal
h 115	19.17	26	PJ Singh, K Sethuraman, JY Lam	Impact of corporate social responsibility dimensions on firm value: Some evidence from Hong Ko...	2017	Sustainability
h 92	5.11	19	PJ Singh, A Smith, AS Sohal*	Strategic supply chain management issues in the automotive industry: an Australian perspective	2005	International Journal of Production ...
h 92	5.41	64	K Burgess, PJ Singh	A proposed integrated framework for analysing supply chains	2006	Supply Chain Management: An Internatior
h 90	10.00	10	PJ Singh, D Power	Innovative knowledge sharing, supply chain integration and firm performance of Australian manu...	2014	International Journal of Production Resear
✓ 86	28.67	56	SS Ng, F De Labastida Rivera, J...	The NK cell granule protein NKG7 regulates cytotoxic granule exocytosis and inflammation	2020	Nature ...

Reviewing his GS Profile shows that this is because a Google Scholar search misses five of his publications, four of which highly cited (see below), even though they were published with his Melbourne affiliation. All five were published with Elsevier for which Google Scholar doesn't always seem to be able to parse affiliation correctly.

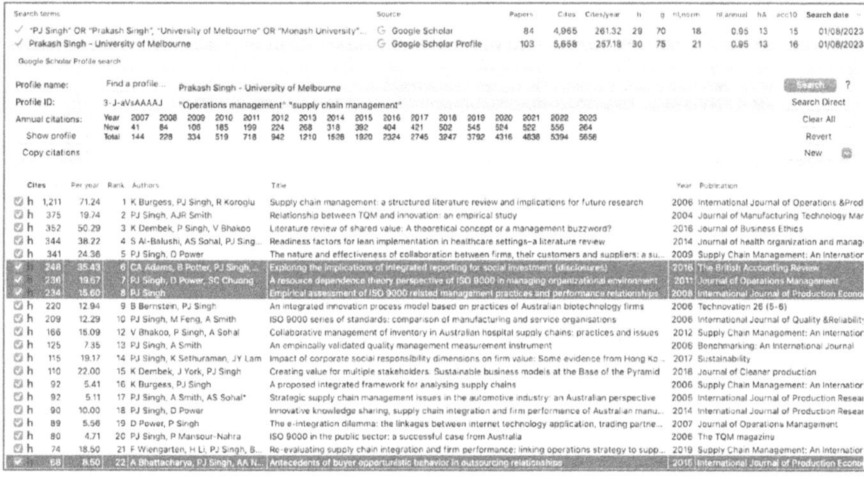

Search terms	Source	Papers	Cites	Cites/year	h	g	hI,norm	hI,annual	hA	acc10	Search date
✓ "PJ Singh" OR "Prakash Singh", "University of Melbourne" OR "Monash University"...	Google Scholar	84	4,965	261.32	29	70	18	0.95	13	15	01/08/2023
✓ Prakash Singh - University of Melbourne	Google Scholar Profile	103	5,658	257.18	30	75	21	0.95	13	16	01/08/2023

Google Scholar Profile search

Profile name: Find a profile... Prakash Singh - University of Melbourne [Search] ?
Profile ID: 3-J-aVsAAAAJ — Search Direct
"Operations management" "supply chain management"

Annual citations:	Year	2007	2008	2009	2010	2011	2012	2013	2014	2015	2016	2017	2018	2019	2020	2021	2022	2023
	New	41	84	106	185	199	224	268	318	392	404	421	502	545	524	522	556	264
	Total	144	228	334	519	718	942	1210	1526	1920	2324	2745	3247	3792	4316	4838	5394	5658

Show profile — Clear All
Copy citations — Revert — New

Cites	Per year	Rank	Authors	Title	Year	Publication
h 1,211	71.24	1	K Burgess, PJ Singh, R Koroglu	Supply chain management: a structured literature review and implications for future research	2006	International Journal of Operations &Prod
h 375	19.74	2	PJ Singh, AJR Smith	Relationship between TQM and innovation: an empirical study	2004	Journal of Manufacturing Technology Mar
h 352	50.29	3	K Dembek, P Singh, V Bhakoo	Literature review of shared value: A theoretical concept or a management buzzword?	2016	Journal of Business Ethics
h 344	38.22	4	S Al-Balushi, AS Sohal, PJ Sing...	Readiness factors for lean implementation in healthcare settings–a literature review	2014	Journal of health organization and manag
h 341	24.36	5	PJ Singh, D Power	The nature and effectiveness of collaboration between firms, their customers and suppliers: a su...	2009	Supply Chain Management: An Internatior
✓ 248	35.43	6	CA Adams, B Potter, PJ Singh,...	Exploring the implications of integrated reporting for social investment (disclosures)	2018	The British Accounting Review
✓ 236	19.67	7	PJ Singh, D Power, SC Chuong	A resource dependence theory perspective of ISO 9000 in managing organizational environment	2011	Journal of Operations Management
✓ 234	15.60	8	PJ Singh	Empirical assessment of ISO 9000 related management practices and performance relationships	2008	International Journal of Production Econo
h 220	12.94	9	B Bernstein, PJ Singh	An integrated innovation process model based on practices of Australian biotechnology firms	2006	Technovation 26 (5-6)
h 209	12.29	10	PJ Singh, M Feng, A Smith	ISO 9000 series of standards: comparison of manufacturing and service organisations	2006	International Journal of Quality &Reliabilit
h 166	15.09	12	V Bhakoo, P Singh, A Sohal	Collaborative management of inventory in Australian hospital supply chains: practices and issues	2012	Supply Chain Management: An Internatior
h 125	7.35	13	PJ Singh, A Smith	An empirically validated quality management measurement instrument	2006	Benchmarking: An International Journal
h 115	19.17	14	PJ Singh, K Sethuraman, JY Lam	Impact of corporate social responsibility dimensions on firm value: Some evidence from Hong Ko...	2017	Sustainability
h 110	22.00	15	K Dembek, J York, PJ Singh	Creating value for multiple stakeholders: Sustainable business models at the Base of the Pyramid	2018	Journal of Cleaner production
h 92	5.41	16	K Burgess, PJ Singh	A proposed integrated framework for analysing supply chains	2006	Supply Chain Management: An Internatior
h 92	5.11	17	PJ Singh, A Smith, AS Sohal*	Strategic supply chain management issues in the automotive industry: an Australian perspective	2005	International Journal of Production Resear
h 90	10.00	18	PJ Singh, D Power	Innovative knowledge sharing, supply chain integration and firm performance of Australian manu...	2014	International Journal of Production Resear
h 89	5.56	19	D Power, P Singh	The e-integration dilemma: the linkages between internet technology application, trading partne...	2007	Journal of Operations Management
h 80	4.71	20	PJ Singh, P Mansour-Nahra	ISO 9000 in the public sector: a successful case from Australia	2006	The TQM magazine
h 74	18.50	21	F Wiengarten, H Li, PJ Singh, B...	Re-evaluating supply chain integration and firm performance: linking operations strategy to supp...	2019	Supply Chain Management: An Internatior
✓ 68	8.50	22	A Bhattacharya, PJ Singh, AA N...	Antecedents of buyer opportunistic behavior in outsourcing relationships	2015	International Journal of Production Econo

Remember that Google Scholar is **not** a bibliometric database like the Web of Science or Scopus. Google Scholar only has fields for authors, title, source, and year. It does not have a dedicated field for affiliation. As we have seen above this means that affiliation searches might not always give a perfect result. Moreover, just like other data sources, Google Scholar will also match any records where a co-author is working at the relevant university. Hence, I would only recommend affiliation searches as a quick-and-dirty option.

Option 9: Use multiple names

So far, we have explained how to *restrict* the number of results. However, there may also be a need to *expand* the number of results if an author has published under multiple names. You can use the logical **OR** operator in the author field in Publish or Perish to search for an author who has published under different names. This will allow you to get a complete record for this author.

The most frequent reason for this is women publishing under their maiden and married name or under different married names. For instance, Rebecca Piekkari started out publishing as under her maiden name Rebecca Marschan in 1996, adopted Rebecca Marschan-Piekkari in 1998, before finally settling on Rebecca Piekkari in 2005. Below you can see how a combination of three names ensures a complete publication record under these circumstances. This search provides a nearly identical result to her Google Scholar profile.

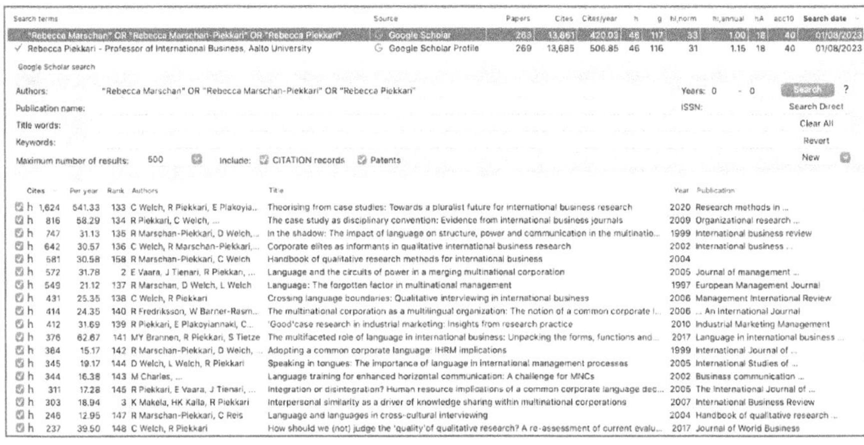

Analyse co-author pairs

You can also use this feature for another purpose, namely, to analyse co-author pairs. To search for articles co-written by specific authors, enter all their names in the Authors field. For instance: "A Harzing" "M Pudelko" will return only articles that have *both* authors in their author list.

As you can see below, excluding minor conference papers and book chapters, Markus and I have published 14 papers together between 2007 and 2016. Using multiple authors searches is a good option to investigate co-authorship patterns.

Google Scholar search

Authors: "A Harzing" "M Pudelko" Years: 0 – 0 Search ?
Publication name: ISSN: Search Direct
Title words: Clear All
Keywords: Revert
Maximum number of results: 500 Include: CITATION records Patents New

Cites	Per year	Rank	Authors	Title	Year
h 515	32.19	4	M Pudelko, AW Harzing	Country-of-origin, localization, or dominance effect? An empirical investigation of HRM practices in fore...	2007
h 387	43.00	5	H Tenzer, M Pudelko, AW Harzi...	The impact of language barriers on trust formation in multinational teams	2014
h 268	26.80	1	AW Harzing, M Pudelko	Language competencies, policies and practices in multinational corporations: A comprehensive review...	2013
h 235	33.57	6	AW Harzing, M Pudelko...	The bridging role of expatriates and inpatriates in knowledge transfer in multinational corporations	2016
h 187	23.38	7	BS Reiche, AW Harzing, M Pud...	Why and how does shared language affect subsidiary knowledge inflows? A social identity perspective	2015
h 180	18.00	2	..., BS Reiche, M Pudelko	Challenges in international survey research: A review with illustrations and suggested solutions for best...	2013
h 173	24.71	8	AW Harzing, M Pudelko	Do we need to distance ourselves from the distance concept? Why home and host country context mig...	2016
h 117	7.80	9	M Pudelko, AW Harzing	The golden triangle for MNCs: Standardization towards headquarters practices, standardization toward...	2008
h 101	11.22	3	AW Harzing, M Pudelko	Hablas vielleicht un peu la mia language? A comprehensive overview of the role of language differences...	2014
h 46	5.75	10	M Pudelko, H Tenzer, AW Harzi...	Cross-cultural management and language studies within international business research: past and pres...	2015
h 35	2.19	11	M Pudelko, AW Harzing	HRM practices in subsidiaries of US, Japanese and German MNCs: Country-of-origin, localization or do...	2007
h 30	1.88	12	M Pudelko, AW Harzing	How European is management in Europe? An analysis of past, present and future management practice...	2007
h 23	1.77	13	M Pudelko, AW Harzing	Japanese human resource management	2010
4	0.25	19	M Pudelko, AW Harzing	How European Is Management in Europe?	2007

Option 10: Use all tactics

For many authors using just *one* of the above options will already provide you with a good result. However, if you are searching for John Smith or Yang Zhang and the authors do not have a Google Scholar Profile, you are likely to need to resort on *all* of these tactics combined. You could for instance combine the multiple initials or given name strategy with the exclusion of stray citations, restriction of the year range, and restriction by research fields.

Even then, it might be really hard to get an accurate result, especially for Asian academics who often only have one given name. In addition, Google Scholar only allows up to 256 characters for all fields combined. With complicated author searches you may rapidly run up against these limitations.

So, in those cases, I suggest you try one of the other data sources which we will discuss in the last section of this chapter. They might not provide you with as many citations per publication as Google Scholar does, but they generally make it easier to at least get a comprehensive record of an author's journal publications.

Address data quality issues

After gathering the correct set of results for your focal author there are several things you can do to improve data quality. First, verify whether the range of years published makes sense. Second consider merging duplicate publications. Third, pay special attention to merging publications around the h-index cut-off.

Check the year makes sense

If you haven't manually included a specific year range, carefully check the years that are reported in Publish or Perish to see whether they make sense. Clearly, if the value is >100 for an author, something is wrong. However, even finding values of >40 for authors should lead you to be suspicious, unless the academic is close to retirement.

Sorting by year is a good way to spot Google Scholar parsing errors. Below is a screenshot of a search for another one of my former University of Melbourne colleagues – David Merrett, a business historian – in which it is clear that Google Scholar parsed the year wrongly.

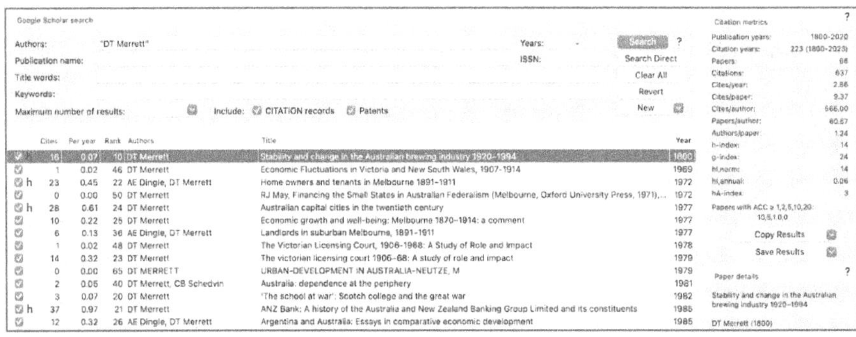

Cites	Per year	Rank	Authors	Title	Year
16	0.07	10	DT Merrett	Stability and change in the Australian brewing industry 1920-1994	1800
1	0.02	46	DT Merrett	Economic Fluctuations in Victoria and New South Wales, 1907-1914	1969
h 23	0.45	22	AE Dingle, DT Merrett	Home owners and tenants in Melbourne 1891-1911	1972
0	0.00	50	DT Merrett	RJ May, Financing the Small States in Australian Federalism (Melbourne, Oxford University Press, 1971),...	1972
h 28	0.61	24	DT Merrett	Australian capital cities in the twentieth century	1977
10	0.22	25	DT Merrett	Economic growth and well-being: Melbourne 1870-1914: a comment	1977
6	0.13	36	AE Dingle, DT Merrett	Landlords in suburban Melbourne, 1891-1911	1977
1	0.02	48	DT Merrett	The Victorian Licensing Court, 1906-1968: A Study of Role and Impact	1978
14	0.32	23	DT Merrett	The victorian licensing court 1906-68: A study of role and impact	1979
0	0.00	65	DT MERRETT	URBAN-DEVELOPMENT IN AUSTRALIA-NEUTZE, M	1979
2	0.05	40	DT Merrett, CB Schedvin	Australia: dependence at the periphery	1981
3	0.07	20	DT Merrett	'The school at war': Scotch college and the great war	1982
h 37	0.97	21	DT Merrett	ANZ Bank: A history of the Australia and New Zealand Banking Group Limited and its constituents	1986
12	0.32	26	AE Dingle, DT Merrett	Argentina and Australia: Essays in comparative economic development	1985

Although David does have a long publication history – his thesis was published in 1969 – he clearly did not publish an article about the Australian brewing industry between 1920 and 1994 in the year 1800! Google Scholar inaccurately parsed part of the title of the book in which this chapter appeared (*The Dynamics of the International Brewing Industry since 1800*) as the book chapter's publication year.

Sorting by year also allows you to review whether metrics based on "academic age" (i.e., the number of years since your first publication) are a reasonable reflection of the academic's career. If, for instance, you find that someone has published an article without citations or with very few citations in a fairly obscure journal (maybe in another language) or published a master's thesis many years before a steady stream of articles emerged (as is the case for David Merrett), it might be justifiable to simply exclude this publication from the analysis.

Merge duplicate publications

In spite of all your efforts to reduce the number of results to a clean list of publications, your Google Scholar results might still report multiple occurrences of the same publication, called "stray citations". Stray citations are more frequent for publications that are of a "non-standard" format, such as books, book chapters, conference papers, and software as – unlike journal articles – there is no universally agreed way to reference them. The Publish or Perish software itself for instance is referenced in nearly 100 different ways. Below are some examples.

Publish or perish
Publish or perish (4.6)
Publish or Perish (Version 2.8), software program
Publish or perish (Version 3.6)[Computer software]
Publish or perish (Version 3.6)[Software]
Publish or Perish (Version 4.17. 0)
Publish or Perish (Version: 4.25. 1)[Software]
Publish or Perish 2.0
Publish or Perish 3.1
Publish or Perish 4 user's manual. 2007
Publish or Perish [computer program]
Publish or perish [computer software]
Publish or Perish [computer software](8.1. 3625)
Publish or Perish [Computer software](Version 6)

Publish or Perish Website.(2016)
Publish or Perish, Available
Publish or Perish, revisado 27 de noviembre 2011
Publish or Perish, version 2.5. 3171
Publish or Perish, version 2.8
Publish or Perish, version 2.8. 3644
Publish or Perish, version 3
Publish or Perish, version 3.0. 1813; 2010
Publish or perish, version 3.0. 3869
Publish or perish, version 3.0. 3883 (18 August 2010)
Publish or perish, version 3.0. 4084
Publish or Perish, version 3.1. 4004
Publish or Perish, version 3.2. 4150
Publish or Perish, version 4.4. 8

How to merge "stray citation" records?

So, what to do if one of your Publish or Perish searches shows up a lot of stray citation records? If these stray citation records have no citations and if you are only interested in total citation counts or the h-index, I suggest you simply ignore them as they will not impact on these metrics.

If you are interested in an accurate count of *publications*, I suggest you simply deselect them, either one-by-one or by selecting all of them and right-clicking to access the context menu, which will allow you to "uncheck" them all on one go.

532	40.92	16	AW Harzing	The publish or perish book	2010
53	4.42	79	AW Harzing	The publish or perish book	2011
18	1.50	160	AW Harzing	The Publish or Perish Book, Part 2: Citation analysis for a...	2011
2	0.15	343	AW Harzing	The publish or perish book. Melbourne, Australia: Tarma...	2010
3	0.23	301	AW Harzing	The publish or perish book. Tarma Software Research	2010
10	0.77	210	AW Harzing	The publish or perish book: Tarma software research Mel...	2010
2	0.15	384	AWK Harzing	The publish or perish book: Tarma software research Mel...	2010
2	0.15	352	AW Harzing	The publish or perish book: Tarma Software Research Pt...	2010
3	0.23	279	AW Harzing	The publish or perish book: Tarma Software Research Pt...	2010
3	0.23	288	AW Harzing	The Publish or Perish book: Your guide to effective and r...	2010
2	0.20	372	AW Harzing	The publish or perish book: Your guide to effective and r...	2013
2	0.50	336	AW Harzing	The Publish or Perish Book: Your guide to Effective and R...	2019
2	0.17	391	AW Harzing	The publish or perish book: Your guide to effective and r...	2011

If, however, one or more of these stray citation records have a non-negligible number of citations [as in the screenshot above], you can merge them into their master record. Duplicates can be merged into the master record by dragging the stray citation(s) onto the master record. The merged record will have a symbol with stacked documents in front of it. Note that I used a different example here as for the PoP book the stacked documents' symbol was partially obscured by the h-index symbol.

	52	2.17	162	AWK Harzing	MNC Staffing policies for the CEO-position in foreign sub...

Create a Google Scholar Citation Profile for persistent merging

Please note that merging records in Publish or Perish is NOT persistent. As soon as you conduct a new search, Publish or Perish will need to "refresh" the data coming from Google Scholar. If the records are still separate in the underlying data sources, they will appear as separate records again in Publish or Perish. I would therefore not spend too much time on merging records, unless you are doing this for an important occasion, such as a performance appraisal, tenure, or promotion application.

If you would like your stray records to be persistently merged, set up a Google Scholar Citation Profile and merge the relevant records there. Publish or Perish allows you to conduct Google Scholar Profile searches. Thus, any work you put into cleaning up your Google Scholar Profile is well worth the effort. We will show how to search for Google Scholar Profiles later in this chapter.

Selective merging around the h-index cut-off

Selective merging in Publish or Perish saves time if you are only interested in the h-index. This involves checking whether you have any publications that are close to becoming part of the h-index and verify whether any stray references can be found for those. These references can then be merged into their master record.

Selective merging might increase your h-index

I recommend checking publications within five citations of reaching the required number of citations to be included in the h-index. Let's work through an example of how this works. I need to use an old example here. At 71, my current h-index is too high for stray citations to be likely to increase it further. The screenshot below shows publications in my raw citation record – back in 2009 – that might qualify for inclusion in the h-index. The Expatriate Failure article with Christensen is the last paper to be included in my then h-index of 23.

✓	25	5.00	AW Harzing, N Noorder...	Knowledge flows in MNCs: an empirical test and extension of Gupta and C
✓	24	3.43	AW Harzing, C Christen...	Expatriate failure: time to abandon the concept?
✓	21	4.20	AW Harzing	Response styles in cross-national survey research: A 26-country study
✓	21	4.20	AW Harzing	Response styles in cross-national survey research
✓	21	2.33	AW Harzing, M Maznevski	The interaction between language and culture: A test of the cultural acco
✓	20	5.00	AW Harzing	Publish or perish
✓	18	2.57	AW Harzing	Journal quality list

The next paper [*Response styles in cross-national survey research*] has 21 citations, but there is a duplicate paper with an equal number of citations. The duplicate paper does not include the subtitle, but a quick verification of the citing articles shows that they are indeed different from those citing the paper with the subtitle. Hence this would be a prime candidate for merging, which increases the h-index to 24.

Merging duplicates can also decrease the h-index

However, in this process I also noticed that one my most-cited publications – the book *Managing the Multinationals* – actually appeared twice. It appeared once with a subtitle and 160 citations and once without a subtitle and 37 citations, thus contributing to the h-index twice. Obviously, these two titles need to be merged, bringing us back to an h-index of 23.

Although this whole process sounds fairly involved, with a little practice it can usually be done in a couple of minutes, whereas a full merge of stray citations can easily take 15-20 minutes. Hence selective merging might be a good compromise. This process has also taught us two important generic lessons for selective merging:

- Publications with subtitles can often appear twice, once with and once without the subtitle, so it is worthwhile to check them.
- Your most highly cited publications might appear in the h-index twice if the number of stray citations is large enough to enter as a separate publication.

Author searches in other data sources

Below I provide brief suggestions for author searches in each of the remaining data sources. The search syntax below refers to what works best when you search the data source *through* PoP. This is not always identical to the most effective search syntax in the data sources' web interfaces as these might be structured differently.

Every data source has its own unique syntax that – oftentimes – is not fully documented. Below you will find the most important tips and known problems, but to get the best out of the different data sources you need to be prepared to experiment with different search strategies. If you find that some things are not working as you expected, please share your findings by contacting me at anne@harzing.com, so that, collectively, we can improve these instructions.

Crossref

Reliably identifying authors is very difficult in Crossref, so it is best to only try this for authors that you are very familiar with.

Preferred search syntax

1. Last name only [only if the last name is fully unique, which is rare].

2. Full given name + Family name. Sort by rank and then move to last consecutive *accurate* result. From there onwards, accurate results will be infrequent, typically occurring in batches. The screenshot below provides an example for one of my co-authors: Helene Tenzer.

3. **Do not**: search for Initial + Family Name as CR implements an OR search, i.e., *J Bloggs* will result in all academics with initial J + all academics with last name Bloggs.

4. **Do not**: use AND or OR searches. They are not supported and will not provide the results you expect.

Most common problems

1. Might report too many homonyms (namesakes). A search can still work if you can identify a comprehensive, but distinctive enough, set of words in articles titles (in **Title words**) or in title and abstract (in **Keywords**) to be included or excluded. You can also use a combination of inclusions and exclusions.

2a. Might still miss some publications, esp. in fields where publishing with initials only is common.

2b. Relevant publications without citations will often be ranked low, so are likely to be missed with the above strategy.

2c. Works best for academics with mostly first-authored publications and authors with few co-authors (leading to high "rank" score).

Google Scholar Profiles

Reliably identifying authors in Google Scholar Profiles is typically quite easy and – if an author has a (clean) Google Scholar Profile is by far the best option of all data sources. To search for an academic's Google Scholar profile just enter any part of their first or last name and/or their affiliation. Note that a Google Scholar Profile search is very "forgiving", unlike structured databases which have a restrictive syntax.

For instance, if you can't recall someone's last name, a search with their first name and university might provide a good result. The screenshot below shows a search for anyone with the first name Paul at Middlesex University. However, note that Google Scholar does not place any limitations on what you include and do *not* include in your profile name. Hence, some profiles might not have given names or universities included.

Select Google Scholar Profile

Profile search terms: Paul Middlesex University   Search

Profile labels: ?

Check the boxes next to the desired profiles in the list below, then click Select to open the profiles in Publish or Perish.

Cites	Profile name	Affiliation
6,721	Paul Gibbs	Middlesex and East European University
5,088	Paul Gooderham	Middlesex University & Norges Handelshøyskole
4,460	Paul Cobley	Middlesex University
773	Paul de Mornay Davies	Psychology Department, Middlesex University
608	Paul Jarvis	Associate Lecturer, Middlesex University
496	Prof. Paul Kleiman	Ciel Associates, Middlesex University & Rose Bruford College of Theatre &Performa
2	Paul Oatt	Middlesex University
1	Paul Taylor-Pitt	Middlesex University

After you have found the Paul you were looking for (in my case Paul Gooderham who works in the Business School), tick the box in front of their name and click on search. This will call up the academic's full citation profile in the Publish or Perish software (see screenshot for the first dozen results).

This will provide you with a full list of publications that can then be filtered and sorted in any way. It will also provide all relevant citation metrics. Moreover, using the "Copy citations" button will copy the yearly citations to the clipboard for pasting into e.g., Excel for further analysis or creation of a longitudinal citation graph.

OpenAlex

The OpenAlex's API does not support regular authors searches in Publish or Perish. It is possible, however, to search for authors if you know either the OpenAlex author ID or an author's ORCID. You can find OpenAlex author IDs on their website. ORCID, which stands for **O**pen **R**esearcher and **C**ontributor **ID** is a unique, persistent identifier, which is free of charge to researchers and can be found on the ORCID website.

After a major update in Author profiles in August 2023, OpenAlex author IDs appear to be complete and reliable. However, the OpenAlex website is still in alpha version and is carries the warning *"buggy, incomplete and changing daily"*.

Preferred search syntax

1. Look up an author's ORCID ID on the ORCID website and enter it in the Author ID or ORCID field.

2. Look up an author's OpenAlex ID on the OpenAlex website and enter it in the Author ID or ORCID field.

Below is a screenshot of an OpenAlex ORCID search for my own OR-CID profile. As you can see OpenAlex presents a very clean and complete set of results, even including the Publish or Perish software. Hence it is a very good alternative to Google Scholar in terms of data quality.

Its coverage also compares very well with the other data sources. OpenAlex doesn't find as many papers and citations as Google Scholar does. Disregarding stray cites, OpenAlex finds 80-85% of the publications that Google Scholar finds, but reports only about half as many citations as Google Scholar.

The main publications that *are* included in Google Scholar, but are missing from OpenAlex are conference papers, book chapters and white papers on my website. However, OpenAlex finds more papers than Scopus (+30%), Crossref (+10%) and the Web of Science (+55%). Its citation levels are respectively 20% (Scopus), 30% (Crossref) and 70% higher (Web of Science).

Most common problems

1. This search strategy only works if the author you are searching for has created an ORCID profile and has kept it up to date.

2. This search strategy relies on the accuracy of OA author profiles. This seems good after a recent update, but needs further verification.

PubMed

PubMed is a longstanding and well-respected free data source in the biomedical disciplines. As such it is a good option for author searches in this field. Its main problem is that it cannot be used to conduct a comprehensive author search for many authors. This is because this would require *all* the author's publications to be covered by PubMed. For instance, Mariachiara Di Cesare (see below) is working in Public Health. A search for her name results in 90 publications in Google Scholar, but only 25 in PubMed. Note that PubMed doesn't report citations, hence we have sorted the search by year.

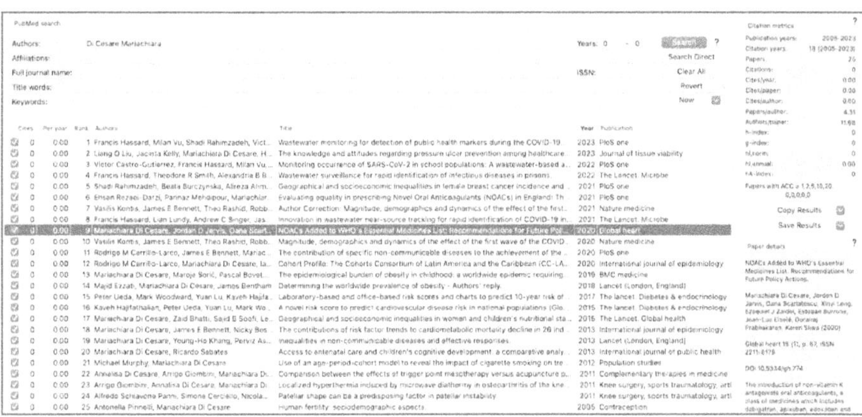

Part of this difference is caused by the fact that GS covers a wider set of document types (including books, book chapters, and conference papers). However, Mariachiara has also published in journals that that are not covered in PubMed such as Nature Food. Hence, I cannot recommend PubMed if your purpose is to get a complete record of an academic's publications.

Preferred search syntax

1. Family name + one or more initials or given name [**please note:** PubMed requires family name first].

2. Two (or more) author names separated by AND will report only papers, co-authored by these academics.

3. Two author names separated by OR will report papers authored by either author (or name variants of one author).

Most common problems

1. Might report too many homonyms. A search can still work if you can identify a comprehensive, but distinctive enough, set of words in articles titles (in **Title words**) or in title and abstract (in **Keywords**) to be included or excluded. You can also use a combination of inclusions and exclusions.

Scopus

Reliably identifying authors is difficult when using the free Scopus API that Publish or Perish needs to rely on. This is because it implements an AND search within the *entire* author record, not within a *single* author name. For instance, a search for C Kulik – a researcher in HRM and Diversity & Inclusion – will also match JA Marrero, LM Kulik, CB Sirlin, … (as in the first result in the screenshot below). Moreover, as the free Scopus version only lists the first author, it can be hard to establish whether the results refer to your focal author if they are not the first author.

Note: The Scopus API is limited to 200 results. Hence if your focal author has more than 200 publications only the most cited publications will be shown. Typically, this means you will miss the author's recent publications. If you need a full record of an author's publications, I recommend you split up your search and then aggregate the individual searches. For details on how to do this see Chapter 2.

Alternatively, if you do have access to the Scopus web interface, you can conduct your search there and import it into Publish or Perish (see Chapter 2 on Importing Scopus data). This will also ensure you have complete author records, listing all authors for each paper.

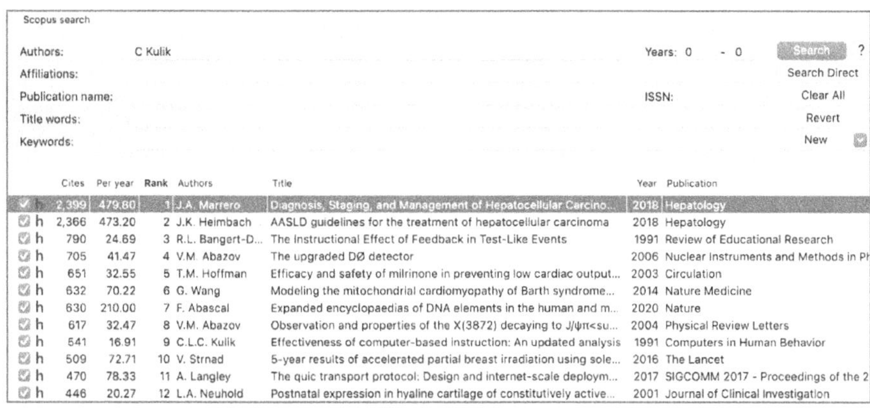

Preferred search syntax

1. Scopus ID. This ID can be found on the Scopus website, e.g.: https://www.scopus.com/authid/detail.uri?authorId=6602836555. An example for my own record is provided in the screenshot below.

2. Single initial + Family name. Because of the limitations identified above, this *only* works for academics with a fully unique last name, who have not published with co-authors with the same initial.

3. Two (or more) author names separated by AND reports papers co-authored by these academics reliably (as far as I have been able to establish).

4. **Do not:** search for Full given name + Family name as this will only give a sub-set of an academic's publications. Searching for my name as Anne-Wil Harzing provides only 7 (out of 103) results, searching for Anne Harzing provides 30.

5. **Do not:** search for Full given name + Multiple initials as this will normally not give any results.

Most common problems

1. Will only provide complete and accurate results if your Scopus profile is complete and accurate. This is less likely for common names. However, you can submit change requests to Scopus.

2a. Might report too many homonyms, but can be narrowed down by year and by including non-relevant article title words in the **Title words** or **Keywords** field preceded by NOT (or -), separated by OR; e.g. medical terms for a Social Sciences scholar. If you are uncertain whether an article belongs to the author you are searching for, right-click and select **Open article in browser** to get more detail.

[**Note:** The use of NOT (or -) as the first word provides inconsistent results, so is not advised. So, it is best to combine a first *inclusion* term with subsequent *exclusion* terms]

2b. Can be narrowed down by excluding namesakes in the author field (see second example below).

2c. Can also be narrowed down by including *relevant* title words in **Title words** or **Keywords** fields separate title words by OR to change this field into "any of the words".

2d. Can also be narrowed down by university affiliation(s) if known and the author you are searching for has not worked at too many different institutions (see first example below).

Below is an example for Carol Kulik, a researcher in HRM and Diversity & Inclusion. We were unable to search for her with her name C Kulik. Carol worked at the University of Melbourne between 2002 and 2007. So, I narrowed down the search by adding this university.

This worked very well in terms of narrowing down the results, even *beyond* Carol's tenure at the University of Melbourne as she had continued to co-author with her former colleagues Cregan, Brown, and Metz. However, there were several results that were incorrect. They all combined an author with the same last name (Kulik) and an author (not necessarily Kulik) working at the University of Melbourne.

Scopus search

Authors: C Kulik   Years: 0 - 0   Search ?

Affiliations: "University of Melbourne"   Search Direct

Publication name: ISSN: Clear All

Title words: Revert

Keywords: New

	Cites	Per year	Rank	Authors	Title	Year	Publication
	0	0.00	41	C. Cregan	When time is running out: A growth curve analysis of older work...	2023	Journal of Organizational Behavior
	4	4.00	36	Y. Kowsar	Shape-Sphere: A metric space for analysing time series by their...	2022	Information Sciences
	2	2.00	38	Y. Kowsar	An Online Unsupervised Dynamic Window Method to Track Repe...	2022	IEEE Transactions on Cybernetics
	1	1.00	39	M. Brown	Managing voluntary collective turnover: the impact of a cynical...	2022	Personnel Review
	0	0.00	42	C. Cregan	Sweated Labour among Clothing Outworkers at the Start of the...	2022	Labour History
	18	9.00	24	C. Cregan	The influence of calculative ("hard") and collaborative ("soft") H...	2021	Human Resource Management Journal
	5	2.50	31	C. Cregan	Benefit of the doubt: the buffering influence of normative contra...	2021	International Journal of Human Resource
h	38	12.67	8	J. Qi	Effectively learning spatial indices	2020	Proceedings of the VLDB Endowment
h	28	7.00	13	Y. Li	Inclusion climate: A multilevel investigation of its antecedents an...	2019	Human Resource Management
	5	1.25	32	T. Hashem	Protecting privacy for distance and rank based group nearest ne...	2019	World Wide Web
	4	1.00	37	Y. Kowsar	Demo: LiftSmart: A monitoring and warning wearable for weight...	2019	UbiComp/ISWC 2019- - Adjunct Proceedi
h	23	3.83	19	M. Brown	Understanding the Change–Cynicism Cycle: The Role of HR	2017	Human Resource Management
	11	1.83	27	I. Metz	The manager as employer agent: The role of manager personalit...	2017	Personnel Review
	7	1.17	29	C. Cregan	Differences in Well-being among People with Disabilities in Paid...	2017	Social Policy and Administration

You can, however, *exclude* certain author names too. The "offending publications" were all authored by Lars Kulik. So, excluding this name in the author field resulted in removal of these publications and a clean record for our focal author (see below). As Scopus only shows this first author, this will require looking up the inaccurate matches (use right-click/Open in browser). Hence, this is a time-consuming process, which is only feasible for important author searches.

Once you have established the feasibility of an affiliation search for your focal author, you can then add additional university names. Note, however, that this will only work if your focal author's name is relatively unique. Otherwise, it will pull in lots of authors with the same last name (or initial) working at the same university.

Semantic Scholar

Semantic Scholar's API does not support authors searches in Publish or Perish.

Web of Science

Note: The WoS API is limited to only 200 results. Therefore, if your focal author has more than 200 publications only their most cited publications will be shown. Typically, this means you will miss the author's recent publications. If you need a full record of an author's publications, I recommend you split up your search and aggregate the individual searches. For details on how to do this see Chapter 2. Alternatively, if you have access to the WoS web interface, you can conduct your search there and import it into Publish or Perish (see Chapter 2 on Importing WoS data).

Although limited to registered users, the Web of Science is a good option for reliable author searches.

Preferred search syntax

1. Family name + Single Initial [**please note:** WoS requires family name first!]. The screenshot below provides an example of this search.

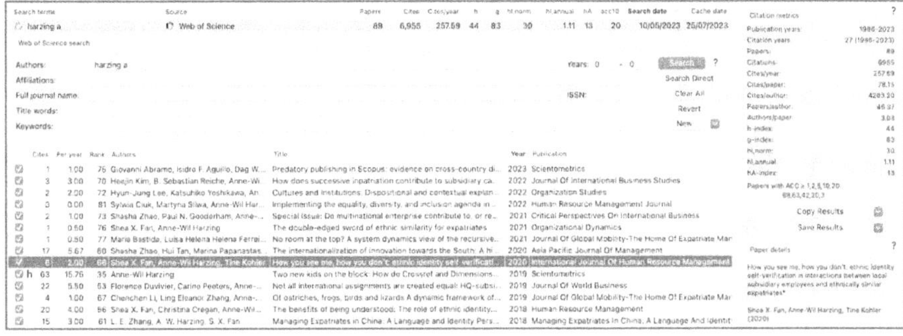

2. Family name + Full given name. This works reliably for publications after 2007 only, but may work for pre-2007 too.

3. Two (or more) author names separated by AND will report papers that are co-authored by these academics.

4. Two author names separated by OR will report paper authored by either author (or name variants of one author).

Most common problems

1. Might report too many homonyms, but can be narrowed down by year and/or including words in article title in **Title words**, separated by OR. [*Can use wildcards, e.g., global* for global, globally, globalize, globalise, globalization, globalisation, globalizing, globalising*]

2. Might still miss some publications even after 2007, esp. in fields where publishing with initials only is common.

In sum

In this chapter, I explained in detail how to conduct effective author searches. Most academics predominantly use Google Scholar for their searches and disambiguation of authors in Google Scholar can be challenging. In this chapter, I therefore provided a large range of options to ensure your Google Scholar author searches result in a clean set of results.

In the last section of this chapter, I also discussed author searches the other data sources (Crossref, Google Scholar Profiles, OpenAlex, PubMed, Semantic Scholar, Scopus, and the Web of Science), reviewing their strengths and weaknesses. In the next chapter, we will turn to journal searches.

Chapter 8: Journal searches

This chapter explains how to conduct effective journal searches in Publish or Perish. Most PoP users mainly use Google Scholar for their searches and journal disambiguation in Google Scholar is not always straightforward. Hence, the instructions in this chapter will focus mainly on this data source. However, the last section of this chapter will also discuss journal searches in the other data sources.

Journal search: The basics

Publish or Perish allows you to perform an analysis of a journal's publications and their impact. Just type the journal's name in the **Publication name** field. Use quotes around the name to ensure that the terms stay together (see screenshot below).

Search terms	Source	Papers	Cites	Cites/year	h	g	hi,norm	hi,annual	hA	acc10	Search date
✓ "Management International Review" from 2017 to 2017	Scopus	33	754	125.67	17	27	17	2.83	6	1	03/08/2023
✓ "Management International Review" from 2017 to 2017	Google Scholar	36	1,350	225.00	21	36	14	2.33	9	8	03/08/2023

Google Scholar search

Authors:

Publication name: "Management International Review"

Title words:

Keywords:

Maximum number of results: 1000   Include: CITATION records   Patents

Years: 2017 - 2017   Search   ?

ISSN: Search Direct   Clear All   Revert   New

	Cites	Per year	Rank	Authors	Title	Year	Publication	Publisher	Type
h	224	37.33	1	H Tenzer, S Terjesen, AW Har…	Language in international business: A review and ag…	2017	Management international review	Springer	HTML
h	92	15.33	2	QTK Nguyen	Multinationality and performance literature: A critical…	2017	Management International Review	Springer	
h	63	10.50	3	H Zhao, J Ma, J Yang	30 years of research on entry mode and performanc…	2017	Management International Review	Springer	
h	101	16.83	4	A Mohr, G Batsakis	Internationalization speed and firm performance: A s…	2017	Management International Review	Springer	
h	95	15.83	5	V Shirodkar, P Konara	Institutional distance and foreign subsidiary perform…	2017	Management International Review	Springer	HTML
h	70	11.67	6	RJ Bryan Jean, RR Sinkovics,…	Antecedents and outcomes of supplier innovativenes…	2017	Management International Review	Springer	
h	63	10.50	7	F Garcia-Lillo, E Claver-Corté…	Mapping the intellectual structure of research on 'bo…	2017	… International Review	Springer	
h	60	10.00	8	J Fortwengel	Understanding when MNCs can overcome institution…	2017	Management International Review	Springer	
h	55	9.17	9	A Jiménez, M Russo, JM Kraa…	Corruption and private participation projects in Centr…	2017	Management International …	Springer	
h	51	8.50	10	HL Chen, CY Chang, WT Hsu	Does board co-working experience influence directo…	2017	Management International …	Springer	
h	42	7.00	11	J Kang, JY Lee, PN Ghauri	The interplay of Mahalanobis distance and firm capa…	2017	Management International Review	Springer	
h	36	6.00	12	H Wechtler, A Koveshnikov, C…	Career anchors and cross-cultural adjustment amon…	2017	Management International Review	Springer	
h	37	6.17	13	R Berger, R Herstein, A Silbig…	Developing international business relationships in a…	2017	Management International …	Springer	
h	31	5.17	14	S Song, JY Lee	Relationship with headquarters and divestments of f…	2017	Management International Review	Springer	
h	32	5.33	15	M Musteen, M Ahsan, T Park	SMEs, Intellectual Capital, and Offshoring of Service…	2017	Management International Review	Springer	
h	30	5.00	16	N Pogrebnyakov	A cost-based explanation of gradual, regional intern…	2017	Management International Review	Springer	
h	27	4.50	17	B Decreton, H Dellestrand, P .	Beyond simple configurations: the dual involvement…	2017	Management International …	Springer	HTML
h	28	4.67	18	PJ Buckley, X Tian	Transnationality and financial performance in the era…	2017	Management International Review	Springer	
h	26	4.33	19	C Holmström Lind, OH Kang	The value-adding role of the corporate headquarters…	2017	Management International Review	Springer	HTML
	20	3.33	20	P Thakur-Wernz, O Bruyaka	Co-evolutionary perspective on sourcing portfolios:…	2017	Management International Review	Springer	
h	22	3.67	21	N Djodat, D zu Knyphausen-A…	Revisiting Ghoshal and Bartlett's theory of the multin…	2017	Management International Review	Springer	
h	21	3.50	22	M Dittfeld	Multinationality and performance: A context-specific…	2017	Management International Review	Springer	
	21	3.50	23	B Swoboda, C Huber, T Schus…	Corporate reputation effects across nations: the imp…	2017	Management International …	Springer	
	14	2.33	24	S Song	Ownership increase in international joint ventures: T…	2017	Management International Review	Springer	
	15	2.50	25	N Yasuda, H Mitsuhashi	Learning from political change and the development…	2017	Management International Review	Springer	
	15	2.50	26	Z Deng, RJB Jean, RR Sinkovi…	Polarizing effects of early exporting on exit	2017	Management International Review	Springer	
	15	2.50	27	PX Meschi, A Norheim-Hanse…	Match-making in international joint ventures in emer…	2017	Management International …	Springer	
	13	2.17	28	S Arvanitis, T Bolli, T Stucki	In or out. how insourcing foreign input production aff…	2017	Management International Review	Springer	
	7	1.17	29	BE James, PM Vaaler	Experience, equity and foreign investment risk: a PIC…	2017	Management International Review	Springer	
	6	1.00	30	PH Sadarangani, A Krishnamu…	Shared Consumer Needs Across India and China: A P…	2017	Management International …	Springer	
	5	0.83	31	C Giachetti, E Spadafora	Conformity or nonconformity in multinationality? Perf…	2017	Management International Review	Springer	
	4	0.67	32	KS Powell	Understanding 'misfits': aspirations and systematic…	2017	Management International Review	Springer	
✓	4	0.67	33	S Song, JR Lee	The hysteresis effects of investment relationships wi…	2017	Management International Review		CITATION
✓	2	0.33	34	P Thakur-Wernz, O Bruyaka	Evolution of offshoring and outsourcing configuratio…	2017	Management International Review		CITATION
	0	0.00	35	RYK Chan, KHY Ma	Erratum to: Environmental orientation of exporting S…	2017	MIR: Management International Rev…	JSTOR	
✓	3	0.50	36	JRJ Bryan	Sinkovics Rudolf R. ve Kim Deakwan (2017). Anteced…	2017	Mir Management International Review		CITATION

A search like this generally provides very good results for journals with (fairly) unique names such as *"Management International Review"* or *"International Journal of Cross Cultural Management"*. The above search provides a complete record of all 33 articles published in *Management International Review* in 2017. You can verify this by checking its website. However, a quicker triangulation option is to search for the same journal in data sources that are known to provide "clean" results such as Scopus or the Web of Science.

The Publisher's column shows that Google Scholar draws most of its results from Springer itself. Wondering why some searches show HTML in the Type column? This is Google Scholar's way to indicate that the article is available in "Gold Open Access", i.e., in the official publisher's format at the publisher's website (rather than for instance a paper repository). Hence, right-clicking on it and selecting "Open Article in Browser" takes you directly the full-text of these articles.

Option 1: Exclude stray citations and patents

In the above search for *Management International Review* there were three articles (highlighted in the screenshot), that had a low relevance rank (ranked 33-36) and carried the CITATION label. CITATION results are records where Google Scholar *has* found citing works, but has been unable to find the cited work itself online. Oftentimes, these records are what are commonly called "stray citations", i.e., citations where the citing authors have made small mistakes in citing a work.

This is clearly the case for the above three articles. Although these articles might increase citation levels for individual articles, the effect of this is usually small. Usually, these stray citations are pure "noise" and do not contribute anything useful to your search

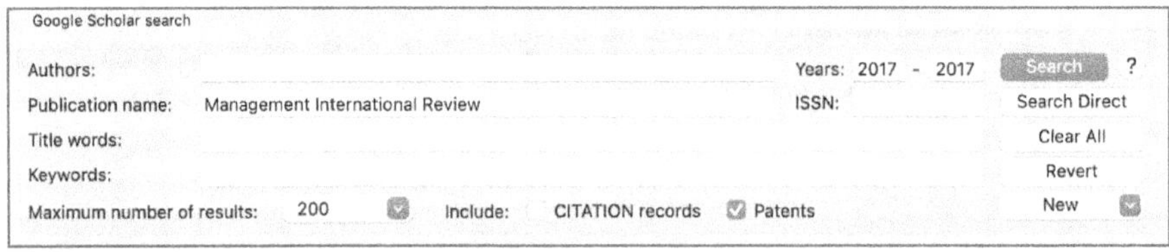

The quickest way to reduce the number of low-quality results in a Google Scholar journal search is thus to exclude CITATION records. The Publish or Perish interface includes an option to include or exclude both CITATION results and patents in Google Scholar searches (see screenshot above). Excluding patents is not necessary as patent results do not occur for journal searches, although it doesn't harm to exclude them. However, the exclusion of CITATION results makes a lot of sense and reduces "noise" in your journal searches.

Option 2: Exclude through sorting rank order

Just like individuals, journals sometimes have very common names, leading to PoP results not related to the journal you are searching for. Searching for *"Journal of Management"* will also result in:
- Journals with prefixes before *"Journal of Management "*, e.g., Australian / Baltic / British / European / Scandinavian / Sri Lankan Journal of Management
- Journals with additional words after *"Journal of Management"*, such as Development / Education / Inquiry / Studies / and Organization / Information Studies / in Engineering

A search for "Journal of Management" gives us more than 1,000 results, even for 2023 alone, even though the journal has only published just over 100 articles. The easiest way to find only the relevant hits is to simply sort the results by rank order, rather than using the Publish or Perish default order on citations (see below).

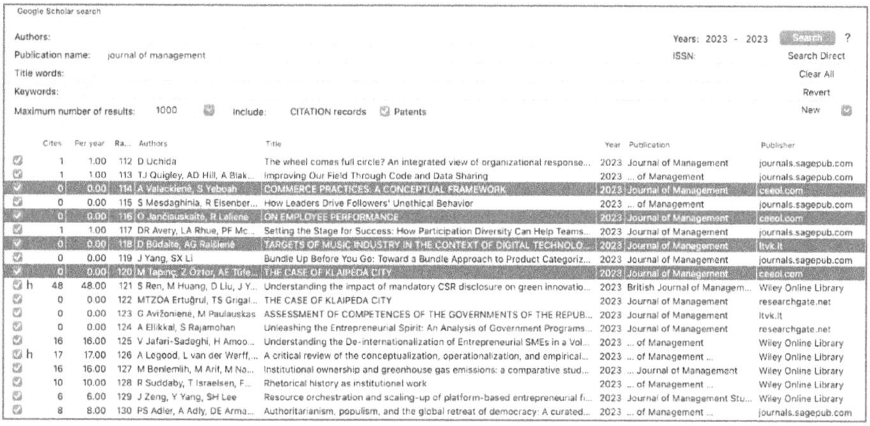

Google Scholar search

Authors:					Years: 2023 - 2023	Search	?
Publication name:	journal of management				ISSN:	Search Direct	
Title words:						Clear All	
Keywords:						Revert	
Maximum number of results:	1000		Include:	CITATION records Patents		New	

	Cites	Per year	Ra...	Authors	Title	Year	Publication	Publisher
	1	1.00	112	D Uchida	The wheel comes full circle? An integrated view of organizational response...	2023	Journal of Management	journals.sagepub.com
	1	1.00	113	TJ Quigley, AD Hill, A Blak...	Improving Our Field Through Code and Data Sharing	2023	... of Management	journals.sagepub.com
	0	0.00	114	A Valackienė, S Yeboah	COMMERCE PRACTICES: A CONCEPTUAL FRAMEWORK	2023	Journal of Management	ceeol.com
	0	0.00	115	S Mesdaghinia, R Eisenber...	How Leaders Drive Followers' Unethical Behavior	2023	... of Management	journals.sagepub.com
	0	0.00	116	O Jančiauskaitė, R Lalienė	ON EMPLOYEE PERFORMANCE	2023	Journal of Management	ceeol.com
	1	1.00	117	DR Avery, LA Rhue, PF Mc...	Setting the Stage for Success: How Participation Diversity Can Help Teams...	2023	Journal of Management	journals.sagepub.com
	0	0.00	118	D Būdaitė, AG Raišienė	TARGETS OF MUSIC INDUSTRY IN THE CONTEXT OF DIGITAL TECHNOLO...	2023	Journal of Management	ltvk.lt
	0	0.00	119	J Yang, SX Li	Bundle Up Before You Go: Toward a Bundle Approach to Product Categoriz...	2023	Journal of Management	journals.sagepub.com
	0	0.00	120	M Tapınç, Z Öztor, AE Tüfe...	THE CASE OF KLAIPĖDA CITY	2023	Journal of Management	ceeol.com
h	48	48.00	121	S Ren, M Huang, D Liu, J Y...	Understanding the impact of mandatory CSR disclosure on green innovatio...	2023	British Journal of Managem...	Wiley Online Library
	0	0.00	122	MTZOA Ertuğrul, TS Grigal...	THE CASE OF KLAIPĖDA CITY	2023	Journal of Management	researchgate.net
	0	0.00	123	G Avižonienė, M Paulauskas	ASSESSMENT OF COMPETENCES OF THE GOVERNMENTS OF THE REPUB...	2023	Journal of Management	ltvk.lt
	0	0.00	124	A Ellikkal, S Rajamohan	Unleashing the Entrepreneurial Spirit: An Analysis of Government Programs...	2023	Journal of Management	researchgate.net
	16	16.00	125	V Jafari-Sadeghi, H Amoo...	Understanding the De-internationalization of Entrepreneurial SMEs in a Vol...	2023	... of Management	Wiley Online Library
h	17	17.00	126	A Legood, L van der Werff,...	A critical review of the conceptualization, operationalization, and empirical...	2023	... of Management ...	Wiley Online Library
	16	16.00	127	M Benlemlih, M Arif, M No...	Institutional ownership and greenhouse gas emissions: a comparative stud...	2023	... Journal of Management	Wiley Online Library
	10	10.00	128	R Suddaby, T Israelsen, F...	Rhetorical history as institutional work	2023	... of Management ...	Wiley Online Library
	6	6.00	129	J Zeng, Y Yang, SH Lee	Resource orchestration and scaling-up of platform-based entrepreneurial f...	2023	Journal of Management Stu...	Wiley Online Library
	8	8.00	130	PS Adler, A Adly, DE Arma...	Authoritarianism, populism, and the global retreat of democracy: A curated...	2023	... of Management ...	journals.sagepub.com

That way articles are ranked by what Google Scholar thinks are the most *relevant* results first. As the screenshot above shows, GS does a good job in matching these to your query as the first 113 results are all publications in the *Journal of Management* that we are looking for. This can be verified by looking at the publisher (Sage Publications). There are a few articles in *Vadyba Journal of Management*, a Lithuanian journal (ranked 114, 116, 118, 120, highlighted in the above screenshot), mixed up with the last two articles in our *Journal of Management* at rank 115 and 117, but apart from that the result for the first 120-odd articles is very clean.

The only partially incorrect result is at rank 1068: a forthcoming article in *Journal of Management* that was found in a university repository. Unfortunately, because of truncation (see section on GS limitations in Chapter 5), distinguishing journal titles is difficult, though the publisher's column can help. From rank 121 onwards, most of the next 100 articles are published in *British Journal of Management* or *Journal of Management Studies* (both Wiley), interspersed with a sprinkling of articles in the *Australian Journal of Management, Journal of Management Education* and *Journal of Management Inquiry* (all Sage), *Journal of Management Development* and *Baltic Journal of Management* (both Emerald), and *Scandinavian Journal of Management* (Elsevier).

As there are only a dozen articles published by SAGE in this next tranche, most of which have initial or final truncation (i.e., before or after Journal of Management), it is easy to verify that there are no additional *Journal of Management* results. When in doubt, you can easily check by right-clicking and clicking **Open article in browser**. Thus, simply unchecking all articles after 113, manually unchecking 106 and manually checking 115, 117, and 119 provides you with a clean and complete record of the 115 articles published in *Journal of Management* in 2023 (to date).

This strategy appears to work well even when searching for multiple years or the journal's entire publication history to date. Google Scholar's relevance matching seems to ensure that only articles from the journal in question are included. A search for *Journal of Management* without year limitations only displayed articles published in the journal in question. This was also true for the *Journal of Marketing*. For other journals, however, results were more mixed.

Relying on Google Scholar's relevance matching may provide good results and is worth a try. However, what if this is not true for the journal that you are searching for? And what if you do not want to have to exclude false matches manually every time you rerun your search? In that case, you can exclude false matches *during* the search, rather than filtering them out *afterwards*. This is what we will discuss in the next section.

Option 3: Exclude by journal name

If the journal name you are searching for is not unique and you want to exclude its namesakes during the search, do this by including words you do not want to appear in the journal title in the journal field prefaced by NOT (or -). Below is an example for *Journal of Management*, excluding many of its most common prefixes and postfixes.

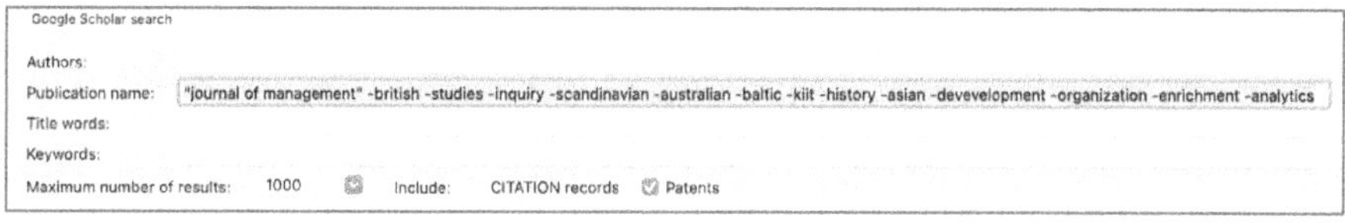

Unfortunately, for journals with a very common name this strategy is unlikely to be successful, especially after the proliferation of online journals – of sometimes rather dubious quality – in recent years. After excluding all of the more common namesakes, your search will be likely to draw in increasingly obscure journals. Whilst you can try and exclude these too, Google Scholar only allows a maximum of 256 characters for your search. So, you are likely to run into this before having listed all exclusion terms. That was indeed my problem in the above search.

However, this strategy can be successful for journals that only have a few namesakes. The first screenshot below provides an example for the journal *International Business Review* which, in a search for a single year, was be mixed up with *Thunderbird International Business Review*. However, using Thunderbird as a single exclusion term cleans up the result to show only articles published in *International Business Review* itself as can be seen in the second screenshot.

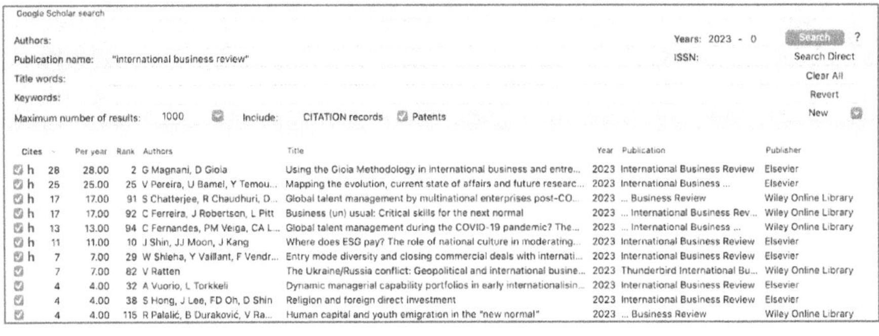

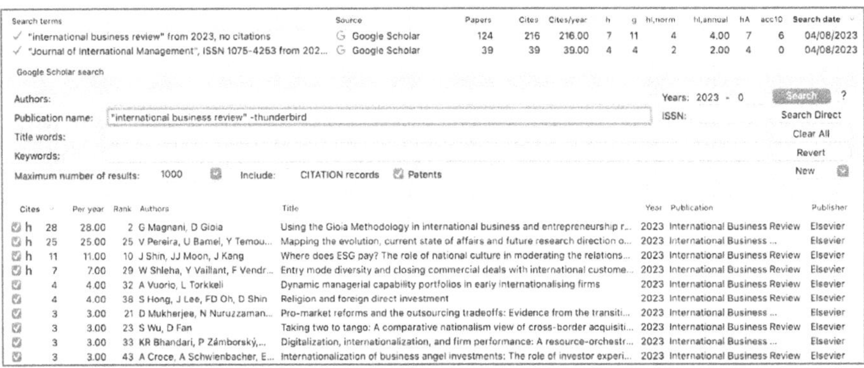

Likewise, as can be seen in the screenshot below, a search for *Journal of International Management* published by Elsevier is confounded with the Inderscience journal *European Journal of International Management* and (not visible in the screenshot) two Turkish journals: the *Journal of International Management Research and Applications* and the *Journal of International Management, Educational and Economics Perspectives.*

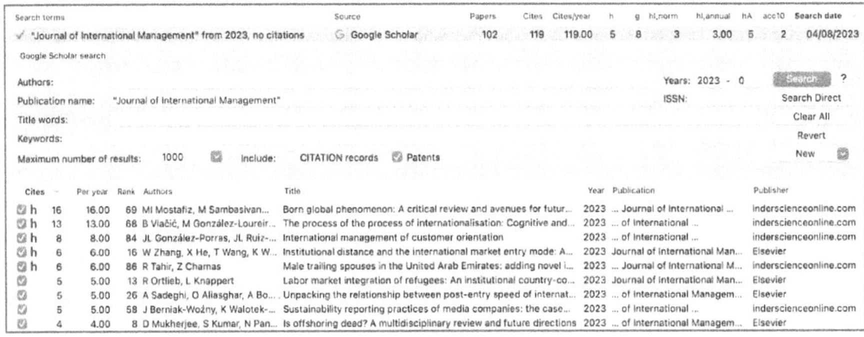

By using European, Educational and Research as exclusion terms in the journal field we get a very clean result incorporating only the 39 articles published in *Journal of International Management* in 2023 to date.

Search terms	Source	Papers	Cites	Cites/year	h	g	hi,norm	hl.annual	hA	acc10	Search date
"Journal of International Management" from 2023, no citations	Google Scholar	102	119	119.00	5	8	3	3.00	5	2	04/08/2023
"Journal of International Management" -European -Educational -R...	Google Scholar	39	39	39.00	4	4	2	2.00	4	0	04/08/2023

Google Scholar search

Authors: Years: 2023 - 0   Search ?

Publication name: "Journal of International Management" -European -Educational -Research   ISSN: Search Direct

Title words: Clear All

Keywords: Revert

Maximum number of results: 1000   Include: CITATION records   Patents   New

Cites		Per year	Rank	Authors	Title	Year	Publication	Publisher
✓ h	6	6.00	16	W Zhang, X He, T Wang, K W...	Institutional distance and the international market entry mode: A...	2023	Journal of International Man...	Elsevier
✓ h	5	5.00	13	R Ortlieb, L Knappert	Labor market integration of refugees: An institutional country-co...	2023	Journal of International Man...	Elsevier
✓ h	5	5.00	26	A Sadeghi, O Aliasghar, A Bo...	Unpacking the relationship between post-entry speed of internat...	2023	... of International Managem...	Elsevier
✓ h	4	4.00	8	D Mukherjee, S Kumar, N Pan...	Is offshoring dead? A multidisciplinary review and future directions	2023	... of International Managem...	Elsevier
✓	3	3.00	14	H Do, B Nguyen, H Shipton	Innovation and internationalization in an emerging market contex...	2023	Journal of International Man...	Elsevier
✓	3	3.00	23	M Tajeddin, M Farashahi, K...	Internationalization of emerging economy SMEs: a tripod approach	2023	Journal of International ...	Elsevier
✓	2	2.00	20	S Wei, Z Su, D Ahlstrom, Z Wu	State fragility and informal entrepreneurship: The moderating eff...	2023	Journal of International Man...	Elsevier
✓	2	2.00	21	E Mavroudi, M Kafouros, F Ji...	How can MNEs benefit from internationalizing their R&D across c...	2023	... of International Managem...	Elsevier
✓	2	2.00	30	M Lee, C Mutlu, SH Lee	Bribery and Firm Growth: Sensemaking in CEE and Post-Soviet C...	2023	Journal of International Man...	Elsevier
✓	2	2.00	34	F Donbesuur, N Zahoor, O Al...	On the performance of platform-based international new venture...	2023	Journal of International ...	Elsevier

Option 4: Searching by ISSN

Rather than searching for journals by name, we can also search for them by ISSN in Publish or Perish, which – as it is a unique journal identifier – should give us much cleaner results. You can search by ISSN simply by including the ISSN in the ISSN search field. It doesn't matter whether you use eight digits or four digits hyphen four digits format. Publish or Perish provides exactly the same results with both. Remember, however, that Google Scholar is not a bibliographic database, and it does not have an ISSN field as such. Hence ISSNs are matched *anywhere* in the document and might thus result in incorrect matches.

This strategy gives good results for most journals. The advantage is that searching by ISSN tends to limit results to hits coming from the publisher's official website, thus automatically removing the more dubious stray citations from other sources. However, this strategy is only successful if the publisher has structured their website sufficiently well for Google Scholar to parse their ISSN. Fortunately, most journals seem to have improved their websites in this respect.

For instance, whereas in 2010 a search for the *Australian Journal of Management* by ISSN provided no results, it now presents a comprehensive set of articles. Below is a screenshot for all articles published in 2005; the journal only published two issues a year with eight articles in each issue, the last article was an editorial.

A combination of journal name and ISSN for *Journal of Management* in 2023 shows an identical result (115 articles published to date) to our earlier experiment of getting a clean record for *Journal of Management* by excluding by rank. There is one incorrect result at rank #116. This may have been caused by the ISSN appearing somewhere else in the document. However, this offending record is easily spotted by its low rank, its different journal name, and its publisher.

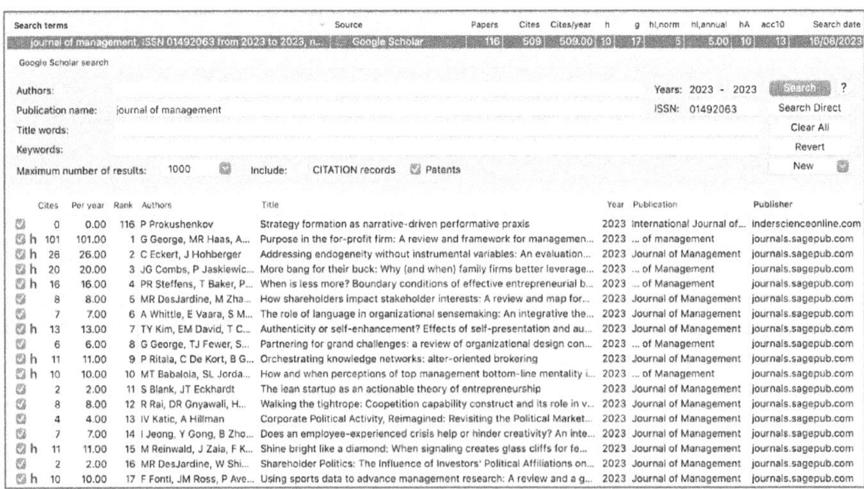

My experiments suggest that the best results are achieved through a combination of journal name and ISSN. Searching for ISSN alone for *Journal of Management* provided me with an additional 100+ results. The ISSN was matched in the list of references of articles published in other journals with "journal of management" in their name. This is because the DOI for an article often includes the ISSN. So, articles referring to an article in *Journal of Management* **and** including the DOI in their reference would also be shown in the search results.

Specific use cases for journal searches

In addition to searching for the results of a specific journal, there are many other things you can do with the journal search. Chapter 12 on literature reviews also includes journal searches as does Chapter 14 on bibliometrics research. Chapter 13 explains how to use a journal search to decide which journal you want to submit your article to. Here I discuss three other frequent use cases: searching for multiple journals, analysing journal impact for specific years, and searching for chapters in an edited volume.

Searching for multiple journals

You do not need to limit your search to a single journal. You can add multiple journal names in the publication name field separated by OR. That way you could for instance do a thematic analysis of all publications in a given year in the five key International Business Journals: *Journal of International Business Studies*, *Journal of World Business*, *International Business Review*, *Management International Review* and *Journal of International Management* (see screenshot below).

Google Scholar doesn't provide fully complete abstracts. However, reviewing titles and parts of the abstracts should give you a good idea of what themes are deemed important in the field recently. Obviously, you can also look at which papers are particularly highly cited, which would give you an indication of "hot topics".

Search terms	Source	Papers	Cites	Cites/year	h	g	hI,norm	hI,annual	hA	acc10	Search date	Cache date
✓ "Journal of International Business Studies" OR "Journal...	Google Scholar	448	3,447	3,447.00	25	36	12	12.00	25	108	04/08/2023	04/08/2023

Cites	Per year	Rank	Authors	Title	Year	Publication	Publisher
86	86.00	172	L Ciravegna, S Michailova	Why the world economy needs, but will not get, more glo...	2022	Journal of International Business Studies	Springer
76	76.00	45	G George, SJD Schillebeeckx	Digital transformation, sustainability, and purpose in the...	2022	Journal of World Business	Elsevier
70	70.00	187	Y Luo	A general framework of digitization risks in international...	2022	Journal of international business studies	Springer
64	64.00	4	D Tolstoy, ER Nordman, U Vu	The indirect effect of online marketing capabilities on th...	2022	International Business Review	Elsevier
60	60.00	55	A Ferraris, WY Degbey, SK Singh, S...	Microfoundations of strategic agility in emerging market...	2022	... of World Business	Elsevier
59	59.00	181	C Welch, E Paavilainen-Mantymaki,...	Reconciling theory and context: How the case study can...	2022	... of International Business ...	Springer
58	58.00	74	B Orlando, D Tortora, A Pezzi, N Bit...	The disruption of the international supply chain: Firm res...	2022	... of International Management	Elsevier
46	46.00	217	J Li, A Van Assche, L Li, G Qian	Foreign direct investment along the Belt and Road: A poli...	2022	Journal of International Business Studies	Springer
45	45.00	197	Y Luo	Illusions of techno-nationalism	2022	Journal of International Business Studies	Springer
44	44.00	73	J Child, J Karmowska, O Shenkar	The role of context in SME internationalization–A review	2022	Journal of World Business	Elsevier
44	44.00	78	S Zhao, X Liu, U Andersson, O She...	Knowledge management of emerging economy multinati...	2022	Journal of World Business	Elsevier
40	40.00	9	Z Khan, J Amankwah-Amoah, YK L...	Strategic ambidexterity and its performance implications...	2022	International Business ...	Elsevier
33	33.00	5	I Kalinic, KD Brouthers	Entrepreneurial orientation, export channel selection, an...	2022	International Business Review	Elsevier
33	33.00	87	M Kafouros, ST Cavusgil, TM Devin...	Cycles of de-internationalization and re-internationalizat...	2022	... of World Business	Elsevier
30	30.00	11	Y Liu, S Collinson, C Cooper, D Bagl...	International business, innovation and ambidexterity: A...	2022	International Business Review	Elsevier
30	30.00	86	H Yu, M Fletcher, T Buck	Managing digital transformation during re-internationaliz...	2022	Journal of International Management	Elsevier
30	30.00	98	M Elo, FA Täube, P Servais	Who is doing "transnational diaspora entrepreneurship"?...	2022	Journal of World Business	Elsevier
30	30.00	201	SA Zahra, O Petricevic, Y Luo	Toward an action-based view of dynamic capabilities for...	2022	Journal of International Business Studies	Springer
29	29.00	6	Z Deng, Z Zhu, M Johanson, M Hil...	Rapid internationalization and exit of exporters: The role...	2022	International Business Review	Elsevier
29	29.00	219	CH Oh, J Oetzel	Multinational enterprises and natural disasters: Challeng...	2022	Journal of International Business Studies	Springer
29	29.00	225	JW Lu, H Ma, X Xie	Foreignness research in international business: Major str...	2022	Journal of International Business Studies	Springer
29	29.00	234	O Guedhami, A Knill, WL Megginso...	The dark side of globalization: Evidence from the impact...	2022	... of International Business ...	Springer
28	28.00	1	AA Ahi, N Sinkovics, Y Shildibekov, ...	Advanced technologies and international business: A mu...	2022	International Business ...	Elsevier
27	27.00	89	NF Richter, S Hauff	Necessary conditions in international business research...	2022	Journal of World Business	Elsevier
25	25.00	130	Y Ponomareva, T Uman, V Bodolica...	Cultural diversity in top management teams: Review and...	2022	... of World Business	Elsevier

Obviously, such an analysis would only be possible for disciplines in which journals typically publish only 50-200 articles a year, which is the case for most top journals in Business & Management. In other disciplines you might overwhelm the Google Scholar limitation of 1,000 results with a single journal.

However, as journal titles can be quite long you are likely to run up against Google Scholar's 256-character limitation. If you had wanted to add *European Journal of International Management* and *Thunderbird International Business Review* to the above that would not be possible within the character limitation.

It so happens that this is not a problem in this case as EJIM is matched when searching for JIM and TIBR is matched when searching for IBR. However, if one wanted to have only the five top journals in the field, you could exclude these two journals with the exclusion strategies discussed above, i.e., excluding European and Thunderbird, which just fit within the character limitation (see screenshot below).

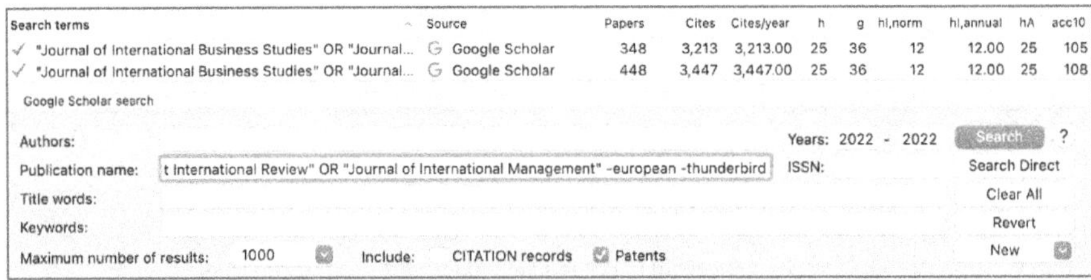

Search terms	Source	Papers	Cites	Cites/year	h	g	hI,norm	hI,annual	hA	acc10
✓ "Journal of International Business Studies" OR "Journal...	Google Scholar	348	3,213	3,213.00	25	36	12	12.00	25	105
✓ "Journal of International Business Studies" OR "Journal...	Google Scholar	448	3,447	3,447.00	25	36	12	12.00	25	108

Analyse impact for specific years

As we have seen in some of the examples above, you can analyse the impact of a journal over a specific period by entering the start or end years in the **Years** fields in Publish or Perish. For instance, you could look at a journal's publications, citations, and h-index in the last three or five years alone. Below for instance you will find the results for the last three years of the *Journal of International Business Studies*.

By sorting the results on citations per year, we can review the most highly cited papers in the past three years. We can also see the average number of citations per paper, which at 32.5 citations is quite high for recently published articles in the Social Sciences. Do note, however, that for any searches in the last 6-12 months the year listed might be the online first year, rather than the year in which the publication appeared in print. For details on this see the section on Google Scholar limitations in Chapter 5.

Searching chapters in an edited volume

Although journals are the most common sources of publications, a search in the Publication name field can also be used to search for publications in other sources. Edited book volumes are a common source in the Social Sciences and Humanities.

Typically, authors will refer to individual chapters within an edited book. Hence, in order to assess the overall impact of an edited book, one would need to search for citations to individual chapters as well as citations to the book as a whole.

Stewart Clegg, Thomas Lawrence, and Cynthia Hardy co-edited the *Handbook of Organisation Studies*. If we want to establish the impact that this handbook has had on the field, we need to be able to accumulate citations to all chapters in this handbook. When searching for the editors, I found nearly 1500 citations to the Handbook as such. This can be done easily by including the three family names in the **Authors** field. This produced two results (see below), one of which appears to have drawn in one of the chapter authors as editor.

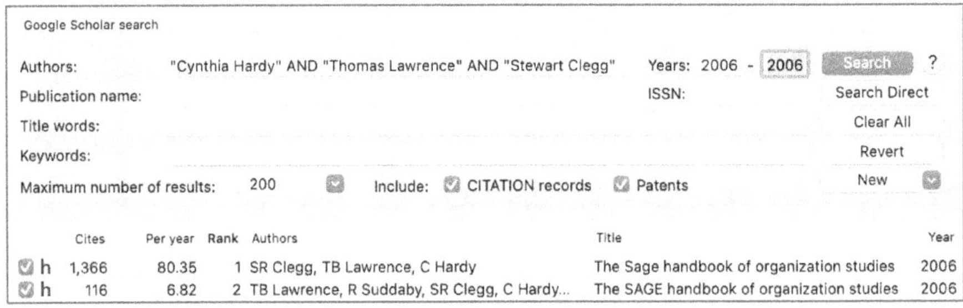

Google Scholar search

Authors:	"Cynthia Hardy" AND "Thomas Lawrence" AND "Stewart Clegg"	Years: 2006 - 2006	Search	?
Publication name:		ISSN:	Search Direct
Title words:			Clear All
Keywords:			Revert
Maximum number of results: 200	Include: ✓ CITATION records ✓ Patents		New

	Cites	Per year	Rank	Authors	Title	Year
✓ h	1,366	80.35	1	SR Clegg, TB Lawrence, C Hardy	The Sage handbook of organization studies	2006
✓ h	116	6.82	2	TB Lawrence, R Suddaby, SR Clegg, C Hardy...	The SAGE handbook of organization studies	2006

However, the screenshot below shows that well over 10,000 citations can be found to individual chapters within the handbook. Hence, only just over 10% of the total citations to the handbook were to the handbook as a whole. Note that unlike for the journal searches that I conducted in this chapter, for this search I didn't untick the CITATION records box as book chapters are often CITATION records.

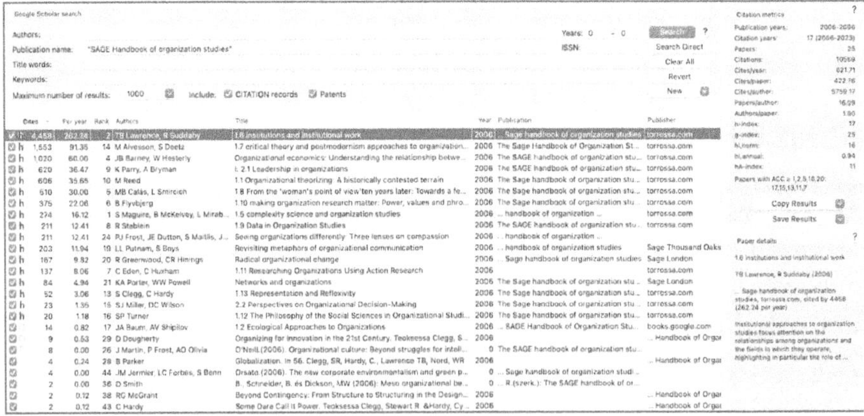

Google Scholar search

Authors:
Publication name: "SAGE Handbook of organization studies"
Title words:
Keywords:
Maximum number of results: 1000   Include: ✓ CITATION records ✓ Patents
Years: 0 - 0   Search   ?   ISSN: Search Direct   Clear All   Revert   New

	Cites	Per year	Rank	Authors	Title	Year	Publication	Publisher
✓ h	4,458	262.24	2	TB Lawrence, R Suddaby	1.6 Institutions and institutional work	2006	Sage handbook of organization studies	torrossa.com
✓ h	1,553	91.35	14	M Alvesson, S Deetz	1.7 critical theory and postmodernism approaches to organization...	2006	The Sage Handbook of Organization St...	torrossa.com
✓ h	1,020	60.00	4	JB Barney, W Hesterly	Organizational economics: Understanding the relationship betwe...	2006	The SAGE handbook of organization stu...	torrossa.com
✓ h	620	36.47	9	K Parry, A Bryman	I: 2.1 Leadership in organizations	2006	The SAGE handbook of organization stu...	torrossa.com
✓ h	606	35.65	10	M Reed	1.1 Organizational theorizing: A historically contested terrain	2006	The Sage handbook of organization stu...	torrossa.com
✓ h	510	30.00	5	MB Calás, L Smircich	1.8 From the 'woman's point of view'ten years later: Towards a fe...	2006	The Sage handbook of organization stu...	torrossa.com
✓ h	375	22.06	6	B Flyvbjerg	1.10 making organization research matter: Power, values and phro...	2006	The Sage handbook of organization stu...	torrossa.com
✓ h	274	16.12	1	S Maguire, B McKelvey, L Mirab...	1.5 complexity science and organization studies	2006	... handbook of organization ...	torrossa.com
✓ h	211	12.41	8	R Stablein	1.9 Data in Organization Studies	2006	The SAGE handbook of organization stu...	torrossa.com
✓ h	211	12.41	24	PJ Frost, JE Dutton, S Maitlis, J...	Seeing organizations differently: Three lenses on compassion	2006	... handbook of organization ...	
✓ h	203	11.94	19	LL Putnam, S Boys	Revisiting metaphors of organizational communication	2006	... handbook of organization studies	Sage Thousand Oaks
✓ h	187	9.82	20	R Greenwood, CR Hinings	Radical organizational change	2006	... Sage handbook of organization studies	Sage London
✓ h	137	8.06	7	C Eden, C Huxham	1.11 Researching Organizations Using Action Research	2006		torrossa.com
✓ h	84	4.94	21	KA Porter, WW Powell	Networks and organizations	2006	The Sage handbook of organization stu...	Sage London
✓ h	52	3.06	13	S Clegg, C Hardy	1.13 Representation and Reflexivity	2006	The Sage handbook of organization stu...	torrossa.com
✓ h	23	1.35	15	SJ Miller, DC Wilson	2.2 Perspectives on Organizational Decision-Making	2006	The Sage handbook of organization stu...	torrossa.com
✓ h	20	1.18	16	SP Turner	1.12 The Philosophy of the Social Sciences in Organizational Studi...	2006	The Sage handbook of organization stu...	torrossa.com
✓	14	0.82	17	JA Baum, AV Shipilov	1.2 Ecological Approaches to Organizations	2006	... SAGE Handbook of Organization Stu...	books.google.com
✓	9	0.53	29	D Dougherty	Organizing for Innovation in the 21st Century. Teoksessa Clegg, S...	2006		... Handbook of Organ...
✓	8	0.00	26	J Martin, P Frost, AO Olivia	O'Neill.(2006). Organizational culture: Beyond struggles for intell...	0	The SAGE handbook of organization stu...	
✓	4	0.24	28	B Parker	Globalization. In 56. Clegg, SR, Hardy, C., Lawrence TB, Nord, WR	2006		... Handbook of Organ...
✓	4	0.00	44	JM Jermier, LC Forbes, S Benn	Orsato (2006). The new corporate environmentalism and green p...	0	... Sage handbook of organization studi...	
✓	2	0.00	36	D Smith	B., Schneider, B. és Dickson, MW (2006): Meso organizational be...	0	... R.(szerk.): The SAGE handbook of or...	
✓	2	0.12	38	RG McGrant	Beyond Contingency: From Structure to Structuring in the Design...	2006		... Handbook of Organ...
✓	2	0.12	43	C Hardy	Some Dare Call It Power. Teoksessa Clegg, Stewart R &Hardy, Cy...	2006		... Handbook of Organ...

Citation metrics ?

Publication years:	2006-2006
Citation years:	17 (2006-2023)
Papers:	25
Citations:	10589
Cites/year:	621.71
Cites/paper:	422.76
Cites/author:	5759.17
Papers/author:	16.09
Authors/paper:	1.90
h-index:	17
g-index:	25
hi,norm:	16
hi,annual:	0.94
hA-index:	11

Papers with ACC ≥ 1,2,5,10,20: 17,15,13,11,7

Copy Results
Save Results

Paper details ?

1.6 Institutions and institutional work

TB Lawrence, R Suddaby (2006)

... Sage handbook of organization studies, torrossa.com, cited by 4458 (262.24 per year)

Institutional approaches to organization studies focus attention on the relationships among organizations and the fields in which they operate, highlighting in particular the role of ...

Needless to say, the editors of the Handbook above could make a much stronger case for the impact of the Handbook if they conducted a comprehensive citation search as described above. Edited volumes are an important way to publish state-of-the art research in some disciplines. Hence, it is important to conduct a comprehensive citation search for all references to the edited volume.

Unfortunately, Google Scholar doesn't seem to find *all* chapters in this handbook. Out of the thirty chapters in this handbook, Google Scholar finds only twenty-five with the above search. Moreover, out of the twenty-five chapters that *are* found, at least seven appear to be substantively incomplete. They are all CITATION records and have very few citations. The missing chapters *can* be found with their title, though Google Scholar generally finds few citations for them. Some of the incomplete records can also be found with their title, but – with one exception – they also tend to have few citations.

Whilst this may be a limitation of Google Scholar, it may also simply be the case that some chapters attracted few citations. The fact that half of the chapters attracted more than 100 citations and six of them more than 500 citations is an impressive result for book chapters. Although this incomplete coverage is disappointing, we should place this in the context of other data sources that generally would not find *any* of this handbook's chapters as they focus on journal publications only. The other data sources *are* useful, however, in getting quicker, and often cleaner results for journal than Google Scholar. The next section therefore provides details on how to use Publish or Perish for journal searches in other data sources.

Journal searches in other data sources

Below I provide brief suggestions for each of the other seven data sources that PoP interfaces with, except for Google Scholar Profiles and Semantic Scholar which do not support journal searches. The search syntax below refers to what works best when you search the data source *through* Publish or Perish. This is not always identical to the most effective search syntax in the web interfaces of the respective databases as these might be structured differently.

Note that every data source has its own unique syntax that is not always fully documented. Below, I will provide the most important tips and problems, but to get the best out of the different data sources you will need to be prepared to experiment a little with different search strategies. If some things are not working as you expect, please share your findings with me at anne@harzing.com, so that, collectively, we can improve the instructions.

Journal searches by ISSN

Crossref, OpenAlex, PubMed, Scopus and the Web of Science all give excellent results for ISSN searches. In contrast to Google Scholar, these data sources do have dedicated ISSN fields, so there is no risk of false matches where the ISSN is found in the list of references. As such, there is no need to add the journal title as well.

For instance, if we repeat the search we conducted for the *Australian Journal of Management* with ISSN only, we get 17 results for 2005 for *each* of the data sources, just like we did in a Google Scholar search with the CITATION records box unticked. All data sources report fewer citations than Google Scholar. OpenAlex (see below) comes closest to Google Scholar and also provides complete abstracts, so is much more useful for content analyses.

It should also be noted, however, that – unlike the other data sources – OpenAlex matches the publication year with the online first year. This means that for many journals it is not possible to get an accurate overview of the articles published in a journal in a specific year.

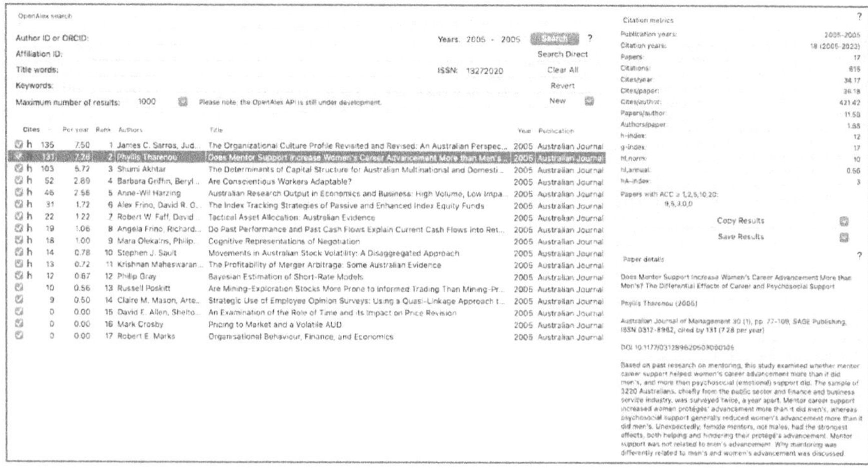

Diving into the history of Science

PubMed obviously doesn't find the *Australian Journal of Management* as this is not a biomedical journal, but it is equally effective in finding complete journal results with an ISSN search. It found the 919 articles published in Science back in 1940 within 10 seconds.

The results (see first screenshot below) provide a fascinating insight into the impact of the 2nd world war on scientific research, from spatial and perceptual disorientation when landing airplanes to bombs on the Royal Botanical Gardens at Kew.

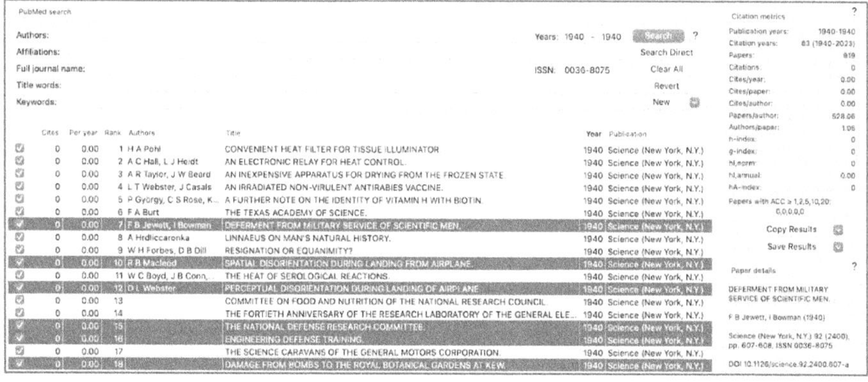

PubMed even allows us to go back to 1880, the first year of publication of Science, for which it reports 312 articles within seconds. Unfortunately, it doesn't (yet) provide abstracts for these older articles. Moreover, its website returns a "404 not found" page for nearly all of the articles. However, the searches still provide us with intriguing insights into the history of Science (in both meanings of the word).

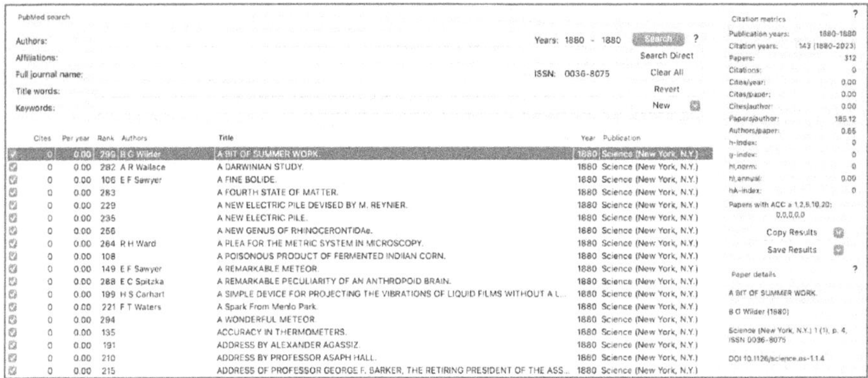

Cites	Per year	Rank	Authors	Title	Year	Publication
0	0.00	299	B G Wilder	A BIT OF SUMMER WORK.	1880	Science (New York, N.Y.)
0	0.00	282	A R Wallace	A DARWINIAN STUDY.	1880	Science (New York, N.Y.)
0	0.00	106	E F Sawyer	A FINE BOLIDE.	1880	Science (New York, N.Y.)
0	0.00	283		A FOURTH STATE OF MATTER.	1880	Science (New York, N.Y.)
0	0.00	229		A NEW ELECTRIC PILE DEVISED BY M. REYNIER.	1880	Science (New York, N.Y.)
0	0.00	235		A NEW ELECTRIC PILE.	1880	Science (New York, N.Y.)
0	0.00	256		A NEW GENUS OF RHINOCERONTIDAe.	1880	Science (New York, N.Y.)
0	0.00	264	R H Ward	A PLEA FOR THE METRIC SYSTEM IN MICROSCOPY.	1880	Science (New York, N.Y.)
0	0.00	108		A POISONOUS PRODUCT OF FERMENTED INDIIAN CORN.	1880	Science (New York, N.Y.)
0	0.00	149	E F Sawyer	A REMARKABLE METEOR.	1880	Science (New York, N.Y.)
0	0.00	288	E C Spitzka	A REMARKABLE PECULIARITY OF AN ANTHROPOID BRAIN.	1880	Science (New York, N.Y.)
0	0.00	199	H S Carhart	A SIMPLE DEVICE FOR PROJECTING THE VIBRATIONS OF LIQUID FILMS WITHOUT A L...	1880	Science (New York, N.Y.)
0	0.00	221	F T Waters	A Spark From Menlo Park.	1880	Science (New York, N.Y.)
0	0.00	294		A WONDERFUL METEOR	1880	Science (New York, N.Y.)
0	0.00	135		ACCURACY IN THERMOMETERS.	1880	Science (New York, N.Y.)
0	0.00	191		ADDRESS BY ALEXANDER AGASSIZ.	1880	Science (New York, N.Y.)
0	0.00	210		ADDRESS BY PROFESSOR ASAPH HALL.	1880	Science (New York, N.Y.)
0	0.00	215		ADDRESS OF PROFESSOR GEORGE F. BARKER, THE RETIRING PRESIDENT OF THE ASS...	1880	Science (New York, N.Y.)

The first issue of Science featured the article "A Bit of Summer Work" (see below) with reflections on what teachers should do during the Summer holidays. I found it absolutely fascinating for three reasons. First, the reference to teachers rather than academics/researchers shows *Science* didn't just cater for researchers.

Second, the suggestion that at least a fortnight should elapse before any intellectual labour is undertaken, with an equal period of repose recommended just before the renewal of teaching sounds positively luxurious in today's pressured times. That is until we discover that that still leaves another two *months* of Summer leave.

Third, the suggestion to spend much of that time on dissecting brains might sound a bit gruesome to many, but I guess it makes perfect sense for medical researchers. However, I couldn't help wondering what the author meant by focusing on cat brains because they are "always and everywhere obtainable".

A Bit of Summer Work

BURT G. WILDER   Authors Info & Affiliations

SCIENCE · 3 Jul 1880 · Vol os 1, Issue 1 · p 4 · DOI: 10.1126/science.os-1.1.4

A BIT OF SUMMER WORK.

BY PROFESSOR BURT G. WILDER, M. D.

Notwithstanding the number of " Summer Schools of Science" to be in operation this season, many teachers are likely to pass the vacation at a distance from the facilities afforded by organized laboratories. How shall they employ their time?

Doubtless they all need rest, and in most cases at least a fortnight should elapse before any intellectual labor is undertaken. An equal period of repose may well occur just before the renewal of teaching in the Fall. But the teacher who hopes to make his instruction each year more thorough and successful than the last, will be pretty sure to spend the remaining month or two in the search of help from books, and, while regretting the vagueness of the information thus obtained, may seldom think of making it more real by personal observation.

Now it is true that in some branches of science this may require appliances not readily obtained. This is the case with Chemistry and Physics, and some parts of Natural History. But Botany and Entomology may be pursued under almost any circumstances, and I venture to suggest that at least one kind of *anatomical* work may be carried on with but a slight amount of apparatus.

Obviously, the summer is not the most favorable time for study of the viscera, while anatomical details respecting the muscles, vessels and nerves are not especially required for ordinary instruction. But the *brain* is not only the organ least satisfactorily treated in the text-books, but at the same time the one concerning which the most should be known, from the double standpoint of physiology and psychology.

But how can the teacher procure brains, and how shall he preserve them when obtained?

The question is a perfectly natural one in view of the prevailing impression that cerebral structure is to be learned from the human brain alone. So far from correct is this idea, that from a single animal brain, perfectly fresh or well preserved, more may be gained than the average medical student learns from the human brains usually examined in the dissecting-room.

This is due to the fact that, excepting the absence of the occipital lobes of the hemispheres, the brains of the cat, the dog, the rabbit and the sheep present nearly all of the structural features of the human brain, while their smaller size and greater accessibility better adapt them for manipulation and for the preservation of the numerous specimens which are needed to display all parts of the organ.

Of the animals above named the cat seems to be the most favorable subject. It is always and everywhere obtainable; the brain is larger than that of the rabbit, and more easily extracted than those of the sheep and most dogs.

Some features of the brain, as the coloration of different parts, and especially the relation of the gray and white substances, are better seen upon fresh specimens; but the beginner will do well to examine hardened brains first, so as to become familiar with the form and relative position of the parts, and with their names.

Among the instruments needed for the removal and dissection of the brain the most essential are a very sharp knife, and a pair of "wire-nippers" with the blades set at a slight angle with the handles. *

As an aid to the study of the brain any work upon Human Anatomy will be found useful. The best are those of "Quain" and "Gray." Descriptions, without figures, of the brains of the sheep, and of the dog and rabbit, are given in the little works of Morrell and Foster and Langley. With some modification these apply to the brain of the cat. †

Finally, it is hardly necessary to urge that outline drawings be made of the brain as a whole, and of its parts as exposed by dissection. If this is done, by the end of the summer the teacher will have become better able to appreciate the peculiarities of the human brain when one comes in his way, and will have laid a substantial foundation for the physiological and psychological instruction which he may be called upon to impart.

ANTIPATHARIA OF THE " BLACK " EXPEDITION.—In vol. iv. No. 4 of the *Bulletin* of the Museum of Comparative Zoology at Harvard College, Cambridge, Mass. (February), L. F. Pourtales describes twelve species of this interesting group taken in the Caribbean Sea (1878-79). In determining the species an attempt has been made to use the differences in the shape of the polyps, as well as the disposition and form of the spines to draw characters for a much-needed revision of their classification. It would seem as if there were at least two different types of spines: the triangular compressed and the more cylindrical. These latter are generally more densely set, even assuming sometimes a brush-like appearance, as in *Antipathes humilis*, a new and wonderfully spinous species, figured but not described by Pourtales. These cylindrical spines are also unequal on the two sides of the pinnules, being longer on the side occupied by the polyps, with a very few around the polyps. The triangular spines are disposed regularly in a quincuncial order around the pinnules, and in a cleaned specimen nothing indicates the place formerly occupied by the polyps. In one series, however, *A. desbonsi*, the spines are in regular verticils. There would appear to be a connection between the shape of the polyps and the shape and disposition of the spines. Those species with triangular spines have polyps with longer tentacles than those with cylindrical spines, and the tentacles have a greater tendency to become regular in shape.

---

* These nippers are imported from Germany by H. Boker & Co., of New York, and are for sale by A. J. Wilkinson & Co., of Boston, and Treman, King & Co., of Ithaca, N. Y. They cost about 75 cents.

† Hektograph copies of instructions for the removal, preservation and dissection of the cat's brain may be had upon application to Mr. F. L. Kilborne, Anatomical Laboratory, Cornell University, Ithaca, N. Y.

Journal searches by name

Of the five additional data sources that allow journal searches, Open-Alex cannot search for journals by name. Hence OpenAlex journal searches need to be conducted by ISSN only. Below we discuss the four other data sources in alphabetical order.

Crossref searches are complicated

Crossref can search for journals by name, but as it implements an OR search it is very hard to get correct result. If you search for the journal *Management International Review*, Crossref also reports *Management Review*, *International Journal of Health Management Review* and many others (see below). What you can do is sort the results by rank as in the screenshot below.

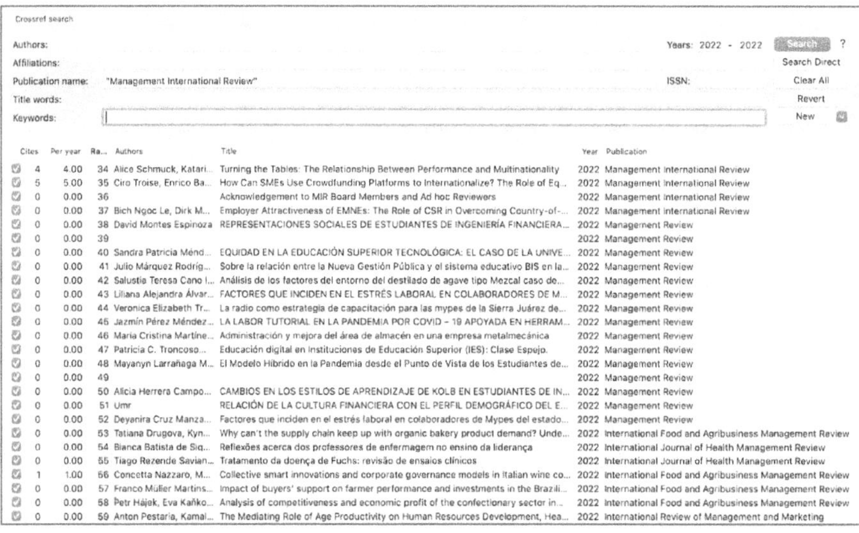

For some journals Crossref shows all relevant results are at the top of the ranking (in the case of the above search the first 37). You can then simply uncheck all remaining results. However, this doesn't work for journals with very common names. None of the results for a search for *"Journal of Management"* actually lists the journal itself. Hence, I would recommend that you use journal searches by name only as a last resort in Crossref.

PubMed and Web of Science

PubMed and the Web of Science can search by name, but you will need to include the full and exact journal title. The advantage is though that PubMed and the Web of Science *only* provide results for the journal that you are searching for.

Partial titles do not provide any results. However, the Web of Science can search for partial titles if you include wildcards. For instance, *Journal of International Ma** will result in *Journal of International <u>Man-agement</u>* and *Journal of International <u>Marketing</u>*).

Scopus requires some work for common titles

Scopus can search for both full and partial journal titles and performs well for journals with (fairly) unique names. However, for journals with quite common names Scopus is likely to provide many irrelevant results, especially if you use partial titles. This is because unlike PubMed and the Web of Science – which only search with full journal titles – it also matches journals that include more than the search terms as the screenshot below illustrates.

	Cites	Per year	Ra...	Authors	Title	Year	Publication
h	65	65.00	1	J.R. Busenbark	Omitted Variable Bias: Examining Management Research With the Impact Thres...	2022	Journal of Management
h	61	61.00	2	L.D.W. Thomas	Ecosystem Legitimacy Emergence: A Collective Action View	2022	Journal of Management
h	48	48.00	3	X. Zhao	The Influence of Corporate Social Responsibility on Incumbent Employees: A Me...	2022	Journal of Management
h	43	43.00	4	L. Chen	Governance and Design of Digital Platforms: A Review and Future Research Dire...	2022	Journal of Management
h	41	41.00	5	A. Maseda	Mapping women's involvement in family firms: A review based on bibliographic...	2022	International Journal of Management Reviews
h	41	41.00	6	G. Maheshwari	Investigating the relationship between educational support and entrepreneurial i...	2022	International Journal of Management Education
h	41	41.00	7	Q. Chen	Green finance and outward foreign direct investment: evidence from a quasi-nat...	2022	Asia Pacific Journal of Management
h	40	40.00	8	B.G. Hwang	Challenges and Strategies for the Adoption of Smart Technologies in the Constr...	2022	Journal of Management in Engineering
h	37	37.00	9	D. Fan	Advancing literature review methodology through rigour, generativity, scope and...	2022	International Journal of Management Reviews
h	37	37.00	10	G.D. Bruton	Indigenous Theory Uses, Abuses, and Future	2022	Journal of Management Studies
h	37	37.00	11	S. Bacq	Stakeholder Governance for Responsible Innovation: A Theory of Value Creation...	2022	Journal of Management Studies
h	35	35.00	12	L. Chen	Platform Governance Design in Platform Ecosystems: Implications for Complem...	2022	Journal of Management
h	34	34.00	13	V. Naciti	Corporate governance and sustainability: a review of the existing literature	2022	Journal of Management and Governance

In addition to Journal of Management, Scopus returns *International Journal of Management Reviews*, *Asia Pacific Journal of Management*, *Journal of Management Studies*, and many others.

Given that Scopus ranks its results based on citations rather than on relevance, we cannot implement the same exclusion strategy as for Crossref. Results for *Journal of Management* are spread throughout the list. The free Scopus version is also limited to 200 results, which for this search only resulted in articles with at least 9 citations. Therefore, *Journal of Management* articles published in 2022 with fewer than 9 citations will be missing from the list.

However, given that – unlike Google Scholar – Scopus does not have a constraint on the number of search terms, you could iteratively add exclusion terms starting the most cited partial namesakes and adding new terms as new journals with fewer citations are pulled in. A search string "Journal of Management" -international -asia -studies -engineering -inquiry -education -european -africa -british -mathematics -australian -governance -organization -systems -scandinavian -analytics -baltic -indian -accounting -development -control -history -religion -asian -serbian -business ensured that only *Journal of Management* articles were reported (see screenshot below).

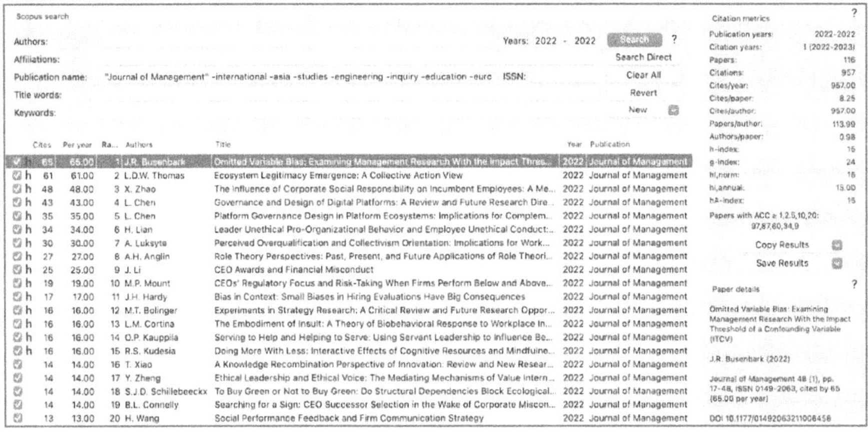

Cites	Per year	Ra...	Authors	Title	Year	Publication
h 65	65.00	1	J.R. Busenbark	Omitted Variable Bias: Examining Management Research With the Impact Thres...	2022	Journal of Management
h 61	61.00	2	L.D.W. Thomas	Ecosystem Legitimacy Emergence: A Collective Action View	2022	Journal of Management
h 48	48.00	3	X. Zhao	The Influence of Corporate Social Responsibility on Incumbent Employees: A Me...	2022	Journal of Management
h 43	43.00	4	L. Chen	Governance and Design of Digital Platforms: A Review and Future Research Dire...	2022	Journal of Management
h 35	35.00	5	L. Chen	Platform Governance Design in Platform Ecosystems: Implications for Complem...	2022	Journal of Management
h 34	34.00	6	H. Lian	Leader Unethical Pro-Organizational Behavior and Employee Unethical Conduct:...	2022	Journal of Management
h 30	30.00	7	A. Luksyte	Perceived Overqualification and Collectivism Orientation: Implications for Work...	2022	Journal of Management
h 27	27.00	8	A.H. Anglin	Role Theory Perspectives: Past, Present, and Future Applications of Role Theori...	2022	Journal of Management
h 25	25.00	9	J. Li	CEO Awards and Financial Misconduct	2022	Journal of Management
h 19	19.00	10	M.P. Mount	CEOs' Regulatory Focus and Risk-Taking When Firms Perform Below and Above...	2022	Journal of Management
h 17	17.00	11	J.H. Hardy	Bias in Context: Small Biases in Hiring Evaluations Have Big Consequences	2022	Journal of Management
h 16	16.00	12	M.T. Bolinger	Experiments in Strategy Research: A Critical Review and Future Research Oppor...	2022	Journal of Management
h 16	16.00	13	L.M. Cortina	The Embodiment of Insult: A Theory of Biobehavioral Response to Workplace In...	2022	Journal of Management
h 16	16.00	14	O.P. Kauppila	Serving to Help and Helping to Serve: Using Servant Leadership to Influence Be...	2022	Journal of Management
h 16	16.00	15	R.S. Kudesia	Doing More With Less: Interactive Effects of Cognitive Resources and Mindfulne...	2022	Journal of Management
14	14.00	16	T. Xiao	A Knowledge Recombination Perspective of Innovation: Review and New Resear...	2022	Journal of Management
14	14.00	17	Y. Zheng	Ethical Leadership and Ethical Voice: The Mediating Mechanisms of Value Intern...	2022	Journal of Management
14	14.00	18	S.J.D. Schillebeeckx	To Buy Green or Not to Buy Green: Do Structural Dependencies Block Ecological...	2022	Journal of Management
14	14.00	19	B.L. Connelly	Searching for a Sign: CEO Successor Selection in the Wake of Corporate Miscon...	2022	Journal of Management
13	13.00	20	H. Wang	Social Performance Feedback and Firm Communication Strategy	2022	Journal of Management

Searching for multiple journals

All five data sources allow searching for multiple journals. Simply include OR between the search terms. When searching for journals by name the problems we experienced for Crossref and Scopus in uniquely identifying journals are obviously multiplied.

Conclusion

Journal searches within other data sources than Google Scholar can be a good option if, rather than prioritising comprehensive coverage of citations, you are more interested in getting both a quick and clean result for your searches. Crossref, OpenAlex, PubMed, Scopus and the Web of Science all give excellent results if you are willing to use ISSN searches. If you need only a limited number of results all these data sources are useful.

However, if you need more than 200 results Crossref, OpenAlex and PubMed have the edge as they all return 1,000 results. If you need full abstracts and as many results as possible both PubMed and OpenAlex are good options. If you need citation levels and as many results as possible, Crossref and OpenAlex are the best option.

Overall, OpenAlex emerges as the best option overall as it returns 1,000 results, allows searching for all journals, not just bio-medical journals as PubMed does, provides abstracts for most papers and provides the most comprehensive citation count of all data sources except Google Scholar.

If you prefer searching for journals by name rather than ISSN, note that this is not possible in OpenAlex and a bit more complicated than an ISSN search in Scopus and especially in Crossref. However, it does provide good results in PubMed and the Web of Science, though the first data source is limited to bio-medical research and the latter data source is limited by providing only 200 results.

In sum

In this chapter we explained how to conduct effective journal searches. Most Publish or Perish users mainly use Google Scholar for their searches and journal disambiguation in Google Scholar is not always straightforward. Hence, in this chapter we focused mainly on this data source.

However, in the last section of this chapter I also discussed journal searches in the five other data sources that allow journal searches (Crossref, OpenAlex, PubMed, Scopus, and the Web of Science). We found that different data sources have different strengths, but that overall OpenAlex is probably the best alternative to Google Scholar.

In the next chapter, we will discuss the two final search options in Publish or Perish: topic and affiliation searches.

Chapter 9: Topic and affiliation searches

This chapter explains how to conduct effective topic and affiliation searches. Most Publish or Perish users mainly use Google Scholar for their searches. Unfortunately, topic and affiliation searches in Google Scholar are not always straightforward. Hence, the instructions in this chapter will focus mainly on this data source. However, in the last two sections of this chapter, I will also discuss topic and affiliation searches in the other data sources.

The basics

The Publish or Perish **Keywords** and **Title words** search fields will allow you to perform a topic or affiliation search in Google Scholar and analyse its results. These search fields can be used for instance to:

- Find particular articles

- Find particular academics

- Conduct advanced author searches

- Conduct advanced journal searches

- Conduct an institutional search

- Conduct a literature review

- Find the best journal for your paper

- Do bibliometric research.

In the remainder of this chapter, we will discuss each of these options. First, however, we will explain the basics of a topic search.

How to do a topic search?

To do a topic search simply enter any words that should or should not appear in the returned papers. Here are some key tips.

- You can a single word or multiple words separated by AND or OR.
  - o AND is not strictly necessary. Google Scholar uses an implicit AND if you enter multiple words. However, you may find it helpful to keep track of the logic of your searches.

- You can *exclude* words by prefacing them with NOT (or use the – symbol).

- You can use "quotes" around the words to ensure that they will appear in that sequence.
  - o If you include the search terms *without* quotes, it will provide many matches as the search will match words in any order.

- If you use the **Keywords field**, terms will appear *anywhere* in the publication. If you use the **Title words** field, they will appear in the *title* of the publication (and most likely in other parts of the publication too).

Below is an example of a search where I used a combination of the above techniques. One of my research areas over the years has been in expatriation, so I am interested in publications on the topic. As Google Scholar does not recognise wildcards, I cannot use expatriat* to cover expatriate, expatriates, and expatriation. I therefore need to include all three words separated by OR.

In recent years, my PhD students have focused on expatriation in the Chinese context. So, I added "China OR Chinese" in the title words field. Many studies in this field of research have dealt with expatriate adjustment and expatriate failure which are areas I am less interested in. Hence, I have excluded them respectively in the title and key-words field. I used the keywords field – which searches in the entire full-text document - for expatriate failure as there are likely to be few articles with these words in the title anyway.

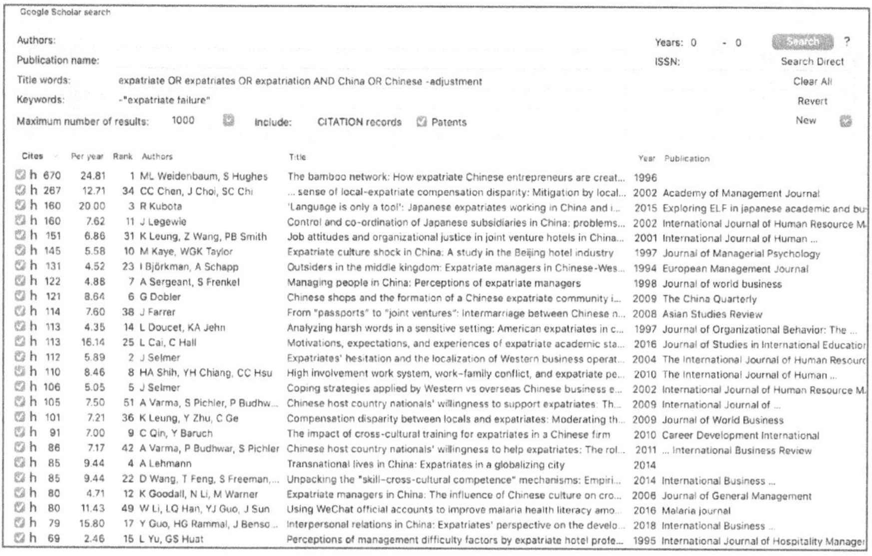

Authors:				Years: 0 - 0	Search ?
Publication name:				ISSN:	Search Direct
Title words:	expatriate OR expatriates OR expatriation AND China OR Chinese -adjustment				Clear All
Keywords:	-"expatriate failure"				Revert
Maximum number of results:	1000	Include:	CITATION records ☑ Patents		New ☑

Cites	Per year	Rank	Authors	Title	Year	Publication
h 670	24.81	1	ML Weidenbaum, S Hughes	The bamboo network: How expatriate Chinese entrepreneurs are creat...	1996	
h 267	12.71	34	CC Chen, J Choi, SC Chi	... sense of local-expatriate compensation disparity: Mitigation by local...	2002	Academy of Management Journal
h 160	20.00	3	R Kubota	'Language is only a tool': Japanese expatriates working in China and i...	2015	Exploring ELF in japanese academic and bu...
h 160	7.62	11	J Legewie	Control and co-ordination of Japanese subsidiaries in China: problems...	2002	International Journal of Human Resource M...
h 151	6.86	31	K Leung, Z Wang, PB Smith	Job attitudes and organizational justice in joint venture hotels in China...	2001	International Journal of Human ...
h 145	5.58	10	M Kaye, WGK Taylor	Expatriate culture shock in China: A study in the Beijing hotel industry	1997	Journal of Managerial Psychology
h 131	4.52	23	I Björkman, A Schapp	Outsiders in the middle kingdom: Expatriate managers in Chinese-Wes...	1994	European Management Journal
h 122	4.88	7	A Sergeant, S Frenkel	Managing people in China: Perceptions of expatriate managers	1998	Journal of world business
h 121	8.64	6	G Dobler	Chinese shops and the formation of a Chinese expatriate community i...	2009	The China Quarterly
h 114	7.60	38	J Farrer	From "passports" to "joint ventures": Intermarriage between Chinese n...	2008	Asian Studies Review
h 113	4.35	14	L Doucet, KA Jehn	Analyzing harsh words in a sensitive setting: American expatriates in c...	1997	Journal of Organizational Behavior: The ...
h 113	16.14	25	L Cai, C Hall	Motivations, expectations, and experiences of expatriate academic sta...	2016	Journal of Studies in International Education
h 112	5.89	2	J Selmer	Expatriates' hesitation and the localization of Western business operat...	2004	The International Journal of Human Resourc...
h 110	8.46	8	HA Shih, YH Chiang, CC Hsu	High involvement work system, work–family conflict, and expatriate pe...	2010	The International Journal of Human ...
h 106	5.05	5	J Selmer	Coping strategies applied by Western vs overseas Chinese business e...	2002	International Journal of Human Resource M...
h 105	7.50	51	A Varma, S Pichler, P Budhw...	Chinese host country nationals' willingness to support expatriates: Th...	2009	International Journal of ...
h 101	7.21	36	K Leung, Y Zhu, C Ge	Compensation disparity between locals and expatriates: Moderating th...	2009	Journal of World Business
h 91	7.00	9	C Qin, Y Baruch	The impact of cross-cultural training for expatriates in a Chinese firm	2010	Career Development International
h 86	7.17	42	A Varma, P Budhwar, S Pichler	Chinese host country nationals' willingness to help expatriates: The rol...	2011	... International Business Review
h 85	9.44	4	A Lehmann	Transnational lives in China: Expatriates in a globalizing city	2014	
h 85	9.44	22	D Wang, T Feng, S Freeman,...	Unpacking the "skill–cross-cultural competence" mechanisms: Empiri...	2014	International Business ...
h 80	4.71	12	K Goodall, N Li, M Warner	Expatriate managers in China: The influence of Chinese culture on cro...	2006	Journal of General Management
h 80	11.43	49	W Li, LQ Han, YJ Guo, J Sun	Using WeChat official accounts to improve malaria health literacy amo...	2016	Malaria journal
h 79	15.80	17	Y Guo, HG Rammal, J Benso ..	Interpersonal relations in China: Expatriates' perspective on the develo...	2018	International Business ..
h 69	2.46	15	L Yu, GS Huat	Perceptions of management difficulty factors by expatriate hotel profe...	1995	International Journal of Hospitality Managel

In topic searches we are often more interested in the *relevance* of the results than the number of citations. Hence, you may wish to sort the results by rank rather than by citations. However, in the example I used above the first-ranked result in terms of citations also has the highest relevance ranking and is indeed very relevant to my search. It is a book, which would not be found in other data sources. This clearly illustrates the advantage of using Google Scholar, despite its slow searches and data quality issues.

We can now review all 300+ individual articles for relevance. There are, however, a lot more things we can conclude from this search. First, judging from the publication years in the citation metrics pane it appears the topic has only been of academic interest since 1991. This probably reflects the increasing role of China in the world economy in the past decade. Indeed, a search without the two China terms includes much older literature.

Second, we can also see that most of the publications on expatriation were published in Business & Management journals. This reflects the fact that expatriates are normally defined as having been assigned to a foreign position by their employer. If we interpreted expatriation as part of the wider concept of global mobility, as the research field of expatriation is increasingly doing, we would draw in a much wider set of publications.

When sorting publications on the number of citations per year (see screenshot below), more recent papers that generated a high level of interest rise to the top of the list. This allows for a third conclusion, namely that there is a clear host country effect in terms of academics studying the topic. Judging by their names, most academics studying expatriates in China or Chinese expatriates in other countries appear to originate from those countries.

Google Scholar search

Authors: | Years: 0 - 0 | Search | ?
Publication name: | ISSN: | Search Direct
Title words: expatriate OR expatriates OR expatriation AND China OR Chinese -adjustment | Clear All
Keywords: -"expatriate failure" | Revert
Maximum number of results: 1000 | Include: CITATION records ☑ Patents | New

	Cites	Pe...	Rank	Authors	Title	Year
☑	25	25.00	55	L Fu, P Charoensukmongkol	Effect of cultural intelligence on burnout of Chinese expatriates in Thailand: The med...	2023
☑ h	670	24.81	1	ML Weidenbaum, S Hughes	The bamboo network: How expatriate Chinese entrepreneurs are creating a new eco...	1996
☑ h	160	20.00	3	R Kubota	'Language is only a tool': Japanese expatriates working in China and implications for...	2015
☑	39	19.50	24	P Charoensukmongkol	How Chinese expatriates' cultural intelligence promotes supervisor-subordinate Gua...	2021
☑	17	17.00	13	S Kozhakhmet, A Nurgabdes...	Knowledge acquisition of Chinese expatriates: managing Chinese MNEs in Kazakhstan	2022
☑ h	113	16.14	25	L Cai, C Hall	Motivations, expectations, and experiences of expatriate academic staff on an intern...	2016
☑ h	79	15.80	17	Y Guo, HG Rammal, J Benso...	Interpersonal relations in China: Expatriates' perspective on the development and us...	2018
☑ h	47	15.67	21	X Guang, P Charoensukmon...	The effects of cultural intelligence on leadership performance among Chinese expatr...	2020
☑	15	15.00	69	MT Jannesari, SE Sullivan	Leaving on a jet plane? The effect of challenge–hindrance stressors, emotional resilie...	2022
☑ h	267	12.71	34	CC Chen, J Choi, SC Chi	... sense of local-expatriate compensation disparity: Mitigation by local referents, ide...	2002
☑ h	80	11.43	49	W Li, LQ Han, YJ Guo, J Sun	Using WeChat official accounts to improve malaria health literacy among Chinese ex...	2016
☑	33	11.00	29	Y Liu, CC Self	Laowai as a discourse of Othering: unnoticed stereotyping of American expatriates in...	2020
☑ h	53	10.60	39	IYS Chan, M Leung, Q Liang	The roles of motivation and coping behaviours in managing stress: Qualitative intervi...	2018
☑ h	60	10.00	16	H Rui, M Zhang, A Shipman	Chinese expatriate management in emerging markets: A competitive advantage pers...	2017
☑	10	10.00	53	T Bunnell, A Poole	(Re) Considering "precarious privilege" within international schooling: expatriate teac...	2022
☑ h	58	9.67	33	D Wang, D Fan, S Freeman,...	Exploring cross-cultural skills for expatriate managers from Chinese multinationals: C...	2017

This is only natural as data collection with a particular population is facilitated by local connections. However, in the early years the topic was investigated mainly by Western researchers, reflection the strong dominance of Western academics at that time (see screenshot below).

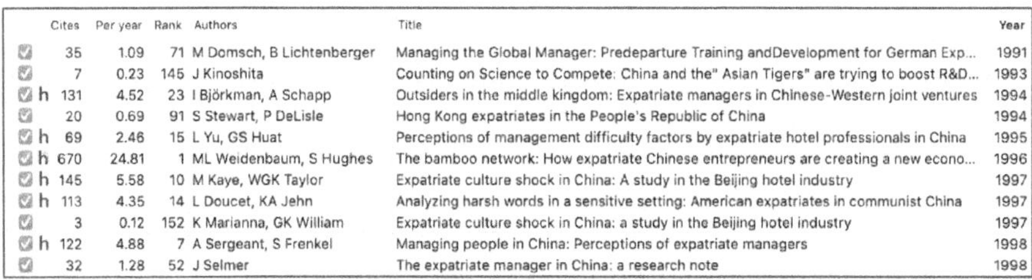

	Cites	Per year	Rank	Authors	Title	Year
☑	35	1.09	71	M Domsch, B Lichtenberger	Managing the Global Manager: Predeparture Training andDevelopment for German Exp...	1991
☑	7	0.23	145	J Kinoshita	Counting on Science to Compete: China and the" Asian Tigers" are trying to boost R&D...	1993
☑ h	131	4.52	23	I Björkman, A Schapp	Outsiders in the middle kingdom: Expatriate managers in Chinese-Western joint ventures	1994
☑	20	0.69	91	S Stewart, P DeLisle	Hong Kong expatriates in the People's Republic of China	1994
☑ h	69	2.46	15	L Yu, GS Huat	Perceptions of management difficulty factors by expatriate hotel professionals in China	1995
☑ h	670	24.81	1	ML Weidenbaum, S Hughes	The bamboo network: How expatriate Chinese entrepreneurs are creating a new econo...	1996
☑ h	145	5.58	10	M Kaye, WGK Taylor	Expatriate culture shock in China: A study in the Beijing hotel industry	1997
☑ h	113	4.35	14	L Doucet, KA Jehn	Analyzing harsh words in a sensitive setting: American expatriates in communist China	1997
☑	3	0.12	152	K Marianna, GK William	Expatriate culture shock in China: a study in the Beijing hotel industry	1997
☑ h	122	4.88	7	A Sergeant, S Frenkel	Managing people in China: Perceptions of expatriate managers	1998
☑	32	1.28	52	J Selmer	The expatriate manager in China: a research note	1998

Finally, remember that after seeing the initial results you can adapt a search any way you like. I suggest that before adapting a search you duplicate it so that the original results is retained for comparison.

You may feel that 300+ results is too much to review one by one. So, if, for instance, you wanted to focus on the role of language in expatriation in a Chinese context adding the word language to the title words field would provide you with a much smaller set of results (see screenshot below).

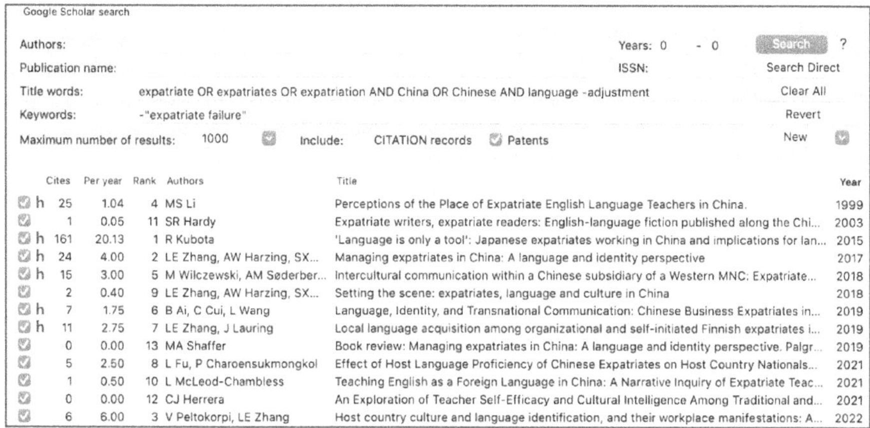

Google Scholar search

| Authors: | | | | | Years: 0 | - 0 | Search | ? |

| Publication name: | | | | | ISSN: | | Search Direct |

Title words: expatriate OR expatriates OR expatriation AND China OR Chinese AND language -adjustment — Clear All

Keywords: -"expatriate failure" — Revert

Maximum number of results: 1000 — Include: CITATION records — Patents — New

	Cites	Per year	Rank	Authors	Title	Year
h	25	1.04	4	MS Li	Perceptions of the Place of Expatriate English Language Teachers in China.	1999
	1	0.05	11	SR Hardy	Expatriate writers, expatriate readers: English-language fiction published along the Chi...	2003
h	161	20.13	1	R Kubota	'Language is only a tool': Japanese expatriates working in China and implications for lan...	2015
h	24	4.00	2	LE Zhang, AW Harzing, SX...	Managing expatriates in China: A language and identity perspective	2017
h	15	3.00	5	M Wilczewski, AM Søderber...	Intercultural communication within a Chinese subsidiary of a Western MNC: Expatriate...	2018
	2	0.40	9	LE Zhang, AW Harzing, SX...	Setting the scene: expatriates, language and culture in China	2018
h	7	1.75	6	B Ai, C Cui, L Wang	Language, Identity, and Transnational Communication: Chinese Business Expatriates in...	2019
h	11	2.75	7	LE Zhang, J Lauring	Local language acquisition among organizational and self-initiated Finnish expatriates i...	2019
	0	0.00	13	MA Shaffer	Book review: Managing expatriates in China: A language and identity perspective. Palgr...	2019
	5	2.50	8	L Fu, P Charoensukmongkol	Effect of Host Language Proficiency of Chinese Expatriates on Host Country Nationals...	2021
	1	0.50	10	L McLeod-Chambless	Teaching English as a Foreign Language in China: A Narrative Inquiry of Expatriate Teac...	2021
	0	0.00	12	CJ Herrera	An Exploration of Teacher Self-Efficacy and Cultural Intelligence Among Traditional and...	2021
	6	6.00	3	V Peltokorpi, LE Zhang	Host country culture and language identification, and their workplace manifestations: A...	2022

Beyond two early results in the area of Education and Literature, the topic doesn't seem to have generated any interest until the mid-2010s. Four of the eleven publications since 2015 include LE Zhang (Ling Eleanor Zhang) as one of the authors. A fifth publication is a book review of her book on *Managing Expatriates in China: a Language and Identity Perspective*. Ling was one of my PhD students and language is a strong interest of hers. Hence, topic searches can also allow you to find key authors in a field.

Finding a specific paper

The Publish or Perish **Title words** search is also very effective if you want to find a specific article. Does this scenario sound familiar? In a conversation you had at a conference on evaluating academic publication records, someone mentioned a recent article that you should really read. Unfortunately, you forgot both the author and the journal the paper was published in.

All you remember is some words in the title: Google Scholar and h-index. Of course, you could search for the article in Google, but this is likely to provide you with many false hits. Using a Google Scholar search in Publish or Perish can, within seconds, provide you with a list of the likely candidates. The screenshot shows the twenty most highly cited results for this search which resulted in some 50 hits.

Google Scholar search

Authors:					Years: 0 - 0	Search ?
Publication name:					ISSN:	Search Direct
Title words:	"Google Scholar" h-index					Clear All
Keywords:						Revert
Maximum number of results: 200		Include: CITATION records ☑ Patents				New

Cites	Per year	Rank	Authors	Title	Year	Publication
☑ h 1,063	70.87	1	J Bar-Ilan	Which h-index?—A comparison of WoS, Scopus and Google Scholar	2008	Scientometrics
☑ h 438	31.29	3	AW Harzing, R Van der Wal	A Google Scholar h-index for journals: An alternative metric to measure journal impact in econo...	2009	Journal of the American Society ...
☑ h 170	15.45	4	SL De Groote, R Raszewski	Coverage of Google Scholar, Scopus, and Web of Science: A case study of the h-index in nursi...	2012	Nursing outlook
☑ h 157	10.47	2	P Jacso'	The pros and cons of computing the h-index using Google Scholar	2008	Online information review
☑ h 153	10.20	7	P Jacsó	Testing the calculation of a realistic h-index in Google Scholar, Scopus, and Web of Science for...	2008	Library trends
☑ h 124	10.33	6	DR Hodge, JR Lacasse	Ranking disciplinary journals with the Google Scholar h-index: A new tool for constructing case...	2011	Journal of Social Work Education
☑ h 95	6.79	11	P Jacsó	Calculating the h-index and other bibliometric and scientometric indicators from Google Schola...	2009	Online information review
☑ h 88	8.80	8	B Minasny, AE Hartemink, A M...	Citations and the h index of soil researchers and journals in the Web of Science, Scopus, and G...	2013	PeerJ
☑ h 60	4.00	15	AW Harzing, R van der Wal	A Google Scholar H-Index for journals: A better metric to measure journal impact in economics...	2008	Proceedings of the Academy of ...
☑ h 50	4.55	16	P Jacsó	Using Google Scholar for journal impact factors and the h-index in nationwide publishing asses...	2012	Online information review
☑ h 45	6.43	13	JA Jacobs	Journal rankings in sociology: Using the H Index with Google Scholar	2016	The American Sociologist
☑ h 44	4.40	5	A Cabezas-Clavijo, E Delgado-...	Google Scholar and the h-index in biomedicine: the popularization of bibliometric assessment	2013	Medicina Intensiva (English ...
☑ h 28	2.33	17	A Thor, L Bornmann	The calculation of the single publication h index and related performance measures: A web app...	2011	Online Information Review
☑ h 28	1.87	19	AW Harzing, R van der Wal	Comparing the Google Scholar h-index with the ISI journal impact factor	2008	Res Int Manag Prod Serv Acad
☑ h 27	2.70	18	R Repiso, ED López-Cózar	H Index Communication Journals according to Google Scholar Metrics (2008-2012)	2013	arXiv preprint arXiv:1310.7378
☑ h 22	4.40	9	JA Teixeira da Silva	The Google Scholar h-index: useful but burdensome metric	2018	Scientometrics
☑ h 18	3.60	20	MT Kalcioglu, Y Ileri, OI Ozda...	... productivity of the top 100 worldwide physicians in the field of otorhinolaryngology and head...	2018	The Journal of ...
☑ 14	4.67	12	A Furnham	What I have learned from my Google Scholar and H index	2020	Scientometrics
☑ 14	2.80	22	W Darmalaksana, WDI Aziz, S...	Analisis Ranking Produktivitas Publikasi Ilmiah Berbasis h-index Google Scholar	2018	... : Pusat Penelitian dan ...
☑ 13	6.50	14	JA Teixeira da Silva	The i100-index, i1000-index and i10,000-index: expansion and fortification of the Google Schol...	2021	Scientometrics

Although it was the most-cited article by Bar-Ilan you were interested in, you now also have a list of related articles that might also be of interest to you. Moreover, by sorting the results by year, you can also review recently published papers about the topic. The highly cited, and often early papers, on the topic focused on comparisons between data sources and a general application of the h-index. More recent papers tended to look at increasingly specialised applications of the h-index as well as potential for manipulation.

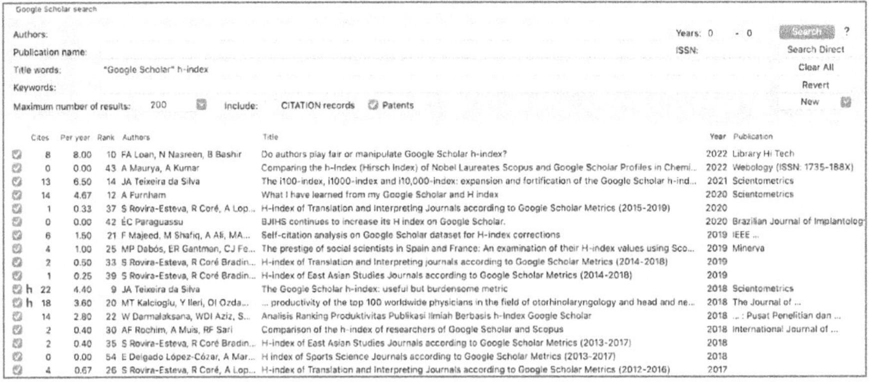

Google Scholar search

Authors:					Years: 0 - 0	Search ?
Publication name:					ISSN:	Search Direct
Title words:	"Google Scholar" h-index					Clear All
Keywords:						Revert
Maximum number of results: 200		Include: CITATION records ☑ Patents				New

Cites	Per year	Rank	Authors	Title	Year	Publication
☑ 8	8.00	10	FA Loan, N Nasreen, B Bashir	Do authors play fair or manipulate Google Scholar h-index?	2022	Library Hi Tech
☑ 0	0.00	43	A Maurya, A Kumar	Comparing the h-Index (Hirsch Index) of Nobel Laureates Scopus and Google Scholar Profiles in Chemi...	2022	Webology (ISSN: 1735-188X)
☑ 13	6.50	14	JA Teixeira da Silva	The i100-index, i1000-index and i10,000-index: expansion and fortification of the Google Scholar h-ind...	2021	Scientometrics
☑ 14	4.67	12	A Furnham	What I have learned from my Google Scholar and H index	2020	Scientometrics
☑ 1	0.33	37	S Rovira-Esteva, R Coré, A Lop...	H-Index of Translation and Interpreting Journals according to Google Scholar Metrics (2015-2019)	2020	
☑ 0	0.00	42	ÉC Paraguassu	BJIHS continues to increase its H index on Google Scholar.	2020	Brazilian Journal of Implantolog
☑ 6	1.50	21	F Majeed, M Shafiq, A Ali, MA...	Self-citation analysis on Google Scholar dataset for H-index corrections	2019	IEEE ...
☑ 4	1.00	25	MP Dabós, ER Gantman, CJ Fe...	The prestige of social scientists in Spain and France: An examination of their H-index values using Sco...	2019	Minerva
☑ 2	0.50	33	S Rovira-Esteva, R Coré Bradin...	H-index of Translation and Interpreting journals according to Google Scholar Metrics (2014-2018)	2019	
☑ 1	0.25	39	S Rovira-Esteva, R Coré Bradin...	H-index of East Asian Studies Journals according to Google Scholar Metrics (2014-2018)	2019	
☑ h 22	4.40	9	JA Teixeira da Silva	The Google Scholar h-index: useful but burdensome metric	2018	Scientometrics
☑ h 18	3.60	20	MT Kalcioglu, Y Ileri, OI Ozda...	... productivity of the top 100 worldwide physicians in the field of otorhinolaryngology and head and ne...	2018	The Journal of ...
☑ 14	2.80	22	W Darmalaksana, WDI Aziz, S...	Analisis Ranking Produktivitas Publikasi Ilmiah Berbasis h-index Google Scholar	2018	... : Pusat Penelitian dan ...
☑ 2	0.40	30	AF Rochim, A Muis, RF Sari	Comparison of the h-index of researchers of Google Scholar and Scopus	2018	International Journal of ...
☑ 2	0.40	35	S Rovira-Esteva, R Coré Bradin...	H-index of East Asian Studies Journals according to Google Scholar Metrics (2013-2017)	2018	
☑ 0	0.00	54	E Delgado López-Cózar, A Mar...	H index of Sports Science Journals according to Google Scholar Metrics (2013-2017)	2018	
☑ 4	0.67	26	S Rovira-Esteva, R Coré, A Lop...	H-index of Translation and Interpreting Journals according to Google Scholar Metrics (2012-2016)	2017	

Finding a specific academic

A Publish or Perish **Keywords** search can also be used to find specific academics. Does this scenario sound familiar? You have attended your field's major academic conference and had a good conversation with someone you really want to follow up with. However, you did not get their business card and forgot their name.

The only two things that you *can* remember is that they were working at the University of Melbourne and had published an article in the *Academy of Management of Learning & Education*, which is the journal you were talking about. You could go to the University of Melbourne website and review their staff list, but that might be a tedious process. You could also go through the full table of contents of the *Academy of Management Learning & Education* over the years hoping you would remember their name if you saw it.

However, what would be a much simpler option is to conduct the search below, entering the journal in the **Publication name** field and the University in the **Keywords** field. This would allow you to refresh your memory in seconds and realise that you had been talking to me ☺. This search strategy will not always lead to such a quick result, but it is worth a try.

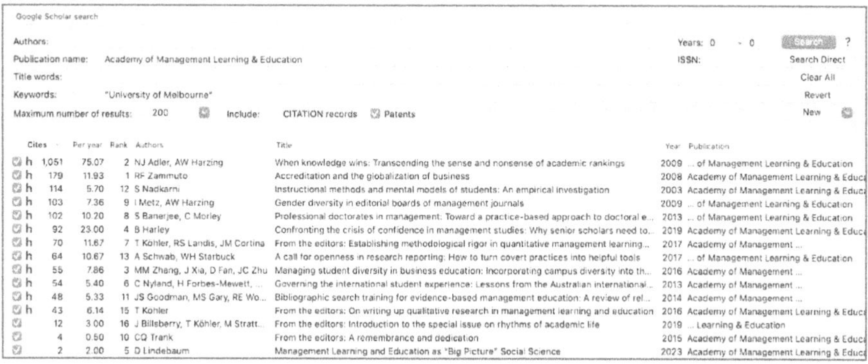

Google Scholar search

		Years: 0	- 0	Search	?
Authors:					
Publication name:	Academy of Management Learning & Education	ISSN:		Search Direct	
Title words:				Clear All	
Keywords:	"University of Melbourne"			Revert	
Maximum number of results:	200	Include: CITATION records ☑ Patents		New	

	Cites	Per year	Rank	Authors	Title	Year	Publication
☑ h	1,051	75.07	2	NJ Adler, AW Harzing	When knowledge wins: Transcending the sense and nonsense of academic rankings	2009	... of Management Learning & Education
☑ h	179	11.93	1	RF Zammuto	Accreditation and the globalization of business	2008	Academy of Management Learning & Educa
☑ h	114	5.70	12	S Nadkarni	Instructional methods and mental models of students: An empirical investigation	2003	Academy of Management Learning & Educa
☑ h	103	7.36	9	I Metz, AW Harzing	Gender diversity in editorial boards of management journals	2009	... of Management Learning & Education
☑ h	102	10.20	8	S Banerjee, C Morley	Professional doctorates in management: Toward a practice-based approach to doctoral e...	2013	... of Management Learning & Education
☑ h	92	23.00	4	B Harley	Confronting the crisis of confidence in management studies: Why senior scholars need to...	2019	Academy of Management Learning & Educa
☑ h	70	11.67	7	T Köhler, RS Landis, JM Cortina	From the editors: Establishing methodological rigor in quantitative management learning...	2017	Academy of Management ...
☑ h	64	10.67	13	A Schwab, WH Starbuck	A call for openness in research reporting: How to turn covert practices into helpful tools	2017	... of Management Learning & Education
☑ h	55	7.86	3	MM Zhang, J Xia, D Fan, JC Zhu	Managing student diversity in business education: Incorporating campus diversity into th...	2016	Academy of Management ...
☑ h	54	5.40	6	C Nyland, H Forbes-Mewett, ...	Governing the international student experience: Lessons from the Australian international...	2013	Academy of Management ...
☑ h	48	5.33	11	JS Goodman, MS Gary, RE Wo...	Bibliographic search training for evidence-based management education: A review of rel...	2014	Academy of Management ...
☑ h	43	6.14	15	T Kohler	From the editors: On writing up qualitative research in management learning and education	2016	Academy of Management Learning & Educa
☑	12	3.00	16	J Billsberry, T Köhler, M Stratt...	From the editors: Introduction to the special issue on rhythms of academic life	2019	... Learning & Education
☑	4	0.50	10	CQ Trank	From the editors: A remembrance and dedication	2015	Academy of Management Learning & Educa
☑	2	2.00	5	D Lindebaum	Management Learning and Education as "Big Picture" Social Science	2023	Academy of Management Learning & Educa

Please note that this search is not flawless. Google Scholar does not have an "affiliation" field as such. Hence you need to use the Keywords field and the name of the university will be matched *anywhere* in the document. The results of our search contain fifteen articles. Of these only eight match our intention of finding an author affiliated by the University of Melbourne: two by me, three by Tine Köhler, and one each by Ray Zammuto, Robert Wood, and Bill Harley. The seven other articles refer to the University of Melbourne somewhere in their paper, often in the references, but also as a location of research, as the PhD institution of one of the authors or in the acknowledgments.

Advanced author searches

The Publish or Perish **Title words** and **Keywords** search fields can also be used for advanced author searches. In the search we showed above on the Google Scholar h-index, you noticed that there were two author names (Harzing and Jacsó) that occurred several times. You therefore wonder whether these authors have published additional work on Google Scholar.

To find out run an advanced author search by combining an author name search with the words Google Scholar in the **Title Words** field. The result of this search is below, sorted by citations per year. It shows that both authors have a considerable oeuvre on the topic, 14 publications for Peter Jacsó and 10 for me.

Cites	Per year	Rank	Authors	Title	Year	Publication
h 1,377	196.71	7	AW Harzing, S Alakangas	Google Scholar, Scopus and the Web of Science: a longitudinal and cross-discipl...	2016	Scientometrics
h 902	60.13	6	AWK Harzing, R Van der Wal	Google Scholar as a new source for citation analysis	2008	Ethics in science and environmental ...
h 744	41.33	10	P Jacso	As we may search—comparison of major features of the Web of Science, Scopus...	2005	Current science
h 601	33.39	4	P Jacsó	Google Scholar: the pros and the cons	2005	Online information review
h 438	31.29	12	AW Harzing, R Van der Wal	A Google Scholar h-index for journals: An alternative metric to measure journal i...	2009	Journal of the American Society ...
h 296	19.73	5	P Jacsó	Google scholar revisited	2008	Online information review
h 240	24.00	2	AW Harzing	A preliminary test of Google Scholar as a source for citation data: a longitudinal s...	2013	Scientometrics
h 197	15.15	1	P Jacsó	Metadata mega mess in Google Scholar	2010	Online Information Review
h 185	30.83	11	A Martín-Martín, E Orduña-Malea, AW Harzing...	Can we use Google Scholar to identify highly-cited documents?	2017	Journal of ...
h 158	17.56	8	AW Harzing	A longitudinal study of Google Scholar coverage between 2012 and 2013	2014	Scientometrics
h 157	10.47	13	P Jacso'	The pros and cons of computing the h-index using Google Scholar	2008	Online information review
h 153	10.20	16	P Jacsó	Testing the calculation of a realistic h-index in Google Scholar, Scopus, and Web...	2008	Library trends
h 152	38.00	14	AW Harzing	Two new kids on the block: How do Crossref and Dimensions compare with Goo...	2019	Scientometrics
h 95	6.79	17	P Jacsó	Calculating the h-index and other bibliometric and scientometric indicators from...	2009	Online information review
h 93	6.20	15	AW Harzing	Google Scholar-a new data source for citation analysis	2008	University of Melbourne
h 65	5.91	19	P Jacsó	Google Scholar Metrics for Publications: The software and content features of a...	2012	Online information review
h 61	5.08	9	P Jacsó	Google Scholar duped and deduped--the aura of "robometrics"	2011	Online Information Review
h 60	4.00	3	AW Harzing, R van der Wal	A Google Scholar H-Index for journals: A better metric to measure journal impact...	2008	Proceedings of the Academy of ...
h 55	5.00	18	P Jacsó	Google Scholar author citation tracker: is it too little, too late?	2012	Online Information Review
h 50	4.55	21	P Jacsó	Using Google Scholar for journal impact factors and the h-index in nationwide pu...	2012	Online information review
h 42	2.33	20	P Jacso	Comparison and analysis of the citedness scores in Web of Science and Google...	2005	International Conference on Asian Dig
h 32	2.46	23	P Jacsó	... and quality of research through rating and ranking of researchers based on pe...	2010	Online information review
h 28	1.75	25	AW Harzing	Comparing the Google Scholar h-index with the ISI Journal Impact Factor http://...	2007	

You can also do this with the search terms in the **Keywords** search field. However, as this will match the search terms *anywhere* in the document you will draw in articles in which Google Scholar is only mentioned casually or is included in one of the references. This is reflected in the fact that this search results in nearly 150 articles. Hence, in most cases starting out with a title words search is advisable.

Ideally, we would want these types of searches to be conducted with the search term being matched in either the title or abstract, but this is unfortunately not possible in Google Scholar. The only choice is between a search in the title and a search in the *entire* publication.

Advanced journal searches

The Publish or Perish **Title words** and **Keywords** search fields are also very useful if you want to know what a particular journal or set of journals has published about a particular topic. For instance, if you want to know what *Science* has published about HIV before 1990, an advanced journal search like the one below will give you the answer in less than a minute.

<table>
<tr><td colspan="5">Google Scholar search</td><td></td><td></td></tr>
<tr><td>Authors:</td><td></td><td></td><td colspan="2">Years: 0   - 1989</td><td>Search</td><td>?</td></tr>
<tr><td>Publication name:</td><td colspan="2">Science</td><td colspan="2">ISSN: 0036-8075</td><td colspan="2">Search Direct</td></tr>
<tr><td>Title words:</td><td colspan="2">HIV</td><td></td><td></td><td colspan="2">Clear All</td></tr>
<tr><td>Keywords:</td><td></td><td></td><td></td><td></td><td colspan="2">Revert</td></tr>
<tr><td colspan="2">Maximum number of results:</td><td>200</td><td>Include:</td><td colspan="2">CITATION records Patents</td><td>New</td></tr>
</table>

Cites	Per year	Rank	Authors	Title	Year	Publication
h 1,323	35.76	7	CM Walker, DJ Moody, DP S...	CD8+ Lymphocytes Can Control HIV Infection in Vitro by Suppressing Virus Replication	1986	Science
h 487	13.16	25	QJ Sattentau, AG Dalgleish,...	Epitopes of the CD4 antigen and HIV infection	1986	Science
h 450	12.16	26	JA Hoxie, JD Alpers, JL Rac...	Alterations in T4 (CD4) protein and mRNA synthesis in cells infected with HIV	1986	Science
h 1,036	28.78	8	TM Folks, J Justement, A Ki...	Cytokine-induced expression of HIV-1 in a chronically infected promonocyte cell line	1987	Science
h 491	13.64	16	AG Fisher, B Ensoli, L Ivanof...	The sor Gene of HIV-1 Is Required for Efficient Virus Transmission in Vitro	1987	Science
h 551	15.31	17	M Siekevitz, SF Josephs, M...	Activation of the HIV-1 LTR by T cell mitogens and the trans-activator protein of HTLV-I	1987	Science
h 664	18.44	18	DH Smith, RA Byrn, SA Mar...	Blocking of HIV-1 infectivity by a soluble, secreted form of the CD4 antigen	1987	Science
h 348	9.67	32	MW Vogt, KL Hartshorn, PA...	Ribavirin antagonizes the effect of azidothymidine on HIV replication	1987	Science
h 239	6.64	47	JW Gnann Jr, JB McCormic...	Synthetic peptide immunoassay distinguishes HIV type 1 and HIV type 2 infections	1987	Science
h 178	4.94	54	DM Knight, FA Flomerfelt, J...	Expression of the art/trs protein of HIV and study of its role in viral envelope synthesis	1987	Science
h 104	2.89	61	J Laurence, A Saunders, J K...	Characterization and clinical association of antibody inhibitory to HIV reverse transcript...	1987	Science
h 1,635	46.71	1	RW Price, B Brew, J Sidtis,...	The brain in AIDS: central nervous system HIV-1 infection and AIDS dementia complex	1988	Science
h 1,345	38.43	3	BD Preston, BJ Poiesz, LA L...	Fidelity of HIV-1 reverse transcriptase	1988	Science
h 1,431	40.89	4	JD Roberts, K Bebenek, TA...	The accuracy of reverse transcriptase from HIV-1	1988	Science
h 1,252	35.77	9	CY Ou, S Kwok, SW Mitchell...	DNA amplification for direct detection of HIV-1 in DNA of peripheral blood mononuclear...	1988	Science
h 617	17.63	12	K Strebel, T Klimkait, MA M...	A Novel Gene of HIV-1, vpu, and Its 16-Kilodalton Product	1988	Science
h 785	22.43	13	JW Curran, HW Jaffe, AM H...	Epidemiology of HIV infection and AIDS in the United States	1988	Science
h 892	25.49	14	C Cheng-Mayer, D Seto, M...	Biologic features of HIV-1 that correlate with virulence in the host	1988	Science
h 581	16.60	15	H Mitsuya, DJ Looney, S Ku...	Dextran Sulfate Suppression of Viruses in the HIV Family: Inhibition of Virion Binding to...	1988	Science
h 437	12.49	19	R Namikawa, H Kaneshima,...	Infection of the SCID-hu mouse by HIV-1	1988	Science
h 545	15.57	20	A Takeda, CU Tuazon, FA E...	Antibody-enhanced infection by HIV-1 via Fc receptor-mediated entry	1988	Science
h 519	14.83	21	N Ahmad, S Venkatesan	Nef Protein of HIV-1 Is a Transcriptional Repressor of HIV-1 LTR	1988	Science
h 573	16.37	22	Y Koyanagi, WA O'Brien, JQ...	Cytokines alter production of HIV-1 from primary mononuclear phagocytes	1988	Science
h 222	6.34	23	W Blattner, RC Gallo, HM Te...	HIV causes aids	1988	Science
h 443	12.66	24	TM Folks, SW Kessler, JM O...	Infection and replication of HIV-1 in purified progenitor cells of normal human bone mar...	1988	Science
h 191	5.46	33	P Duesberg	HIV is not the cause of AIDS	1988	Science

I used both the journal name and its ISSN as using the journal name only drew in publications in outlets that had Science in their title such as *Social Science & Medicine* and *Forensic Science International*. The search resulted in 69 papers. Sorting them by year clearly shows that research on the topic exploded in 1988, including two articles with completely opposite conclusions (#23 and #33).

Likewise, if you would like to know what the *Journal of International Business Studies* has published about emerging markets or emerging economies, you will find its 43 publications on the topic in just a few seconds. I ordered them by citations per year to focus on the most impactful articles first. However, sorting by years shows that interest in the topic has been stable over the years.

Google Scholar search

Authors: | Years: 0 - 0 | Search ?
Publication name: Journal of International Business Studies | ISSN: | Search Direct
Title words: "emerging markets" OR "emerging economies" | Clear All
Keywords: | Revert
Maximum number of results: 200 | Include: CITATION records ✓ Patents | New

	Cites	Pe…	Rank	Authors	Title	Year
h	3,868	257.87	1	MW Peng, DYL Wang, Y Jiang	An institution-based view of international business strategy: A focus on emerging economies	2008
h	2,158	113.58	2	T London, SL Hart	Reinventing strategies for emerging markets: beyond the transnational model	2004
h	752	68.36	4	C Wang, J Hong, M Kafouro…	Exploring the role of government involvement in outward FDI from emerging economies	2012
h	645	53.75	6	P Sharma	Country of origin effects in developed and emerging markets: Exploring the contrasting role…	2011
h	722	51.57	5	I Filatotchev, X Liu, T Buck,…	The export orientation and export performance of high-technology SMEs in emerging marke…	2009
h	572	40.86	7	D Miller, J Lee, S Chang, I L…	Filling the institutional void: The social behavior and performance of family vs non-family tec…	2009
h	76	38.00	22	AL Genin, J Tan, J Song	State governance and technological innovation in emerging economies: State-owned enterp…	2021
h	712	37.47	3	KE Meyer	Perspectives on multinational enterprises in emerging economies	2004
h	70	35.00	14	J Anand, G McDermott, R M…	Innovation in and from emerging economies: New insights and lessons for international busi…	2021
h	547	34.19	8	I Filatotchev, R Strange, J Pi…	FDI by firms from newly industrialised economies in emerging markets: corporate governanc…	2007
h	377	29.00	10	X Liu, J Lu, I Filatotchev, T…	Returnee entrepreneurs, knowledge spillovers and innovation in high-tech firms in emerging…	2010
h	331	27.58	11	GD Santangelo, KE Meyer	Extending the internationalization process model: Increases and decreases of MNE commit…	2011
h	325	27.08	12	GD Bruton, S Khavul, H Cha…	Microlending in emerging economies: Building a new line of inquiry from the ground up	2011
h	47	23.50	40	SG Lazzarini, LF Mesquita,…	Leviathan as an inventor: An extended agency model of state-owned versus private firm inv…	2021
h	460	20.91	9	KE Meyer, S Estrin	Brownfield entry in emerging markets	2001
h	117	19.50	25	H Kim, J Song	Filling institutional voids in emerging economies: The impact of capital market development…	2017
h	128	18.29	23	C Zhou, J Xie, Q Wang	Failure to complete cross-border M&As:"to" vs."from" emerging markets	2016
h	159	17.67	17	RA Corredoira, GA McDerm…	Adaptation, bridging and firm upgrading: How non-market institutions and MNCs facilitate k…	2014
h	158	17.56	16	M Zhao, SH Park, N Zhou	MNC strategy and social adaptation in emerging markets	2014
h	144	16.00	21	MA Sartor, PW Beamish	Offshoring innovation to emerging markets: Organizational control and informal institutional…	2014
h	47	15.67	29	MA Sartor, PW Beamish	Integration-oriented strategies, host market corruption and the likelihood of foreign subsidia…	2020
h	237	13.94	13	KZ Zhou, DK Tse, JJ Li	Organizational changes in emerging economies: Drivers and consequences	2006
	25	12.50	34	R Parente, M Melo, D Andre…	Public sector organizations and agricultural catch-up dilemma in emerging markets: The orc…	2021

Affiliation searches

The Publish or Perish **Keywords** search can be used for very generic affiliation searches. GS does not have a bibliographic field for affiliation. This means that affiliation searches are often not very accurate as GS will match the name of the university *anywhere* in the document (e.g., acknowledgements, main body, and references).

Moreover, GS appears to be unable to parse affiliations on most articles in Elsevier journals. I therefore do not recommend Google Scholar for systematic affiliation searches. The only exception would be very generic searches, such as establishing whether a university generates any academic papers at all. This might be quite useful when evaluating potential international collaborations.

JIBS articles at the University of Melbourne

In spite of these limitations, Google Scholar does seem to have *some* use in finding out whether there are any academics in an institution working on a specific topic or publishing in a specific journal. This could be useful for instance for PhD students looking for a supervisor or for academics looking for an institution to visit on their sabbatical. The screenshot below shows an example of such a search focusing on articles published in the *Journal of International Business Studies* at the University of Melbourne, my previous employer.

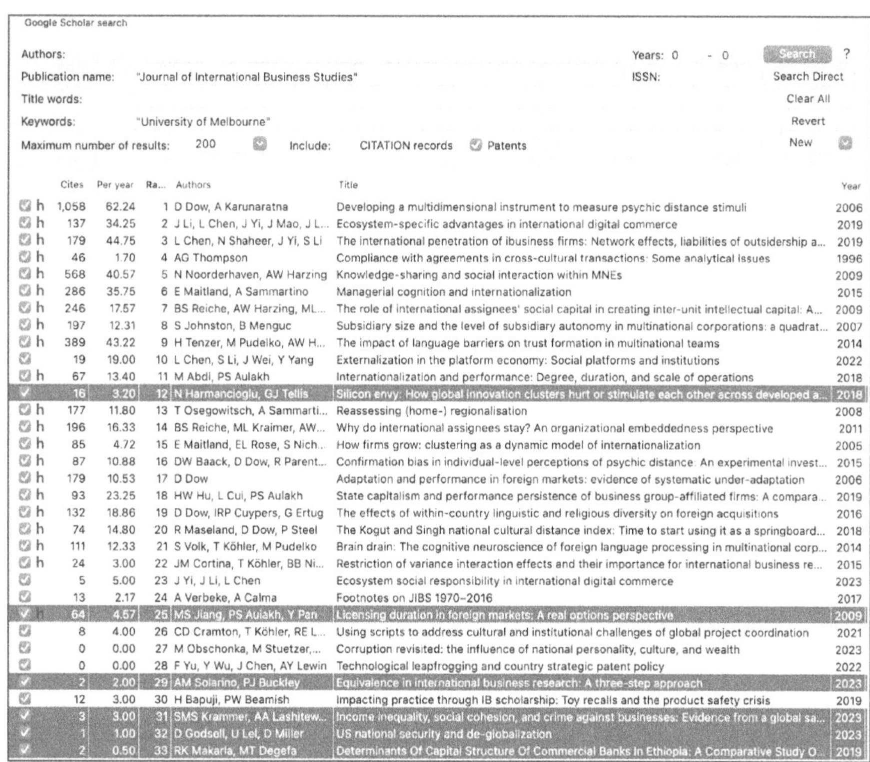

Google Scholar search

| Authors: | | | | | Years: 0 - 0 | Search ? |

| Publication name: "Journal of International Business Studies" | ISSN: | Search Direct |

Title words: | Clear All

Keywords: "University of Melbourne" | Revert

Maximum number of results: 200   Include: CITATION records ☑ Patents   New

	Cites	Per year	Ra...	Authors	Title	Year
☑ h	1,058	62.24	1	D Dow, A Karunaratna	Developing a multidimensional instrument to measure psychic distance stimuli	2006
☑ h	137	34.25	2	J Li, L Chen, J Yi, J Mao, J L...	Ecosystem-specific advantages in international digital commerce	2019
☑ h	179	44.75	3	L Chen, N Shaheer, J Yi, S Li	The international penetration of ibusiness firms: Network effects, liabilities of outsidership a...	2019
☑ h	46	1.70	4	AG Thompson	Compliance with agreements in cross-cultural transactions: Some analytical issues	1996
☑ h	568	40.57	5	N Noorderhaven, AW Harzing	Knowledge-sharing and social interaction within MNEs	2009
☑ h	286	35.75	6	E Maitland, A Sammartino	Managerial cognition and internationalization	2015
☑ h	246	17.57	7	BS Reiche, AW Harzing, ML...	The role of international assignees' social capital in creating inter-unit intellectual capital: A...	2009
☑ h	197	12.31	8	S Johnston, B Menguc	Subsidiary size and the level of subsidiary autonomy in multinational corporations: a quadrat...	2007
☑ h	389	43.22	9	H Tenzer, M Pudelko, AW H...	The impact of language barriers on trust formation in multinational teams	2014
☑	19	19.00	10	L Chen, S Li, J Wei, Y Yang	Externalization in the platform economy: Social platforms and institutions	2022
☑ h	67	13.40	11	M Abdi, PS Aulakh	Internationalization and performance: Degree, duration, and scale of operations	2018
☑	16	3.20	12	N Harmancioglu, GJ Tellis	Silicon envy: How global innovation clusters hurt or stimulate each other across developed a...	2018
☑ h	177	11.80	13	T Osegowitsch, A Sammarti...	Reassessing (home-) regionalisation	2008
☑ h	196	16.33	14	BS Reiche, ML Kraimer, AW...	Why do international assignees stay? An organizational embeddedness perspective	2011
☑ h	85	4.72	15	E Maitland, EL Rose, S Nich...	How firms grow: clustering as a dynamic model of internationalization	2005
☑ h	87	10.88	16	DW Baack, D Dow, R Parent...	Confirmation bias in individual-level perceptions of psychic distance: An experimental invest...	2015
☑ h	179	10.53	17	D Dow	Adaptation and performance in foreign markets: evidence of systematic under-adaptation	2006
☑ h	93	23.25	18	HW Hu, L Cui, PS Aulakh	State capitalism and performance persistence of business group-affiliated firms: A compara...	2019
☑ h	132	18.86	19	D Dow, IRP Cuypers, G Ertug	The effects of within-country linguistic and religious diversity on foreign acquisitions	2016
☑ h	74	14.80	20	R Maseland, D Dow, P Steel	The Kogut and Singh national cultural distance index: Time to start using it as a springboard...	2018
☑ h	111	12.33	21	S Volk, T Köhler, M Pudelko	Brain drain: The cognitive neuroscience of foreign language processing in multinational corp...	2014
☑ h	24	3.00	22	JM Cortina, T Köhler, BB Ni...	Restriction of variance interaction effects and their importance for international business re...	2015
☑	5	5.00	23	J Yi, J Li, L Chen	Ecosystem social responsibility in international digital commerce	2023
☑	13	2.17	24	A Verbeke, A Calma	Footnotes on JIBS 1970–2016	2017
☑ h	64	4.57	25	MS Jiang, PS Aulakh, Y Pan	Licensing duration in foreign markets: A real options perspective	2009
☑	8	4.00	26	CD Cramton, T Köhler, RE L...	Using scripts to address cultural and institutional challenges of global project coordination	2021
☑	0	0.00	27	M Obschonka, M Stuetzer,...	Corruption revisited: the influence of national personality, culture, and wealth	2023
☑	0	0.00	28	F Yu, Y Wu, J Chen, AY Lewin	Technological leapfrogging and country strategic patent policy	2022
☑	2	2.00	29	AM Solarino, PJ Buckley	Equivalence in international business research: A three-step approach	2023
☑	12	3.00	30	H Bapuji, PW Beamish	Impacting practice through IB scholarship: Toy recalls and the product safety crisis	2019
☑	3	3.00	31	SMS Krammer, AA Lashitew...	Income inequality, social cohesion, and crime against businesses: Evidence from a global sa...	2023
☑	1	1.00	32	D Godsell, U Lel, D Miller	US national security and de-globalization	2023
☑	2	0.50	33	RK Makarla, MT Degefa	Determinants Of Capital Structure Of Commercial Banks In Ethiopia: A Comparative Study O...	2019

In this type of search, it is generally best to sort the results by Google Scholar rank (by clicking on the rank column), rather than the standard sort for the number of citations. The latter privileges publications that have more citations, but these might be less relevant for the search in question.

Most of the 33 papers were written by one or more authors affiliated with Melbourne. However, the authors of highlighted publications #12, #25, #29 and #31-32 have no links to Melbourne. Two of them refer to the University of Melbourne in their list of references. The remaining three mention the institution in the acknowledgements, having presented their work at a seminar at this university. Hit #33 is the *Osmanian Journal of International Business Studies*. This false hit could have been prevented by searching for ISSN instead.

Thus, this search might enable you to identify relevant individuals easily and very quickly in a particular university. However, it should always be combined with alternative search strategies, such as perusing university web sites, for the best results.

Obviously, this search only shows articles that have been published in the journal whilst the author was affiliated with the university in question. It will not show articles published before the author joined this university, nor does it guarantee that the authors are *still* affiliated with the university. This is a limitation Google Scholar shares with all other data sources as bibliographic data sources show affiliations of authors are the time of publishing. If you want to maximise your chances of finding someone who is currently affiliated with the institution, sort by year.

Literature reviews, journal submission, bibliometric research

There are three further important reasons for doing topic searches in Publish or Perish, which are so important that they each deserve a separate chapter.

The first is doing a literature review, as a student for your studies or when doing research as an academic. Chapter 12 explains how to do this effectively. Another important reason for topical searches is journal selection for academic papers. Chapter 13 illustrates how to use a topic search to decide which journal to submit your paper to. Finally, topic searches are also important for bibliometric research, which we will discuss in detail in Chapter 14.

Topic searches in other data sources

So far, we have focused on searching in Google Scholar only. Below, I provide brief suggestions for keyword searches in each of the other data sources, except Google Scholar Profiles which only allows for author searches. The search syntax below refers to what works best when you search the data source through Publish or Perish. This is not always identical to the most effective search syntax in the web interfaces of the respective databases as these might be structured differently.

Every data source has its own unique syntax that – oftentimes – is not fully documented. Below you will find the most important tips and problems, but to get the best out of the different data sources you need to be prepared to experiment with different search strategies. If you find that some searches are not working as you expected, please share your findings by contacting me at anne@harzing.com, so that, collectively, we can improve these instructions.

Crossref

This data source can be used for basic topic searches. However, it has many limitations (see below). Hence, I would not recommend it as a first point of call. Its complete search syntax and most common problems are listed below.

Search syntax and advantages

- Can search for *any of the words* by using **OR**
- Can search for **Title words**, which matches words in title only
- Can search for a combination of the **Title words/Keywords** and **Publication name/ISSN**, **Authors**, and **Affiliations** fields

Most common problems

- Cannot search for *all of the words*, when using **AND** Crossref simply reverts to **OR**
- Cannot restrict search, when using **NOT** Crossref reverts to **OR**
- Cannot do an "exact phrase" search
- Cannot search for terms in abstract or full text of articles. A search in the **Keywords** field provides results that are identical to the **Title words** fields.
- Exact match only, expatriate doesn't match expatriates

Given that Crossref interprets every search as an OR search when multiple terms are included in the same search field, the only way to achieve a manageable set of results is to strategically use *multiple* search fields to narrow down your search. Let's assume I wanted to learn about articles published on the role of language in expatriation.

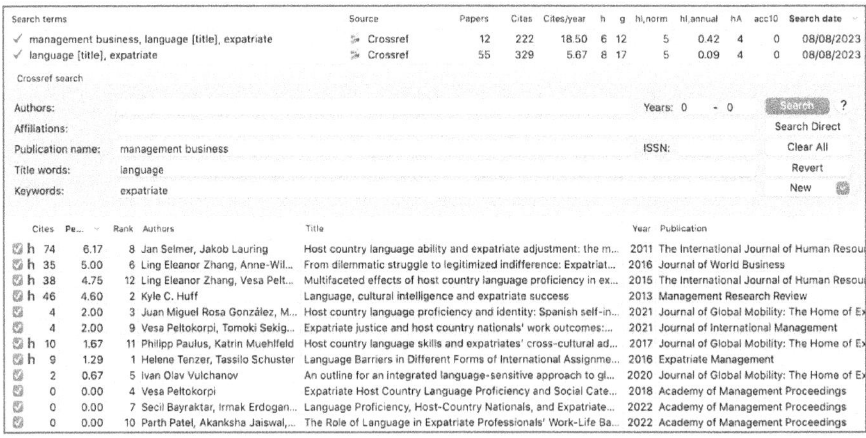

Search terms	Source	Papers	Cites	Cites/year	h	g	hI,norm	hI,annual	hA	acc10	Search date
✓ management business, language [title], expatriate	Crossref	12	222	18.50	6	12	5	0.42	4	0	08/08/2023
✓ language [title], expatriate	Crossref	55	329	5.67	8	17	5	0.09	4	0	08/08/2023

Crossref search

Authors:		Years: 0 - 0	Search	?
Affiliations:			Search Direct	
Publication name:	management business	ISSN:	Clear All	
Title words:	language		Revert	
Keywords:	expatriate		New	

Cites	Pe...	Rank	Authors	Title	Year	Publication
h 74	6.17	8	Jan Selmer, Jakob Lauring	Host country language ability and expatriate adjustment: the m...	2011	The International Journal of Human Resou...
h 35	5.00	6	Ling Eleanor Zhang, Anne-Wil...	From dilemmatic struggle to legitimized indifference: Expatriat...	2016	Journal of World Business
h 38	4.75	12	Ling Eleanor Zhang, Vesa Pelt...	Multifaceted effects of host country language proficiency in ex...	2015	The International Journal of Human Resou...
h 46	4.60	2	Kyle C. Huff	Language, cultural intelligence and expatriate success	2013	Management Research Review
4	2.00	3	Juan Miguel Rosa González, M...	Host country language proficiency and identity: Spanish self-in...	2021	Journal of Global Mobility: The Home of Ex
4	2.00	9	Vesa Peltokorpi, Tomoki Sekig...	Expatriate justice and host country nationals' work outcomes:...	2021	Journal of International Management
h 10	1.67	11	Philipp Paulus, Katrin Muehlfeld	Host country language skills and expatriates' cross-cultural ad...	2017	Journal of Global Mobility: The Home of Ex
h 9	1.29	1	Helene Tenzer, Tassilo Schuster	Language Barriers in Different Forms of International Assignme...	2016	Expatriate Management
2	0.67	5	Ivan Olav Vulchanov	An outline for an integrated language-sensitive approach to gl...	2020	Journal of Global Mobility: The Home of Ex
0	0.00	4	Vesa Peltokorpi	Expatriate Host Country Language Proficiency and Social Cate...	2018	Academy of Management Proceedings
0	0.00	7	Secil Bayraktar, Irmak Erdogan...	Language Proficiency, Host-Country Nationals, and Expatriate...	2022	Academy of Management Proceedings
0	0.00	10	Parth Patel, Akanksha Jaiswal,...	The Role of Language in Expatriate Professionals' Work-Life Ba...	2022	Academy of Management Proceedings

In the above search, I first searched for expatriate and language in the **Title words** and **Keywords** fields. This already provided a limited number of results. I then restricted my search including the search terms management and business in the **Publication Name** field. This meant that only publications in the field of Business & Management were included, which led to a dozen very relevant results.

OpenAlex

This data source can be used for advanced topic searches, because of its ability to search in title and/or abstract, its stemming options and the fact that it provides up to 1,000 results within 40-50 seconds. It is limited, however, by its inability to conduct OR and NOT searches and the restriction of a single search term in the **Title words** field. Its complete search syntax and most common problems are listed below.

Search syntax and advantages

- Can search for *all of the words* by using **AND** [not essential as OpenAlex uses an implicit AND]
- Can search for title words only or for matches in title and abstract or use a combination of both fields. Note: In some cases, Open-Alex also appears to match the search term in additional prelims such as funding source as well as author bios. In some cases, OA also seems to match search terms in the full text of publications.
- Can search for an *exact phrase* by putting the phrase in "quotes"
- Can search for keywords in full text of articles
- Uses stemming which allows effective searches, e.g.,
    o expatriate also matches expatriates
    o organization also matches organizational
    o global also matches globalization
    o politics also matches political
- Can search for a combination of the **Title words/Keywords** and **ISSN** as well as **Author** and **Affiliation ID**

Most common problems

- Cannot search for *any of the words* by using **OR**
- Cannot restrict search by using **NOT**

- Can only search for *one* word in the **Title words** field (can search for multiple words in the **Keywords** field)
- Cannot search for keywords in the full text of articles. This needs further investigation as it does seem to work in some cases.
- Stemming is sometimes applied (too) aggressively
  - when searching for globalization most hits match with global
  - when searching for harzing most of the hits match with harz

The screenshot below shows the result of a search which attempted to establish how much had been published on politics in the research field of international business in the last three years. It did provide a manageable set of 62 relevant results.

PubMed

This data source can be used for advanced topic searches on biomedical topics, because of its ability to search in title and/or abstract, and the fact that it provides up to 1,000 results within 15 seconds. It is limited, however, by its lack of stemming, its inability to conduct NOT searches and the fact that for some combined searches PubMed limits the number of results to 199 or 398. Its complete search syntax and most common problems are listed below.

Search syntax and advantages

- Can search for *all of the words* by using **AND** [not essential as PubMed uses an implicit AND]
- Can search for *any of the words* by using **OR**
- Can search for an *exact phrase* by putting the phrase in "quotes"
- Can search for title words only or for matches in title and abstract (including the article's keywords)
- Can search for a combination of the **Title words/Keywords** and **Publication name/ISSN**, **Authors**, and **Affiliations** fields

Most common problems

- Exact match only, vaccine doesn't match vaccines
- Cannot restrict search with **NOT**, when using **NOT** PubMed reverts to **AND**
- Cannot search for keywords in full text of articles
- Limits results for *some* keywords to a max of 199 or 398 results

OpenAlex search

Author ID or ORCID:					Years: 2020 - 0	Search	?
Affiliation ID:						Search Direct	
Title words:	covid-19			ISSN:		Clear All	
Keywords:	"international business"					Revert	
Maximum number of results:	1000	Please note: the OpenAlex API is still under development.				New	

	Cites	Per year	Ra...	Authors	Title	Year
☑ h	303	101.00	1	Paula Caligiuri, Helen De Ci...	International HRM insights for navigating the COVID-19 pandemic: Implications for future re...	2020
☑ h	117	39.00	2	Stephen Brammer, Timothy...	COVID-19 and Management Education: Reflections on Challenges, Opportunities, and Poten...	2020
☑ h	116	38.67	3	Alain Verbeke	Will the COVID-19 Pandemic Really Change the Governance of Global Value Chains?	2020
☑ h	96	32.00	4	May McMaster, Charlie Nett...	Risk Management: Rethinking Fashion Supply Chain Management for Multinational Corporati...	2020
☑ h	60	20.00	5	Sébastien Miroudot	Reshaping the policy debate on the implications of COVID-19 for global supply chains	2020
☑ h	58	29.00	6	Luciano Ciravegna, Snejina...	Why the world economy needs, but will not get, more globalization in the post-COVID-19 de...	2021
☑ h	57	19.00	7	Tyler McKechnie, Marc Levi...	Virtual Surgical Training During COVID-19	2020
☑ h	47	15.67	8	Alain Verbeke, W. L. Yuan	A Few Implications of the COVID-19 Pandemic for International Business Strategy Research	2020
☑ h	39	13.00	9	Ari Van Assche, Sarianna M....	From the editor: COVID-19 and international business policy	2020
☑ h	37	12.33	10	Karl L. Evans, John G. Ewen...	Conservation in the maelstrom of Covid-19 – a call to action to solve the challenges, exploit...	2020
☑ h	35	11.67	11	Steven Brakman, Harry Garr...	The turn from just-in-time to just-in-case globalization in and after times of COVID-19	2020
☑ h	33	11.00	12	Ilan Alon	COVID-19 and International Business: A Viewpoint	2020
☑ h	32	16.00	13	Steven Brakman, Harry Garr...	Robots do not get the coronavirus: The COVID-19 pandemic and the international division of...	2021
☑ h	26	8.67	14	Simon J. Evenett	Chinese whispers: COVID-19, global supply chains in essential goods, and public policy	2020
☑ h	26	13.00	15	Abu Baker Sheikh, Prabal C...	Association of Guillain-Barre syndrome with COVID-19 infection: An updated systematic revi...	2021
☑ h	24	8.00	16	Eulália Santos, Margarida Ol...	A reflection on explanatory factors for <scp>COVID</scp> -19: A comparative study betwee...	2020
☑ h	20	10.00	17	Louise Curran, Jappe Eckha...	The trade policy response to COVID-19 and its implications for international business	2021
☑ h	18	18.00	18	Carla Santos-Pereira, Bruno...	The influence of technological innovations on international business strategy before and dur...	2022
☑	15	5.00	19	Kriswanda Krishnapatria	From 'Lockdown' to Letdown: Students' Perception of E-learning amid the COVID-19 Outbre...	2020
☑	12	4.00	20	Daniel Muzio, Jonathan P. D...	Introduction to the COVID-19 Commentaries	2020
☑	11	3.67	21	Hinrich Voss	Implications of the COVID-19 pandemic for human rights and modern slavery vulnerabilities...	2020

The search above for a combination of a medical term (Covid-19) in the **Title words** field and a business term ("international business") in the **Keywords** field results in 21 records and shows that PubMed does have *some* coverage of journals outside the biomedical field, but only for articles its judges to deal with biomedical issues. A comparison with OpenAlex also shows that even this coverage is by no means complete.

Hence, it is advisable to stick to topics squarely in the biomedical field when searching in PubMed. Below is a more appropriate search for 2023 articles dealing with covid-19 and breast cancer.

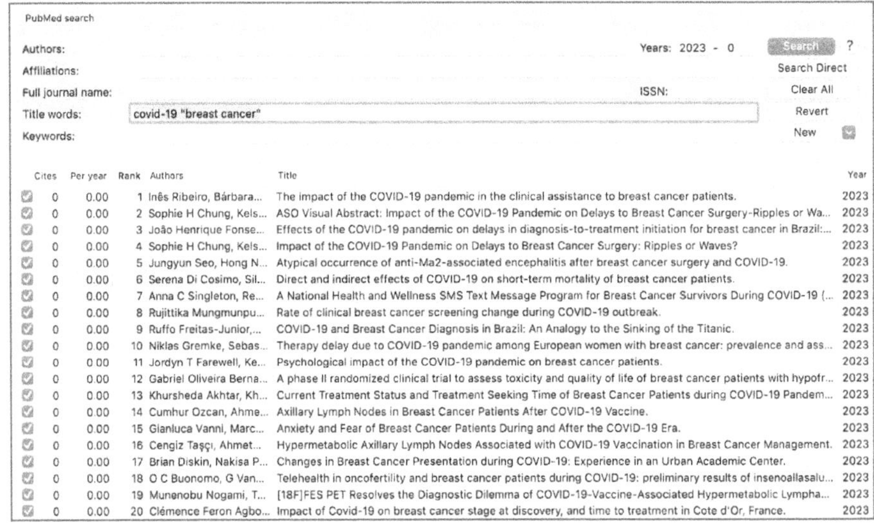

Cites	Per year	Rank	Authors	Title	Year
0	0.00	1	Inês Ribeiro, Bárbara...	The impact of the COVID-19 pandemic in the clinical assistance to breast cancer patients.	2023
0	0.00	2	Sophie H Chung, Kels...	ASO Visual Abstract: Impact of the COVID-19 Pandemic on Delays to Breast Cancer Surgery-Ripples or Wa...	2023
0	0.00	3	João Henrique Fonse...	Effects of the COVID-19 pandemic on delays in diagnosis-to-treatment initiation for breast cancer in Brazil:...	2023
0	0.00	4	Sophie H Chung, Kels...	Impact of the COVID-19 Pandemic on Delays to Breast Cancer Surgery: Ripples or Waves?	2023
0	0.00	5	Jungyun Seo, Hong N...	Atypical occurrence of anti-Ma2-associated encephalitis after breast cancer surgery and COVID-19.	2023
0	0.00	6	Serena Di Cosimo, Sil...	Direct and indirect effects of COVID-19 on short-term mortality of breast cancer patients.	2023
0	0.00	7	Anna C Singleton, Re...	A National Health and Wellness SMS Text Message Program for Breast Cancer Survivors During COVID-19 (...	2023
0	0.00	8	Rujittika Mungmunpu...	Rate of clinical breast cancer screening change during COVID-19 outbreak.	2023
0	0.00	9	Ruffo Freitas-Junior,...	COVID-19 and Breast Cancer Diagnosis in Brazil: An Analogy to the Sinking of the Titanic.	2023
0	0.00	10	Niklas Gremke, Sebas...	Therapy delay due to COVID-19 pandemic among European women with breast cancer: prevalence and ass...	2023
0	0.00	11	Jordyn T Farewell, Ke...	Psychological impact of the COVID-19 pandemic on breast cancer patients.	2023
0	0.00	12	Gabriel Oliveira Berna...	A phase II randomized clinical trial to assess toxicity and quality of life of breast cancer patients with hypofr...	2023
0	0.00	13	Khursheda Akhtar, Kh...	Current Treatment Status and Treatment Seeking Time of Breast Cancer Patients during COVID-19 Pandem...	2023
0	0.00	14	Cumhur Ozcan, Ahme...	Axillary Lymph Nodes in Breast Cancer Patients After COVID-19 Vaccine.	2023
0	0.00	15	Gianluca Vanni, Marc...	Anxiety and Fear of Breast Cancer Patients During and After the COVID-19 Era.	2023
0	0.00	16	Cengiz Taşçı, Ahmet...	Hypermetabolic Axillary Lymph Nodes Associated with COVID-19 Vaccination in Breast Cancer Management.	2023
0	0.00	17	Brian Diskin, Nakisa P...	Changes in Breast Cancer Presentation during COVID-19: Experience in an Urban Academic Center.	2023
0	0.00	18	O C Buonomo, G Van...	Telehealth in oncofertility and breast cancer patients during COVID-19: preliminary results of insenoallasalu...	2023
0	0.00	19	Munenobu Nogami, T...	[18F]FES PET Resolves the Diagnostic Dilemma of COVID-19-Vaccine-Associated Hypermetabolic Lympha...	2023
0	0.00	20	Clémence Feron Agbo...	Impact of Covid-19 on breast cancer stage at discovery, and time to treatment in Cote d'Or, France.	2023

Scopus

This data source can be used for advanced topic searches, because of its ability to search in title and/or abstract, its useful plural stemming as well as wildcard options and its ability to restrict searches by using **NOT**. It provides up to 200 results.

Scopus is limited, however, by its slower searches, taking as long for 200 results as OpenAlex does for 1,000, and its lack of abstracts. Its complete search syntax and most common problems are listed below.

Search syntax and advantages

- Can search for *all of the words* by using **AND** [not essential as Scopus uses an implicit AND]
- Can search for *any of the words* by using **OR**
- Can search for an *exact phrase* by putting the phrase in "quotes"
- Can restrict search by using **NOT**
- Can search for title words only or for matches in title and abstract
- Uses stemming for plural of the search term, expatriate also matches expatriates, organization also matched organizations
- Allows wildcards, e.g., organization* to included organizational
- Can search for a combination of the **Title words/Keywords** and **Publication name/ISSN**, **Authors**, and **Affiliations** fields

Most common problems

- Cannot use **NOT** as the *first* operator in a search field, e.g., "NOT expatriate" will give an error message, but "language NOT expatriate" is fine.
- Cannot search for search terms in full text of articles

Search terms		Source	Papers	Cites	Cites/year	h	g	hI,norm	hI,annual	hA	acc10	Search date
✓	politics [title], "international business" from 2020	OpenAlex	62	183	61.00	8	13	5	1.67	6	5	08/08/2023
✓	politics [title], "international business" from 2020	Scopus	10	22	7.33	2	4	2	0.67	2	0	08/08/2023

Scopus search

Authors:		Years: 2020 - 0	Search ?
Affiliations:			Search Direct
Publication name:		ISSN:	Clear All
Title words:	politics		Revert
Keywords:	"international business"		New

Cites	Per year	Rank	Authors	Title	Year	Publication
h 9	9.00	1	A.Y. Lewin	China's Belt and Road Initiative and international business: The overlo...	2022	Journal of International Business Policy
h 6	6.00	2	N.V. Wilmot	Englishization and the politics of translation	2023	Critical Perspectives on International Business
2	2.00	3	I. Lyan	"Start-up Nation" vs "the Republic of Samsung": power and politics in...	2022	Critical Perspectives on International Business
2	0.67	4	C. Perold	IBM's world citizens: Valentim bouças and the politics of IT expansion...	2020	IEEE Annals of the History of Computing
2	0.67	5	B. Zesik	The Rhetoric, Politics and Reality of Talent Management: Insider Persp...	2020	Managing Talent: A Critical Appreciation
1	0.33	6	F.N.K. Ofori	Business geo-politics, geo-economics and the fourth Industrial Revol...	2020	South African Journal of Business Management
0	0.00	7	I. Saittakari	Publisher Correction: A review of location, politics, and the multinatio...	2023	Journal of International Business Studies
0	0.00	8	M. Kriegsbaum	Stakeholder Politics and PBL Curriculum: A Learner's Perspective	2020	Populism and Higher Education Curriculum Develo
0	0.00	9	I. Saittakari	A review of location, politics, and the multinational corporation: Bringi...	2023	Journal of International Business Studies
0	0.00	10	L.c. Lo	Facilitating the Market with a Gift: The Politics of the ECFA between C...	2023	Asian Studies Review

Repeating the search that we conducted for OpenAlex (see above screenshot) shows the differences between the two data sources. OpenAlex provides many more results for two reasons. First, Open-Alex has a broader coverage. It includes more books, book chapters, conference papers, as well as journals not covered in Scopus. Second, it applies much more extensive stemming. In OpenAlex politics also matches political, in Scopus it only matches politics.

The latter can be seen as an advantage of Scopus, however. It allows for a more precise way of searching. Scopus is also able to provide results for politics and political by either searching for politics OR political or by using the wildcard search politic*. Doing so, provides 40 results rather than the original ten (see screenshot below).

Search terms	Source	Papers	Cites
✓ politics [title], "international business" from 2020	OpenAlex	62	183
✓ politics OR political [title], "international business" from 2020	Scopus	40	196
✓ politic* [title], "international business" from 2020	Scopus	40	196
✓ politics [title], "international business" from 2020	Scopus	10	22

Semantic Scholar

This data source can be used for basic topic searches. It provides up to 1,000 results in less than 30 seconds. However, the Semantic Scholar API interface we use in Publish or Perish cannot limit results by searching for **Title words** only, nor is it able to restrict searches by year, author, affiliation, or publication name. It also matches search terms *anywhere* in the article. This means that most searches will provide far too many results to be useful. Hence, I would not recommend it as a first point of call. Its complete search syntax and most common problems are listed below.

Search syntax and advantages

- Can search for *all of the words* by using **AND** [not essential as Semantic Scholar uses an implicit AND]
- Can search for an *exact phrase* by putting the phrase in "quotes"
- Can search for search terms in full text of articles

Most common problems

- Cannot search for *any of the words* by using **OR,** when using **OR** Semantic Scholar matches this as a search term
- Cannot restrict search, when using **NOT** Semantic Scholar matches this as a search term
- Cannot search for **Title words**, which matches words in title only
- Cannot restrict search to Abstract only, search terms will be matched anywhere in the full text of the article (if available).
- Cannot search for a combination of the **Title words/Keywords** and **Publication name/ISSN**, **Authors**, and **Affiliations** fields
- Cannot restrict by year
- Exact match only, expatriate doesn't match expatriate

Most searches in Semantic Scholar will provide 1,000 results. Below I have provided a very restrictive search with many search terms. This presents us with five results that appear to be relevant to the search terms. However, it also shows six results where search terms have been matched anywhere in the document. These publications do not seem to have a strong relevance to our search terms.

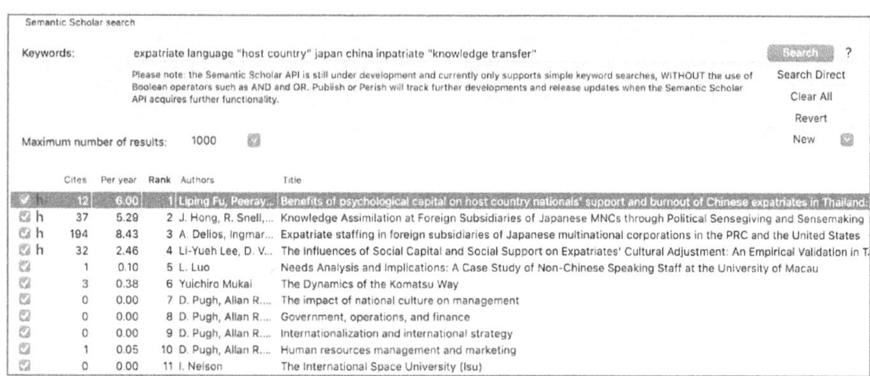

Web of Science

This data source can be used for advanced topic searches, because of its ability to search in title and/or abstract, its useful plural stemming as well as wildcard options and its ability to restrict searches by using **NOT**. It provides up to 200 results. It also is quicker than Scopus and provides complete abstracts, as well as all authors.

Its main disadvantage is that WoS is only accessible to researchers with a subscription. The WoS complete search syntax and most common problems are listed below.

Search syntax and advantages

- Can search for *all of the words* by using **AND** [not essential as WoS uses an implicit AND]
- Can search for *any of the words* by using **OR**
- Can search for an *exact phrase* by putting the phrase in "quotes"
- Can restrict search by using **NOT**
- Can search for title words only or for matches in title and abstract
- Uses stemming, expatriate also matches expatriates
- Allows wildcards, e.g. organization* to included organizational
- Can search for a combination of the **Title words/Keywords** and **Publication name/ISSN**, **Authors**, and **Affiliations** fields

Most common problems

- Cannot use **NOT** as the *first* operator in a search field, e.g., "NOT expatriate" will give an error message, but "language NOT expatriate" is fine.
- Cannot search for search terms in full text of articles

Affiliation searches in other data sources

So far, we have focused on searching in Google Scholar only. Below I provide brief suggestions for keyword searches in each of the other data sources, except Google Scholar Profiles which only allows for author searches and Semantic Scholar which only allows for topic searches.

Every data source has its own unique syntax that – oftentimes – is not fully documented. The search syntax below refers to what works best when you search the data source through Publish or Perish. This is not always identical to the most effective search syntax in the web interfaces of the respective databases as these might be structured differently.

Below you will find the most important tips and problems, but to get the best out of the different data sources you need to be prepared to experiment with different search strategies. If you find that some searches are not working as you expected, please share your findings by contacting me at anne@harzing.com, so that, collectively, we can improve these instructions.

Crossref

Affiliation attribution in Crossref is substantially incomplete. Currently, it includes affiliation information for only a (small) subset of publishers. Springer, Elsevier, and Emerald are among the publishers not covered. Its only advantage is that it appears to cover more conference proceedings papers than other data sources.

The screenshot below lists the results for a search for my publications at Middlesex University, an institution that I have been affiliated with since 2014. It provides a mere 12 results (including four conference papers in the Academy of Management proceedings not found in the other data sources). Scopus provided 34 results, and OpenAlex 28.

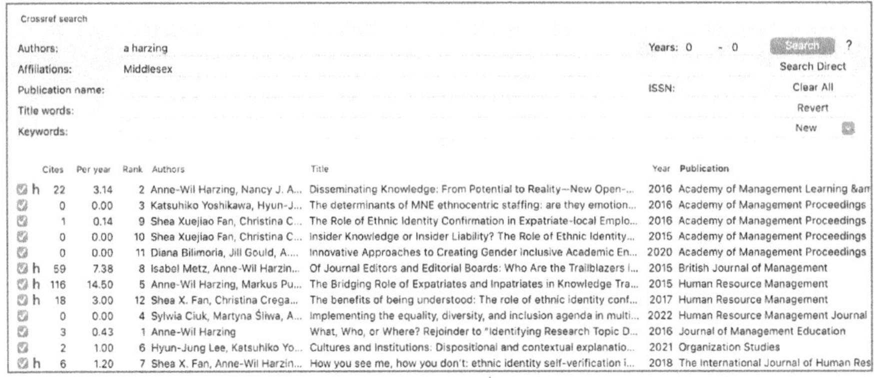

The screenshot below lists the results for a search for my publications at the University of Melbourne, an institution that I have been affiliated with between 2001 and 2014. It provides a mere 16 results (again including four AoM proceedings papers). In contrast, Scopus provides 63 results, and OpenAlex 57.

The results include some articles that were published when I was no longer affiliated with Melbourne. This is because the affiliation is linked to *papers*, not *individuals*. Hence, a combined author/affiliation search will report results even if it is one of the author's co-authors that has the requested affiliation, in this case my co-authors Isabel Metz and Christina Cregan who were both affiliated with Melbourne.

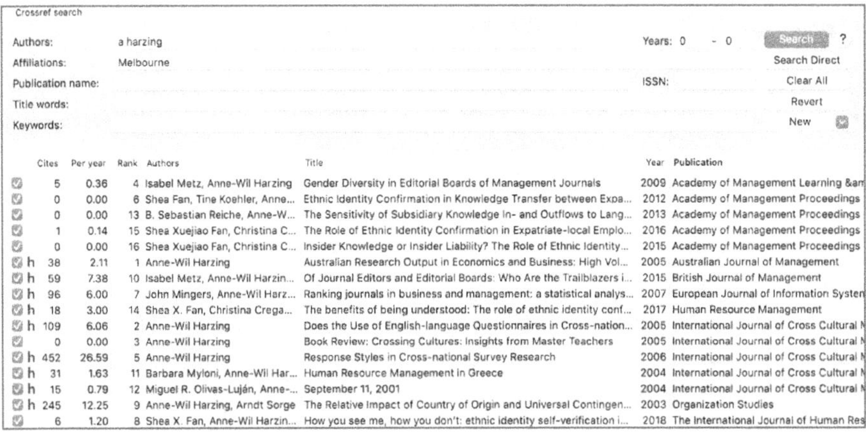

As Crossref's affiliation coverage is so limited, we do not recommend using this data source for affiliation searches. If you still want to use it, remember that Crossref interprets every search as an OR search.

Hence, Middlesex University matches Middlesex University, but also *every other university* with University in their name. Therefore, using only the most unique part of a university's name is the best solution.

OpenAlex

The OA API does not support regular affiliation searches by name in Publish or Perish. It is possible to search for affiliations, however, if you know the OA affiliation ID. You can find OA affiliation IDs on their website by searching for the university in question.

Checking affiliation accuracy through author searches

A good way to check the affiliation accuracy in a data source is to review a known author's record (in this case my own) during their affiliation at a university. As the screenshot below shows, searching by affiliation ID (in this case Middlesex University) in OpenAlex provides reasonably good results.

Search terms	Source	Papers	Cites	Cites/year	h	g	hi,norm	hi,annual	hA	acc10	Search date
0000-0003-1509-3003, I60488453	OpenAlex	28	1,729	216.13	18	28	13	1.63	7	6	17/08/2023
a harzing, Middlesex University	Scopus	34	1,865	233.13	19	34	19	2.38	8	8	17/08/2023
a harzing, Middlesex	Crossref	12	228	28.50	5	12	4	0.50	3	1	17/08/2023

OpenAlex search

Author ID or ORCID: 0000-0003-1509-3003	Years: 0 - 0 Search ?
Affiliation ID: I60488453	Search Direct
Title words:	ISSN: Clear All
Keywords:	Revert
Maximum number of results: 1000 Please note: the OpenAlex API is still under development.	New

	Cites	Per year	Rank	Authors	Title	Year	Publication
	6	6.00	20	Mariana Dodourova, Shasha…	Ambidexterity in MNC knowledge sourcing in emerging econ…	2023	International Business Review
	5	5.00	21	Giovanni Abramo, Isidro F. A…	Retraction of Predatory publishing in Scopus: evidence on cr…	2022	Scientometrics
	5	5.00	22	Heejin Kim, B. Sebastian Rei…	How does successive inpatriation contribute to subsidiary c…	2022	Journal of International Business Studie
	1	1.00	28	Sylwia Ciuk, Martyna Śliwa,…	Implementing the equality, diversity, and inclusion agenda in…	2022	Human Resource Management Journal
	2	1.00	24	Shasha Zhao, Paul N. Good…	Guest editorial	2021	Critical Perspectives on International B
	2	1.00	25	María Bastida Domínguez, L…	No room at the top? A system dynamics view of the recursiv…	2021	Journal of global mobility
	2	1.00	26	Hyun Jung Lee, Katsuhiko Y…	Cultures and Institutions: Dispositional and contextual expla…	2021	Organization Studies
h	71	17.75	6	Anne-Wil Harzing	Two new kids on the block: How do Crossref and Dimension…	2019	Scientometrics
h	26	6.50	12	Florence Duvivier, Christian…	Not all international assignments are created equal: HQ-sub…	2019	Journal of World Business
h	19	4.75	18	Shasha Zhao, Hui Tan, Mari…	The internationalization of innovation towards the South: A h…	2019	Asia Pacific Journal of Management
	7	1.40	19	Shea Xuejiao Fan, Anne-Wil…	How you see me, how you don't: ethnic identity self-verificat…	2018	International Journal of Human Resourc
h	99	16.50	4	Helene Tenzer, Siri Terjesen…	Language in International Business: A Review and Agenda fo…	2017	Management International Review
h	97	16.17	5	Alberto Martín-Martín, Enriq…	Can we use Google Scholar to identify highly-cited documen…	2017	Journal of Informetrics
h	42	7.00	9	Anne-Wil Harzing, Satu Alak…	Microsoft Academic is one year old: the Phoenix is ready to l…	2017	Scientometrics
h	21	3.50	15	Shea Xuejiao Fan, Anne-Wil…	Host country employees' ethnic identity confirmation: Evide…	2017	Journal of World Business
h	19	3.17	17	Shea Xuejiao Fan, Christina…	The benefits of being understood: The role of ethnic identity…	2017	Human Resource Management
	2	0.33	27	Ling Eleanor Zhang, Anne-…	Host Country Language: Why It Matters, and Why Expatriate…	2017	Palgrave Macmillan UK eBooks
h	63	9.00	7	Anne-Wil Harzing, Satu Alak…	Microsoft Academic: is the phoenix getting wings?	2016	Scientometrics
h	42	6.00	10	Ling Eleanor Zhang, Anne-…	From dilemmatic struggle to legitimized indifference: Expatri…	2016	Journal of World Business
h	35	5.00	11	Anne-Wil Harzing	Microsoft Academic (Search): a Phoenix arisen from the ash…	2016	Scientometrics
h	24	3.43	14	Anne-Wil Harzing, Nancy J.…	Disseminating Knowledge: From Potential to Reality—New O…	2016	Academy of Management Learning and
h	20	2.86	16	Anne-Wil Harzing	Why replication studies are essential: learning from failure a…	2016	Cross cultural & strategic management
	4	0.57	23	Anne-Wil Harzing	What, Who, or Where? Rejoinder to "Identifying Research To…	2016	Journal of Management Education
h	835	104.38	1	Anne-Wil Harzing, Satu Alak…	Google Scholar, Scopus and the Web of Science: a longitudi…	2015	Scientometrics
h	100	12.50	2	Anne-Wil Harzing, Markus P…	Do We Need to Distance Ourselves from the Distance Conce…	2015	Management International Review
h	100	12.50	3	B. Sebastian Reiche, Anne-…	Why and how does shared language affect subsidiary knowl…	2015	Journal of International Business Studie
h	56	7.00	8	Isabel Metz, Anne-Wil Harzi…	Of Journal Editors and Editorial Boards: Who Are the Trailbla…	2015	British Journal of Management
h	24	3.00	13	Anne-Wil Harzing	Health warning: might contain multiple personalities—the pr…	2015	Scientometrics

However, when compared to Scopus OpenAlex misses three of my journal articles, one of these is without affiliation in their data base, and two assign me to the wrong affiliation (the Indonesian *Centre for Innovation Policy and Government*). It also misses four of my book chapters, two are without affiliation, one is not included in Open-Alex, and one is attributed to the Indonesian Centre. However, it does find a book chapter not found in Scopus.

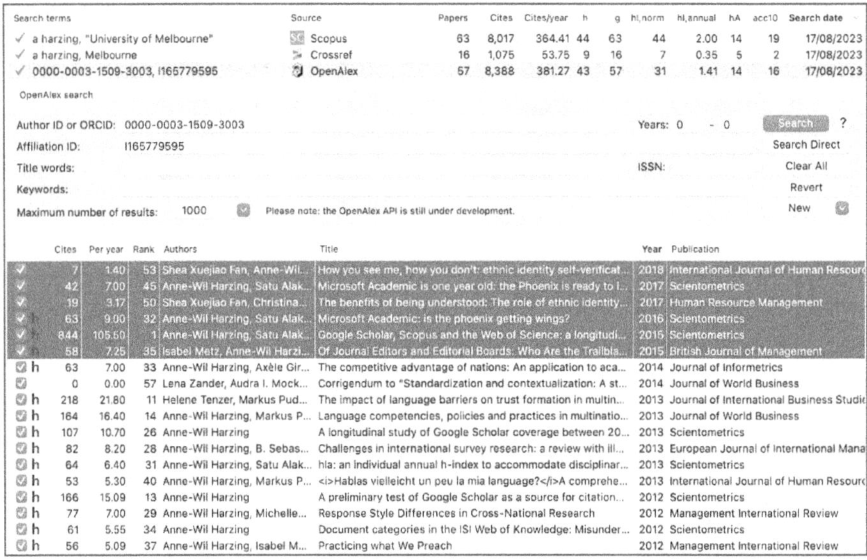

		Source	Papers	Cites	Cites/year	h	g	hi,norm	hi,annual	hA	acc10	Search date
✓	a harzing, "University of Melbourne"	Scopus	63	8,017	364.41	44	63	44	2.00	14	19	17/08/2023
✓	a harzing, Melbourne	Crossref	16	1,075	53.75	9	16	7	0.35	5	2	17/08/2023
✓	0000-0003-1509-3003, I165779595	OpenAlex	57	8,388	381.27	43	57	31	1.41	14	16	17/08/2023

	Cites	Per year	Rank	Authors	Title	Year	Publication
✓	7	1.40	53	Shea Xuejiao Fan, Anne-Wil...	How you see me, how you don't: ethnic identity self-verificat...	2018	International Journal of Human Resour...
✓	42	7.00	45	Anne-Wil Harzing, Satu Alak...	Microsoft Academic is one year old: the Phoenix is ready to l...	2017	Scientometrics
✓	19	3.17	50	Shea Xuejiao Fan, Christina...	The benefits of being understood: The role of ethnic identity...	2017	Human Resource Management
✓	63	9.00	32	Anne-Wil Harzing, Satu Alak...	Microsoft Academic: is the phoenix getting wings?	2016	Scientometrics
✓	844	105.50	1	Anne-Wil Harzing, Satu Alak...	Google Scholar, Scopus and the Web of Science: a longitudi...	2015	Scientometrics
✓	58	7.25	35	Isabel Metz, Anne-Wil Harzi...	Of Journal Editors and Editorial Boards: Who Are the Trailbla...	2015	British Journal of Management
✓ h	63	7.00	33	Anne-Wil Harzing, Axèle Gir...	The competitive advantage of nations: An application to aca...	2014	Journal of Informetrics
✓	0	0.00	57	Lena Zander, Audra I. Mock...	Corrigendum to "Standardization and contextualization: A st...	2014	Journal of World Business
✓ h	218	21.80	11	Helene Tenzer, Markus Pud...	The impact of language barriers on trust formation in multin...	2013	Journal of International Business Studie...
✓ h	164	16.40	14	Anne-Wil Harzing, Markus P...	Language competencies, policies and practices in multinatio...	2013	Journal of World Business
✓ h	107	10.70	26	Anne-Wil Harzing	A longitudinal study of Google Scholar coverage between 20...	2013	Scientometrics
✓ h	82	8.20	28	Anne-Wil Harzing, B. Sebas...	Challenges in international survey research: a review with ill...	2013	European Journal of International Mana...
✓ h	64	6.40	31	Anne-Wil Harzing, Satu Alak...	hIa: an individual annual h-index to accommodate disciplinar...	2013	Scientometrics
✓ h	53	5.30	40	Anne-Wil Harzing, Markus P...	Hablas vielleicht un peu la mia language?A comprehe...	2013	International Journal of Human Resour...
✓ h	166	15.09	13	Anne-Wil Harzing	A preliminary test of Google Scholar as a source for citation...	2012	Scientometrics
✓ h	77	7.00	29	Anne-Wil Harzing, Michelle...	Response Style Differences in Cross-National Research	2012	Management International Review
✓ h	61	5.55	34	Anne-Wil Harzing	Document categories in the ISI Web of Knowledge: Misunder...	2012	Scientometrics
✓ h	56	5.09	37	Anne-Wil Harzing, Isabel M...	Practicing what We Preach	2012	Management International Review

Likewise, a search for my publications at the University of Melbourne (see above) provides reasonably good results. However, OpenAlex misses three of my journal articles and two of my conference papers, all without affiliation in their data base. It also missed two more early journal articles, a book chapter and a conference paper which are not included at all. A search in OpenAlex does find a book review not found in Scopus, an additional book chapter, as well as two articles in *European Management Review* in 2008 *Management International* in 2003, journals which was not yet included in Scopus at that time.

The latter differences are simply differences in coverage, which are to be expected in different data sources. However, the six articles that are listed without affiliation in OpenAlex do indicate that currently its coverage is not (yet) fully accurate.

In sum, OpenAlex thus does not yet seem to provide a fully complete record of affiliation searches. It does, however, find 85-90% of my publications through an affiliation search and finds nearly all of my significant publications. As their data base is still under active development, coverage may well improve in the near future.

Affiliation search only

In addition to combined author and affiliation searches, OpenAlex can also search for all publications affiliated with a particular university in a particular (as long as there are less than 1,000).

The screenshot above shows the results the large variety of research topics published at Middlesex University in 2015. If a university has published more than 1,000 papers, only the 1,000 most cited papers will be shown.

Combined affiliation and topic searches

Finally, it is also possible to search for a combination of affiliation ID and topic. If for instance I wanted to search for publications on COVID-19 at my university (Middlesex University) I would get this result (see screenshot), retrieving some 115 papers in a few seconds.

You could broaden out this search by including this term in the **Keywords** field, which would ensure it is matched not just in the title, but also in the abstract, leading to an additional 50-odd papers. Note that OpenAlex only accepts one search term in the **Title words** field, but it accepts multiple terms in the **Keywords** field.

OpenAlex search

Author ID or ORCID:

Affiliation ID: I60488453

Title words: covid-19

Keywords:

Maximum number of results: 1000   Please note: the OpenAlex API is still under development

Years: -   Search   ?
Search Direct
ISSN: Clear All
Revert
New

Cites	Per year	Rank	Authors	Title	Year	Publication
☑ h 2,722	907.33	1	Jay Joseph Van Bavel, Katherine Baicker, P...	Using social and behavioural science to support COVID-19 pandemic response	2020	Nature Human Behaviour
☑ h 361	120.33	2	Eleonora Pantano, Gabriele Pizzi, Daniele S...	Competing during a pandemic? Retailers' ups and downs during the COVID-19 outbr...	2020	Journal of Business Research
☑ h 279	93.00	3	Vasilis Kontis, James E. Bennett, Theo Rash...	Magnitude, demographics and dynamics of the effect of the first wave of the COVID-...	2020	Nature Medicine
☑ h 141	47.00	4	Jay Joseph Van Bavel, Katherine Baicker, P...	Using social and behavioural science to support COVID-19 pandemic response	2020	
☑ h 97	32.33	5	Tahmina Zebin, Shahadate Rezvy	COVID-19 detection and disease progression visualization: Deep learning on chest X...	2020	Applied Intelligence
☑ h 87	43.50	6	Pantea Foroudi, S. Asieh Hosseini Tabaghde...	The gloom of the COVID-19 shock in the hospitality industry: A study of consumer ri...	2021	International Journal of Hospitality Management
☑ h 65	21.67	7	Phalguni Kotabagi, Lorna Fortune, Sandra E...	Anxiety and depression levels among pregnant women with COVID-19	2020	Acta Obstetricia et Gynecologica Scandinavica
☑ h 55	27.50	8	Christian Espinosa, Jose Arias	COVID-19 effect on herding behaviour in European capital markets	2021	Finance Research Letters
☑ h 47	15.67	9	Abha Govind, Sandra Essien, Athikkattuvala...	Re: Novel Coronavirus COVID-19 in late pregnancy: Outcomes of first nine cases in a...	2020	European Journal of Obstetrics & Gynecology and
☑ h 44	22.00	10	Valerio Capraro, Hélène Barcelo	Telling people to 'rely on their reasoning' increases intentions to wear a face coverin...	2021	Applied Cognitive Psychology
☑ h 40	20.00	11	Francis Hassard, Lian Lundy, Andrew C. Sin...	Innovation in wastewater near-source tracking for rapid identification of COVID-19 in...	2021	The Lancet microbe
☑ h 39	19.50	12	Shuihua Wang, Yin Zhang, Xiaochun Cheng...	PSSPNN: PatchShuffle Stochastic Pooling Neural Network for an Explainable Diagno...	2021	Computational and Mathematical Methods in Medi
☑ h 34	17.00	13	Keith Hawton, Lisa Marzano, Lorna Fraser,...	Reporting on suicidal behaviour and COVID-19—need for caution	2021	The Lancet Psychiatry
☑ h 33	11.00	14	Johannes Thome, Jocelyn Deloyer, Andrew...	The impact of the early phase of the COVID-19 pandemic on mental-health services i...	2020	World Journal of Biological Psychiatry
☑ h 32	10.67	15	Melanie Coates	Covid-19 and the rise of racism	2020	BMJ
☑ h 31	15.50	16	Silvia Bartolic, David Boud, Jenilyn Agapito,...	A multi-institutional assessment of changes in higher education teaching and learnin...	2021	Educational review
☑ h 30	15.00	17	Abeer Hassan, Ahmed A. Elamer, Suman Lo...	The future of <scp>non-financial</scp> businesses reporting: Learning from the Cov...	2021	Corporate Social Responsibility and Environmental
☑ h 27	9.00	18	Monomita Nandy, Suman Lodh, Audrey Tang	Lessons from Covid-19 and a resilience model for higher education	2020	Industry and higher education
☑ h 27	9.00	19	Christian Espinosa, Jose Arias	Herding Behaviour in Asutralian stock market: Evidence on COVID-19 effect	2020	Applied Economics Letters
☑ h 23	11.50	20	Irena Papadopoulos, Runa Lazzarino, Steve...	Spiritual Support During COVID-19 in England: A Scoping Study of Online Sources	2021	Journal of Religion & Health
☑ h 21	7.00	21	José Manuel Hernández-Padilla, José Gran...	Design and Psychometric Analysis of the COVID-19 Prevention, Recognition and Ho...	2020	International Journal of Environmental Research an
☑ 21	21.00	22	Neil Guppy, Dominique Verpoorten, David B...	The post-COVID-19 future of digital learning in higher education: Views from educat...	2022	British Journal of Educational Technology
☑ 21	7.00	23	Dalia Dawoud, Khaled Y. Soliman	Cost-Effectiveness of Antiviral Treatments for Pandemics and Outbreaks of Respirat...	2020	Value in Health
☑ 21	7.00	24	Sakib Rokadiya, Eliza Gil, Claire Stubbs, Da...	COVID-19: Outcomes of patients with confirmed COVID-19 re-admitted to hospital.	2020	Journal of Infection
☑ 20	10.00	25	Lin Yu, Kitty Kioskli, Lance M. McCracken	The Psychological Functioning in the COVID-19 Pandemic and Its Association With P...	2021	The Journal of Pain

However, you can also *restrict* your search. If you wanted to know whether anyone in your institution (or another institution) had done research on racism in a COVID-19 context you would simply enter both words in the keywords field. Below are the first few of 22 results for this search for the University of Oxford.

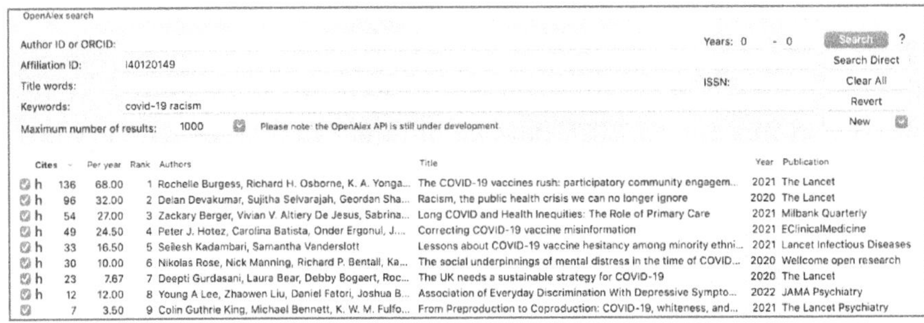

OpenAlex search

Author ID or ORCID: Years: 0 - 0   Search   ?

Affiliation ID: I40120149   Search Direct

Title words: ISSN: Clear All

Keywords: covid-19 racism   Revert

Maximum number of results: 1000   Please note: the OpenAlex API is still under development   New

Cites	Per year	Rank	Authors	Title	Year	Publication
☑ h 136	68.00	1	Rochelle Burgess, Richard H. Osborne, K. A. Yonga...	The COVID-19 vaccines rush: participatory community engagem...	2021	The Lancet
☑ h 96	32.00	2	Delan Devakumar, Sujitha Selvarajah, Geordan Sha...	Racism, the public health crisis we can no longer ignore	2020	The Lancet
☑ h 54	27.00	3	Zackary Berger, Vivian V. Altiery De Jesus, Sabrina...	Long COVID and Health Inequities: The Role of Primary Care	2021	Milbank Quarterly
☑ h 49	24.50	4	Peter J. Hotez, Carolina Batista, Onder Ergonul, J...	Correcting COVID-19 vaccine misinformation	2021	EClinicalMedicine
☑ h 33	16.50	5	Seilesh Kadambari, Samantha Vanderslott	Lessons about COVID-19 vaccine hesitancy among minority ethni...	2021	Lancet Infectious Diseases
☑ h 30	10.00	6	Nikolas Rose, Nick Manning, Richard P. Bentall, Ka...	The social underpinnings of mental distress in the time of COVID...	2020	Wellcome open research
☑ h 23	7.67	7	Deepti Gurdasani, Laura Bear, Debby Bogaert, Roc...	The UK needs a sustainable strategy for COVID-19	2020	The Lancet
☑ h 12	12.00	8	Young A Lee, Zhaowen Liu, Daniel Fatori, Joshua B...	Association of Everyday Discrimination With Depressive Sympto...	2022	JAMA Psychiatry
☑ 7	3.50	9	Colin Guthrie King, Michael Bennett, K. W. M. Fulfo...	From Preproduction to Coproduction: COVID-19, whiteness, and...	2021	The Lancet Psychiatry

PubMed

PubMed is limited in terms of its coverage to bio-medical research, and it doesn't report citations. However, as far as we can establish it accurately and comprehensively reports affiliations of papers. This does not preclude occasional errors, but affiliation search in PubMed can generally be trusted. Note that the following apply.

- Like other data sources, PubMed assigns university affiliation to papers, i.e., reports the affiliation of the author(s) at the time the paper was published.
- The affiliation is linked to individuals, not the full author record. Hence a combined author/affiliation search can be conducted with more accuracy than other sources.

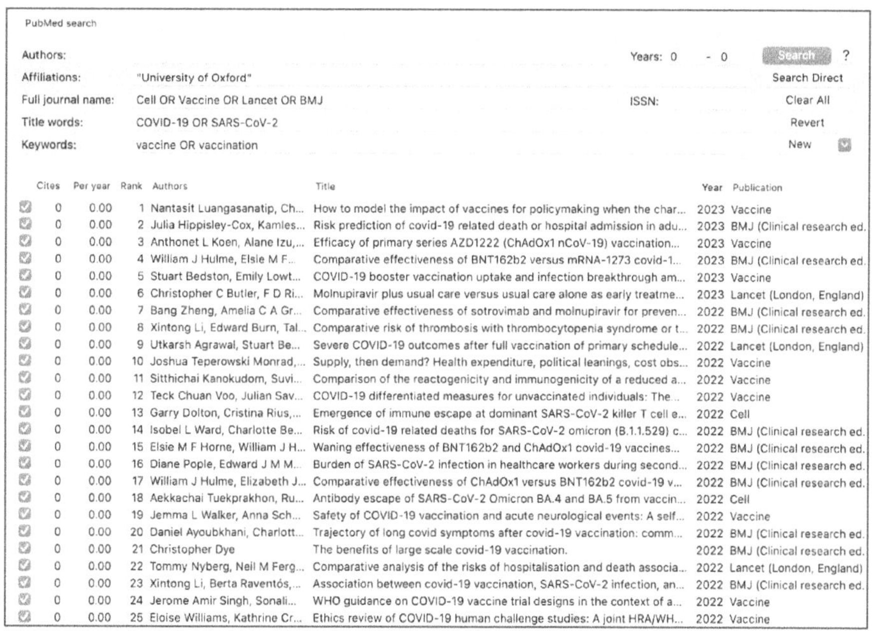

Cites	Per year	Rank	Authors	Title	Year	Publication
0	0.00	1	Nantasit Luangasanatip, Ch...	How to model the impact of vaccines for policymaking when the char...	2023	Vaccine
0	0.00	2	Julia Hippisley-Cox, Kamles...	Risk prediction of covid-19 related death or hospital admission in adu...	2023	BMJ (Clinical research ed.
0	0.00	3	Anthonet L Koen, Alane Izu,...	Efficacy of primary series AZD1222 (ChAdOx1 nCoV-19) vaccination...	2023	Vaccine
0	0.00	4	William J Hulme, Elsie M F...	Comparative effectiveness of BNT162b2 versus mRNA-1273 covid-1...	2023	BMJ (Clinical research ed.
0	0.00	5	Stuart Bedston, Emily Lowt...	COVID-19 booster vaccination uptake and infection breakthrough am...	2023	Vaccine
0	0.00	6	Christopher C Butler, F D Ri...	Molnupiravir plus usual care versus usual care alone as early treatme...	2023	Lancet (London, England)
0	0.00	7	Bang Zheng, Amelia C A Gr...	Comparative effectiveness of sotrovimab and molnupiravir for preven...	2022	BMJ (Clinical research ed.
0	0.00	8	Xintong Li, Edward Burn, Tal...	Comparative risk of thrombosis with thrombocytopenia syndrome or t...	2022	BMJ (Clinical research ed.
0	0.00	9	Utkarsh Agrawal, Stuart Be...	Severe COVID-19 outcomes after full vaccination of primary schedule...	2022	Lancet (London, England)
0	0.00	10	Joshua Teperowski Monrad,...	Supply, then demand? Health expenditure, political leanings, cost obs...	2022	Vaccine
0	0.00	11	Sitthichai Kanokudom, Suvi...	Comparison of the reactogenicity and immunogenicity of a reduced a...	2022	Vaccine
0	0.00	12	Teck Chuan Voo, Julian Sav...	COVID-19 differentiated measures for unvaccinated individuals: The...	2022	Vaccine
0	0.00	13	Garry Dolton, Cristina Rius,...	Emergence of immune escape at dominant SARS-CoV-2 killer T cell e...	2022	Cell
0	0.00	14	Isobel L Ward, Charlotte Be...	Risk of covid-19 related deaths for SARS-CoV-2 omicron (B.1.1.529) c...	2022	BMJ (Clinical research ed.
0	0.00	15	Elsie M F Horne, William J H...	Waning effectiveness of BNT162b2 and ChAdOx1 covid-19 vaccines...	2022	BMJ (Clinical research ed.
0	0.00	16	Diane Pople, Edward J M M...	Burden of SARS-CoV-2 infection in healthcare workers during second...	2022	BMJ (Clinical research ed.
0	0.00	17	William J Hulme, Elizabeth J...	Comparative effectiveness of ChAdOx1 versus BNT162b2 covid-19 v...	2022	BMJ (Clinical research ed.
0	0.00	18	Aekkachai Tuekprakhon, Ru...	Antibody escape of SARS-CoV-2 Omicron BA.4 and BA.5 from vaccin...	2022	Cell
0	0.00	19	Jemma L Walker, Anna Sch...	Safety of COVID-19 vaccination and acute neurological events: A self...	2022	Vaccine
0	0.00	20	Daniel Ayoubkhani, Charlott...	Trajectory of long covid symptoms after covid-19 vaccination: comm...	2022	BMJ (Clinical research ed.
0	0.00	21	Christopher Dye	The benefits of large scale covid-19 vaccination.	2022	BMJ (Clinical research ed.
0	0.00	22	Tommy Nyberg, Neil M Ferg...	Comparative analysis of the risks of hospitalisation and death associa...	2022	Lancet (London, England)
0	0.00	23	Xintong Li, Berta Raventós,...	Association between covid-19 vaccination, SARS-CoV-2 infection, an...	2022	BMJ (Clinical research ed.
0	0.00	24	Jerome Amir Singh, Sonali...	WHO guidance on COVID-19 vaccine trial designs in the context of a...	2022	Vaccine
0	0.00	25	Eloise Williams, Kathrine Cr...	Ethics review of COVID-19 human challenge studies: A joint HRA/WH...	2022	Vaccine

As evidenced in the screenshot above, PubMed can be very useful to find out what a university (or author) has published on COVID-19 or any other medical topic. You can make your search as broad or as narrow as you like as PubMed has a fairly flexible search syntax.

In the above screenshot, I have defined a restrictive search looking at what Oxford University academics have published in one of the key medical journals in the area of Covid vaccination. At the time of the search this resulted in seventy publications published in a range of journals. Initially articles were mostly published in the *Lancet*, more recently *BMJ* and *Vaccine* dominate the list.

Scopus and Web of Science

As was shown in the OpenAlex searches above, both Scopus and the Web of Science typically report affiliations of papers accurately and comprehensively. This does not preclude occasional errors, but affiliation search can generally be trusted. Note that, like most other data sources the following conditions apply for both Scopus and the Web of Science:

- Assign university affiliation to papers, i.e., report the affiliation of the author(s) at the time the paper was published.
- As the affiliation is linked to *papers*, not *individuals*, a combined author/affiliation search will report results even if it is one of the author's co-authors that has the requested affiliation.

As both Scopus and the Web of Science APIs only allow 200 results, they are less useful for generic affiliation searches as they will only report the most cited publications. Moreover, Scopus only reports the first author and does not report abstracts. The Web of Science is only available for academics with a university subscription. Hence, I will not provide any further examples for these two data sources.

Searching for multiple universities

Four of the five data sources discussed in this section allow searching for multiple universities in the same search (verify WoS once available). The fifth, OpenAlex, only allows *one* term in the affiliation search.

A search for my name and the University of Melbourne and Middlesex University as affiliation in Scopus resulted in 91 publications, correctly filtering out the articles that were duplicated in separate searches because of matches on the co-author affiliation (see below).

Search terms	Source	...	Cites	Cites/year	h	g	hi,norm	hi,annual	hA	acc10
a harzing, "University of Melbourne" OR "Middlesex University"	SC Scopus	91	8,868	403.09	47	91	47	2.14	16	25

Scopus search

Authors: a harzing — Years: 0 – 0 — Search — ?
Affiliations: "University of Melbourne" OR "Middlesex University" — Search Direct
Publication name: — ISSN: — Clear All
Title words: — Revert
Keywords: — New

	Cites	Per year	Rank	Authors	Title	Year	Publication
h	828	118.29	1	A. Harzing	Google Scholar, Scopus and the Web of Science: a longit...	2016	Scientometrics
h	587	41.93	2	N.J. Adler	When knowledge wins: Transcending the sense and non...	2009	Academy of Management Learning and Education
h	470	27.65	3	A.W. Harzing	Response styles in cross-national survey research: A 26...	2006	International Journal of Cross Cultural Management
h	465	31.00	4	A. Harzing	Google Scholar as a new source for citation analysis	2008	Ethics in Science and Environmental Politics
h	346	15.73	5	A.W. Harzing	Of bears, bumble-bees, and spiders: The role of expatria...	2001	Journal of World Business
h	320	15.24	6	A.W. Harzing	Acquisitions versus greenfield investments: International...	2002	Strategic Management Journal
h	276	13.80	7	A.J. Feely	Language management in multinational companies	2003	Cross Cultural Management: An International Journal
h	276	19.71	8	N. Noorderhaven	Knowledge-sharing and social interaction within MNEs	2009	Journal of International Business Studies
h	264	16.50	9	M. Pudelko	Country-of-origin, localization, or dominance effect? An...	2007	Human Resource Management
h	263	13.15	10	A.W. Harzing	The relative impact of country of origin and universal co...	2003	Organization Studies
h	229	16.36	11	A. Harzing	A google scholar h-index for journals: An alternative met...	2009	Journal of the American Society for Information Sci...
h	214	9.73	12	A.W. Harzing	Who's in charge? An empirical study of executive staffin...	2001	Human Resource Management
h	213	14.20	13	A.W. Harzing	The language barrier and its implications for HQ-subsidi...	2008	Cross Cultural Management: An International Journal
h	197	21.89	14	H. Tenzer	The impact of language barriers on trust formation in mu...	2014	Journal of International Business Studies
h	177	14.75	15	A.W. Harzing	Babel in business: The language barrier and its solutions...	2011	Journal of World Business
h	147	14.70	16	A.W. Harzing	A preliminary test of Google Scholar as a source for citat...	2013	Scientometrics
h	142	10.14	17	B.S. Reiche	The role of international assignees' social capital in creat...	2009	Journal of International Business Studies

Research collaborations

As we have discussed above Crossref only allows OR searches, but the three other data sources allow both OR and AND sources. The latter would allow us to verify whether universities have collaborated. Scopus appears to conduct this search within a single author record, and thus only reports only authors with dual affiliation. Whilst this may be of interest in itself, it doesn't allow us to establish research collaborations more broadly.

However, it is possible to do this in PubMed. When searching for two research-intensive universities in the Biomedical Sciences like the University of Melbourne and the University of Oxford, you will quickly run into the 399 results limitation of PubMed. However, when searching for universities that do not have a strong emphasis in the Biomedical Sciences like Middlesex University, you will find a complete record of co-authored publications (see screenshot below).

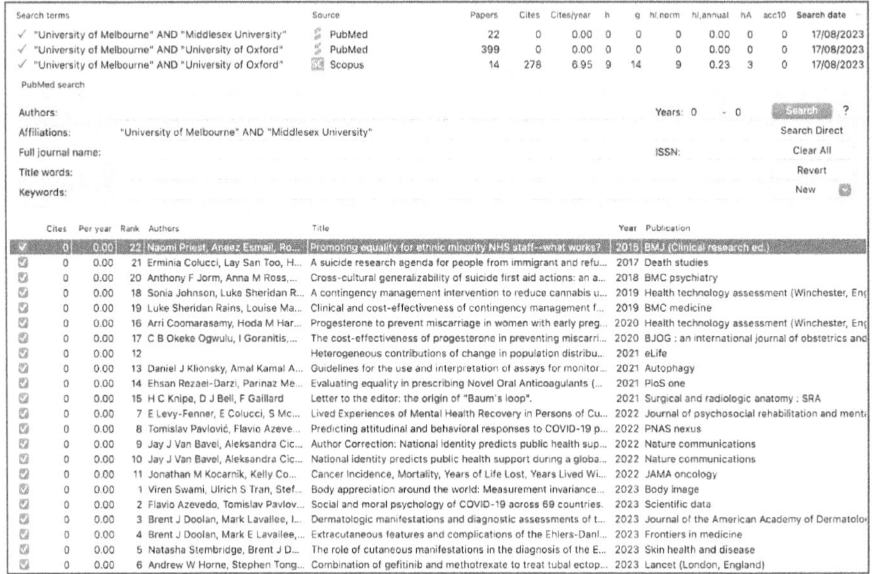

Search terms	Source	Papers	Cites	Cites/year	h	g	hl,norm	hl,annual	hA	acc10	Search date
✓ "University of Melbourne" AND "Middlesex University"	PubMed	22	0	0.00	0	0	0	0.00	0	0	17/08/2023
✓ "University of Melbourne" AND "University of Oxford"	PubMed	399	0	0.00	0	0	0	0.00	0	0	17/08/2023
✓ "University of Melbourne" AND "University of Oxford"	Scopus	14	278	6.95	9	14	9	0.23	3	0	17/08/2023

PubMed search

Authors:
Affiliations: "University of Melbourne" AND "Middlesex University"
Full journal name:
Title words:
Keywords:

Years: 0 – 0   Search   ?
Search Direct
Clear All
Revert
New

Cites	Per year	Rank	Authors	Title	Year	Publication
0	0.00	22	Naomi Priest, Aneez Esmail, Ro...	Promoting equality for ethnic minority NHS staff--what works?	2015	BMJ (Clinical research ed.)
0	0.00	21	Erminia Colucci, Lay San Too, H...	A suicide research agenda for people from immigrant and refu...	2017	Death studies
0	0.00	20	Anthony F Jorm, Anna M Ross,...	Cross-cultural generalizability of suicide first aid actions: an a...	2018	BMC psychiatry
0	0.00	18	Sonia Johnson, Luke Sheridan R...	A contingency management intervention to reduce cannabis u...	2019	Health technology assessment (Winchester, Eng
0	0.00	19	Luke Sheridan Rains, Louise Ma...	Clinical and cost-effectiveness of contingency management f...	2019	BMC medicine
0	0.00	16	Arri Coomarasamy, Hoda M Har...	Progesterone to prevent miscarriage in women with early preg...	2020	Health technology assessment (Winchester, Eng
0	0.00	17	C B Okeke Ogwulu, I Goranitis,...	The cost-effectiveness of progesterone in preventing miscarri...	2020	BJOG : an international journal of obstetrics and
0	0.00	12		Heterogeneous contributions of change in population distribu...	2021	eLife
0	0.00	13	Daniel J Klionsky, Amal Kamal A...	Guidelines for the use and interpretation of assays for monitor...	2021	Autophagy
0	0.00	14	Ehsan Rezaei-Darzi, Parinaz Me...	Evaluating equality in prescribing Novel Oral Anticoagulants (...	2021	PloS one
0	0.00	15	H C Knipe, D J Bell, F Gaillard	Letter to the editor: the origin of "Baum's loop".	2021	Surgical and radiologic anatomy : SRA
0	0.00	7	E Levy-Fenner, E Colucci, S Mc...	Lived Experiences of Mental Health Recovery in Persons of Cu...	2022	Journal of psychosocial rehabilitation and menta
0	0.00	8	Tomislav Pavlović, Flavio Azeve...	Predicting attitudinal and behavioral responses to COVID-19 p...	2022	PNAS nexus
0	0.00	9	Jay J Van Bavel, Aleksandra Cic...	Author Correction: National identity predicts public health sup...	2022	Nature communications
0	0.00	10	Jay J Van Bavel, Aleksandra Cic...	National identity predicts public health support during a globa...	2022	Nature communications
0	0.00	11	Jonathan M Kocarnik, Kelly Co...	Cancer Incidence, Mortality, Years of Life Lost, Years Lived Wi...	2022	JAMA oncology
0	0.00	1	Viren Swami, Ulrich S Tran, Stef...	Body appreciation around the world: Measurement invariance...	2023	Body Image
0	0.00	2	Flavio Azevedo, Tomislav Pavlov...	Social and moral psychology of COVID-19 across 69 countries.	2023	Scientific data
0	0.00	3	Brent J Doolan, Mark Lavallee, I...	Dermatologic manifestations and diagnostic assessments of t...	2023	Journal of the American Academy of Dermatolo
0	0.00	4	Brent J Doolan, Mark E Lavallee,...	Extracutaneous features and complications of the Ehlers-Danl...	2023	Frontiers in medicine
0	0.00	5	Natasha Stembridge, Brent J D...	The role of cutaneous manifestations in the diagnosis of the E...	2023	Skin health and disease
0	0.00	6	Andrew W Horne, Stephen Tong...	Combination of gefitinib and methotrexate to treat tubal ectop...	2023	Lancet (London, England)

In sum

In this chapter, we illustrated how you can conduct effective topic and affiliation searches. Most Publish or Perish users primarily use Google Scholar for their searches. Hence, the instructions in this chapter focused mainly on this data source. In the last two sections, however, we also discussed topic and affiliation searches the other data sources.

This chapter ends the section on basic use cases: author, journal, topic, and affiliation searches. In the next five chapters, we will look at more advanced use cases. We start with presenting your case for tenure and promotion (Chapter 10), before moving on to evaluating other academics (Chapter 11), doing a literature review (Chapter 12), deciding on where to submit your paper (Chapter 13) and doing bibliometric research (Chapter 14).

Chapter 10: Presenting your case for tenure or promotion

Many academics using the Publish or Perish software do so because they need to make a case for tenure, promotion, or any other type of research evaluation. In this chapter, I will provide some pointers on how to report your case for citation impact more effectively. Note that my suggestions refer to citation impact only. They do not relate to the *content* of your research, nor to teaching or service/external engagement activities. For tips on those you may want to refer to one of my other books: *Writing effective promotion applications*.

First, please understand that it is *your* job to convince and educate your tenure or promotion panel of the impact of your research. Many senior academics, having grown up in an age in which citations were relatively unimportant, have a limited knowledge of their own or other academics' citation records. Moreover, many academics have the tendency to subconsciously overestimate what their own records were when they went up for tenure or promotion. Hence, they are implicitly using an inappropriate reference group.

If you have an excellent record, you might think it is unfair to have to do all this work to get tenure or promotion. You may also think senior academics should know better. That might well be true, but remember that they are only human and are very busy academics. Moreover, many other processes in academia (e.g., any further promotions, job applications, funding applications, research awards, and fellowship applications) depend on you making a case for the impact of your research. Hence it is not a bad idea to get some skills in "selling" your record!

In this chapter, I discuss five key strategies: pick your metrics wisely, create your own reference group, compare your papers to the journal average, present comprehensive citation counts for edited volumes, and find the pearls in your record. Just pick and mix the ones that suit your record best. Finally, I also provide some advice on what to do if you have very few citations overall.

Pick your metrics wisely

Publish or Perish provides you with a very wide range of metrics. If your university prescribes the metrics you should use, you have little choice. However, in many cases there is more flexibility. So, what metrics do you pick? The screenshot below shows a summary of my own citation record. My h-index and g-index are relatively high in comparison to other academics in my field, so it is quite easy for me to make my case.

Citation metrics	?		Papers/author:	114.56
			Authors/paper:	2.05
Publication years:	1995–2023		h-index:	71
Citation years:	28 (1995–2023)		g-index:	160
Papers:	180		hI,norm:	56
Citations:	25864		hI,annual:	2.00
Cites/year:	923.71		hA-index:	25
Cites/paper:	143.69		Papers with ACC ≥ 1,2,5,10,20:	
Cites/author:	17568.19		129,111,84,60,29	

However, if I had a free choice and was applying for a professorial position, I would probably point out that my individual h-index (hI,norm) is relatively high in comparison to my regular h-index. I would also point out my relatively high hI,annual and hA-index, as well as my high ACCs (annualised citation counts). This would allow me to make the case that:

- **My most-cited work is single-authored**. This makes it easy to substantiate that I made a significant intellectual contribution. It also shows that my citation record is not inflated by citations from (famous) co-authors and their networks.

- **I have made a sustained contribution over the years**, reflected in my high hI,annual, i.e., on average I published two single-authored equivalent impactful articles every year in the last 27 years. Most academics will see their hI,annual decline gradually after a mid-career highpoint. It becomes harder to increase your h-index once it is at a fairly high level and without a further increase in the h-index, the hI,annual will decline gradually with each passing year.

- **I have published a significant number of sustainably impactful publications**, reflected by my high hA-index, i.e., I have 25 articles with at least 25 citations per year. This is confirmed by my high ACCs. I have 60 articles with 10 or more citations *per year* and 29 articles with 20 or more citations per year.

Advice for early to mid-career academics

Whether it is beneficial for you to use the individual h-index rather than the regular h-index and g-index depends on your number of highly cited single-authored articles. Note that Publish or Perish will provide you with three implementations of the individual h-index: hI,norm, hI-index, and hm-index; the latter two are only visible when you export the metrics. So, feel free to pick the one that shows of your case to its best advantage!

The hI,annual can be particularly useful if you are an early or mid-career academic as this metric is often relatively high at this career stage. Using the hIa allows you to compare yourself against more senior academics on an equal footing. Of course, you need to inspire confidence that you will be able to sustain this level of performance. It is not easy to keep publishing new impactful articles every year!

Create your own reference group

You can make your case for citation impact by comparing your citation record to a *relevant* group of peers. Many evaluators have very little idea of what typical norm scores for the various metrics are. So, unless you make an *explicit* comparison, they will – consciously or subconsciously - use their own reference group. This might not work to your advantage.

There are vast disciplinary differences in typical citations levels. This is especially true when using the Web of Science as a data source (see Chapter 4). Therefore, if your university has tenure or promotion committees that include academics in related, or even unrelated, disciplines, it is even more important to position your case for tenure or promotion within an appropriate reference group. Below I first show how citations can vary dramatically even within sub-disciplines, and then explain how to pick your reference group.

Differences in citation levels within sub-disciplines

The area of Human Resource Management, as a sub-discipline of Management, includes scholars working on industrial relations and labour unions, as well as scholars working on more psychologically oriented topics such as motivation or job attitudes, which is generally classified as organisational behaviour. The latter academics might be able to publish in one of the mainstream Psychology journals such as *Psychological Bulletin.* The former academics would feel fortunate if they were able to publish in the top US journal in their field: *Industrial Relations.* The journal impact factor of *Psychological Bulletin* is nearly eight times as high as the journal impact factor of *Industrial Relations.*

Moreover, as their research is very context specific, many academics in Industrial Relations will not be able to publish in mainstream US-American Industrial Relations journals. They are likely to publish in lower-impact journals such as *British Journal of Industrial Relations, European Journal of Industrial Relations*, or the Australian *Labour History.* Therefore, even within the sub-discipline of HRM, academics in the areas of Industrial Relations can be expected to be cited far less frequently than academics in the area of Organisational Behaviour.

The screenshot below shows a Publish or Perish analysis comparing *Psychological Bulletin* with Industrial Relations journals for 2016-2020. It shows how articles in the former can expect much higher citation rates. Even within the set of industrial relations journals there is a clear difference between the well-established British journal, the (much younger) European journal and the very localised Australian journal. Looking at how your article compares with other articles in the journal is therefore another good strategy (see the next section).

Search terms	Source	Papers	Cites	Cites/year	h
✓ Psychological Bulletin, ISSN 0033-2909...	G Google Scholar	206	35,899	5,983.17	109
✓ British Journal of Industrial Relations, IS...	G Google Scholar	268	4,204	700.67	33
✓ European Journal of Industrial Relations,...	G Google Scholar	129	2,343	390.50	27
✓ Labour History, ISSN 0023-6942 from 2...	G Google Scholar	248	53	8.83	3

How to pick your reference group?

It is very important to pick your reference group wisely. It should be narrow enough to reflect any of the differences in citation behaviours across disciplines, sub-disciplines, or even sub-sub-disciplines that we discussed above. However, it should not be so narrow that it leads your committee to discard your selection as biased or irrelevant. I have found the following two strategies to be particularly effective: a national or international discipline-based strategy and an institution-based strategy.

For the discipline-based strategy, you compare your citation record with a *representative* selection of academics in your field of research at the level you are applying for. Depending on your field, the level you are applying for, and the country you work in this could be either a national or an international group of scholars. To make your case more convincing, it is often best to pick academics at institutions of a similar or higher level of prestige. If you can demonstrate that you are performing at the same level as the average of academics in more prestigious institutions who have been in position for a while, you have a very strong case.

The institution-based strategy is a more local strategy. Here you compare your record with academics in your *own* institution at the level you are applying for. If you have access to the length of tenure of your academic colleagues, you might be able to compare your own record with that of both long-established academics and those who were recently promoted to the same level. The former is effective if promotion criteria have not changed over time. The latter might be more effective if they have become more stringent in recent years. More generally, this strategy might be useful if your institution has more stringent norms for promotion than comparable institutions.

I used a combination of both strategies in my promotion application at the University of Melbourne (see screenshot below), comparing my own metrics with recent promotions in the same department, professors in the field of International Business in Australia, and more established professors in the department. Note the h-indices and citation levels in this table might appear very low by today's standards. That is because - with publications expanding at 10% per year - average citation levels have increased dramatically in the last 15 years. The general principle of comparison is still valid, however.

Table 1: Bibliometric comparison with other professors, mean and range are given for each indicator.

Group	h-index	1st authored papers in h-index	Single-authored papers in h-index	Number of ISI citing articles (2006 only)	Number of years as professor
2005/2006 promotions	Mean: 6.3 Range: 4-8	Mean: 4.3 Range: 3-5	Mean: 3.0 Range: 2-4	Mean: 15 Range: 3-34	Recently appointed
IB professors at top Oz unis	Mean: 9.0 Range: 4-16	Mean: 3.3 Range: 1-6	Mean: 1.5 Range: 0-3	Mean: 10 Range: 3-21	15 years (4-28 years)
DoMM established professors	Mean: 14.0 Range: 6-22	Mean: 5.0 Range: 0-11	Mean: 2.0 Range: 0-4	Mean: 46 Range: 8-102	14 years (10-19 years)
Anne-Wil Harzing	13	13	10	63	N/A

Please note that you will normally need at least 3-4 academics in your reference group to be able to make a credible comparison. Larger numbers are advisable. I would generally advise against listing names of individuals as this can easily lead to a hostile response. However, be prepared to substantiate your averages if so requested. You might wish to create folders for your reference groups in the Publish or Perish Multi-searches centre. That way you can store and update your analyses easily.

Compare papers to the journal average

The previous section suggested you pick your own reference group, focusing on academics in your discipline or university. But what better reference group than other articles published at the same time in the same journal? In this section, I will show you how you can make your case for academic research impact by strategically comparing your papers to their journal reference group. To do so, simply search for the journal you published in, and set the years to the year of your publication. To make your case you can pursue several avenues.

Most cited paper in the journal that year

The Publish or Perish screenshot below compares my 2001 paper published in *Journal of World Business* with other papers published in the same year. You can see it is the most highly cited paper in the journal in that particular year and its citations compared well with the journal average. You could write this up in your case as: *"My 2001 paper in Journal of World Business was the most cited paper out of 25 papers published that year and had nearly four times as many citations as the average paper in the journal that year."*

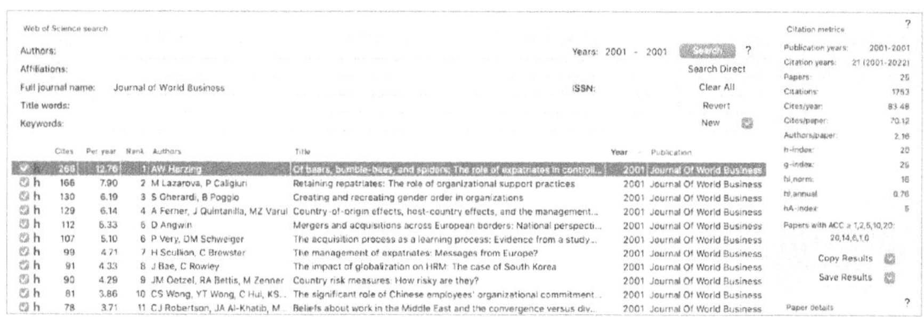

Most cited single-authored paper

Now of course it won't happen very often that your paper is the most cited article in the journal. So, you can be a bit creative in this as well. The Publish or Perish screenshot below shows my 2000 publication in the *Journal of International Business Studies*.

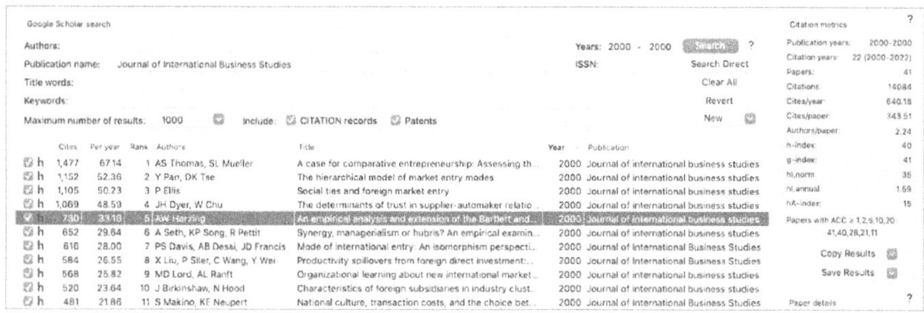

My paper was not the most cited paper in the journal that year, but it was the 2nd most cited single-authored paper and the 5th most cited paper overall (out of 42), which in a top US journal might be seen as a significant achievement. In my promotion application, I combined this observation with a statement that: *"I am one of only two academics affiliated with an Australian university who has ever published a single-authored article in Journal of International Business Studies (JIBS) since it was established 37 years ago."*

If you work outside North America and have published in a North American journal, you could also make an argument that publishing in these journals is more difficult from outside North America. Check whether your paper is (one of) the most cited article by a non-North American academic or whether it is (one of) the most cited article by an academic from your own country.

Paper in top 5% or top 10% most cited

Of course, it will not happen very often that your paper is one of the most-cited papers in the journal in question. However, even being able to say that it is within the top 5% or top 10% most cited papers that year would make a very significant contribution to your case.

If you are lucky, you might have articles that are amongst the most-cited articles in a particular journal over a longer period. If you could say that your article was among the top 5% or top 10% most cited articles in a particular journal over its entire history of publication that would make a very strong case, especially if the journal was a particularly well-known journal.

	Cites	Per year	Rank	Authors	Title	Year
☑ h	7,047	414.53	1	AY Kolb, DA Kolb	Learning styles and learning spaces: Enhancing experiential learning in higher education	2005
☑ h	5,362	315.41	2	S Ghoshal	Bad management theories are destroying good management practices	2005
☑ h	2,576	128.80	3	J Pfeffer, CT Fong	The end of business schools? Less success than meets the eye	2002
☑ h	1,374	98.14	4	F Luthans, JB Avey, JL Patera	Experimental analysis of a web-based training intervention to develop positive psycholo...	2008
☑ h	1,288	71.56	5	B Honig	Entrepreneurship education: Toward a model of contingency-based business planning	2004
☑ h	1,229	76.81	6	D Dunne, R Martin	Design thinking and how it will change management education: An interview and discus...	2006
☑ h	1,217	110.64	7	RJ Ely, H Ibarra, DM Kolb	Taking gender into account: Theory and design for women's leadership development pr...	2011
☑ h	1,111	61.72	8	PC Earley, RS Peterson	The elusive cultural chameleon: Cultural intelligence as a new approach to intercultural...	2004
☑ h	1,023	204.60	10	G Nabi, F Liñán, A Fayolle, N Kru...	The impact of entrepreneurship education in higher education: A systematic review and...	2017
☑ h	1,004	77.23	9	NJ Adler, AW Harzing	When knowledge wins: Transcending the sense and nonsense of academic rankings	2009
☑ h	919	57.44	11	DL McCabe, KD Butterfield...	Academic dishonesty in graduate business programs: Prevalence, causes, and propose...	2006
☑ h	914	45.70	12	DC Kayes	Experiential learning and its critics: Preserving the role of experience in management le...	2002
☑ h	910	50.56	13	DR DeTienne, GN Chandler	Opportunity identification and its role in the entrepreneurial classroom: A pedagogical a...	2004
☑ h	833	64.08	14	KY Ng, L Van Dyne, S Ang	From experience to experiential learning: Cultural intelligence as a learning capability fo...	2009
☑ h	784	39.20	15	RE Boyatzis, EC Stubbs, SN Tayl...	Learning cognitive and emotional intelligence competencies through graduate manage...	2002
☑ h	782	39.10	16	C Argyris	Double-loop learning, teaching, and research	2002

My 2009 article with Nancy Adler in the *Academy of Management Learning & Education* was in the top 1% of articles (10th out of more than 1,000 papers) published in AMLE since its inception in 2002 with a total of 1,000 (Google Scholar) citations (see above). This would be a strong claim for its impact.

However, it is not such a good idea to use this strategy if your paper was published early in the period you are reporting on. For instance, if you claim that your paper is amongst the 25% most cited articles in a journal between 2000-2022, and your paper was published in 2000/2001, it is likely that your paper was cited less than average for articles published in 2000 and 2001.

Sorting publications by the number of citations per year (the second column) is a good way to avoid this problem as this automatically corrects for the age of the article. If we sort the above screenshot on citations per year, my article with Nancy moves up to #8 and several recent contributions, published between 2015 and 2020, now rank much higher in the list.

Compare a body of work

If you do not have any papers that really stand out, but your papers are generally well cited in comparison to the journals that they are published in, you could emphasise this. For instance, you could say something like: *"on average my articles are amongst the top 20%-30% most cited papers when compared to papers published in the same journal in the same year"*.

You will need to be a little careful with this strategy though. Unless you have some papers that have been published in journals that your evaluation committee will recognise as top journals, it will only elicit the comment that you tend to "waste your work" by publishing it in low impact journals. So, you may need to combine this strategy with some evidence that the journals you have published in have high standards of peer review.

Present comprehensive citation counts for edited volumes

In some disciplines it is common to publish edited volumes. In these cases, the volume's editor might need to invest considerable effort coaching its contributors to submit their chapters in time. Editors might also provide significant editorial input. Edited volumes can make a major contribution to their field of study as they often provide a collection of the latest research on a particular topic. Unfortunately, edited volumes are often not appreciated as much as monographs or journal articles. Their citation impact might also be modest.

However, one reason for this modest citation count might be that few academics will refer to the edited volume as a whole. Authors more commonly refer to individual chapters within an edited volume. Moreover, some edited volumes, such as handbooks or companions go through various editions. Thus, collating the citation counts of the individual chapters and editions will provide a more comprehensive case of the publication's its impact.

Worked example: IHRM textbook

In 1995, I published an edited textbook on the topic of International Human Resource Management, with new editions published in 2004, 2010, 2014, 2019, and 2022. Although it was a textbook, Publish or Perish demonstrates that it generated quite a lot of citations in the academic literature. Many of these citations were to the book as a whole, with a combined number of nearly 700 citations for the various editions.

However, as the three screenshots below show, there were a further 575 citations to individual chapters in the 1994/1995 edition, 775 to chapters the 2004 edition and 313 to chapters in the 2010/2011 edition. Overall, the book therefore had nearly 2,500 citations, a number that would allow me to more easily argue the case that this edited volume has had a very significant impact in the field of International Human Resource Management.

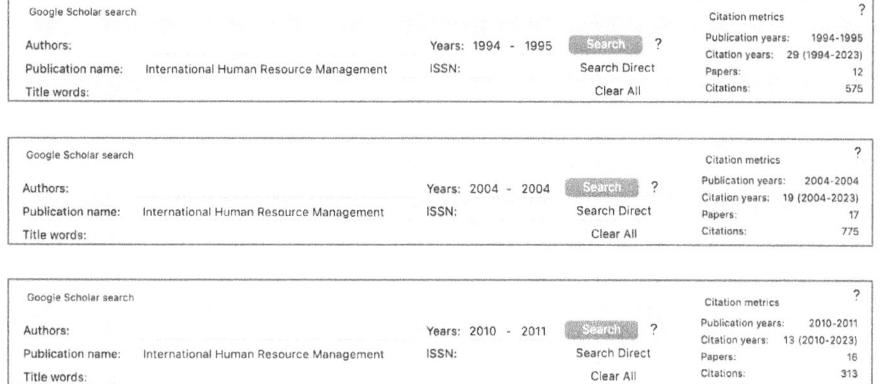

Interestingly, Google Scholar didn't show significant citations to the 2014, 2019, and 2022 editions (a total of 50). This might have been due by Google Scholar attributing book citations to the wrong version. In this case, however, this is immaterial as our aim was to provide a comprehensive count for various editions combined.

Find the pearls in your record

The most important realisation in presenting your case for tenure, promotion, or grant applications is that every case is different. We all have "pearls" in our research portfolio. You just need to find and polish them, so they shine brightly. Of course, sometimes you are prescribed to list a number of metrics, maybe total citation counts, or h-index, or your number of publications. However, even in that case you can always add additional information.

Different profiles, different stories

Over a decade ago, I had a colleague at the University of Melbourne – Maria Kraimer – whose total Google Scholar citation level was very similar to mine. Even now our total citations are less than 6% apart and as she started publishing 2 years later, our citations/per year counts are virtually identical. However, I would suggest two very different ways of presenting our records to our best advantage.

Ground-breaking contributions

As Maria, I would indicate that I had no less than five articles that have gathered more than 100 citations per year. I would also point out that four of my articles have gathered more than 2,000 citations and six more than 1,000 (see screenshot below), indicating they are truly ground-breaking. I would also mention that I had made these ground-breaking contributions very early in my career; Maria's seven most highly cited articles were all published shortly after her PhD completion.

Cites	Per year	Rank	Authors	Title	Year
h 3,732	169.64	1	SE Seibert, ML Kraimer, RC Liden	A social capital theory of career success	2001
h 2,827	128.50	2	RT Sparrowe, RC Liden, SJ Wayne, ML Kraimer	Social networks and the performance of individuals and groups	2001
h 2,579	107.46	3	SE Seibert, JM Crant, ML Kraimer	Proactive personality and career success.	1999
h 2,343	106.50	4	SE Seibert, ML Kraimer, JM Crant	What do proactive people do? A longitudinal model linking proactive personality and c...	2001
h 1,389	63.14	5	SE Seibert, ML Kraimer	The five-factor model of personality and career success	2001
h 1,055	47.95	6	ML Kraimer, SJ Wayne, RAA Jaworski	Sources of support and expatriate performance: The mediating role of expatriate adju...	2001
h 821	34.21	7	SJ Wayne, RC Liden, ML Kraimer, IK Graf	The role of human capital, motivation and supervisor sponsorship in predicting career...	1999
h 808	42.53	8	B Erdogan, ML Kraimer, RC Liden	Work value congruence and intrinsic career success: The compensatory roles of lead...	2004
h 716	37.68	9	ML Kraimer, SJ Wayne	An examination of perceived organizational support as a multidimensional construct i...	2004
h 715	59.58	10	ML Kraimer, SE Seibert, SJ Wayne, RC Liden,...	Antecedents and outcomes of organizational support for development: the critical rol...	2011
h 697	41.00	11	B Erdogan, RC Liden, ML Kraimer	Justice and leader-member exchange: The moderating role of organizational culture	2006
h 655	59.55	12	MA Shaffer, ML Kraimer, YP Chen, MC Bolino	Choices, challenges, and career consequences of global work experiences: A review...	2012
h 589	196.33	13	J Akkermans, J Richardson, ML Kraimer	The Covid-19 crisis as a career shock: Implications for careers and vocational behavior	2020

I would probably not discuss co-authorship patterns in any detail as this is not a particular strength of Maria's record. Many of her highly cited publications were lead-authored by someone else. One could of course consider pointing to well-known co-authors, but this is a bit of a double-edged sword. To some readers this is a very positive sign, others might wonder about the academic's own contribution.

Finally, I would point to a recent article about Covid-19 (last line of the screenshot). Published in 2020, it is Maria's most cited article on a citations per year basis.

Sustained and single-authored contributions

As Anne-Wil, I would make a very different case, given that I do not have any articles with very high citation levels (i.e., above 2,000). I do have three publications that have more than 1,000 citations, but none of these are in my main research area (International Business). I would, however, indicate that I have no less than 25 articles that have each gathered more than 25 or more citations per year (see screenshot below).

	Cites	Per year ⌄	Rank	Authors	Title	Year
☑ h	1,073	178.83	2	AW Harzing, S Alakan...	Google Scholar, Scopus and the Web of Science: A longitudinal and...	2016
☑ h	1,420	94.67	1	AW Harzing	Publish or Perish	2007
☑ h	1,002	77.08	3	NJ Adler, AW Harzing	When knowledge wins: Transcending the sense and nonsense of a...	2009
☑ h	845	60.36	5	AW Harzing, R van der...	Google Scholar as a new source for citation analysis?	2008
☑ h	668	55.67	9	AW Harzing, A Pinning...	International Human Resource Management	2010
☑ h	832	52.00	6	AW Harzing	Response styles in cross-national survey research: A 26-country St...	2006
☑ h	515	42.92	15	AW Harzing	The Publish or Perish Book: Your guide to Effective and Responsibl...	2010
☑ h	851	42.55	4	AW Harzing	Acquisitions versus greenfield investments: International strategy a...	2002
☑ h	337	42.13	22	H Tenzer, M Pudelko,...	The impact of language barriers on trust formation in multinational...	2014
☑ h	545	41.92	13	N Noorderhaven, AW...	Knowledge-sharing and social interaction within MNEs	2009
☑ h	114	38.00	55	AW Harzing	Two new kids on the block: How do Crossref and Dimensions comp...	2019
☑ h	525	35.00	14	M Pudelko, AW Harzing	Country-of-origin, localization, or dominance effect? An empirical i...	2007
☑ h	204	34.00	35	AW Harzing, M Pudelk...	The bridging role of expatriates and inpatriates in knowledge transf...	2016
☑ h	730	33.18	7	AW Harzing	An empirical analysis and extension of the Bartlett and Ghoshal typ...	2000
☑ h	459	32.79	19	AW Harzing, AJ Feely	The language barrier and its implications for HQ-subsidiary relation...	2008
☑ h	678	32.29	8	AW Harzing	Of bears, bumble-bees, and spiders: The role of expatriates in cont...	2001
☑ h	419	32.23	20	AW Harzing, R van der...	A Google Scholar h-index for journals: An alternative metric to mea...	2009
☑ h	353	32.09	21	AW Harzing, K Köster,...	Babel in business: The language barrier and its solutions in the HQ-...	2011
☑ h	159	31.80	46	H Tenzer, S Terjesen,...	Language in International Business: A Review and Agenda for Futur...	2017
☑ h	578	30.42	11	AJ Feely, AW Harzing	Language management in multinational companies	2003
☑ h	149	29.80	48	A Martin-Martin, E Or...	Can we use Google Scholar to identify highly-cited documents?	2017
☑ h	253	28.11	29	AW Harzing, M Pudelko	Language competencies, policies and practices in multinational cor...	2013
☑ h	503	26.47	16	AW Harzing, A Sorge	The relative impact of country of origin and universal contingencies...	2003
☑ h	606	26.35	10	AW Harzing	Managing the multinationals: An international study of control mec...	1999
☑ h	234	26.00	34	AW Harzing	A preliminary test of Google Scholar as a source for citation data: a...	2013
☑ h	150	25.00	47	AW Harzing, M Pudelko	Do we need to distance ourselves from the distance concept? Why...	2016

I would also point out that my most highly cited work is largely first or single-authored and that much of it was published in the second half of my career, thus indicating that my impact has not slowed down after being promoted to Full Professor in 2006. That said, I would probably also emphasise that my PhD thesis (*Managing the Multinationals*, 3rd from below) has turned out to be quite influential, with more than 600 citations.

Creating effective stories

So, my story and that of Maria would be very different, despite our similar citation levels. As I indicated in the introduction of my 2010 Publish or Perish book.

> *Citations are not only a reflection of the impact that a particular piece of academic work has generated. Citations can also be used to tell stories about academics, journals, and fields of research. This guide is meant to help you create effective stories.*

So go ahead: find the pearls in your record, polish them and string them into a beautifully arranged necklace that presents your citation story effectively.

What if you have very few citations?

Of course, it is rather difficult to make your case for citation impact if you have very few citations overall. This will often be the case if you are a junior researcher who has started publishing quite recently. In this instance, there are three things you can do beyond making the general argument that citation scores in your discipline are low as we discussed in Section 2 (only if that's the case of course).

Argue for the use of Google Scholar

First, if your University prefers the Web of Science as a data source and you have very few citations in the Web of Science, but quite a respectable number of citations in Google Scholar, you can argue that Google Scholar citations are a more accurate measurement of citation impact for junior scholars.

This is true because Google Scholar includes citations in Masters and Doctoral theses, conference proceedings and working papers that, in most cases, will ultimately be reflected in Web of Science citations. As we discussed in Chapter 4, Google Scholar also includes books, book chapters, and a wider range of journals than Web of Science, especially in the Social Sciences and Humanities.

Argue citations are slow to pick up

Second, explain that citations can take a long time to pick up. This is particularly true for the Social Sciences and Humanities, where the publication process is generally more drawn-out with many rounds of revisions. Even accepted publications can take a very long time to finally appear in print. In contrast, in disciplines such as Molecular Biology & Genetics or Astrophysics the time lapse between research and publication and publication and citation is generally much shorter. Hence, whereas one can expect a PhD student or postdoc in these fields to have citations, this is rarely ever the case in the Social Sciences and Humanities.

My current Web of Science citation record puts me in the top 1% most cited academics in my field and I receive around 1400 new Web of Science citations a year. However, my citations took rather a long time to take off. My first publication appeared in 1995 and by 2000 I had about a dozen publications printed or in press/accepted. However, at the start of 2000 I only had nine Web of Science citations (with 20 new citations in 2000 and 27 new citations in 2001). If I had had to make my tenure case after just 5 years, I wouldn't have had much to show for in terms of research impact!

You might be able to apply this strategy by doing some analyses for top people in your field and look at their first five years after they published their first article. This strategy is probably most effective when combined with the next strategy.

Argue for quality "by association"

Third, if you have only a few citations, it might be worth tracking each of them down to find out who is citing your work. It is more impressive if some famous academics in your field have cited work, or if many of your citations occur in the top journals in your field. Some of the fame and quality image of the academics and journals citing your work might rub off on you in the eyes of your evaluation committee.

	Cites	Per year	Rank	Authors	Title	Year
✓	1,420	94.67	1	AW Harzing	Publish or Perish	07
h	1,073	178.83	2	AW Harzing, S Alakan…	Google Scholar, Scop	16
h	1,002	77.08	3	NJ Adler, AW Harzing	When knowledge wir	09
h	851	42.55	4	AW Harzing	Acquisitions versus g	02
h	845	60.36	5	AW Harzing, R van der…	Google Scholar as a	08
h	832	52.00	6	AW Harzing	Response styles in cr	06
h	730	33.18	7	AW Harzing	An empirical analysis	00
h	678	32.29	8	AW Harzing	Of bears, bumble-be	01
h	668	55.67	9	AW Harzing, A Pinning…	International Human	10
h	606	26.35	10	AW Harzing	Managing the multina	99
h	578	30.42	11	AJ Feely, AW Harzing	Language manageme	03
h	559	20.70	12	AW Harzing	The persistent myth	95
h	545	41.92	13	N Noorderhaven, AW…	Knowledge-sharing a	09
h	525	35.00	14	M Pudelko, AW Harzing	Country-of-origin, lo	07
h	515	42.92	15	AW Harzing	The Publish or Perish	10
h	503	26.47	16	AW Harzing, A Sorge	The relative impact o	03
h	484	23.05	17	AW Harzing	Who's in charge? An	01
h	481	19.24	18	AW Harzing	Response rates in int	97
h	459	32.79	19	AW Harzing, AJ Feely	The language barrier	08
h	419	32.23	20	AW Harzing, R van der…	A Google Scholar h-i	09
h	353	32.09	21	AW Harzing, K Köster,…	Babel in business: Th	11
h	337	42.13	22	H Tenzer, M Pudelko,…	The impact of language barriers on trust formation in multinational…	2014
h	309	16.26	23	AW Harzing	The role of culture in entry-mode studies: from neglect to myopia?	2003

Open Article in Browser
Open Full Text in Browser
Open Citing Works in Browser
Open Related Works in Browser
Retrieve Citing Works in Publish or Perish
Find Article with Unpaywall

Split Citations

Copy Results
Save Results

Select All
Check All
Check Selection

Uncheck All
Uncheck Selection
Uncheck 0 Cites
Uncheck CITATION Results

Quality of citing works

To find out who is citing your work and where, right-click on the publication in question and click "**Retrieve Citing Works in Publish or Perish**" (see screenshot above). Publish or Perish will now retrieve all citing works. Currently, this option is only available for Google Scholar, Google Scholar Profiles and OpenAlex.

You can also do this for a set of articles. The screenshot below shows the results of a citing works search for the seven articles I published in the *Journal of International Business Studies*. As you can see in the screenshot below – which shows the first 10 citing works – I limited the search to citations from 2016 onwards to retrieve only recent citations. To find out the journals in which your work is cited simply sort the results by journal. Note that to change the **Display title** and the years you are searching for, you will need to stop the search. You can then edit these fields and resume the search.

Google Scholar citing references

Display title: Citations for seven articles in JIBS — Years: 2016 - 0 — Retrieve ?

Retrieve Direct

Cited works:
An empirical analysis and extension of the Bartlett and Ghoshal typology of multinational companies
Knowledge-sharing and social interaction within MNEs
The impact of language barriers on trust formation in multinational teams
The role of international assignees' social capital in creating inter-unit intellectual capital: A cross-level model
Why do international assignees stay? An organizational embeddedness perspective

Apply
Revert
New

	Cites	Per year	Rank	Authors	Title	Year
☑ h	250	83.33	3	DG Collings, K Mellahi, WF Ca...	Global talent management and performance in multinational enterprises: A mul...	2019
☑ h	162	32.40	4	M Andresen, F Bergdolt	A systematic literature review on the definitions of global mindset and cultural...	2017
☑ h	145	36.25	5	T Kostova, PC Nell, AK Hoenen	Understanding agency problems in headquarters-subsidiary relationships in m...	2018
☑ h	142	28.40	6	PM Wright, MD Ulrich	A road well traveled: The past, present, and future journey of strategic human...	2017
☑ h	140	70.00	7	KE Meyer, C Li, APJ Schotter	Managing the MNE subsidiary: Advancing a multi-level and dynamic research...	2020
☑ h	131	21.83	8	S Morris, S Snell, I Björkman	An architectural framework for global talent management	2016
☑ h	107	21.40	9	JE Tulung	Resource availability and firm's international strategy as key determinants of e...	2017
☑ h	96	16.00	10	D Cerrato, L Crosato, D Depp...	Archetypes of SME internationalization: A configurational approach	2016
☑ h	79	15.80	11	R Grünig, D Morschett	Developing international strategies	2017
☑ h	75	12.50	12	H Mun, HC Moon	The strategy for Korea's economic success	2016

Quality of journal outlets

If you cannot find any famous scholars citing your work, you could instead focus on the quality of the journals that your work appeared in. In general, this is not appropriate, as some papers in top journals never get cited. However, *on average* papers in top journals do get cited more than papers in lower-ranked journals. That's why these journals have higher Journal Impact Factors. Therefore, if your work has been published in high-impact journals, you could make the case that it is *more likely* that your work will be highly cited in the future.

In addition, you could make the argument that these journals have generally higher quality standards for the work they publish and a more rigorous review process. However, that's a quality argument, not a citation impact argument, and although the two are related, they are not necessarily identical.

Highly influential citations

Finally, you could use Semantic Scholar to track down all citations to your work that are "highly influential" (see also Chapter 2). This may allow you to spot high profile academics or important articles that have built significantly on your work. Obviously, this would be a very time-consuming exercise for more senior scholars with a large number of citations, and thus a substantial number of "highly influential" citations. However, for a junior academic with only a dozen highly influential citations, it could be very useful to find out which articles were highly influenced by your own work.

In sum

In this chapter I showed you how you can make your case for citation impact, discussing five specific strategies: picking your metrics wisely, creating your own reference group, comparing your papers to the journal average, presenting comprehensive citation counts for edited volumes, and finding the pearls in your record. Finally, I also provided some advice on what to do if you have very few citations overall. In the next chapter I will look at how you can use Publish or Perish to evaluate *other* academics.

Chapter 11: Evaluating other academics

When searching for other academics with the Publish or Perish software, you can obviously use the results to assess their publication output and citation metrics for tenure, promotion, or performance appraisals. This type of usage simply mirrors searching for your own record for this purpose. However, there are many other reasons why you might want to use the PoP software to evaluate other academics. In this chapter I discuss the most important ones:

- finding reviewers, examiners, speakers, or referees.
- preparing for a meeting with a visitor or your academic hero.
- writing laudations or obituaries.
- assessing papers for publication awards.
- preparing for a job interview.
- evaluating an author's output by affiliation.
- narrower purposes useful for any of the above and other cases: finding an author's citations in a specific journal, finding citation connections, and analysing co-authorship pairs, including supervisor/supervisee pairs.

Reviewers, examiners, speakers, referees

PoP can be very useful to find an academic who is suitable for the one of the many academic service roles in our profession: reviewers for journals or conferences, editorial board members, examiners for PhD theses, keynote speakers, discussants, track chairs or session chairs for conferences, academic mentors, referees, etc. Here, I discuss how to use PoP to select someone as an editorial board member. However, the mechanisms that are involved are very similar for most of the functions. Typically, there are several things that you would like an incumbent to display: academic credibility, some expertise in the (sub)discipline, some experience with the journal, and – in some cases – expertise in specific geographic areas.

Academic credibility

The first question would be: Does the prospective editorial board member (or reviewer or examiner or speaker or referee…) have a credible publication record? If one is selecting an editorial board member for a prestigious journal, there should be some evidence of publications that have had an impact on the field and of a sustained stream of research output. This can be easily evaluated looking at the number of publications and citations that PoP reports.

Expertise in the area in question

The prospective editorial board member should also have expertise in the disciplinary orientation of the journal or the sub-discipline that is currently underrepresented. A quick perusal of the titles of their publications should be sufficient to establish this.

For some journals it might be important to have a broad orientation so that one is able to review in a range of different, but related areas. Other journals might prefer specialists, either because the journal is a specialist journal itself (e.g., *International Journal of Nuclear Desalination*), or because the journal has a more general orientation, but only publishes the very best research in each sub-discipline (e.g., *Science*).

Experience with the journal

An editor will also want to know whether the prospective editorial board member has experience with the journal. Most journals will keep systematic files on their ad-hoc reviewers. So, if the prospective board member has been a successful ad hoc reviewer, they can be expected to have sufficient experience with the journal.

However, editors would normally give preference to academics that have published in the journal themselves. Publish or Perish makes it very easy to run a quick search on this using a combination of author and journal field searches or – for a cleaner result – review someone's GS Profile, sorting by publication name.

Google Scholar search

	Cites	Per ye...	Rank	Authors	Title	Year
☑ h	246	17.57	1	BS Reiche, AW Harzing, ML Kraimer	The role of international assignees' social capital in creat...	2009
☑ h	230	38.33	2	BS Reiche, A Bird, ME Mendenhall...	Contextualizing leadership: A typology of global leaders...	2017
☑ h	196	16.33	3	BS Reiche, ML Kraimer, AW Harzing	Why do international assignees stay? An organizational e...	2011
☑ h	187	23.38	4	BS Reiche, AW Harzing, M Pudelko	Why and how does shared language affect subsidiary kn...	2015
☑ h	52	26.00	5	FJ Froese, S Stoermer, BS Reiche, S...	Best of both worlds: How embeddedness fit in the host u...	2021
☑ h	27	13.50	6	J Cerar, PC Nell, BS Reiche	The declining share of primary data and the neglect of th...	2021
☑ h	12	12.00	7	H Kim, BS Reiche, AW Harzing	How does successive inpatriation contribute to subsidiar...	2022
☑	0	0.00	8	BS Reiche	Research handbook of global leadership: Making a differ...	2021

The screenshot above displays the results of a search for one of my former PhD students – Sebastian Reiche – and the top journal in our field: *Journal of International Business Studies* (JIBS). A search for an academic's full publication record would allow an editor to assess whether the academic had knowledge of the publication process in other key journals in the field. Below you can see the results of a GS Profile search for my own name, sorted by journal with two of the key journals in my field visible.

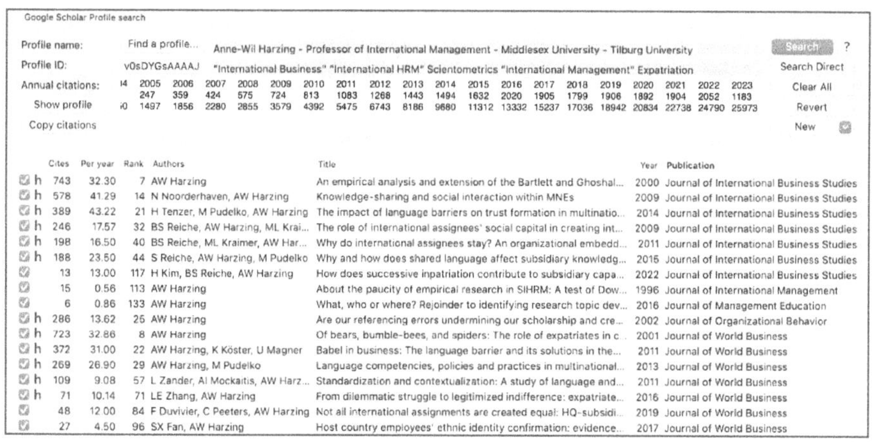

Google Scholar Profile search

Profile name: Find a profile... Anne-Wil Harzing - Professor of International Management - Middlesex University - Tilburg University

Profile ID: vOsDYGsAAAAJ "International Business" "International HRM" Scientometrics "International Management" Expatriation

Annual citations:

	2005	2006	2007	2008	2009	2010	2011	2012	2013	2014	2015	2016	2017	2018	2019	2020	2021	2022	2023
i4	247	359	424	575	724	813	1083	1268	1443	1494	1632	2020	1905	1799	1906	1892	1904	2052	1183
i0	1497	1856	2280	2855	3579	4392	5475	6743	8186	9680	11312	13332	15237	17036	18942	20834	22738	24790	25973

	Cites	Per year	Rank	Authors	Title	Year	Publication
☑ h	743	32.30	7	AW Harzing	An empirical analysis and extension of the Bartlett and Ghoshal...	2000	Journal of International Business Studies
☑ h	578	41.29	14	N Noorderhaven, AW Harzing	Knowledge-sharing and social interaction within MNEs	2009	Journal of International Business Studies
☑ h	389	43.22	21	H Tenzer, M Pudelko, AW Harzing	The impact of language barriers on trust formation in multinatio...	2014	Journal of International Business Studies
☑ h	246	17.57	32	BS Reiche, AW Harzing, ML Krai...	The role of international assignees' social capital in creating int...	2009	Journal of International Business Studies
☑ h	198	16.50	40	BS Reiche, ML Kraimer, AW Har...	Why do international assignees stay? An organizational embedd...	2011	Journal of International Business Studies
☑ h	188	23.50	44	S Reiche, AW Harzing, M Pudelko	Why and how does shared language affect subsidiary knowledg...	2015	Journal of International Business Studies
☑	13	13.00	117	H Kim, BS Reiche, AW Harzing	How does successive inpatriation contribute to subsidiary capa...	2022	Journal of International Business Studies
☑	15	0.56	113	AW Harzing	About the paucity of empirical research in SIHRM: A test of Dow...	1996	Journal of International Management
☑	6	0.86	133	AW Harzing	What, who or where? Rejoinder to identifying research topic dev...	2016	Journal of Management Education
☑ h	286	13.62	25	AW Harzing	Are our referencing errors undermining our scholarship and cre...	2002	Journal of Organizational Behavior
☑ h	723	32.86	8	AW Harzing	Of bears, bumble-bees, and spiders: The role of expatriates in c...	2001	Journal of World Business
☑ h	372	31.00	22	AW Harzing, K Köster, U Magner	Babel in business: The language barrier and its solutions in the...	2011	Journal of World Business
☑ h	269	26.90	29	AW Harzing, M Pudelko	Language competencies, policies and practices in multinational...	2013	Journal of World Business
☑ h	109	9.08	57	L Zander, AI Mockaitis, AW Harz...	Standardization and contextualization: A study of language and...	2011	Journal of World Business
☑ h	71	10.14	71	LE Zhang, AW Harzing	From dilemmatic struggle to legitimized indifference: expatriate...	2016	Journal of World Business
☑	48	12.00	84	F Duvivier, C Peeters, AW Harzing	Not all international assignments are created equal: HQ-subsidi...	2019	Journal of World Business
☑	27	4.50	96	SX Fan, AW Harzing	Host country employees' ethnic identity confirmation: evidence...	2017	Journal of World Business

Both searches would also show whether the academic's experience with the journal is recent. As can be seen above Sebastian published three articles and a book review in JIBS in the last two years, whereas my publication frequency in JIBS and *Journal of World Business* has declined, reflecting my changing research interests.

Geographical scope

Many journals in the Social Sciences will publish work conducted in different countries. To the extent that the country context matter for the research in question, it is important to have editorial board members with a broad geographical experience. Although it is not always possible to deduce this from the articles titles, in many cases a quick perusal of the PoP results should provide the editor with a feel for the experience the prospective board members has with research in different countries. Looking at their co-authors might also give some clues, to the extent one can deduce nationality from names.

If expertise in specific countries is essential, then using a combination of author and keyword search might help. The screenshot below for instance shows a Web of Science search with the number of articles I have published that included China in the title or abstract. Note that if you conducted this search with Google Scholar, China would be matched anywhere in the document making the search less useful for our current purpose.

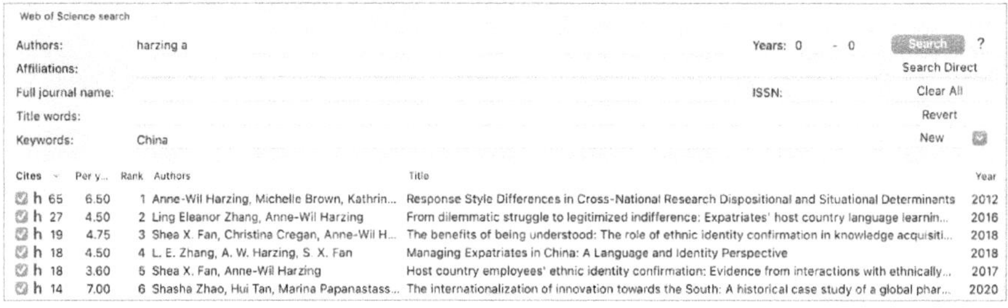

Caveats

None of the factors discussed above – academic credibility, expertise in the field, experience with the journal, and geographical scope – can be established with absolute certainty through a simple Publish or Perish search. However, through these searches, the editor should get a feel for the prospective board members that are worthy of further investigation. The same would apply to reviewers, keynote speakers, examiners, or referees.

Meeting an academic visitor

Do you recognise the following scenario? You are about to meet an official guest of some standing, but you do not know the academic in question very well and hence do not have a clear idea of what s/he is well-known for. You have been running around all day and only have 5-10 minutes before the meeting. How do you ensure you are well prepared and don't blunder your way through the meeting?

You could of course start searching on the web for the academic's university staff page. However, this might not always be easy to find, especially if the academic has a relatively common name. Moreover, not all universities allow their staff to create their own web pages. Even if they do, they often are out of date as most academics are not very diligent in maintaining them. Here Publish or Perish comes to the rescue with a quick solution. If you know the academic's given and family name you can use these for a very quick author search, which can allow you to deduce quite a lot in just a couple of minutes.

What are you best known for?

Even though a "quick-and-dirty" search might not be able to give you fully accurate citation metrics, looking at the most cited works will give you a very quick idea of what the academic you are meeting is best-known for. It might also give you a good insight into their publication strategy.

- Do they have a large number of papers that have gathered a reasonable number of citations? That might point to a more diversified publication strategy.

- Do they have one or two papers with a huge number of citations and other less cited work? This might point to a very focused publication strategy.

Who are you working with?

By sorting the search results on the author column, you can quickly find who the academic's co-authors are. You might have an academic acquaintance or even collaborator in common? Nothing is better to get a conversation going than talking about people you both know. Looking at an academic's earliest collaborators might also give you a clue about who their PhD advisor was. Finding that someone mostly publishes on their own is also useful to know. You might not bring up collaborative work in that case, certainly not in a first meeting.

What are you working on recently?

Sorting the search results on the year column helps you finding out what the academic in question has been working on most recently. Most academics don't like it too much if you only talk about papers they published decades ago (even they are classics). The research in question might be more than fifteen years old and they might have moved on to completely different topics by now.

How long have you been in the business?

Reviewing the years active statistic gives you some feel for how much academic experience the person you are meeting is likely to have. Of course, this might not be of great importance, but again it might change what you will be talking about with this person. Knowing this ahead of time might be helpful. Your conversations with someone in a mid-career stage might be different from those with someone who is close to retirement.

What journals have you published in?

Sorting on the publication column will allow you to find out which journals the academic has published in, giving you an idea of their disciplinary orientation and publication strategy.

- Have they published in general or specialised journals?

- Do they publish mostly conceptual or empirical work?

- Have they published in the top journals in their field?

- Have they published in lots of different journals or focused their output in a small number of journals?

Worked Example: Rabi Bhagat

In 2010, two colleagues at the University of Melbourne organised a 2-day workshop on Global Teams. One of the keynote speakers was Rabi Bhagat. Although I had seen his name in press before, I could not recall clearly in what context, and I had never met him before. However, as Head of the International Business group, I wanted to make sure that I had some conversation topics ready. I therefore ran a quick Publish or Perish search for his name. The results for his most cited works are below.

Authors	Title	Year
DN Den Hartog, RJ House, PJ Hanges, ...	Culture specific and cross-culturally generalizable implicit leadership the...	1999
K Leung, RS Bhagat, NR Buchan, M Erez, ...	Culture and international business: Recent advances and their implication...	2005
RS Bhagat, BL Kedia, PD Harveston, ...	Cultural variations in the cross-border transfer of organizational knowled...	2002
BL Kedia, RS Bhagat	Cultural constraints on transfer of technology across nations: Implication...	1988
SE Sullivan, RS Bhagat	Organizational stress, job satisfaction and job performance: where do we...	1992
RS Bhagat, SJ McQuaid	Role of subjective culture in organizations: A review and directions for fut...	1982
TA Beehr, RS Bhagat	Human stress and cognition in organizations: An integrated perspective	1985
RS Bhagat	Effects of stressful life events on individual performance effectiveness an...	1983
RS Bhagat, SJ McQuaid, H Lindholm, ...	Total life stress: A multimethod validation of the construct and its effects...	1985
A Phatak, RS Bhagat, R Kashlak, A Phata...	International management	2008
TA Beehr, RS Bhagat	Introduction to human stress and cognition in organizations	1985
RS Bhagat, KO Prien	Cross-cultural training in organizational contexts.	1996
RD Arvey, RS Bhagat, E Salas	Cross-cultural and cross-national issues in personnel and human resourc...	1991
LH Peters, RS Bhagat, ...	An Examination of the I ndependent and Joint Contributions of Organizati...	1981
RS Bhagat	Conditions under which stronger job performance–job satisfaction relatio...	1982
RS Bhagat, B Krishnan, TA Nelson, ...	Organizational stress, psychological strain, and work outcomes in six nati...	2010

Influential work on culture and knowledge transfer

It was immediately apparent that he had participated in the GLOBE leadership project (see the first publication) and had published influential papers on the impact of culture on transfer of technology and knowledge across borders. The latter is most likely where I had seen his name, as some of my own work has been on the transfer of human resource management practices across cultures.

OB/Psychology scholar rather than Strategy scholar

However, I also noticed that he had published a fairly large body of work related to stress and stressors in the workplace, stretching from 1985 to 1995. This made me realise that his disciplinary background might be in Organisational Behaviour or even Psychology. His work on technology transfer had led me to the erroneous assumption that he was a macro-oriented Strategy scholar.

Working with a varied group of co-authors on conceptual work

The results also showed me that he had worked with a fairly varied group of co-authors and acted both as first and second author. The titles of his papers led me to conclude that he preferred conceptual work rather than empirical work as most of his papers are about building theory, creating frameworks, or providing an integrative perspective on a topic.

Recent work on Asia and global mindsets

Sorting the results by year (see below) showed that in the past couple of years (i.e., between 2007 and 2010) he became interested in the role of Asia in management theories, as well as in global mindsets and global leadership. I also established he had maintained his interest in stress but added a cross-cultural element to it. Finally, I noticed that he had published a textbook (*International Management*). Given that I have published a textbook on International HRM that might provide another conversation starter.

RS Bhagat, B Krishnan, TA Nelson, ...	Organizational stress, psychological strain, and work outcomes in six nati...	2010
RS Bhagat, AS McDevitt, I McDevitt	On improving the robustness of Asian management theories: Theoretical...	2010
MW Peng, RS Bhagat, SJ Chang	Asia and global business	2010
RS Bhagat, B Krishnan, TA Nelson, ...	Organizational stress, psychological strain, and work outcomes in six nati...	2010
RS Bhagat, RM Steers	Cambridge handbook of culture, organizations, and work	2009
RS Bhagat, CA Davis, ML London	Acculturative stress in professional immigrants: Towards a cultural theory...	2009
A Phatak, RS Bhagat, R Kashlak, A Phatak,...	International management	2008
RS Bhagat, PK Steverson, ...	International and cultural variations in employee assistance programmes:...	2007
MH Hoppe, RS Bhagat	Leadership in the United States of America: The leader as cultural hero	2007
RS Bhagat, HC Triandis, BR Baliga, TK Billi...	On becoming a global manager: A closer look at the opportunities and co...	2007
RS Bhagat, PK Steverson, ...	Cultural variations in employee assistance programs in an era of globaliza...	2007
RS Bhagat, JR Van Scotter, PK Steverson, ...	Cultural variations in individual job performance: implications for industria...	2007
RS Bhagat, P Englis-Danskin, ...	Creation, diffusion, and transfer of organizational knowledge in transnatio...	2007

Recent leadership on multi-country projects

Further, I noticed that although his most cited (older) work is mostly conceptual, his recent articles seem to include empirical work, with data collected in a lot of different countries. Given that he is the first author on these articles, I conclude he was leading those projects. As I had led several large-scale multi-country projects myself that might also be a nice conversation topic.

Journals published in

Sorting the results by journals showed (amongst others):

- four articles in the *Academy of Management Review* (a journal that only publishes conceptual work),

- three articles each in *Human Relations* (two of which theoretical) and *Journal of Management*, and

- two articles each in *Journal of Organisational Behavior* and *Journal of Vocational Behavior*.

This set of publications confirmed my earlier impression that my counterpart was strong in conceptual/theoretical work. His publication profile also confirmed to me that he was a micro Organisational Behaviour scholar than a macro International Business scholar. As my own research is in the more micro areas of International Business, I knew this would make it easier to talk about his research.

Ready to meet our keynote speaker in less than 10 minutes

In less than 10 minutes, I was ready to meet our keynote speaker, with a good knowledge of his research interests, co-authors, type of research outlets, and research leadership experience. As it turned out, we only talked about Melbourne (the location of the conference) and the Publish or Perish software. But my preparation meant that I was ready for any conversation about his academic work!

In sum: PoP helps with academic detective work

A simple 5–10-minute author search can give you an excellent quick impression of another academic. Obviously, you could do the same type of search in a more rigorous fashion if you were meeting up with someone who could be a potential co-author or if you are lucky enough to have a meeting with your "academic hero".

The point is: there is much more to Publish or Perish than finding out someone's h-index or citations. With a bit of detective work, you can easily reconstruct a fairly good picture of someone's academic career in a very short space of time.

Writing laudations or obituaries

Writing laudations or obituaries is likely to generate diametrically opposite emotions. However, in both cases it is equally important to get a complete overview of someone's impact on the field. It is all too easy to be heavily influenced by a number of contributions that are well known to you personally, whilst forgetting the broader impact that the academic in question might have had.

As an example of how to use Publish or Perish in writing obituaries or review publications when outlining the impact of a scholar's work for laudations, I will focus on Sumantra Ghoshal. His book *Managing Across Borders* with Christopher Bartlett, first published in 1989, was the key inspiration for my own PhD work on control mechanisms in multinational companies. I was very shocked to learn of his untimely death at only 55 in 2004.

The screenshot below shows that Sumantra Ghoshal's work has had an enormous impact on the field, with 16 of his publications drawing more than 1,000 citation and five of them generating more than 5,000 citations. His body of work generated nearly 100,000 citations in total, even though less than 20 years had passed between his first publication and his death. However, there are other conclusions we can derive from the Publish or Perish data.

Cites	Per year	Rank	Authors	Title	Year	Publication
☑ h 26,747	1,069.88	3	J Nahapiet, S Ghoshal	Social capital, intellectual capital, and the organizational advant...	1998	Academy of management review
☑ h 12,795	609.29	2	CA Bartlett, S Ghoshal	Managing across borders: The transnational solution	2002	
☑ h 9,390	375.60	4	W Tsai, S Ghoshal	Social capital and value creation: The role of intrafirm networks	1998	Academy of management Journal
☑ h 5,621	312.28	5	S Ghoshal	Bad management theories are destroying good management pr...	2005	Academy of Management learning &education
☑ h 4,031	149.30	6	S Ghoshal, P Moran	Bad for practice: A critique of the transaction cost theory	1996	Academy of management Review
☑ h 3,213	97.36	7	S Ghoshal, CA Bartlett	The multinational corporation as an interorganizational network	1990	Academy of management review
☑ h 2,320	64.44	8	S Ghoshal	Global strategy: An organizing framework	1987	Strategic management journal
☑ h 1,649	63.42	77	N Nohria, S Ghoshal	The differentiated network: Organizing multinational corporatio...	1997	(No Title)
☑ h 1,427	41.97	9	S Ghoshal, N Nohria	Internal differentiation within multinational corporations	1989	Strategic management journal
☑ h 1,405	37.97	92	CA Bartlett, S Ghoshal	Tap your subsidiaries for global reach	1986	Harvard business review
☑ h 1,236	35.31	10	S Ghoshal, CA Bartlett	Creation, adoption and diffusion of innovations by subsidiaries...	1988	Journal of international business studies
☑ h 1,227	47.19	11	S Ghoshal, CA Bartlett, PC Kovner	The individualized corporation	1997	
☑ h 1,141	39.34	12	N Nohria, S Ghoshal	Differentiated fit and shared values: Alternatives for managing h...	1994	Strategic management journal
☑ h 1,124	38.76	13	S Ghoshal, CA Bartlett	Linking organizational context and managerial action: The dime...	1994	Strategic management journal
☑ h 1,058	50.38	14	CA Bartlett, S Ghoshal	Building competitive advantage through people	2002	MIT Sloan management review
☑ h 1,053	36.10	15	CA Bartlett, S Ghoshal	Beyond the M-form: Toward a managerial theory of the firm	1993	Strategic Management Journal

Combining rigour and relevance

First, sorting his output by outlet clearly illustrates Ghoshal's fairly unique ability to combine rigorous scholarship with work that has managerial relevance. He has published many influential books that target a wider audience beyond academia. He also published a large part of his body of work in more managerially oriented journals such as *Harvard Business Review* and *Sloan Management Review*.

At the same time, he has published in the top journals in the field of Management and Strategy, such as the *Academy of Management Review /Journal, Strategic Management Journal, Management Science*, and the *Journal of International Business Studies*. There are few academics that have combined rigour and relevance so successfully.

Reflections on our profession

Many academics and students will have been inspired by Ghoshal's last article, published posthumously in the *Academy of Management of Learning & Education*. Provocatively titled *"Bad Management Theories are Destroying Good Management Practice"*, it is a powerful analysis of the potential negative impact of our academic theories in Business and Management. However, I was unaware that Ghoshal's interest in this field was long-standing with his trenchant critique on transaction cost theory published in 1996 (see the 6th publication in the above screenshot).

I was also unaware of another posthumous publication "Scholarship that Endures", that appeared in the probably little-known research annual *Research Methodology in Strategy and Management*, published by Emerald publishers. Even seventeen years after its publication, there are only nine citations it. I can only assume most people are unaware of it. Hence, I am quoting the first paragraph of the article at length, in the hope that it will offer new inspiration for current and future scholars:

> *"As academics, we collectively publish thousands of articles and hundreds of books each year. We spend a large part of our lives producing them, sacrificing, in the process, sleep, time with our families, reading things we want to read, seeing places we wish to see. Most of these books and articles soon vanish without a trace, helping us get tenure perhaps, but talking with them into oblivion very large parts of the best years of our lives. Few – very few – of the outputs of our intellectual endeavors endure. What is it that distinguishes scholarship that endures from scholarship that does not?" (Ghoshal, 2006: 1)*

As an aside, finding Ghoshal's "Scholarship that Endures" article in Google Books also led me to stumble upon another article in the same volume of this research annual that is of substantial relevance to me (Bednar & Westphal, 2006). It deals with improving response rates when surveying corporate elites. I therefore ran a search for articles published in this research annual over the five years between 2004 and 2009 that it was published (screenshot below).

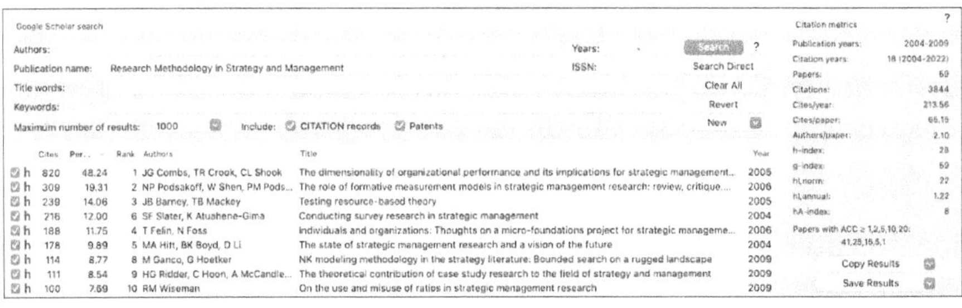

Google Scholar search

| Authors: | | Years: | | Search | ? |

Publication name: Research Methodology in Strategy and Management — ISSN: — Search Direct — Clear All — Revert — New

Title words: | Keywords: | Maximum number of results: 1000 | Include: ✓ CITATION records ✓ Patents

	Cites	Per..	Rank	Authors	Title	Year
✓ h	820	48.24	1	JG Combs, TR Crook, CL Shook	The dimensionality of organizational performance and its implications for strategic management...	2005
✓ h	309	19.31	2	NP Podsakoff, W Shen, PM Pods...	The role of formative measurement models in strategic management research: review, critique....	2006
✓ h	239	14.06	3	JB Barney, TB Mackey	Testing resource-based theory	2005
✓ h	216	12.00	6	SF Slater, K Atuahene-Gima	Conducting survey research in strategic management	2004
✓ h	188	11.75	4	T Felin, N Foss	Individuals and organizations: Thoughts on a micro-foundations project for strategic manageme...	2006
✓ h	178	9.89	5	MA Hitt, BK Boyd, D Li	The state of strategic management research and a vision of the future	2004
✓ h	114	8.77	8	M Ganco, G Hoetker	NK modeling methodology in the strategy literature: Bounded search on a rugged landscape	2009
✓ h	111	8.54	9	HG Ridder, C Hoon, A McCandle...	The theoretical contribution of case study research to the field of strategy and management	2009
✓ h	100	7.69	10	RM Wiseman	On the use and misuse of ratios in strategic management research	2009

Citation metrics

Publication years:	2004-2009
Citation years:	18 (2004-2022)
Papers:	59
Citations:	3844
Cites/year:	213.56
Cites/paper:	65.15
Authors/paper:	2.10
h-index:	28
g-index:	59
hI,norm:	22
hI,annual:	1.22
hA-index:	8
Papers with ACC ≥ 1,2,5,10,20:	41,28,16,5,1

Copy Results — Save Results

I discovered a large number of highly intriguing titles, often written by well-known scholars. Most of these articles seem to have generated relatively little interest so far; only a few drawing more than 10 citations per year. It is exactly these kinds of serendipitous findings that are facilitated by Publish or Perish and Google Scholar.

Getting to an age where my academic heroes are passing away, I have had to use the Publish or Perish software regularly in the past years to conduct bibliometric analyses of a scholar's work and have always discovered hidden treasures in their publication records. Here is the first of a series of bibliographic analyses I am conducting in my role as Academy of International Business Bibliometrician.

A Bibliographic Analysis of the Scholarly Writings of Jean J. Boddewyn

Introduction

One would be hard pushed to find another scholar who has had such a long scholarly writing career as Jean Boddewyn. Boddewyn continued to make major contributions into his nineties. Even in the last five years of his life, he published half a dozen articles in core International Business journals. A complete bibliography of Boddewyn's scholarly work until 2011 can be found in **this article in ISMO**. This article was part of a **Festschrift in his honor**, which included reviews of his contributions to various fields.

Boddewyn's collective scholarly work has been cited more than 8,500 times in Google Scholar, with a h-index of 43. Although he wrote much of his influential work alone, he co-authored with a wide range of academics, both junior and senior. In 2008 Boddewyn also organized and edited a book written by the AIB Fellows: **International Business Scholarship: AIB Fellows on the First 50 Years and Beyond** in the Emerald series *Research in Global Strategic Management*. He repeated this venture in 2014 with ten Fellows elected between 2008 and 2012 sharing their insights on important IB topics in **Multidisciplinary Insights from New AIB Fellows**.

Reviewing Boddewyn's scholarly work is like reviewing the development of the field of International Business. It is impossible to do justice to the breadth and depth of his scholarly contributions in this short overview. Below is a very selective review of his scholarly work, focusing on his early and most recent work, both of which will be less familiar to many.

Publication awards

Many journals give out some type of best paper award on a yearly basis. One of the factors that are often considered when awarding best journal article prizes is the (citation) impact a particular article has had. This is relatively easy to do when the awards are given 10 years after publications, as is for instance the case with the *Journal of International Business Studies* decade award. However, most journal article prizes are awarded 1 or 2 years after the articles are published. Especially in the Social Sciences and Humanities there are few articles that gather significant citation impact in such a short time. It is still possible to get a sense of their impact by searching Google Scholar through Publish or Perish.

Example: AMLE article of the year award

In 2010, my article with Nancy Adler (*When Knowledge Wins: the Sense and Nonsense of Academic Ranking*) won the 2009 outstanding article of the year for the *Academy of Management Learning and Education* journal in which it was published.

I hope this decision was mainly driven by the article's content, which cautioned against an exclusive focus on the use academic rankings and discussed the importance of doing research that has relevance to societal problems. However, it is likely that the decision was partially influenced by the article's citation impact.

Unfortunately, around April 2010, when the award decision was taken, the Web of Science had only incorporated articles from the first (March) issue of the *Academy of Management Learning & Education*, with the three remaining 2009 issues not yet entered in the Web of Science. Of these March articles there was one article with 18 citations (my own paper), two articles with 4 citations and several articles with 1-3 citations for a total of 38 citations for AMLE for 2009. Hence, Web of Science data would not have been very useful to assess the impact of articles published in AMLE in 2009.

When I did a search with Google Scholar data in Publish or Perish in April 2010, the picture was entirely different; *all* 2009 AMLE papers were included. Although, with 56 citations, our awarded article was still the most cited article in the journal, there were fourteen (not two) other articles with at least 4 citations and the total number of citations to AMLE articles published in 2009 was 179, rather than the meagre 38 citations in the Web of Science. From this, I would conclude that many articles published in this journal do have a fairly substantial immediate impact.

Doing the same search again in 2023 (see below) showed that the awarded article remains the most highly cited paper in the journal, no doubt one factor leading to it being awarded a decade award in 2019. However, it is also clear that the journal published many other high-impact articles that year, with no less than 17 of the articles published in 2009 articles gathering more than ten citations per year.

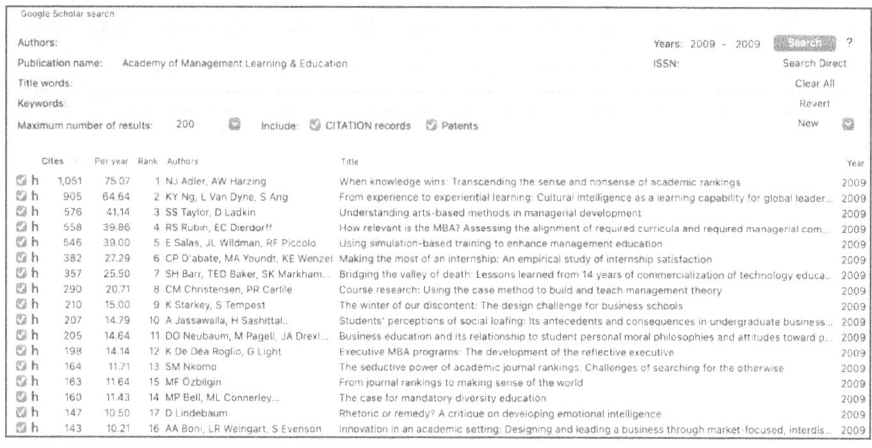

	Cites	Per year	Rank	Authors	Title	Year
☑ h	1,051	75.07	1	NJ Adler, AW Harzing	When knowledge wins: Transcending the sense and nonsense of academic rankings	2009
☑ h	905	64.64	2	KY Ng, L Van Dyne, S Ang	From experience to experiential learning: Cultural intelligence as a learning capability for global leader...	2009
☑ h	576	41.14	3	SS Taylor, D Ladkin	Understanding arts-based methods in managerial development	2009
☑ h	558	39.86	4	RS Rubin, EC Dierdorff	How relevant is the MBA? Assessing the alignment of required curricula and required managerial com...	2009
☑ h	546	39.00	5	E Salas, JL Wildman, RF Piccolo	Using simulation-based training to enhance management education	2009
☑ h	382	27.29	6	CP D'abate, MA Youndt, KE Wenzel	Making the most of an internship: An empirical study of internship satisfaction	2009
☑ h	357	25.50	7	SH Barr, TED Baker, SK Markham...	Bridging the valley of death: Lessons learned from 14 years of commercialization of technology educa...	2009
☑ h	290	20.71	8	CM Christensen, PR Carlile	Course research: Using the case method to build and teach management theory	2009
☑ h	210	15.00	9	K Starkey, S Tempest	The winter of our discontent: The design challenge for business schools	2009
☑ h	207	14.79	10	A Jassawalla, H Sashittal...	Students' perceptions of social loafing: Its antecedents and consequences in undergraduate business...	2009
☑ h	205	14.64	11	DO Neubaum, M Pagell, JA Drexl...	Business education and its relationship to student personal moral philosophies and attitudes toward p...	2009
☑ h	198	14.14	12	K De Déa Roglio, G Light	Executive MBA programs: The development of the reflective executive	2009
☑ h	164	11.71	13	SM Nkomo	The seductive power of academic journal rankings: Challenges of searching for the otherwise	2009
☑ h	163	11.64	15	MF Özbilgin	From journal rankings to making sense of the world	2009
☑ h	160	11.43	14	MP Bell, ML Connerley...	The case for mandatory diversity education	2009
☑ h	147	10.50	17	D Lindebaum	Rhetoric or remedy? A critique on developing emotional intelligence	2009
☑ h	143	10.21	16	AA Boni, LR Weingart, S Evenson	Innovation in an academic setting: Designing and leading a business through market-focused, interdis...	2009

When evaluating papers for publication awards, I would recommend using Publish or Perish with Google Scholar data even in cases where the Web of Science *does* have complete data for the journal. Google Scholar citations are a much better indicator of early impact as they include citations in conference papers and working papers, most of which will eventually find their way to published articles.

Preparing for a job interview

We have all been there: you are invited for a job interview, and you want to be well-prepared. As part of your search, you want to find out what academics in the university you applied for are working on. You might even want to do this *before* applying for the job to decide whether this is the place for you, or simply to tailor your application to the university.

It is all about creating a connection

Most shortlisted applicants for the job are well qualified and will do a good job in their research presentation and teaching demonstration. What matters most is that you create a connection with the people on your interview or shortlist panel. They should be able to picture you as a person they *could*, and would *want to*, work with.

As far as I know, personal chemistry is impossible to engineer. However, you can do to increase the chances of building a connection by being well prepared. There are several ways you could approach this, discussed in more detail below. Note that I am not suggesting you should misrepresent your academic record or compromise your own personal values. However, you can emphasise different aspects of your academic record depending on who is on your panel.

Find out what your panel members are working on

Publish or Perish gives you a quick and easy way to find out what the academics on your interview panel are best known for. Simply do an author search in your preferred data source for the members of your interview panel. You might even want to read some of these articles in order to be able to make intelligent comments about them.

It would also be a good idea to find out the *recent* research interests of the members on your panel by sorting their publications by year. You might discover that some of them have similar interests or are even working on papers together. This is something you could comment positively on in your interview, while indicating that working with colleagues is something you aspire to in your job. This is even more effective if the panel members didn't know they were working on similar topics. Never underestimate how little many academics know about their colleagues! The panel will be mightily impressed if you have spotted synergies they were not even aware of.

Find out where your panel members are publishing

When searching for your panel members' publications, also make sure you sort the results by publication. This allows you to find out whether there are any journals they have published in regularly. Many academics have their favourite journals and they will tend to think positively about applicants targeting the same journals. This might be because targeting the same journals automatically reflects a similarity in academic norms and values, or simply because your panel members are more aware of the (high) quality standards of the journals they are personally familiar with.

I am not suggesting you lie about where you are targeting your work. However, doing a quick search to find out which journals your panel members tend to publish in heavily might give you some clues about which of your research projects to focus on. It might also lead you to mention in your job interview you have been doing ad-hoc reviewing for this particular journal (only if this is true of course).

Reviewing the *type* of outlets that panel members publish in also gives you an idea of what is valued in the institution you are applying to. Are they mainly publishing in top US academic journals, are they publishing in a wider variety of journals, do practice journals feature as an outlet, have any of them written books? None of these publication strategies are inherently superior to others, but it is useful to be aware what seems to be valued most by the institution in question.

You could use this as a lead-in to a question to the panel of what would be expected of you in terms of publication output if you joined the institution. Most interviews panels *really* appreciate it if you ask questions pro-actively rather than just answer theirs. However, what they appreciate most are *informed* questions.

Find out who are citing your panel members' work

In order to *really* impress, you could try to read some of the articles that have built on the panel members' important works and comment intelligently on how they have done this. Many academics are not really aware who is citing their work, so that knowledge might make an excellent impression.

You can find these citing articles easily. Simply right-click on the paper in question; in the pop-up menu, click on **Retrieve citing works in Publish or Perish**. Pick one that is related to a topic you know a lot (or at least something) about, so that you can talk comfortably about it. This might be an easy way to give you a connection to a person in the panel. Alternatively, pick an article written by an academic you know very well. If you are lucky your panel member knows the academic too but didn't know that s/he cited their work. There is nothing like common acquaintances to build a connection!

I can particularly recommend this strategy when some of your panel members are senior administrators such as Deans or Department Chairs. Oftentimes their heavy administrative load has prevented these academics from publishing much in recent years. They will be very pleased to be reminded that their research is still cited!

Find out more about the university

Most junior applicants are too narrowly focused on the job in question and their future department or school. Showing you know more about the university as a whole indicates you have made a real effort. It also signals that you are potential leadership material as you are able to take a broader perspective.

Find out what the university is well known for. You can search for the University's most cited publications using an affiliation search in the data sources that have a dedicated affiliation field. If you prefer to use Google Scholar, you can use the keywords field to approximate this (see next section for an example). Make sure though to double-check that the university in question is listed as an affiliation of the author, not in the references or any other part of the publication.

Having found out what your panel members are working on, try to establish whether there is anyone else in the university working on similar topics. You can do this by including the topic in the keywords field and the university in the affiliation field.

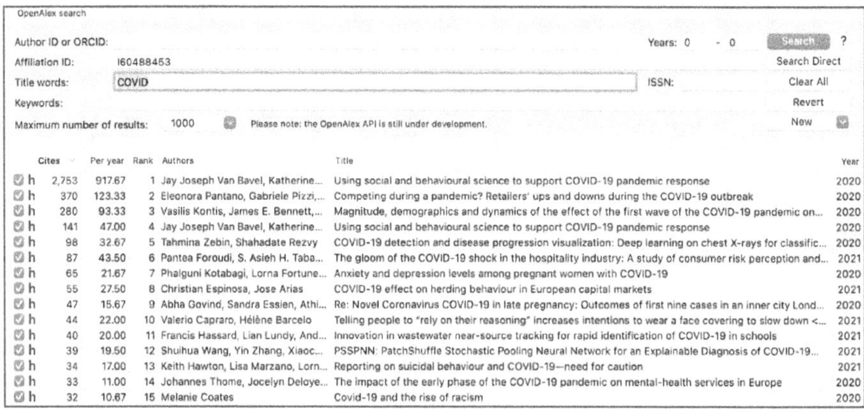

	Cites	Per year	Rank	Authors	Title	Year
☑ h	2,753	917.67	1	Jay Joseph Van Bavel, Katherine...	Using social and behavioural science to support COVID-19 pandemic response	2020
☑ h	370	123.33	2	Eleonora Pantano, Gabriele Pizzi,...	Competing during a pandemic? Retailers' ups and downs during the COVID-19 outbreak	2020
☑ h	280	93.33	3	Vasilis Kontis, James E. Bennett,...	Magnitude, demographics and dynamics of the effect of the first wave of the COVID-19 pandemic on...	2020
☑ h	141	47.00	4	Jay Joseph Van Bavel, Katherine...	Using social and behavioural science to support COVID-19 pandemic response	2020
☑ h	98	32.67	5	Tahmina Zebin, Shahadate Rezvy	COVID-19 detection and disease progression visualization: Deep learning on chest X-rays for classific...	2020
☑ h	87	43.50	6	Pantea Foroudi, S. Asieh H. Taba...	The gloom of the COVID-19 shock in the hospitality industry: A study of consumer risk perception and...	2021
☑ h	65	21.67	7	Phalguni Kotabagi, Lorna Fortune...	Anxiety and depression levels among pregnant women with COVID-19	2020
☑ h	55	27.50	8	Christian Espinosa, Jose Arias	COVID-19 effect on herding behaviour in European capital markets	2021
☑ h	47	15.67	9	Abha Govind, Sandra Essien, Athi...	Re: Novel Coronavirus COVID-19 in late pregnancy: Outcomes of first nine cases in an inner city Lond...	2020
☑ h	44	22.00	10	Valerio Capraro, Hélène Barcelo	Telling people to "rely on their reasoning" increases intentions to wear a face covering to slow down <...	2021
☑ h	40	20.00	11	Francis Hassard, Lian Lundy, And...	Innovation in wastewater near-source tracking for rapid identification of COVID-19 in schools	2021
☑ h	39	19.50	12	Shuihua Wang, Yin Zhang, Xiaoc...	PSSPNN: PatchShuffle Stochastic Pooling Neural Network for an Explainable Diagnosis of COVID-19...	2021
☑ h	34	17.00	13	Keith Hawton, Lisa Marzano, Lorn...	Reporting on suicidal behaviour and COVID-19—need for caution	2021
☑ h	33	11.00	14	Johannes Thome, Jocelyn Deloye...	The impact of the early phase of the COVID-19 pandemic on mental-health services in Europe	2020
☑ h	32	10.67	15	Melanie Coates	Covid-19 and the rise of racism	2020

Above is an example for Middlesex University. Despite the fact that the university doesn't haveg a strong focus on the Life Sciences, Middlesex academics have published quite a few articles about COVID, including one that is very highly cited.

Your interview panel will be mightily impressed if you have identified another academic in their university that shares their research interests, especially if they weren't even aware of them. You could even link this to a more general discussion on multi-disciplinarity and your own views on this. Although some universities might equate multidisciplinary research with a lack of depth, these days most universities acknowledge that big world problems can only be addressed with multidisciplinary research.

Evaluating author output by affiliation

You might need to establish what a particular author has published during the time they were affiliated with a particular university. For instance, this is useful for research administrators who are preparing for a national research evaluation. Publish or Perish was an essential tool in my role as Associate Dean Research at Melbourne University. It allowed us to quickly get a full record of an individual academic's publications for our yearly submission to the government, particularly for academics who consistently ignored our emails. It might also be useful to assess which of an author's publications will be included in international research rankings such as the Times Higher Education, QS, US News or ARWU/Shanghai ranking.

In doing these searches, you will need to strike a balance between accuracy and coverage. Of the currently available data sources in PoP Crossref only provides *very* partial results for affiliation searches and is not recommended. Google Scholar appears to be unable to parse affiliations on most articles in Elsevier journals. The API for OpenAlex and Semantic Scholar do not currently offer the option of running complex combined searches. PubMed is only relevant for biomedical researchers.

Traditional bibliometric data sources such as the Web of Science and Scopus have a dedicated affiliation field and will thus get you a fully accurate list of publications. However, they may miss some publications that are in outlets that are not included in their coverage. Google Scholar doesn't have an affiliation search. Hence, its results might not be fully accurate and complete, but are likely to be more complete.

The best strategy would therefore simply be to triangulate and use different data sources. Each data source has its own limitations, but PoP allows you to run searches in different data sources very easily. It will even pre-populate your new search with the current search terms. Note, however, that every data source has its own specific search syntax, so you may need to adapt these slightly (see Chapters 7-9 for further details on this). The next section shows a detailed example for the discipline of Business & Management.

Triangulating: Scopus, WoS, Google Scholar

Here I searched for my own publications between 2016 and 2018 with a Middlesex University affiliation in three different data sources: Scopus, Web of Science (WoS) and Google Scholar. Although there is a common core of publications covered in each of the data bases there are also important differences.

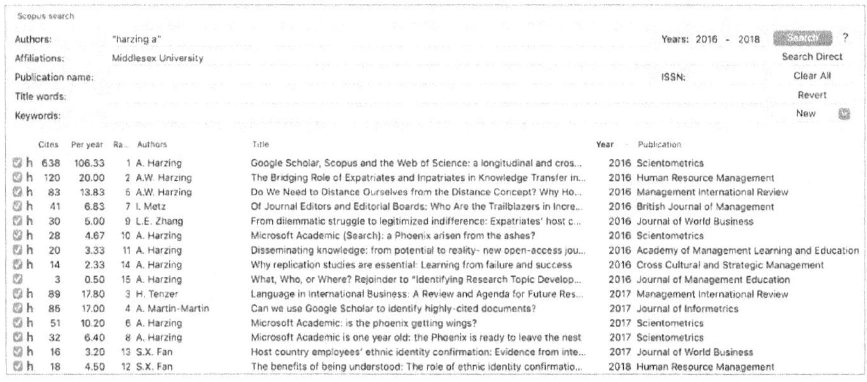

Scopus search

Authors:	"harzing a"		Years: 2016 - 2018	Search	?
Affiliations:	Middlesex University			Search Direct	
Publication name:			ISSN:	Clear All	
Title words:				Revert	
Keywords:				New	

	Cites	Per year	Ra..	Authors	Title	Year	Publication
h	638	106.33	1	A. Harzing	Google Scholar, Scopus and the Web of Science: a longitudinal and cros...	2016	Scientometrics
h	120	20.00	2	A.W. Harzing	The Bridging Role of Expatriates and Inpatriates in Knowledge Transfer in...	2016	Human Resource Management
h	83	13.83	6	A.W. Harzing	Do We Need to Distance Ourselves from the Distance Concept? Why Ho...	2016	Management International Review
h	41	6.83	7	I. Metz	Of Journal Editors and Editorial Boards: Who Are the Trailblazers in Incre...	2016	British Journal of Management
h	30	5.00	9	L.E. Zhang	From dilemmatic struggle to legitimized indifference: Expatriates' host c...	2016	Journal of World Business
h	28	4.67	10	A. Harzing	Microsoft Academic (Search): a Phoenix arisen from the ashes?	2016	Scientometrics
h	20	3.33	11	A. Harzing	Disseminating knowledge: from potential to reality- new open-access jou...	2016	Academy of Management Learning and Education
h	14	2.33	14	A. Harzing	Why replication studies are essential: Learning from failure and success	2016	Cross Cultural and Strategic Management
	3	0.50	15	A. Harzing	What, Who, or Where? Rejoinder to "Identifying Research Topic Develop...	2016	Journal of Management Education
h	89	17.80	3	H. Tenzer	Language in International Business: A Review and Agenda for Future Res...	2017	Management International Review
h	85	17.00	4	A. Martin-Martin	Can we use Google Scholar to identify highly-cited documents?	2017	Journal of Informetrics
h	51	10.20	6	A. Harzing	Microsoft Academic: is the phoenix getting wings?	2017	Scientometrics
h	32	6.40	8	A. Harzing	Microsoft Academic is one year old: the Phoenix is ready to leave the nest	2017	Scientometrics
h	16	3.20	13	S.X. Fan	Host country employees' ethnic identity confirmation: Evidence from inte...	2017	Journal of World Business
h	18	4.50	12	S.X. Fan	The benefits of being understood: The role of ethnic identity confirmatio...	2018	Human Resource Management

With fifteen journal articles Scopus (see above) provides the fewest results for this search, but it doesn't miss any of my journal articles published between 2016 and 2018. Unfortunately, the free Scopus version used in PoP only shows the first author (see Chapter 4) and is also limited to 200 results. Finally, note that a Scopus search in Publish or Perish will provide the best results if you quote the author's name. If you neglect to do so, Scopus will also show records where the author's last name matches with one author and their initial matches with another author.

A WoS search reports nearly all the journal articles that Scopus does but misses my 2016 article in the *Journal of Management Education,* which appears to be covered only until 2014 in WoS. Web of Science does, however, cover all five substantive chapters in my co-authored 2018 book as well as its preface, introduction, and conclusion. Web of Science has substantially increased its coverage of books in recent years, although this hasn't resulted in a back catalogue of books yet.

Google Scholar search

	Authors:	a harzing		Years: 2016 - 2018	Search	?
Publication name:			ISSN:	Search Direct
Title words:				Clear All
Keywords:	"Middlesex University"			Revert
Maximum number of results:	200	Include: CITATION records Patents		New

	Cites	Per ye…	Rank	Authors	Title	Year	Publication
h	236	33.71	1	AW Harzing, M Pudelko…	The bridging role of expatriates and inpatriates in knowle…	2016	Human Resource …
h	27	3.86	3	AW Harzing	Why replication studies are essential: Learning from failu…	2016	Cross Cultural &Strategic Management
h	88	12.57	4	I Metz, AW Harzing, MJ Zyphur	Of journal editors and editorial boards: who are the trailb…	2016	British journal of management
	9	1.29	5	AW Harzing	From h-index to hIa: The ins and outs of research metrics	2016	Research in International Management
h	1,382	197.43	7	AW Harzing, S Alakangas	Google Scholar, Scopus and the Web of Science: a longit…	2016	Scientometrics
	3	0.43	8	AW Harzing	Sacrifice a little accuracy for a lot more comprehensive c…	2016	Humanities
	6	0.86	9	AW Harzing	What, who, or where? Rejoinder to "identifying research…	2016	Journal of Management Education
h	39	5.57	13	AW Harzing, NJ Adler	Disseminating knowledge: From potential to reality—new…	2016	Academy of management learning & …
	2	0.29	17	S Zhao, H Tan, M Papanastass…	The internationalisation of innovation to China: The case…	2016	
h	54	7.71	19	AW Harzing	Microsoft Academic (Search): a Phoenix arisen from the…	2016	Scientometrics
h	174	24.86	20	AW Harzing, M Pudelko	Do we need to distance ourselves from the distance con…	2016	Management International Review
h	58	9.67	2	AW Harzing, S Alakangas	Microsoft Academic is one year old: The Phoenix is read…	2017	Scientometrics
h	103	17.17	16	AW Harzing, S Alakangas	Microsoft Academic: is the phoenix getting wings?	2017	Scientometrics
h	24	4.00	21	LE Zhang, AW Harzing, SX Fan	Managing expatriates in China: A language and identity p…	2017	
	5	0.83	22	AW Harzing, PM Kroonenberg	The mystery of the phantom reference	2017	Accessed
	3	0.60	6	AW Harzing, C Vinkenburg…	How to make career advancement in Economics more in…	2018	Economisch Statistische …
h	30	6.00	10	SX Fan, C Cregan, AW Harzing…	The benefits of being understood: The role of ethnic ide…	2018	Human Resource …
	1	0.20	11	AW Harzing	Internal vs. external promotion, part one: seven reasons…	2018	Impact of Social Sciences Blog
	0	0.00	12	AW Harzing	Internal vs. external promotion, part two: seven advantag…	2018	Impact of Social Sciences Blog
	8	1.60	18	AW Harzing	Running the REF on a rainy Sunday afternoon: Can we ex…	2018	STI 2018 Conference Proceedings
h	670	134.00	23	BS Reiche, H Tenzer, AW Harzi…	International human resource management	2018	International Human Resource …
	5	1.00	24	LE Zhang, AW Harzing, SX Fan…	Host country language: Why it matters, and why expatria…	2018	Managing Expatriates in …
	7	1.40	25	LE Zhang, AW Harzing, SX Fan…	Conclusion: Expatriate language and identity challenges…	2018	Managing Expatriates in …
	3	0.60	26	LE Zhang, AW Harzing, SX Fan…	The impact of host country language skills on expatriate…	2018	Managing Expatriates in …
	2	0.40	27	LE Zhang, AW Harzing, SX Fan…	Setting the scene: expatriates, language and culture in C…	2018	Managing Expatriates in …
	0	0.00	28	LE Zhang, AW Harzing, SX Fan…	The double-edged sword of ethnic similarity	2018	Managing Expatriates in …
	0	0.00	29	LE Zhang, AW Harzing, SX Fan…	Gaining acceptance from local colleagues: Evidence fro…	2018	Managing Expatriates in …

As shown above Google Scholar covers most articles that Scopus does but misses two articles in *Journal of World Business* and one in *Journal of Informetrics.* Both are published by Elsevier, whereas the other articles in my list are all published by other publishers.

As these Elsevier publications are found with a regular Google Scholar search for my name (i.e., without the affiliation restriction) it appears Google Scholar has difficulty parsing the author affiliation data in Elsevier. Like WoS, Google Scholar does cover the five substantive chapters and the conclusion in my 2018 co-authored book, as well as the book as a whole, though it misses the Preface and Introduction. That said, Google Scholar does report significant citation levels for the book, 41 citations in all, 24 to the full book and 17 to its chapters whereas WoS only picks up two citations.

Google Scholar also covers a publication in the professional journal *Economisch Statistische Berichten* on *How to make career advancement in Economics more inclusive*, three white papers (*From h-index to hIa, Sacrifice a little coverage…*, and *The mystery of the phantom reference*), two conference papers (*The internationalisation of innovation to China* and *Running the REF on a rainy Sunday afternoon*), and two blogposts on the Impact of Social Science Blog on internal vs external promotion.

Conclusion and general word of caution

If your main aim is to easily find all relevant journal articles for an academic at a particular university, Scopus might be your best choice, in Business & Management at least. If you wanted to stick to journal articles and books only, WoS might have a slight edge, though only if the book publications are recent. However, if you wanted to have a comprehensive overview of not just the author's academic publications, but also their engagement with more public-facing publication outlets, such as blogs and professionally oriented journals, Google Scholar would be the best choice. That said, the best option would be simply to triangulate as results might differ by discipline.

There are several limitations to an affiliation search, especially for mobile researchers. They might have published papers with a former employer's affiliation during their tenure at their new employer. This is especially true if these papers have been in press for quite a while, something that tends to happen frequently in the Social Sciences. For instance, nearly all of my 2014 publications and several of my 2015 publications still carried a University of Melbourne affiliation, even though I joined Middlesex University in 2014.

Moreover, the affiliation is matched in the *entire* set of co-authors. Thus, you will be able to find results searching for my co-author Markus Pudelko and Middlesex University, even though he has never worked at the university. However, in most cases this is unlikely to provide a serious practical limitation for this use case as you will be searching for an author's actual affiliation. It will only matter if the author you are searching for has collaborated with a co-author in their current university *before* they joined it. These cases can usually be eyeballed easily.

Co-authorships and citation connections

We end the chapter with four very specific searches you can do with the Publish or Perish software, searches that 99% of the PoP users will be unfamiliar with. They will answer questions that might be relevant for any of the above use cases, as well as making your own case for impact. The first two deal with co-authorships, the next two with citation connections. Again, these are just *examples* to inspire you. Feel free to experiment, you can't break the software!

Have two academics ever published together?

You might be interested to establish what two or more academics have published together. There might be lots of reasons for this. You may be looking for a good co-author and want to check whether they have published with someone you know well and trust. You may have read an article by these academics and wonder what else they have written together. Or you might simply be curious whether two academics you know well have ever worked together.

Whatever the reason, finding out whether two academics have published together couldn't be easier. Just add both names in the author field, separated by AND, and you will get a nice list of publications that they have co-authored. As this is a fairly restrictive search, in most cases using family names only is sufficient, though if one or both of the authors' names are very common you might need to add an initial or given name.

For example, the screenshot below shows that between 2007 and 2017 Markus Pudelko and I have co-authored 12 publications. As is reflected in the authorship order, the early publications were mainly based on his research, whereas the later publications were based on a collaborative project that I led. The presence of Sebastian Reiche (my former PhD student) and Helene Tenzer (a junior colleague of Markus at the time) as first authors in later publications shows our natural progression to senior authorship roles.

	Cites	Per year	Ra...	Authors	Title	Year
h	533	35.53	4	M Pudelko, AW Harzing	Country-of-origin, localization, or dominance effect? An empirical investigation of HRM...	2007
h	32	2.13	12	M Pudelko, AW Harzing	How is European management in Europe? An analysis of past, present and future manag..	2007
h	115	8.21	9	M Pudelko, AW Harzing	The golden triangle for MNCs: Standardization towards headquarters practices, standar...	2008
h	24	2.00	13	M Pudelko, A Harzing	Japanese human resource management: inspirations from abroad and current trends of...	2010
h	255	28.33	1	AW Harzing, M Pudelko	Language competencies, policies and practices in multinational corporations: A compre...	2013
h	173	19.22	2	AW Harzing, BS Reiche,...	Challenges in international survey research: A review with illustrations and suggested so...	2013
h	95	11.88	3	AW Harzing, M Pudelko	Hablas vielleicht un peu la mia language? A comprehensive overview of the role of langu...	2014
h	340	42.50	5	H Tenzer, M Pudelko, AW...	The impact of language barriers on trust formation in multinational teams	2014
h	40	5.71	10	M Pudelko, H Tenzer, AW...	Cross-cultural management and language studies within international business research...	2015
h	208	34.67	6	AW Harzing, M Pudelko...	The bridging role of expatriates and inpatriates in knowledge transfer in multinational co...	2016
h	152	25.33	8	AW Harzing, M Pudelko	Do we need to distance ourselves from the distance concept? Why home and host coun...	2016
h	171	34.20	7	BS Reiche, AW Harzing,...	Why and how does shared language affect subsidiary knowledge inflows? A social identi...	2017

Did a job applicant publish without their supervisor?

Usually, early publications of PhD students are co-authored with their supervisors. For example, as can be seen below my PhD student Sebastian Reiche published two journal articles and a handbook chapter out of his PhD with me and his other PhD supervisor, Maria Kraimer. After completing his PhD, he also co-authored three articles and two book chapters with me between 2011 and 2022.

	Cites	Per year	Ra...	Authors	Title	Year
h	236	18.15	2	BS Reiche, AW Harzing, ML Kraimer	The role of international assignees' social capital in creating inter-unit intellect...	2009
h	49	3.77	6	BS Reiche, M Kraimer, AW Harzing	Inpatriates as agents of cross-unit knowledge flows in multinational corporatio...	2009
h	184	16.73	3	BS Reiche, ML Kraimer, AW Harzing	Why do international assignees stay? An organizational embeddedness persp...	2011
h	140	12.73	5	BS Reiche, AW Harzing	International assignments	2011
h	173	19.22	1	AW Harzing, BS Reiche, M Pudelko	Challenges in international survey research: A review with illustrations and sug...	2013
h	171	34.20	4	BS Reiche, AW Harzing, M Pudelko	Why and how does shared language affect subsidiary knowledge inflows? A s...	2017
	1	1.00	9	AW Harzing, BS Reiche, M Pudelko	Intercultural survey research: challenges and suggested solutions	2021
	0	0.00	7	H Kim, BS Reiche, AW Harzing	How does successive inpatriation contribute to subsidiary capability building a...	2022

However, later on in their career we would normally expect our PhD students to work on their own or with other academics to show they can work independently. So how do you find out whether this is the case? You simply run a search with the student's name and the name of their supervisor (preceded by a minus sign "-").

As the screenshot below shows, Sebastian published a large number of articles on his own and with other academics (71 in total to date), even *during* the time he published with his supervisors. No wonder I am so proud of him!

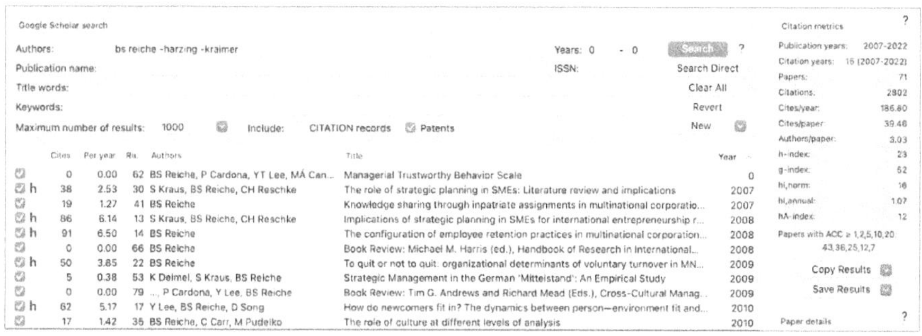

	Cites	Per year	Rn.	Authors	Title	Year
	0	0.00	62	BS Reiche, P Cardona, YT Lee, MÁ Can...	Managerial Trustworthy Behavior Scale	0
h	38	2.53	30	S Kraus, BS Reiche, CH Reschke	The role of strategic planning in SMEs: Literature review and implications	2007
	19	1.27	41	BS Reiche	Knowledge sharing through inpatriate assignments in multinational corporatio...	2007
h	86	6.14	13	S Kraus, BS Reiche, CH Reschke	Implications of strategic planning in SMEs for international entrepreneurship r...	2008
h	91	6.50	14	BS Reiche	The configuration of employee retention practices in multinational corporation...	2008
	0	0.00	66	BS Reiche	Book Review: Michael M. Harris (ed.), Handbook of Research in International...	2008
h	50	3.85	22	BS Reiche	To quit or not to quit: organizational determinants of voluntary turnover in MN...	2009
	5	0.38	53	K Deimel, S Kraus, BS Reiche	Strategic Management in the German 'Mittelstand': An Empirical Study	2009
	0	0.00	79	..., P Cardona, Y Lee, BS Reiche	Book Review: Tim G. Andrews and Richard Mead (Eds.), Cross-Cultural Manag..	2009
h	62	5.17	17	Y Lee, BS Reiche, D Song	How do newcomers fit in? The dynamics between person—environment fit and...	2010
	17	1.42	35	BS Reiche, C Carr, M Pudelko	The role of culture at different levels of analysis	2010

Google Scholar search

Authors: bs reiche -harzing -kraimer

Publication name:

Title words:

Keywords:

Maximum number of results: 1000   Include: CITATION records   Patents

Years: 0 - 0   Search   ?

ISSN: Search Direct

Clear All

Revert

New

Citation metrics

Publication years:	2007-2022
Citation years:	16 (2007-2022)
Papers:	71
Citations:	2802
Cites/year:	186.80
Cites/paper:	39.46
Authors/paper:	3.03
h-index:	23
g-index:	62
hi,norm:	16
hi,annual:	1.07
hA-index:	12

Papers with ACC ≥ 1,2,5,10,20: 43,36,25,12,7

Copy Results

Save Results

Paper details

Figure out "citation connections"

In most data sources you can only search in the title and abstract of publications, even if the publications are available in Open Access. Google Scholar, however, searches for keywords in the entire text of a full-text document. Hence, a simple citation search for your own name in the author field and another academic's name in the **Keywords** field will quickly list the articles in which you have cited this academic's work.

The screenshot below shows all 37 publications in which I have cited Rosalie Tung, one of the first academics writing about international staffing, one of my research topics, sorted chronologically with the earliest citing article first. You can see I have been referring to her work throughout my career, from my first publication in 1995 to one of my most recent publications in 2022. Hence, asking her to act as a referee for my promotion applications, and later for my Academy of International Business Fellowship was a natural choice.

	Cites	Per year	Rank	Authors	Title	Year
✓ h	579	20.68	2	AWK Harzing	The persistent myth of high expatriate failure rates	1995
☑	15	0.56	15	AW Harzing	About the paucity of empirical research in IHRM: A test of Downes framework of staffing foreign subsi...	1996
☑	3	0.11	22	AW Harzing	MNC Staffing policies for the managing director position in foreign subsidiaries: the results of an inno...	1996
☑ h	494	19.00	14	AW Harzing	Response rates in international mail surveys: Results of a 22-country study	1997
☑ h	279	12.13	7	AW Harzing	Cross-national industrial mail surveys: why do response rates differ between countries?	2000
☑ h	242	11.00	8	AW Harzing	An analysis of the functions of international transfer of managers in MNCs	2001
☑ h	725	32.95	25	AW Harzing	Of bears, bumble-bees, and spiders: The role of expatriates in controlling foreign subsidiaries	2001
☑ h	286	13.62	3	AW Harzing	Are our referencing errors undermining our scholarship and credibility? The case of expatriate failure r...	2002
☑	5	0.24	26	AW Harzing	MNE staffing policies for the managing director position in foreign subsidiaries	2002
☑ h	272	14.32	1	J Barry Hocking, M Brown...	A knowledge transfer perspective of strategic assignment purposes and their path-dependent outco...	2004
☑ h	96	5.05	18	AW Harzing	10 Composing an International Staff	2004
☑ h	1,051	75.07	12	NJ Adler, AW Harzing	When knowledge wins: Transcending the sense and nonsense of academic rankings	2009
☑ h	246	17.57	21	BS Reiche, AW Harzing, ML Krai...	The role of international assignees' social capital in creating inter-unit intellectual capital: A cross-lev...	2009
☑ h	53	3.79	30	BS Reiche, M Kraimer, AW Harzing	Inpatriates as agents of cross-unit knowledge flows in multinational corporations	2009
☑ h	94	7.23	35	D Akkermans, AW Harzing...	Cultural accommodation and language priming: Competitive versus cooperative behavior in a prisoner...	2010
☑	4	0.33	6	AW Harzing, I Metz	Practicing what we preach	2011
☑ h	148	12.33	16	BS Reiche, AW Harzing	International assignments	2011
☑ h	196	16.33	19	BS Reiche, ML Kraimer, AW Harzi...	Why do international assignees stay? An organizational embeddedness perspective	2011
☑ h	126	11.45	17	AW Harzing, M Brown, K Köster,...	Response style differences in cross-national research: dispositional and situational determinants	2012
☑ h	33	3.00	23	AW Harzing, I Metz	Explaining geographic diversity of editorial boards: the role of conference participation and English-la...	2012
☑ h	181	18.10	11	AW Harzing, BS Reiche...	Challenges in international survey research: A review with illustrations and suggested solutions for be...	2013
☑ h	77	7.70	13	AW Harzing, I Metz	Practicing what we preach: The geographic diversity of editorial boards	2013
☑ h	102	11.33	10	AW Harzing, M Pudelko	Hablas vielleicht un peu la mia language? A comprehensive overview of the role of language differenc...	2014
☑ h	389	43.22	27	H Tenzer, M Pudelko, AW Harzing	The impact of language barriers on trust formation in multinational teams	2014
☑	0	0.00	42	SX Fan, AW Harzing, T Köhler	How You See Me, How You Don't: Ethnic Identity Self-verification in Interactions	2014
☑ h	47	5.88	24	M Pudelko, H Tenzer, AW Harzing	Cross-cultural management and language studies within international business research: past and pre...	2015
☑ h	88	12.57	4	I Metz, AW Harzing, MJ Zyphur	Of journal editors and editorial boards: who are the trailblazers in increasing editorial board gender eq...	2016
☑ h	173	24.71	5	AW Harzing, M Pudelko	Do we need to distance ourselves from the distance concept? Why home and host country context mi...	2016
☑	24	4.00	33	LE Zhang, AW Harzing, SX Fan	Managing expatriates in China: A language and identity perspective	2017
☑ h	27	4.50	37	SX Fan, AW Harzing	Host country employees' ethnic identity confirmation: Evidence from interactions with ethnically simil...	2017
☑ h	30	6.00	28	SX Fan, C Cregan, AW Harzing...	The benefits of being understood: The role of ethnic identity confirmation in knowledge acquisition by...	2018
☑	0	0.00	41	LE Zhang, AW Harzing, SX Fan, L...	The double-edged sword of ethnic similarity	2018
☑	2	0.40	46	LE Zhang, AW Harzing, SX Fan, L...	Setting the scene: expatriates, language and culture in China	2018
☑	0	0.00	47	LE Zhang, AW Harzing, SX Fan, L...	Gaining acceptance from local colleagues: Evidence from Indian expatriates in China	2018
☑	7	1.75	40	C Li, LE Zhang, AW Harzing	Of ostriches, frogs, birds and lizards: a dynamic framework of cultural identity negotiation strategies i...	2019
☑	9	3.00	20	S Fan, AW Harzing	Moving beyond the baseline: Exploring the potential of experiments in language research	2020
☑	9	3.00	36	SX Fan, AW Harzing, T Köhler	How you see me, how you don't: ethnic identity self-verification in interactions between local subsidia...	2020
☑	4	2.00	34	M Bastida, LHHF Pinto, AW Harzi...	No room at the top? A system dynamics view of the recursive consequences of women's underrepres...	2021
☑	13	6.50	38	M Dodourova, S Zhao, AW Harzing	Ambidexterity in MNC knowledge sourcing in emerging economies: A microfoundational perspective	2021
☑	1	0.50	48	SX Fan, AW Harzing	The double-edged sword of ethnic similarity for expatriates	2021
☑	2	2.00	29	S Ciuk, M Śliwa, AW Harzing	Implementing the equality, diversity, and inclusion agenda in multinational companies: A framework fo...	2022
☑	5	5.00	39	HJ Lee, K Yoshikawa, AW Harzing	Cultures and institutions: Dispositional and contextual explanations for country-of-origin effects in M...	2022

However, this works the other way around as well: you can find out if the other academic has ever cited you. What better way to find out common interests? The screenshot below shows all articles in which Rosalie Tung has cited me. Note that for both searches the actual number of citations might be underestimated as you may well cite more than one of an academic's papers in each article.

	Cites	Per year	Rank	Authors	Title	Year
☑ h	876	35.04	5	RL Tung	American expatriates abroad: From neophytes to cosmopolitans	1998
☑ h	313	13.04	4	PM Caligiuri, RL Tung	Comparing the success of male and female expatriates from a US-based multinational company	1999
☑ h	49	2.72	10	RL Tung	Perspectives—New era, new realities: Musings on a new research agenda... from an old timer	2005
☑ h	26	1.53	12	RL Tung	North American research agenda and methodologies: Past imperfect, future—Limitless possibilities	2006
☑ h	72	4.80	9	RL Tung	Do race and gender matter in international assignments to/from Asia Pacific? An exploratory study of...	2008
☑ h	358	25.57	1	D Bello, K Leung, L Radebaugh, R...	From the editors: Student samples in international business research	2009
☑	11	0.79	13	RL Tung	Cross-cultural research diary: A personal odyssey	2009
☑ h	780	60.00	2	RL Tung, A Verbeke	Beyond Hofstede and GLOBE: Improving the quality of cross-cultural research	2010
☑ h	49	4.90	6	RL Tung, Y Paik, J Bae	Korean human resource management in the global context	2013
☑ h	57	5.70	8	HD Kim, RL Tung	Opportunities and challenges for expatriates in emerging markets: An exploratory study of Korean exp...	2013
☑ h	236	33.71	3	RL Tung	New perspectives on human resource management in a global context	2016
☑ h	181	25.86	7	Y Baruch, Y Altman, RL Tung	Career mobility in a global era: Advances in managing expatriation and repatriation	2016
☑	10	1.43	11	B Bader, RL Tung	Motivations of global careers among expatriates in German companies: a comparison with the year 20...	2016
☑	2	0.33	14	RL Tung	Prologue—Voyages of Self-Discovery: A Reflection on Four Decades of Research on Expatriation and C...	2017

As this type of search relies on Google Scholar searching the list of references and referencing formats and standards differ by journal, you will need to careful with the initials you included in this search. For names that are not that common, it is unlikely that there are two academics with the same family name in a specific sub-discipline. Hence you will normally get a good result with someone's last name only. In any case, if you want to use this as a conversation starter, you will need to download the articles in question, so you can easily spot any inaccurate references.

Estimate self-citations

This also a way in which you can estimate an author's self-citations. Simply include their own name in the **Keywords** field. However, here the limitation that each citing article is only shown once, even if it is citing the academics a dozen times, limits its usefulness. It is quite natural for academics to cite their prior work in their articles; much of our work is cumulative. Typically, most academics would self-cite one of their own articles in at least half of their work. Where self-citation becomes excessive is if academics cite a wide range of their own articles in *each* publication, with sometimes tenuous relevance.

How much is [author x] cited in [journal y]?

You can use the same technique to find out how much a particular author is cited in a particular journal. This gives you a good idea which conversations you are part of; it might thus be useful if you are submitting to the journal in question. It may also be useful for editors looking for reviewers or editorial board members.

The screenshot below shows the first 26 of 188 articles published in *Journal of International Business Studies* (the top journal in my field) citing one or more of my publications. Not surprisingly, the first time my work was cited in JIBS was in my own article in the journal in 2000. Self-citations are likely to occur before other citations.

	Cites	Per ye...	Rank	Authors	Title	Year
☑ h	742	32.26	1	AW Harzing	An empirical analysis and extension of the Bartlett and Ghoshal typology of multinational companies	2000
☑ h	851	38.68	9	KD Brouthers, LE Brouthers	Explaining the national cultural distance paradox	2001
☑ h	143	6.50	30	CM Lau, HY Ngo	Organization development and firm performance: A comparison of multinational and local firms	2001
☑ h	123	5.59	84	S Jun, JW Gentry, YJ Hyun	Cultural adaptation of business expatriates in the host marketplace	2001
☑ h	216	9.82	104	M Laroche, VH Kirpalani, F Po...	A model of advertising standardization in multinational corporations	2001
☑ h	313	15.65	31	J Child, L Chung, H Davies	The performance of cross-border units in China: A test of natural selection, strategic choice and c...	2003
☑ h	129	6.45	82	JK Giacobbe-Miller, DJ Miller,...	Country and organizational-level adaptation to foreign workplace ideologies: A comparative study...	2003
☑ h	167	8.79	87	JP Doh, H Teegen, R Mudambi	Balancing private and state ownership in emerging markets' telecommunications infrastructure: C...	2004
☑ h	230	12.11	90	JP Shay, SA Baack	Expatriate assignment, adjustment and effectiveness: An empirical examination of the big picture	2004
☑ h	1,661	92.28	16	K Leung, RS Bhagat, NR Buch...	Culture and international business: Recent advances and their implications for future research	2005
☑ h	1,385	76.94	24	L Tihanyi, DA Griffith, CJ Russell	The effect of cultural distance on entry mode choice, international diversification, and MNE perfor...	2005
☑ h	369	20.50	33	S Venaik, DF Midgley, TM Devi...	Dual paths to performance: The impact of global pressures on MNC subsidiary conduct and perfo...	2005
☑ h	315	17.50	55	RA Belderbos, MG Heijltjes	The determinants of expatriate staffing by Japanese multinationals in Asia: Control, learning and v...	2005
☑ h	360	20.00	64	JM Mezias, TA Scandura	A needs-driven approach to expatriate adjustment and career development: A multiple mentoring...	2005
☑ h	1,202	70.71	8	BW Husted, DB Allen	Corporate social responsibility in the multinational enterprise: Strategic and institutional approach...	2006
☑ h	2,983	175.47	14	BL Kirkman, KB Lowe, CB Gibs...	A quarter century of Culture's Consequences: a review of empirical research incorporating Hofste...	2006
☑ h	1,384	81.41	15	JP Johnson, T Lenartowicz, S...	Cross-cultural competence in international business: Toward a definition and a model	2006
☑ h	242	14.24	79	U Weitzel, S Berns	Cross-border takeovers, corruption, and related aspects of governance	2006
☑ h	573	35.81	11	D Dikova, A Van Witteloostuijn	Foreign direct investment mode choice: entry and establishment modes in transition economies	2007
☑ h	777	48.56	20	I Björkman, GK Stahl, E Vaara	Cultural differences and capability transfer in cross-border acquisitions: The mediating roles of ca...	2007
☑ h	398	24.88	37	MB Lazarova, JL Cerdin	Revisiting repatriation concerns: Organizational support versus career and contextual influences	2007
☑ h	430	26.88	47	RG Flores, RV Aguilera	Globalization and location choice: an analysis of US multinational firms in 1980 and 2000	2007
☑ h	298	18.63	51	MC Bolino	Expatriate assignments and intra-organizational career success: Implications for individuals and o...	2007
☑ h	229	14.31	68	P Andriani, B McKelvey	Beyond Gaussian averages: redirecting international business and management research toward e...	2007
☑ h	156	9.75	85	VP Lau, MA Shaffer, K Au	Entrepreneurial career success from a Chinese perspective: conceptualization, operationalization,...	2007
☑ h	210	13.13	93	SJ Shin, FP Morgeson, MA Ca...	What you do depends on where you are: Understanding how domestic and expatriate work require...	2007

However, an analysis like this also allows you to verify whether the number of citing articles increases over time by sorting the articles by years as above. To quickly count citations in specific years or range of year, un-select all publications and then select the years you want to count. In my case, citations to my work did increase over the years: from 13 in 2001-2005 to 37 in 2006-2010, 50 in 2011-2015, and 56 in 2016-2020.

So, on average my work was cited in respectively 2, 7, 10 and 11 articles in the *Journal of International Business Studies* a year in the last 20 years. Given that JIBS only publishes between 60 and 90 articles a year, this shows my work has a significant impact on the field, being cited in 10-15% of the articles published in the journal from 2006 onwards. Citations in 2021 and 2022 show that in the two most recent full years citations to my work had stabilised at 11 per year.

Knowing whether your work is cited in your field's top journal, whether it continues to be cited over the years, and what conversations in the field it is contributing to is be useful not just for your own journal submissions or editors looking for reviewers, but also for your tenure and promotion applications. You can find much more guidance on this in my book *Writing effective promotion applications*.

In sum

This chapter outlined six typical use cases for PoP author searches when evaluating other academics: finding reviewers, examiners, speakers, or referees; preparing for a meeting with a visitor or your academic hero; writing laudations or obituaries; assessing papers for publication awards; preparing for a job interview; and finally evaluating authors' output by affiliation.

It also showed you how you can use PoP to assess co-authorships and citation connections between individuals and an individual and a journal community. But remember, these are just examples. There is no end to the number of academic questions that can be answered with Publish or Perish using some smart searching techniques. If you have found a particularly intriguing use case, please do let me know and I will post it in the next edition of this guide.

In the next chapter we will take a deep dive into using Publish or Perish for another very important academic task: conducting literature reviews.

Chapter 12: Conducting a Literature review search

In the early years of Publish or Perish most users mainly used the software as a h-index calculator. Over the years, however, academics have realised its potential as a tool for literature reviews. You can use any data source that is accessible through the Publish or Perish software to do literature reviews. Most users, however, prefer to use Google Scholar for its broader coverage. Hence, my examples in this chapter refer to Google Scholar. For instructions on how to use the other data sources see Chapter 4 on data sources and Chapter 9 on topic searches.

Literature review search: the basics

Doing a literature review in Publish or Perish couldn't be easier. Simply pop your search terms in the **Keywords** field and press search. Depending on how broad you want the results to be, you can either use a single word or multiple words.

If you want the words to appear in the exact order in which they are entered simply quote them, for instance "ethical marketing" or "workplace bullying". Publish or Perish also allows using Boolean operators such as AND, OR, and NOT. You can use them to create more complex searches. For full details on this, refer to Chapter 1 on the main user interface and Chapter 9 on topic searches.

Google Scholar searches in the full text of the document. If you want to narrow down the results, use the **Title words** field. This search only provides publications with the words are included in the title. As you would expect important publications in a field to include the relevant search terms in their title, this might be a good strategy.

Comprehensive literature review:
Born global firms

Let's assume you would like to know what has been written about the concept of "born global" firms. Born globals are firms who start operating internationally from their inception, rather than starting out as domestic firms first and only internationalising gradually. To do so enter "born global" OR "born globals" in the **Title words** field. This results in more than 1,000 papers, ten of which have been cited more than 1,000 times.

Founding authors

Sorting the results by year (just click on the column heading to do this) allows us to identify who the "founding author(s)" of the concept are. Below I have reproduced all articles with "born global" in the title until 2000; the first article was published in 1993 by Rennie in *McKinsey Quarterly*.

The paper talks about a McKinsey study amongst Australian firms. It identified small and medium-sized companies that successfully competed against large, established players in the global arena without first building a home base. Thus, it appears a consulting firm in Australia has first discovered the born global phenomenon.

	Cites	Per ye…	R…	Authors	Title	Year ˄
☑ h	1,779	61.34	2	MW Rennie	Born global	1993
☑ h	115	4.11	1	ST Cavusgil, GA Knight	A quiet revolution in Australian exporters	1994
☑ h	2,674	102.85	5	G Knight, ST Cavusgil,…	The born global firm: a challenge to traditional internationali…	1996
☑	56	2.24	1	ST Cavusgil, GA Knight	Explaining an emerging phenomenon for international marke…	1997
☑ h	337	13.48	31	GA Knight	Emerging paradigm for international marketing: The born glo…	1997
☑	65	2.71	6…	S Kandasaami	Internationalisation of small-and medium-sized born global f…	1998
☑	5	0.22	2	P Servais, ES Rasmussen	Born Globals–connectors between various industrial districts	1999
☑	4	0.17	6	C Gurau, A Ranchhod	The'Born Global'Firms in UK Biotechnology	1999
☑ h	346	15.73	23	TK Madsen, E Rasmuss…	Differences and similarities between born globals and other…	2000
☑ h	171	7.77	65	E Autio, HJ Sapienza	Comparing process and born global perspectives in the inter…	2000
☑	84	3.82	161	PD Harveston	Synoptic versus incremental internationalization: An examina…	2000
☑	49	2.23	1…	T Almor	Born global: the case of small and medium sized, knowledge…	2000
☑	29	1.32	217	G Knight, TK Madsen,…	The born global firm: description and empirical investigation…	2000
☑ h	109	4.95	5…	J Bell, R McNAUGHTON	Born global firms: a challenge to public policy in support of i…	2000
☑	56	2.55	6…	S Kandasaami, X Huang	International marketing strategy of SMEs: A comparison of b…	2000

The second publication is an editorial by a well-known academic in International Marketing, who reports on the results of the McKinsey study that he discovered when spending 6 months as a Fulbright Scholar in Australia. Cavusgil (1994:4) says:

"I would like to comment on an interesting phenomenon in the Australian export scene. It is relevant to those of us in other post-industrial economies and, hopefully, should spur some research interests."

The Australian angle is also displayed in a later conceptual paper published in 1998 by Kandasaami, University of Western Australia. Interestingly, this paper did gather a respectable 65 citations, despite being an unpublished working paper.

Historical development of the field

Our literature search also allows us to follow the development of this field of research over the decades. As shown in the above screenshot, Cavusgil took his recommendations to heart and started researching this phenomenon, leading to a very highly cited publication in 1996 – co-authored with Gary Knight. Knight and Cavusgil went on to publish many other papers in this field. They were joined at an early stage by a Danish academic, Tage Madsen, who, with his Danish co-authors Servais and Rasmussen, also published several papers on the topic. In 1999, the phenomenon was also picked up in the UK, where Gurau & Ranchhod researched biotechnology firms.

By 2000 the topic had spread to researchers in the USA (Harveston et al.), Ireland (Bell), Finland (Autio), and Israel (Almor). Interest in it remained strong amongst researchers these countries, but after 2000 they were also joined by researchers in Sweden, Portugal, and New Zealand. Apart from a few researchers in the USA and Israel, the phenomenon initially attracted most interest from academics in "small" economies at the geographical peripheries of the world.

The mid 2000s saw the interest in the phenomenon expand to other countries such as Germany, Switzerland, Mexico, Korea, with Latin American countries and Italy joining from the late 2000s. In the early 2010s geographical interest had spread to India, China, and Eastern Europe. The year 2012 saw the publication of a *Handbook of Research on Born Globals* with 18 chapters by different researchers in the field, as well as an annotated bibliography.

In 2015, the 2014 JIBS award for the best paper of the decade went to Knight's and Cavusgil's paper *"Innovation, organisational capabilities, and the born-global firm"*. In the same year, Gary Knight published a review article (*"Born global firms: Evolution of a contemporary phenomenon"*) in *Advances in International Marketing*. It appears that after 20 years, the topic of "born globals" had reached maturity.

Since then, the field has blossomed with hundreds of publications since the mid 2010s. The field of born globals clearly continues to be of great interest to international business scholars. Scholars are now branching out into specialised topics such as born global family firms, as well as specific industries such as the music industry, natural cosmetics, and breweries.

Important journals

Sorting our results set on born global firms by journal (again just click on the column heading) allows us to identify the journals that have published articles relating to this topic. It showed that all mainstream IB journals (*Journal of International Business Studies, Journal of World Business, Management International Review*, and *International Business Review*) have published a substantial number of papers on the topic.

More specialised International Marketing journals such as *Journal of International Marketing* and *International Marketing Review* have also published many papers on this topic. Most of the born global firms are exporters rather than multinationals with subsidiaries abroad. Exporting is traditionally a topic of considerable interest to the International Marketing community.

The results also showed many papers in the *International Journal of Globalisation and Small Business* and the *Journal of International Entrepreneurship*. This illustrates that the born global phenomenon often involves small and medium-sized firms and that the early internationalisation decision can be seen in the context of entrepreneurship. Hence, our journal review has allowed us to identify not just the main outlets, but with them also the many subdisciplines in which this phenomenon has attracted substantive interest.

Follow up on key publications in the field

Your literature review will discover the seminal publications in the field. These could be publications that are highly cited or publications that deal with exactly the topic you are interested in. Oftentimes, you will also want to ensure that you review papers that are *citing* this seminal piece of work. These papers might show up in your initial search, but if they look at the phenomenon from a different angle and don't refer to the exact same concepts, they will not be captured.

So how can you use Publish or Perish to follow up on publications that cite your seminal publications? Simply right-click on the seminal article in question and chose **"Retrieve citing works in Publish or Perish"**. This will look up all publications referencing your seminal publication and present them ordered by the number of citations.

The screenshot below shows the ten most highly cited articles that cite the first publication on born globals (Rennie 1996). Of these, four were included in our initial search, as they have "born global" in the title. The three articles by Alba et al., Quelch & Klein, and Teece are probably not very relevant. However, the publications by Rialp et al. and two articles by Jones & Coviello appear to be relevant, even though they do not mention the terms born global in the title.

Cites	Per ye...	R...	Authors	Title
☑ h 4,290	238.33	1	GA Knight, ST Cavusgil	Innovation, organizational capabilities, and the born-global firm
☑ h 3,807	152.28	2	J Alba, J Lynch, B Weit...	Interactive home shopping: consumer, retailer, and manufacturer...
☑ h 2,922	584.40	3	TK Madsen, P Servais	The internationalization of born globals: an evolutionary process?
☑ h 1,811	120.73	4	JA Quelch, LR Klein	The Internet and international marketing
☑ h 1,565	92.06	5	A Rialp, J Rialp, GA Kni...	The phenomenon of early internationalizing firms: what do we kn...
☑ h 1,510	88.82	6	MV Jones, NE Coviello	Internationalisation: conceptualising an entrepreneurial process o...
☑ h 1,461	97.40	7	L Zhou, W Wu, X Luo	Internationalization and the performance of born-global SMEs: th...
☑ h 1,459	132.64	8	MV Jones, N Coviello,...	International entrepreneurship research (1989–2009): a domain...
☑ h 1,344	70.74	9	DD Sharma, A Blomste...	The internationalization process of born globals: a network view
☑ h 1,332	166.50	10	DJ Teece	A dynamic capabilities-based entrepreneurial theory of the multi...

In sum

Using Publish or Perish allows you to quickly establish the seminal publications, founding authors, historical development, and important journal outlets of any field of research.

How to conduct a longitudinal literature review?

Publish or Perish can also be used to analyse the development of the literature on any topic longitudinally. You can search for specific key words and look at how the number of papers published varies over time. To eliminate many irrelevant results, it is a good idea to focus on a small set of journals. You can search for more than one journal at a time using the OR function in the publication name field. Google Scholar limits the character count it accepts, so it will consider only the first 3-5 journals. Other data sources that can be accessed with Publish or Perish do not have such limitations.

Publish or Perish does not provide the ability to further analyse for instance the number of publications per year. However, exporting the data to a spreadsheet or statistical programme allows you to do this very easily. Moreover, by selecting all publications in a given year, clicking "unselect" and looking at the reduction in the number of papers, you can quickly establish the number of papers per year.

Example 1: Culture in the field of IB

Let us assume that you are interested in how research into the role of national culture in the field of International Business has developed over the years. To limit the number of irrelevant hits, you limit your search to the two mainstream International Business journals (*Journal of International Business Studies* and *International Business Review*) and use **Title words**. The screenshot below shows the search, as well as all papers receiving more than 500 citations.

	Cites	Per year	Rank	Authors	Title	Year
h	8,791	251.17	27	B Kogut, H Singh	The effect of national culture on the choice of entry mode	1988
h	2,008	74.37	29	KL Newman, SD Nollen	Culture and congruence: The fit between management practices and national culture	1996
h	1,663	92.39	32	K Leung, RS Bhagat, NR Buchan,...	Culture and international business: Recent advances and their implications for future research	2005
h	1,600	69.57	34	AS Thomas, SL Mueller	A case for comparative entrepreneurship: Assessing the relevance of culture	2000
h	1,437	49.55	1	G Hofstede	The business of international business is culture	1994
h	1,374	57.25	37	BW Husted	Wealth, culture, and corruption	1999
h	1,182	45.46	35	DA Ralston, DH Holt, RH Terpstra...	The impact of natural culture and economic ideology on managerial work values: a study of the United...	1997
h	1,009	25.23	41	NJ Adler	A typology of management studies involving culture	1983
h	871	34.84	47	JF Hennart, J Larimo	The impact of culture on the strategy of multinational enterprises: does national origin affect ownershi...	1998
h	853	44.89	2	CM Lau, HY Ngo	The HR system, organizational culture, and product innovation	2004
h	778	59.85	42	U Stephan, LM Uhlaner	Performance-based vs socially supportive culture: A cross-national study of descriptive norms and en...	2010
h	770	30.80	45	RS Schuler, N Rogovsky	Understanding compensation practice variations across firms: The impact of national culture	1998
h	762	36.29	40	V Pothukuchi, F Damanpour, J Ch...	National and organizational culture differences and international joint venture performance	2002
h	752	44.24	49	CCY Kwok, S Tadesse	National culture and financial systems	2006
h	671	39.47	50	EK Pellegrini, TA Scandura	Leader–member exchange (LMX), paternalism, and delegation in the Turkish business culture: An em...	2006
h	634	30.19	53	ACW Chui, AE Lloyd, CCY Kwok	The determination of capital structure: is national culture a missing piece to the puzzle?	2002
h	625	44.64	55	R Chakrabarti, S Gupta-Mukherje...	Mars–Venus marriages: Culture and cross-border M&A	2009
h	501	38.54	54	S Han, T Kang, S Salter, YK Yoo	A cross-country study on the effects of national culture on earnings management	2010
h	501	13.18	60	JL Graham	The influence of culture on the process of business negotiations: An exploratory study	1985

Highly cited papers and development over time

The most highly cited paper – by a large distance – is Kogut & Singh's paper on the effect of national culture on the choice of entry mode. This was a seminal paper because it introduced culture as a variable to be considered in entry mode studies.

Other highly cited papers over the years are those providing reviews of the field (e.g., Adler in 1983, Hofstede in 1994, and Leung et al. in 2005). However, the study of the impact of culture on managerial work values and practices is also quite popular (Newman & Nollen; Ralston et al.).

Further highly cited papers deal with the impact of culture on specific topics such as wealth and corruption (Husted), strategy (Hennart & Larimo), compensation practices (Schuler & Rogovsky), joint ventures (Pothukuchi et al.), financial systems (Kwok & Tadesse), capital systems (Chui), mergers & acquisitions (Chakrabarti et al.), earnings management (Han) and negotiations (Graham). Not surprisingly, there are also a few articles that deal with organisational or business culture rather national culture (e.g., Lau & Ngo, Stephan & Uhlaner, and Pellegrini & Scandura).

By sorting the articles by year, I can establish that the interest in the role of culture is increasing. Only six articles were published in these two journals in the 1980s that had culture in their title. Likewise, in the first half of the nineties, there were only five articles that dealt with culture to such an extent that they included the word in their title. In the latter half of the nineties, the total number of articles had increased to nearly a dozen.

The first decade of the 21st century produced some 40 articles in JIBS and IBR with the word culture in the title, with another 50-odd published in the next decade. Culture is definitely a topic that appears to be of sustained interest to international business scholars!

Example 2: HIV in Science, Nature, and Cell

Let us assume that you are interested in how research on HIV has developed over the years. You decide to focus your search only on three core journals in the field that are most likely to publish on this topic: *Science*, *Nature*, and *Cell*.

The screenshot below shows all papers with more than 3,000 citations. We can see that each of the three journals has published very highly cited articles in this field: three in *Cell*, six in *Nature* and seven in *Science*. We can also observe that most of the highly cited articles on this topic were published between 1995 and 1998, and in fact ten out of the sixteen most highly cited articles were published in 1996.

Google Scholar search

| Authors: | | | | | | Years: 0 - 0 | Search | ? |

Publication name:	Nature OR Science OR Cell	ISSN:	Search Direct
Title words:	HIV		Clear All
Keywords:			Revert
Maximum number of results:	1000	Include: CITATION records ☑ Patents	New

	Cites	Per year	Rank	Authors	Title	Year	Publication
☑ h	5,864	217.19	8	Y Feng, CC Broder, PE Kennedy,…	HIV-1 entry cofactor: functional cDNA cloning of a seven-transmembrane, G protein…	1996	Science
☑ h	5,650	201.79	4	DD Ho, AU Neumann, AS Perelso…	Rapid turnover of plasma virions and CD4 lymphocytes in HIV-1 infection	1995	Nature
☑ h	4,952	183.41	16	HK Deng, R Liu, W Ellmeier, S Ch…	Identification of a major co-receptor for primary isolates of HIV-1	1996	Nature
☑ h	4,574	169.41	10	AS Perelson, AU Neumann, M Ma…	HIV-1 dynamics in vivo: virion clearance rate, infected cell life-span, and viral gener…	1996	Science
☑ h	4,279	158.48	12	T Dragic, V Litwin, GP Allaway, S…	HIV-1 entry into CD4+ cells is mediated by the chemokine receptor CC-CKR-5	1996	Nature
☑ h	4,036	161.44	14	PD Kwong, R Wyatt, J Robinson,…	Structure of an HIV gp120 envelope glycoprotein in complex with the CD4 receptor…	1998	Nature
☑ h	3,916	145.04	37	R Liu, WA Paxton, S Choe, D Cera…	Homozygous defect in HIV-1 coreceptor accounts for resistance of some multiply-e…	1996	Cell
☑ h	3,826	136.64	7	F Cocchi, AL DeVico, A Garzino-…	Identification of RANTES, MIP-1α, and MIP-1β as the Major HIV-Suppressive Factors…	1995	Science
☑ h	3,787	140.26	30	G Alkhatib, C Combadiere, CC Br…	CC CKR5: a RANTES, MIP-1α, MIP-1β receptor as a fusion cofactor for macrophage…	1996	Science
☑ h	3,779	139.96	6	M Samson, F Libert, BJ Doranz, J…	Resistance to HIV-1 infection in caucasian individuals bearing mutant alleles of the…	1996	Nature
☑ h	3,613	138.96	31	D Finzi, M Hermankova, T Pierso…	Identification of a reservoir for HIV-1 in patients on highly active antiretroviral therapy	1997	Science
☑ h	3,475	128.70	29	JW Mellors, CR Rinaldo Jr, P Gup…	Prognosis in HIV-1 infection predicted by the quantity of virus in plasma	1996	Science
☑ h	3,183	138.39	69	TBH Geijtenbeek, DS Kwon, R Tor…	DC-SIGN, a dendritic cell–specific HIV-1-binding protein that enhances trans-infecti…	2000	Cell
☑ h	3,165	117.22	21	M Dean, M Carrington, C Winkler,…	Genetic Restriction of HIV-1 Infection and Progression to AIDS by a Deletion Allele o…	1996	Science
☑ h	3,114	183.18	13	CL Day, DE Kaufmann, P Klepiela,…	PD-1 expression on HIV-specific T cells is associated with T-cell exhaustion and dis…	2006	Nature
☑ h	3,102	114.89	35	H Choe, M Farzan, Y Sun, N Sulliv…	The β-chemokine receptors CCR3 and CCR5 facilitate infection by primary HIV-1 is…	1996	Cell

Development of research volume over time

However, I am also interested in how the volume of research on HIV has developed over the years. To assess this, I have rerun the search for a single journal only: *Science*. The reason for this is that if I include all journals, only the most highly cited 1,000 results will be shown, as Google Scholar limits its results to 1,000. This will naturally exclude many recent articles as they are not yet highly cited.

I also split my search into two time periods and then aggregated both searches into one. This ensured that I also included less-cited articles (there are over 100 articles without any citations in both periods). This reduces the risk of missing most recently published articles. In doing so I was able to conclude the following.

- **The number of publications on HIV peaked in 1988:** When I sort the results by year, I find that articles on HIV started being published in Science in 1986, when three articles were published on the topic. About a dozen articles were published in 1987, whilst nearly 50 articles were published in 1988. This was the year with the largest number of publications on HIV in *Science*.

- **Another peak in publications appeared in 1996:** Between 1989 and 1995 the number of articles had gone down to about 20-30. However, in 1996 the number of articles reached nearly 50 again, dropping to around 30 again in 1997-1999. Then, from the early 2000s, the number of articles published went down to about 15 a year, with a seeming resurgence from 2013 onwards where we see a return to 25-30 articles a year.

Publication peaks follow major medical developments. The name HIV was introduced in May 1986 by the International Committee on the Taxonomy of Viruses. The current treatment for HIV was introduced in 1996, resulting in a declining number of deaths from HIV /AIDS. So, by studying the scientific interest in HIV (or any illness) through journal publications, we can understand the development of interest in the disease over time.

Using Publish or Perish for meta-analyses

A specific type of literature reviews is required for meta-analyses. The persistent challenge for meta-analytic studies is to keep track of the literature searches a researcher must do when conducting a meta-analysis. It is expected that the Methods section of a meta-analytic paper will report all literature search steps and the results of these searches. It is nearly impossible to keep track of those searches and their results – unless you use Publish or Perish.

Integration between PoP and Endnote

By using PoP in combination with EndNote (or any other reference manager), you can easily collect references for meta-analysis. Vas Taras, who has often used PoP for meta-analyses explains how.

- First, create a list of search terms that are relevant to your literature search. For example, I am working on "roots" tourism, and I need to find all literature on the topic. However, there are multiple names for this phenomenon, so I'll need to search for "roots tourism", "diaspora tourism", "ancestral tourism", "family and friends tourism", and so on.

- So, I type in the first of these search terms in PoP. PoP returns the list of studies on the topic.

- Next, with a couple of clicks, I export these results to EndNote and save them as a new group.

- Then I move on to the next search term in PoP, and again export the results to EndNote.

- I repeat the steps for each of my search terms, each time saving the results as a separate group of references. This way, I now have a list of how many hits I got in Google Scholar for each of my searches. I will report these numbers in my paper when I am describing my literature search.

- Next, I use the "consolidate duplicates" function in EndNote. This allows me to remove papers that used multiple terms. When done, I have a clean list of all studies that mention any of my search terms. I could list multiple search terms in PoP to get the full, consolidated list right away, but I prefer to track the number of hits for each search term first.

Subsequently, I can proceed with the usual screening of the papers for suitability for my meta-analysis, first based on only the title of the publication and outlets, and later based on inspection of the full-text papers.

The good thing is that once all my references are in EndNote, I can now give the list to my graduate student and ask her/him to download full text PDFs and check the studies for the presence of usable data. It would be hard to train a student to do it directly in Google Scholar. Too many mistakes would happen. But when the list is in EndNote, the student can go through it paper by paper. A much more reliable approach.

Advantages of using PoP

PoP gives me the following important advantages over the searches directly in Google Scholar:

1. PoP allows for saving multiple references at once. Google Scholar would require that I export them to EndNote one by one, which can take hours if I am dealing with hundreds or thousands of hits as it often happens.

2. PoP allows me to keep track of the exact number of hits for each search term. It is very useful not only for reporting in the Methods/Literature Search section of the resulting paper, but also for keeping for my own records.

3. By consolidating duplicates in EndNote, I can not only get a total list of hits, but also the unique number of hits for each search term, and for the literature search overall.

In sum

Publish or Perish is an essential tool for literature reviews. Although it can be used with any data source, it is particularly effective with Google Scholar, which has a broader coverage than the other data sources. Publish or Perish allows the user to review, sort, and export results in a way not possible in the Google Scholar web interface. It can also be used to collect articles for meta-analyses.

So, we are now familiar with the best strategies to keep up to date with the literature and how to review it using the Publish or Perish software. This will help you in writing up your paper. The next step though is to decide where to submit your paper. In the next chapter we will demonstrate how Publish or Perish can be used to select appropriate journal outlets for academic papers.

Chapter 13: Researching target journals

Let's assume you have written a paper, but are unsure which journal to submit it to. Normally, you would already have a good idea of suitable journals through your literature review, but there might be good reasons why you haven't been able to settle on a journal yet.

- You might want to ensure you haven't neglected any options.
- You might already know what the most suitable journal for your paper would be, but you have already published several papers there, and are keen to show the impact of your work beyond your immediate academic peer group.
- The most appropriate journal is one where you have recently had a bad experience in the review process (e.g., long delays or shoddy reviewer reports).

Use Publish or Perish to search for keywords

If you are still debating which journal to submit to, use Publish or Perish to conduct a search with the most important keywords in your paper. If you search for a relatively generic topic, many of the hits you get will be books, especially in the Social Sciences and Humanities. Books tend to be highly cited because they contain more citable material than short journal articles. This is especially true for classic works in the field.

We are not currently intending to write a book. So, the best way to find appropriate journals is to sort the results by publication outlet. Do this by clicking on the Publication column. The default sort for Publish or Perish is the number of citations. So, by clicking on the Publication column you will create a list sorted by publication outlet first and then by the number of citations. Scrolling down the list you can easily identify the journals that contain articles on your topic. It also shows us which of these articles are most highly cited.

Worked example: Ethical marketing

Let's assume you have written up a paper about ethical marketing. During your literature review, you have already noticed that the top mainstream marketing journals such as the *Journal of Marketing* and *Journal of Consumer Research* do not seem to publish a lot of papers on this topic. Hence, you are looking for alternative options. To achieve this, use the Publish or Perish software and follow these two simple steps:

1. **Use the quoted terms in the Keywords field**. Enter the words *ethical marketing* in the **Keywords field**. This will result in articles in which the two words *ethical marketing* appear in that order. If you include the search term *ethical marketing* without quotes it will provide many more matches as it matches the words in any order. There will be lots of publications that include both these relatively generic words.

2. **Limit the search to recent years**. As you want to ensure that the journal has published on ethical marketing in *recent* years, you limit the search to the last decade. This search was conducted in 2010. Hence, the results found range between 2000 and 2010.

The search resulted in 874 hits. As expected, many of the most-cited works are books, often generic ones on Marketing Research, Consumer Behaviour, and International Marketing. However, sorting the results by publication allows us to identify the most important journal outlets. Below, you will find screenshots with the most frequently occurring journals in this search, with a brief discussion of the results for each. [Note that if you wanted to limit the number of book results, you could untick the CITATION box, as many books are CITATION records]

Journal of Business Ethics

The *Journal of Business Ethics* is by far the most frequently mentioned journal in our search. The screenshot below shows some of the most cited papers.

Title	Year	Publication
A review of empirical studies assessing ethical decision making in business	2000	Journal of Business Ethics
A cross cultural comparison of the contents of codes of ethics: USA, Canada and …	2000	Journal of Business Ethics
Unpacking the ethical product	2001	Journal of Business Ethics
A partnership model of corporate ethics	2002	Journal of Business Ethics
Cross-cultural methodological issues in ethical research	2000	Journal of Business Ethics
An empirical investigation of the relationships between ethical beliefs, ethical ideo…	2001	Journal of Business Ethics
Ethics in personal selling and sales management: a review of the literature focusi…	2000	Journal of Business Ethics
An ethical exploration of privacy and radio frequency identification	2005	Journal of Business Ethics
Ethics and Marketing on this Internet: Practitioners' Perceptions of Societal, Indu…	2000	Journal of Business Ethics
The questionable use of moral development theory in studies of business ethics: …	2001	Journal of Business Ethics
Packaging ethics: Perceptual differences among packaging professionals, brand …	2000	Journal of Business Ethics
International marketing ethics from an Islamic perspective: a value-maximization …	2001	Journal of Business Ethics
Gender differences in ethical perceptions of salespeople: An empirical examinatio…	2002	Journal of Business Ethics
Ethical judgment and whistleblowing intention: examining the moderating role of I…	2003	Journal of Business Ethics
Is cross-cultural similarity an indicator of similar marketing ethics?	2001	Journal of Business Ethics

Even though there are a few papers relating to marketing, most of the papers seem to deal mostly with general business ethics. Even so, this could be an option for Marketing academics who want to reach out to a more general audience interested in ethics.

Journal of Macromarketing

The second most frequently listed journal in our search is *Journal of Macromarketing*. The screenshot below shows all the hits in order of the number of citations.

Title	Year	Publication
The general theory of marketing ethics: a revision and three questions	2006	Journal of macromarketing
Normative perspectives for ethical and socially responsible marketing	2006	Journal of Macromarketing
Building understanding of the domain of consumer vulnerability	2005	Journal of Macromarketing
Quality-of-life (QOL) marketing: Proposed antecedents and consequences	2004	Journal of Macromarketing
Macro measures of consumer well-being (CWB): a critical analysis and a researc…	2006	Journal of Macromarketing
Globalization and technological achievement: Implications for macromarketing an…	2004	Journal of Macromarketing
Research on marketing ethics: A systematic review of the literature	2007	Journal of Macromarketing
Distributive justice: Pressing questions, emerging directions, and the promise of …	2008	Journal of Macromarketing
Research on consumer well-being (CWB): Overview of the field and introduction…	2007	Journal of Macromarketing
The small and long view	2006	Journal of Macromarketing
Voluntary codes of ethical conduct: Group membership salience and globally inte…	2007	Journal of Macromarketing
On Economic Growth, Marketing Systems, and the Quality of Life	2009	Journal of Macromarketing
Assessing distributive justice in marketing: a benefit-cost approach	2007	Journal of Macromarketing
Globalization, transformation, and quality of life: Reflections on ICMD-8 and par…	2004	Journal of Macromarketing
Limited choice: An exploratory study into issue items and soldier subjective well-…	2006	Journal of Macromarketing
Handbook of Quality-of-Life Research: An Ethical Marketing Perspective, by M. …	2003	Journal of Macromarketing
Applying Catholic Social Teachings to Ethical Issues in Marketing	2009	Journal of Macromarketing
Medicalization and Marketing	2010	Journal of Macromarketing

This journal has published a range of highly cited papers in this field and as such might be an appropriate outlet. However, many of the articles seems to focus on high-level societal issues, quality of life or consumer well-being. This is also reflected in the journal's editorial statement. Whether or not this suits your paper obviously depends on its topic.

> *"The Journal of Macromarketing examines important social issues, how they are affected by marketing, and how society influences the conduct of marketing."*

European Journal of Marketing

The journal that had the third largest number of hits for the search with the keywords "ethical marketing" was the *European Journal of Marketing*. The screenshot below shows all resulting papers in order of number of citations. Unfortunately, Google Scholar sometimes does abbreviate the title of a journal (see the first five hits). For details on Google Scholar limitations see Chapter 5.

Title	Year	Publication
How important are ethics and social responsibility?	2001	European Journal of ...
Moral philosophies of marketing managers	2002	European Journal of ...
An ethical basis for relationship marketing: a virtue ethics perspective	2007	European journal of ...
Corporate social responsibility: investigating theory and research in the marke...	2008	European Journal of ...
Children's impact on innovation decision making	2009	European Journal of ...
Grounded theory, ethnography and phenomenology	2005	European journal of Marketing
Societal marketing and morality	2002	European Journal of Marketing
Marketing as a profession: on closing stakeholder gaps	2002	European Journal of Marketing
Futures dilemmas for marketers: can stakeholder analysis add value?	2005	European Journal of Marketing
Ethics and value creation in business research: comparing two approaches	2006	European Journal of Marketing
An ethical basis for relationship marketing: a virtue ethics perspective The Aut...	2007	European Journal of Marketing

This means that the citation order is not perfect as it starts again with the first article for the non-abbreviated journal title, i.e., the *"Grounded theory, ethnography..."* article has more citations than most of the preceding articles. However, as we are mainly interested in finding journal outlets rather than doing a citation analysis, this is not a serious problem.

Perusing the titles, the *European Journal of Marketing* appears to have a rather broad focus, publishing papers in a variety of areas in marketing. Indeed, this is reflected in its mission statement:

"We welcome novel and ground-breaking contributions from a wide range of research traditions within the broad domain of marketing".

This statement also mentions:

"The EJM is receptive to controversial topics, and new, as well as developments that challenge existing theories and paradigms."

Hence, at first glance, this might not be a bad outlet for a topic that is not yet part of the mainstream in Marketing.

Journal of Consumer Marketing

As shown in the screenshot below, *Journal of Consumer Marketing* has also published a substantial number of papers containing the key words ethical marketing in the past decade. Not surprisingly, most of these papers focus on the ethical consumer. Hence, this journal would be a very appropriate outlet if your paper is focusing on the ethical aspects of consumer behaviour.

Title	Year	Publication
Shopping for a better world? An interpretive study of the potential for ethical...	2004	Journal of Consumer ...
"To legislate or not to legislate": a comparative exploratory study of privacy...	2003	Journal of consumer ...
An inquiry into the ethical perceptions of sub-cultural groups in the US: Hispa...	2002	Journal of Consumer ...
Consumers' Rules of Engagement in Online Information Exchanges	2009	Journal of Consumer ...
The myth of the ethical consumer -do ethics matter in purchase behaviour?	2001	Journal of consumer marketing
The ethicality of altruistic corporate social responsibility	2002	Journal of Consumer Marketing
Consumer privacy and the Internet in Europe: a view from Germany	2003	Journal of Consumer Marketing
Neuromarketing: a layman's look at neuroscience and its potential application...	2007	Journal of Consumer Marketing

Journal of Public Policy & Marketing

Another journal with a fairly large number of papers on this topic is *Journal of Public Policy & Marketing*. Perusing the article titles, its topics appear to have some overlap with the *Journal of Macromarketing*.

Title	Year	Publication
Does Fair Trade deliver on its core value proposition? Effects on income, e...	2009	Journal of Public Policy & ...
The philosophy and methods of deliberative democracy: Implications for p...	2009	Journal of Public Policy & ...
Marketing to the Poor: An Integrative Justice Model for Engaging Impoveri...	2009	Journal of Public Policy & ...
Consumer online privacy: legal and ethical issues	2000	Journal of Public Policy & Marketing
Antiglobal challenges to marketing in developing countries: Exploring the id...	2005	Journal of Public Policy & Marketing
Ethics and Public Policy Implications of Research on Consumer Well-Being	2008	Journal of Public Policy & Marketing
Principle-Based Stakeholder Marketing: Insights from Private Triple-Bottom...	2010	Journal of Public Policy & Marketing
Ethical Beliefs and Information Asymmetries in Supplier Relationships	2010	Journal of Public Policy & Marketing

This is confirmed when we look at its editorial statement:

> *"Journal of Public Policy & Marketing has adopted the noteworthy mission of publishing thoughtful articles on how marketing practice shapes and is shaped by societally important factors such as ..."*

It appears that these two journals would be particularly suitable if your paper focused on societal issues surrounding ethical marketing.

Journal of Marketing Education

A surprising discovery was the realisation that the *Journal of Marketing Education* had published a substantial number of papers in this area. Hence, if your paper had clear links to marketing education, or was investigating perceptions of marketing students, this journal might be an appropriate outlet for your article.

Title	Year	Publication
The effects of marketing education and individual cultural values on marketing...	2002	Journal of Marketing Education
Important factors underlying ethical intentions of students: Implications for m...	2004	Journal of Marketing Education
The Impact of Corporate Culture, the Reward System, and Perceived Moral I...	2005	Journal of Marketing Education
Teaching marketing law: A business law perspective on integrating marketing ...	2000	Journal of Marketing Education
Designing discussion activities to achieve desired learning outcomes: Choices ...	2007	Journal of Marketing Education
Group-Based Assessment as a Dynamic Approach to Marketing Education	2009	Journal of Marketing Education

Journal of the Academy of Marketing science

You already discovered that the mainstream marketing journals have not published that many articles in ethical marketing. It should, therefore, come as a pleasant surprise that *Journal of the Academy of Marketing Science*, one of the top mainstream marketing journals, has published four articles on the topic between 2000 and 2010.

Title	Year	Publication
Representing the perceived ethical work climate among marketing employ...	2000	Journal of the Academy of ...
Consumer online privacy concerns and responses: a power–responsibility...	2007	Journal of the Academy of Marketing
Marketing with integrity: ethics and the service-dominant logic for marketing	2008	Journal of the Academy of Marketing.
A simulation of moral behavior within marketing exchange relationships	2007	Journal of the Academy of Marketing.

Its editorial statement indicates that articles in a very broad range of topics are acceptable, including ethics and social responsibility. Hence, if you judge your article to be of sufficient quality to merit publication in one of the top journals in marketing, this might be an appropriate choice. It would allow you to reach the widest possible audience in the broad field of marketing.

Using the "Title words" field to further refine results

Judging from the titles in the results shown above, some articles didn't really seem to have a major focus on ethical marketing, but instead simply mentioned the words somewhere in the article.

Another option, therefore, would be to narrow down your results by using the **Title words** field. The results will only contain articles that have the words ethical marketing in their title, although the words do not necessarily appear close together. The screenshot below produces the results in order of the number of citations.

Title	Year	Publication
Normative perspectives for ethical and socially responsible marketing	2006	Journal of Macromarketing
Representing the perceived ethical work climate among marketing employees	2000	Journal of the Academy of ...
Important factors underlying ethical intentions of students: Implications for ma...	2004	Journal of Marketing Education
Perceived risk, moral philosophy and marketing ethics: mediating influences on ...	2002	Journal of Business research
Ethical guidelines for marketing practice: A reply to Gaski & some observations ...	2001	Journal of Business Ethics
Consumer interests and the ethical implications of marketing: a contingency fra...	2003	Journal of Consumer Affairs
Ethical marketing for competitive advantage on the Internet	2001	Academy of Marketing Science
The Impact of Corporate Culture, the Reward System, and Perceived Moral In...	2005	Journal of Marketing Education
An ethical basis for relationship marketing: a virtue ethics perspective	2007	European journal of ...
Ethical trends in marketing and psychological research	2001	Ethics & Behavior
Sustainable Tourism: Ethical Alternative or Marketing Ploy?	2007	Journal of business ethics
The impact of cultural values on marketing ethical norms: A study in India and t...	2006	Journal of International ...

Comparing the journal titles with our previous results shows that most of the same journals appear in the list. However, there are five new journals that appear on the scene: *Journal of Business Research, Academy of Marketing Science Review, Journal of Consumer Affairs, Ethics & Behavior,* and *Journal of International Marketing.* These journals did not feature on our list before as they only published one or two papers on ethical marketing. However, if the titles appear relevant to your paper, they might be worth considering.

Review key academics in your field

Another good option to establish which journals are important in your field of study is to look up established academics in your field. The reasoning here is that if successful academics in your field have published in these journals, there is a high likelihood that these journals are appropriate outlets for your own work too.

Below, I have reproduced a Publish or Perish Google Scholar Profile search for two academics who are working in the broader field of "Marketing in society" or "responsible/sustainable marketing". The two journals that we identified earlier in this chapter as being very appropriate outlets for marketing articles focusing on broader societal issues – *Journal of Public Policy & Marketing* and *Journal of Macromarketing* – both feature heavily in the publication lists of these two academics. Hence, this provides additional reassurance that these journals might be a good outlet for your paper.

Google Scholar Profile search

Profile name:	Find a profile... Julie Ozanne - University of Melbourne		Search ?
Profile ID:	7RuKUaAAAAAJ "Transformative Consumer Research"		Search Direct

Annual citations:	2002	2003	2004	2005	2006	2007	2008	2009	2010	2011	2012	2013	2014	2015	2016	2017	2018	2019	2020	2021	2022	2023	
	129	164	156	169	185	205	254	299	335	364	440	450	557	578	647	706	763	786	820	769	784	394	Clear All
Show profile	1198	1362	1518	1687	1872	2077	2331	2630	2965	3329	3769	4219	4776	5354	6001	6707	7470	8256	9076	9845	10629	11023	Revert
Copy citations																						New	

	Cites	Per year	Rank	Authors	Title	Year	Publication
h	83	8.30	25	B Saatcioglu, JL Ozanne	A critical spatial approach to marketplace exclusion and inclusion	2013	Journal of Public Policy &Marketing
h	297	13.50	8	S Dobscha, JL Ozanne	An ecofeminist analysis of environmentally sensitive women using qualitative metho...	2001	Journal of Public Policy &Marketing
h	159	13.25	16	LK Ozanne, JL Ozanne	A child's right to play: the social construction of civic virtues in toy libraries	2011	Journal of Public Policy &Marketing
h	157	12.08	17	JL Ozanne, L Anderson	Community action research	2010	Journal of Public Policy &Marketing
h	142	5.92	18	RG Lee, JL Ozanne, RP Hill	Improving service encounters through resource sensitivity: The case of health care...	1999	Journal of Public Policy &Marketing
h	124	20.67	19	JL Ozanne, B Davis, JB Murray, S...	Assessing the societal impact of research: The relational engagement approach	2017	Journal of Public Policy &Marketing
h	98	14.00	23	B Davis, JL Ozanne, RP Hill	The transformative consumer research movement	2016	Journal of Public Policy &Marketing
h	96	3.84	24	JL Ozanne, RP Hill, ND Wright	Juvenile delinquents' use of consumption as cultural resistance: Implications for juv...	1998	Journal of Public Policy &Marketing
h	80	5.71	27	JL Ozanne, C Corus, B Saatcioglu	The philosophy and methods of deliberative democracy: Implications for public poli...	2009	Journal of Public Policy &Marketing
h	61	6.10	30	JL Ozanne, EM Moscato, DR Kun...	Transformative photography: evaluation and best practices for eliciting social and p...	2013	Journal of Public Policy &Marketing
h	46	3.83	36	JL Ozanne	Introduction to the special issue on transformative consumer research: Creating dial...	2011	Journal of Public Policy &Marketing
	16	8.00	48	LK Ozanne, JL Ozanne	Disaster recovery: How ad hoc marketing systems build and mobilize social capital f...	2021	Journal of Public Policy &Marketing

However, we can also see that a journal that had not yet come up in our earlier **Keywords** searches – *Journal of Marketing Management* – is a popular outlet for one of the academics for a ranges of responsible marketing topics. She has published multiple articles in this journal from 1990 onwards. This includes two papers in 2021, indicating that this journal's mission hasn't changed in this respect as is confirmed by its current mission statement.

> *"The JMM explicitly desires to see all paradigmatic traditions contribute to debates on marketing theory and practice. This includes traditional, predominantly managerial contributions aligned with logical empiricist perspectives, through to interpretive and Consumer Culture Theoretic (CCT) reflections on marketing's role in providing the resources for identity building and self-affirmation, as well as the negative ramifications of consumption on individuals and communities. Studies that engage with both the light-side and dark-side of marketing and consumer practice are welcome. Going beyond these two research orientations, the JMM seeks to support a number of other important paradigmatic traditions including Marxist and Neo-Marxist perspectives, postmodern interpretations of marketing and consumer practice, postcolonial understandings, macromarketing and Transformative Consumer Research (TCR) interventions, to name just a few which further marketing thought. The paradigmatic pluralism of the JMM is underwritten by a belief that marketing scholarship must be theoretically embedded and reflexive if it is to enhance our knowledge of marketing theory and practice(s)."*

Before submission:
Have you missed any papers?

Before submitting to a journal, you can use the PoP software to find out whether the journal you intend to submit to has published any (recent) relevant papers on your topic. You might have missed them whilst working hard on the final version of your paper. There are few things that annoy a journal editor more than receiving a paper for their journal that neglects to refer to relevant papers in the journal in question.

I am not talking here about the practice of less scrupulous journal editors who are demanding you cite papers from their own journal simply to increase their journal's Journal Impact Factor. However, journal editors are rightly annoyed if you have failed to incorporate *relevant* prior papers from their journal. By publishing in a certain journal, you are contributing to a conversation. Not acknowledging the other conversation partners is plain rude. So how do you do a final check to establish that you haven't missed any highly relevant papers in the journal you are targeting? You could simply browse tables of contents on the web or in the library. However, Publish or Perish offers a much quicker way.

Worked example: Entry modes of Japanese MNCs

Let's assume you have written a paper about entry mode choice (the choice between different ways to enter a foreign market) of Japanese MNCs and intend to submit to *Journal of International Business Studies*. Simply search for the term "entry mode" (in quotes) in the **Keywords** field of the with "*Journal of International Business Studies*" in the **Publication name** field. This will provide any articles in which the words *entry mode* appear in that order. The screenshot below provides *all* articles that have been published in *Journal of International Business Studies* since its inception in 1970 that have entry mode in their title, sorted by number of citations, a total of no less than 600 papers. Note I have unclicked the CITATION records box to reduce the number of "stray citations" (see Chapter 5).

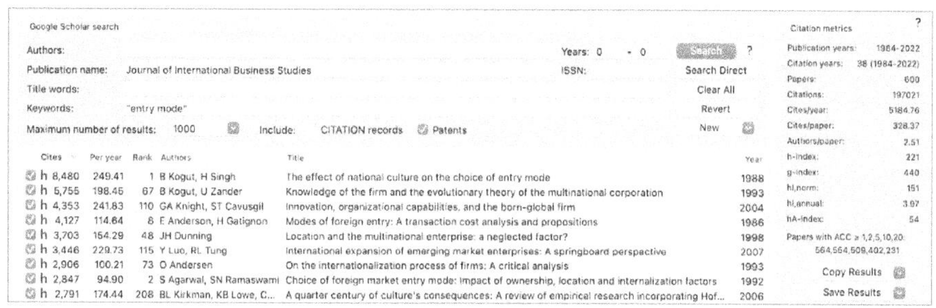

As Google Scholar matches the search terms anywhere in the article, this search provides you with far too many results to cope with. So, you can narrow down your search in three ways:

1. Using a data source that searches only in the title and abstract, such as the Web of Science. However, this will still provide you with 134 results.
2. Limit the search to the last 10 years only. However, this will still provide you with 298 results for Google Scholar and 62 results for the Web of Science.
3. Search in the **Title words** field instead. Combined with the last 10-year criterion, this leads to a very manageable twelve papers (see screenshot below).

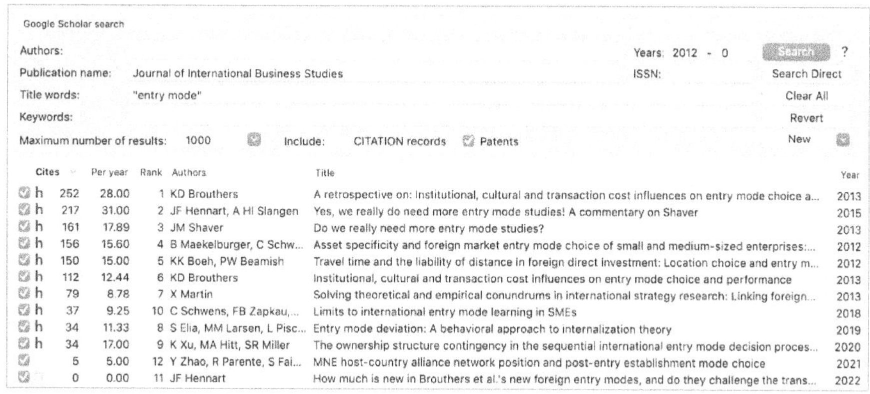

As you can see there is even a discussion going on in the journal on whether more research on entry mode is needed, something you might like to refer to in your paper. If you wanted to double-check whether you missed any papers dealing with Japan, you could relax the last 10 years criterion and search for Japan in the keyword field. Using Google Scholar, you would also be able to capture papers that mentioned Japan in the main text of the article only (see below).

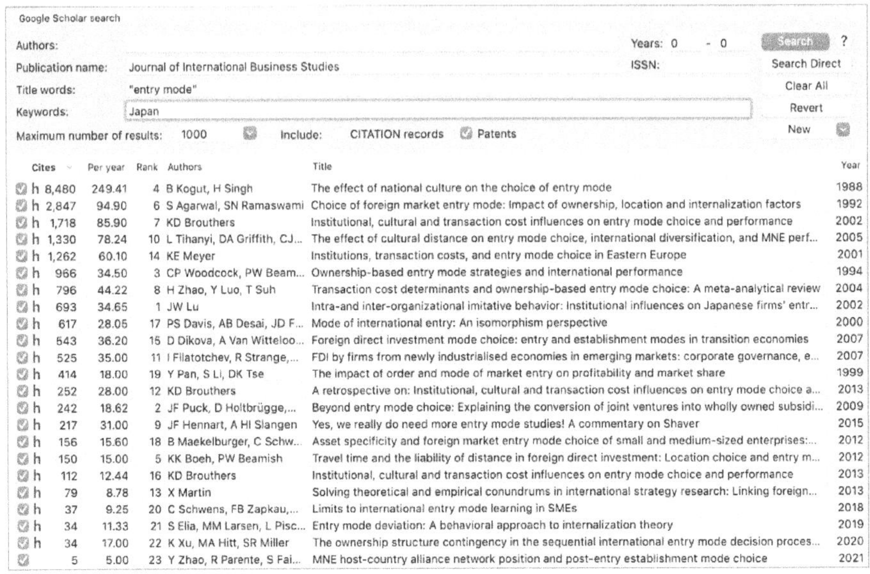

Cites	Per year	Rank	Authors	Title	Year
h 8,480	249.41	4	B Kogut, H Singh	The effect of national culture on the choice of entry mode	1988
h 2,847	94.90	6	S Agarwal, SN Ramaswami	Choice of foreign market entry mode: Impact of ownership, location and internalization factors	1992
h 1,718	85.90	7	KD Brouthers	Institutional, cultural and transaction cost influences on entry mode choice and performance	2002
h 1,330	78.24	10	L Tihanyi, DA Griffith, CJ…	The effect of cultural distance on entry mode choice, international diversification, and MNE perf…	2005
h 1,262	60.10	14	KE Meyer	Institutions, transaction costs, and entry mode choice in Eastern Europe	2001
h 966	34.50	3	CP Woodcock, PW Beam…	Ownership-based entry mode strategies and international performance	1994
h 796	44.22	8	H Zhao, Y Luo, T Suh	Transaction cost determinants and ownership-based entry mode choice: A meta-analytical review	2004
h 693	34.65	1	JW Lu	Intra-and inter-organizational imitative behavior: Institutional influences on Japanese firms' entr…	2002
h 617	28.05	17	PS Davis, AB Desai, JD F…	Mode of international entry: An isomorphism perspective	2000
h 543	36.20	15	D Dikova, A Van Witteloo…	Foreign direct investment mode choice: entry and establishment modes in transition economies	2007
h 525	35.00	11	I Filatotchev, R Strange,…	FDI by firms from newly industrialised economies in emerging markets: corporate governance, e…	2007
h 414	18.00	19	Y Pan, S Li, DK Tse	The impact of order and mode of market entry on profitability and market share	1999
h 252	28.00	12	KD Brouthers	A retrospective on: Institutional, cultural and transaction cost influences on entry mode choice a…	2013
h 242	18.62	2	JF Puck, D Holtbrügge,…	Beyond entry mode choice: Explaining the conversion of joint ventures into wholly owned subsidi…	2009
h 217	31.00	9	JF Hennart, A HI Slangen	Yes, we really do need more entry mode studies! A commentary on Shaver	2015
h 156	15.60	18	B Maekelburger, C Schw…	Asset specificity and foreign market entry mode choice of small and medium-sized enterprises:…	2012
h 150	15.00	5	KK Boeh, PW Beamish	Travel time and the liability of distance in foreign direct investment: Location choice and entry m…	2012
h 112	12.44	16	KD Brouthers	Institutional, cultural and transaction cost influences on entry mode choice and performance	2013
h 79	8.78	13	X Martin	Solving theoretical and empirical conundrums in international strategy research: Linking foreign…	2013
h 37	9.25	20	C Schwens, FB Zapkau,…	Limits to international entry mode learning in SMEs	2018
h 34	11.33	21	S Elia, MM Larsen, L Pisc…	Entry mode deviation: A behavioral approach to internalization theory	2019
h 34	17.00	22	K Xu, MA Hitt, SR Miller	The ownership structure contingency in the sequential international entry mode decision proces…	2020
5	5.00	23	Y Zhao, R Parente, S Fai…	MNE host-country alliance network position and post-entry establishment mode choice	2021

No papers at all?

If your search finds that the journal you intend to submit your paper to has *never* published anything on the topic of your paper or has last published something more than a decade ago, you might need to think again about your choice. Remember: wanting to submit to the journal because it is the top-ranked journal in your field is not a good enough reason!

Of course, there can be good reasons to want to introduce a particular stream of research to a new audience but realise that this is not an easy way to get your paper accepted. Just like other people, many academics find it difficult to relate to ideas that have no connection at all to their knowledge base.

If there is no prior published work on your topic in the journal at all, reviewers of the journal might not be familiar with this field and might not be able to evaluate its merits. It might also mean that the readers of the journal might not be interested in reading your work, even if it should get accepted. Maybe it is a sign you should take a step back and examine which journals publish on your topic?

In sum

Publish or Perish allows you to quickly get a very comprehensive overview of the journals that might be appropriate outlets for your next paper. Give it a try for your next paper and let me know how you fare. In the next chapter, we will discuss how to use Publish or Perish to do bibliometric research.

Chapter 14: Doing bibliometric research

Earlier chapters discussed how to use Publish or Perish to present your case for research impact (Chapter 10), evaluate other academics (Chapter 11), do literature reviews (Chapter 12), and decide where to submit your paper to (Chapter 13). However, Publish or Perish can also be used for research purposes. In this chapter we show how you can use Publish or Perish to do bibliometric analyses. Bibliometric analysis is a method for exploring and analysing large volumes of scientific data relating to publications and citations.

In the past, bibliometric research was mainly done by professional bibliometricians, often with a research background in the discipline of Library and Information Science. The introduction of Google Scholar as a free source of publication and citation data, however, has prompted many academics with a primary research interest in other disciplines to conduct bibliometric research. These academics typically study authors, journals, institutions, or research topics in their own discipline. They often publish in their own disciplinary journals rather than traditional bibliometrics journals such as *Scientometrics*, *Journal of Informetrics* or *Journal of the American Society for Information Science and Technology*.

Professional bibliometricians typically use specialised software to conduct their analyses or create their own software routines using programming languages such as Python. Academics who are conducting incidental bibliometric studies typically rely on Publish or Perish to do their research.

A Google Scholar search for the words: *Harzing "Publish or Perish"* now results in more than 6,000 hits. In 2020, when Covid-19 made fieldwork collection difficult, academics started using the Publish or Perish software to do desk-based research. The graph below shows they haven't stopped. Since 2021, the number of publications using the software has been rising steeply.

In this chapter we therefore explain how Publish or Perish can be used to do bibliometric research for authors, journals, institutions, and research topics. Although most academics use Google Scholar as a data source (see Chapter 5 for Google Scholar's strengths and weaknesses), these analyses can be conducted with any data source. Some studies discussed below even compare data sources.

Bibliometric research for authors

Publish or Perish can be used to do bibliometric research for authors. Before conducting your analyses, please refer to Chapter 7 for details on author searches across data sources. The key question in this type of study is what population of authors to include. Of course, this is largely dependent on your research question. Here we will discuss a few examples, but the possibilities are endless.

Comparing your own research metrics over time

The most basic bibliometric research that can be done easily with Publish or Perish is to compare your own research metrics over time. You could repeat a search for your name every month, quarter, or year. Longitudinal results for individuals can be used to establish progress for a tenure, promotion, or grant application.

Publish or Perish simplifies this process by allowing you to duplicate your original search. Do this by simply selecting the search and use a copy/past command or by using **Duplicate Current Search**. Below is a monthly search of my Google Scholar Profile metrics. Note that some metrics (hI,annual, hA, acc10) decline (temporarily) at the turn of the year as the number of years active increases by one.

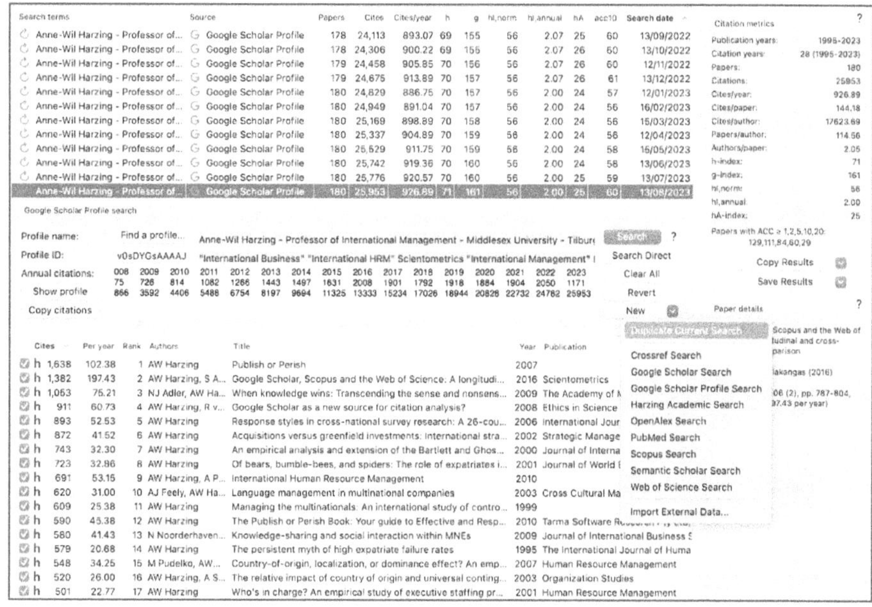

Comparing data sources/metrics across disciplines

If your aim is to study the impact of different data sources or different metrics for comparisons of academic performance across disciplines, you will obviously need to select academics from a broad range of disciplines. This is what we did in this paper where we compared 146 carefully matched academics across five broad disciplines: Sciences, Life Sciences, Engineering, Social Sciences and Humanities.

- Harzing, A.W.; Alakangas, S. (2016) Google Scholar, Scopus, and the Web of Science: A longitudinal and cross-disciplinary comparison, *Scientometrics*, vol. 106, no. 2, pp. 787-804.

The study compared four research metrics (publications, citations, h-index, and hI,annual, an annualised individual h-index, see Chapter 3 for details on these metrics) and three databases (Google Scholar, Scopus, and the Web of Science (see Chapters 4 and 5 for details on these data sources). Its analyses showed that both the data source and the specific metrics used dramatically change the conclusions that can be drawn from cross-disciplinary comparisons.

The study was conducted before Publish or Perish offered the option to *directly* search Scopus and the Web of Science. Data from these sources were therefore imported into the Publish or Perish software (see Chapter 4 for details on how to do this). The screenshot below shows a small part of the folders that were created for this project. I continued to collect data for this sample of academics over the years allowing for longitudinal comparisons. Publish or Perish stores all your old searches and folders making this process very easy.

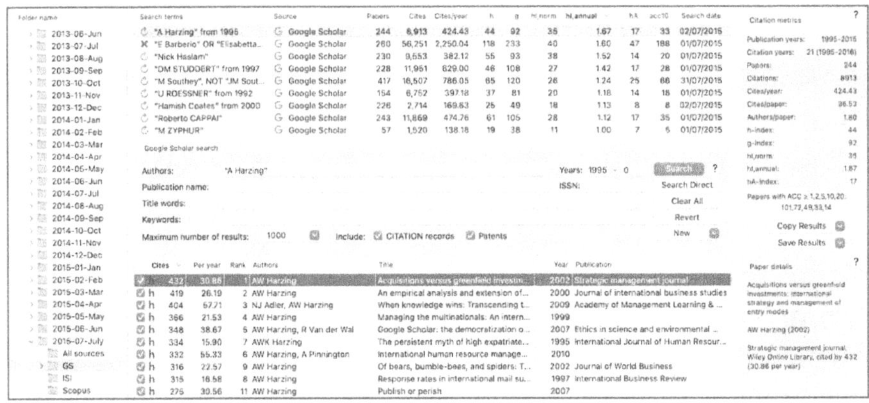

Creating rankings of individual academics

Most academics using Publish or Perish to do bibliometric research for authors intend to create some sort of ranking of individual academics. This necessitates a more focused population. Here are some options you may wish to consider.

Pick a specific discipline

In order for a ranking to make any sense to your readers, it is usually best to limit your population by discipline. However, even within disciplines there can be very substantial differences in typical citation scores. Hence your definition of discipline might need to be fairly narrow.

A good example is Nosek (2010) and his co-authors analysing citation data for more than 600 academics in the field of social psychology in the US and Canada. They used Google scholar and Publish or Perish to gather their data. Data were analysed both at the individual level and at the departmental level. As the number of citations and the h-index are strongly linked to the academic's seniority, they created new indicators unrelated to the number of years since PhD. These indicators were very similar to the various individual h-index indicators that were introduced later and are now included in Publish or Perish.

- Nosek, B. A., Graham, J., Lindner, N. M., Kesebir, S., Hawkins, C. B., Hahn, C., ... & Tenney, E. R. (2010). Cumulative and career-stage citation impact of social-personality psychology programs and their members. *Personality and Social Psychology Bulletin, 36*(10), 1283-1300.

The authors employed exemplary data management and search procedures. Hence, anyone wanting to conduct bibliometric research on authors would be well advised to read their paper. The paper also contains an excellent supplementary page with career-stage impact calculators, additional analyses, and search tips.

Pick a specific country

An additional way to narrow down your population is by country. This both limits the scope of the data collection effort and reduces differences caused by different research traditions in different countries. As most studies aim to produce norm scores of some sort, this is a good thing. Obviously, if your research question is to compare the impact of different research traditions on citation patterns, your choice would be different.

As even narrowing down the population by discipline or country can leave you with a very large number of academics, most studies will narrow down their field even further by studying academics that share specific attributes. These attributes could for instance be:
- Working at the top 5/10/20 universities (however defined) in the country
- Being a fellow of one of the major professional associations in the discipline
- Being editor or editorial board member of one of journals in the discipline
- Having been president of a major professional association in the field
- Having won a major research award (e.g., dissertation award, Nobel prize)
- Having done their PhD at a specified set of institutions.

Obviously, your selection needs to make sense in the context of your research questions. There are only so many exploratory ranking studies that will be published, even if you are personally very interested in the results. However, whatever choice you make, Publish or Perish can be relied on to conduct, manage, and store all of your searches, allowing for longitudinal analyses as well as replication.

Bibliometric research for journals

In addition to calculating the citation impact of specific journals, you can also use Publish or Perish to compare a set of journals various characteristics or test specific hypotheses. Below we provide three examples, but the possibilities are limitless. Before conducting your analyses, please refer to Chapter 8 for details on effective journal searches across data sources.

Creating alternative journal rankings

Shortly after the introduction of Publish or Perish we conducted a study providing an alternative to the then dominant Journal Impact Factor (JIF). It included all 800+ journals listed on my Journal Quality List. This list collates journal rankings in the area of Business & Economics (see https://harzing.com/resources/journal-quality-list).

Our study compared two bibliometric metrics, the JIF and a newly proposed Google Scholar h-index for journals. As it was conducted using a command line version of Publish or Perish, I cannot show screenshots of its searches. However, its procedures are very similar to the other research projects in this chapter.

- Harzing, A.W.; Wal, R. van der (2009) **A Google Scholar h-index for journals: An alternative metric to measure journal impact in Economics & Business?**, *Journal of the American Society for Information Science and Technology*, vol. 60, no. 1, pp 41-46

The study allowed us to draw general conclusions about the reasons for why particular journals scored better on either the JIF or the h-index. The major reason for a high JIF in comparison to the h-index related to journals that published a small number of papers and/or had highly concentrated citations, where the top 10 most cited articles provided the bulk of citations. For these journals, the JIF – which is based on *average* citation levels that can be distorted by a few highly cited papers – presents a less accurate reflection of a journal's overall impact than the h-index.

The single most important determinant of a high h-index compared to the JIF appeared to be the extent to which the journal publishes policy-oriented papers that are highly cited in working papers and policy documents. These publication types are not included in the Web of Science but *are* included in Google Scholar. Publishing a large number of papers overall and being cited in conference papers and non-Web of Science indexed journals were secondary reasons for a high h-index. Overall, the h-index might therefore more suitable to measure a journal's wider economic or social impact rather than its impact on an academic audience only.

Country differences in co-authorship patterns

Publish or Perish can also be used to test specific hypotheses about for instance co-authorship patterns. If I wanted to test the hypothesis that on average North Americans tend to publish more co-authored papers than Europeans, I could use PoP to conduct a large-scale comparison of North American versus European academic authors.

However, that would be quite time-consuming. I can also investigate this on a journal level; it has been well established that North American journals have a larger proportion of North American authors, whilst European journals feature more European authors. This is true in any discipline, but it is even more prominent in the Social Sciences and Humanities where research topics tend to be more "location-bound" than in the Sciences.

Taking Accounting journals as an example, of the six top Accounting journals, four are North America (JAR, AR, CAR, and RAS), whilst the remaining two journals *Accounting, Organisations and Society* and *European Accounting Review* are European. The table below shows the Publish or Perish authorship per paper metrics for Web of Science data exported to Excel. I used the Web of Science as – because of truncation (see Chapter 5) Google Scholar authorship data are not entirely accurate. I looked at a five-year period between 2006 and 2011 and found that co-authorship patterns do indeed differ between the four North American (2.15-2.45 authors per paper) and the two European journals (1.93-2.06 authors per paper).

Query	Authors_Paper
Accounting Review from 2006 to 2011	2.45
Accounting, Organizations and Society from 2006 to 2011	2.06
Contemporary Accounting Research from 2006 to 2011	2.38
European Accounting Review from 2006 to 2011	1.93
Journal of Accounting Research from 2006 to 2011	2.27
Review of Accounting Studies from 2006 to 2011	2.15

As can be seen below in an analysis for 2018-2022, these differences partly persist in recent years, although all journals have increased the average number of authors per paper. Of course, this is only a very small sample of journals, but one could easily expand this to other journals in Accounting or the field of Business more generally.

Query	Authors_Paper
Accounting Review from 2018 to 2022	2.78
Accounting, Organizations and Society from 2018 to 2022	2.49
Contemporary Accounting Research from 2018 to 2022	3.03
European Accounting Review from 2018 to 2022	2.71
Journal of Accounting Research from 2018 to 2022	2.61
Review of Accounting Studies from 2018 to 2022	3.01

Co-authorship patterns across disciplines and time

This same strategy can be used to compare co-authorship patterns across disciplines and time. One could look at a few top journals in every discipline and calculate co-authorship patterns over the years. The table below shows a small-scale comparison of co-authorship patterns between 1995-2022 for two top journals in the Humanities, the Sciences/Medicine, and Management.

Journal name	Mean citations per paper						
	1995-1998	1999-2002	2003-2006	2007-2010	2011-2014	2015-2018	2019-2022
British Journal for the Philosophy of Science	1.08	1.12	1.16	1.16	1.26	1.36	1.35
Evolutionary Anthropology	1.33	1.46	1.42	1.63	1.86	2.42	3.20
Nature Genetics	8.49	9.28	9.27	18.11	23.15	20.90	19.22
Nature Medicine	5.51	6.52	7.00	7.60	9.66	14.16	19.34
Organization Science	1.98	2.05	2.16	2.29	2.32	2.33	2.63
Organization Studies	1.52	1.60	1.84	2.02	2.07	2.31	2.44

Data were collected from OpenAlex using an ISSN journal search and exported to Excel. Bibliometric research often requires significant manual checking and cleaning. In this case, I needed to remove all articles without authors, as well as all editorials and book reviews. The former obviously reduces the average number of authors. The latter two article types are normally written by sole authors and would lead us to underestimate the average number of authors for journals with a high number of publications in these categories.

A comparison of seven consecutive 4-year periods shows that in the Sciences/Medicine papers typically have a much larger number of authors than in both the Humanities and Management – as one of the Social Sciences. In the Humanities and the Social Sciences single-authored articles are common and co-authored articles typically only have 2 or 3 co-authors. In the Sciences/Medicine single-authored article are a rarity. Most articles have at least 6 to 10 authors.

These results can be useful if one wants to make a case for promotion to a panel that is comprised of academics from different disciplines. It helps to explain why it is not realistic to expect the same number of publications from academics in the Social Sciences and Humanities as from academics in the Sciences/Medicine.

Another hypothesis that we could test is whether the number of co-authors tends to increase over time, reflecting the more collaborative nature of academic research and publishing in more recent times. The table above clearly shows that this has indeed been the case. There has been an increase in the average number of authors per paper over time for *all* of the six journals.

For the two Management journals – *Organization Science* and *Organization Studies* – and the *British Journal of the Philosophy of Science*, this has been a steady year-on-year increase. The Science journal *Nature Genetics* saw its biggest rise around 15 years ago and has maintained a high average number of authors at around 20 since then. *Nature Medicine* saw its biggest increase in the last decade and its average number of authors now also sits around 20. Finally, *Evolutionary Anthropology* has changed from a journal with largely single-authored work in the mid-1990s to a journal with an average of more than three authors in the latest period. Although the exact reasons behind this would need further investigation, it might well reflect a change in research methods or topics over the years.

Historical development of a discipline

This section shows how an excellent coverage of some conference proceedings in Crossref, OpenAlex and Google Scholar can be used to unearth historical records that can help tracing the development of a specific discipline. Not quite bibliometric research, but definitely historical research facilitated by bibliometrics data. Crossref provides full coverage of *all* Academy of Management proceedings since 1954. This was several years before the launch of the Association's first journal, the *Academy of Management Journal*. Publishing the extended abstracts of only 10% of the papers presented at the conference, these proceedings are one of the most prestigious conference outlets in the field of Management.

As such, its comprehensive coverage in Crossref allows for fascinating insights into the history of this discipline. Whereas in the first 15 years the proceedings were largely composed of reports by the president and the various committees, from 1969 onwards they included a range of papers presented at the conference. Below are screenshots of the 15 most cited papers in 1969 and 1970.

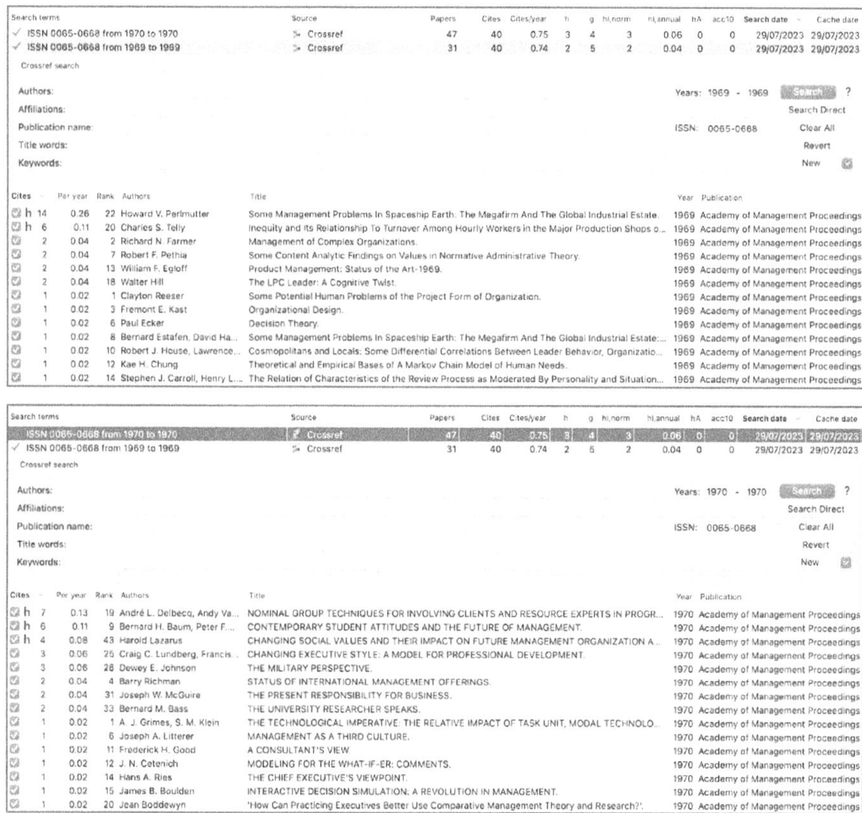

Search terms	Source	Papers	Cites	Cites/year	h	g	hi,norm	hi,annual	hA	acc10	Search date	Cache date
✓ ISSN 0065-0668 from 1970 to 1970	Crossref	47	40	0.75	3	4	3	0.06	0	0	29/07/2023	29/07/2023
✓ ISSN 0065-0668 from 1969 to 1969	Crossref	31	40	0.74	2	5	2	0.04	0	0	29/07/2023	29/07/2023

Crossref search

Authors: Years: 1969 - 1969

Affiliations: Search Direct

Publication name: ISSN: 0065-0668 Clear All

Title words: Revert

Keywords: New

Cites		Per year	Rank	Authors	Title	Year	Publication
h	14	0.26	22	Howard V. Perlmutter	Some Management Problems In Spaceship Earth: The Megafirm And The Global Industrial Estate.	1969	Academy of Management Proceedings
h	6	0.11	20	Charles S. Telly	Inequity and Its Relationship To Turnover Among Hourly Workers in the Major Production Shops o...	1969	Academy of Management Proceedings
	2	0.04	2	Richard N. Farmer	Management of Complex Organizations.	1969	Academy of Management Proceedings
	2	0.04	7	Robert F. Pethia	Some Content Analytic Findings on Values in Normative Administrative Theory.	1969	Academy of Management Proceedings
	2	0.04	13	William F. Egloff	Product Management: Status of the Art-1969.	1969	Academy of Management Proceedings
	2	0.04	18	Walter Hill	The LPC Leader: A Cognitive Twist.	1969	Academy of Management Proceedings
	1	0.02	1	Clayton Reeser	Some Potential Human Problems of the Project Form of Organization.	1969	Academy of Management Proceedings
	1	0.02	3	Fremont E. Kast	Organizational Design.	1969	Academy of Management Proceedings
	1	0.02	6	Paul Ecker	Decision Theory.	1969	Academy of Management Proceedings
	1	0.02	8	Bernard Estafen, David Ha...	Some Management Problems In Spaceship Earth: The Megafirm And The Global Industrial Estate:...	1969	Academy of Management Proceedings
	1	0.02	10	Robert J. House, Lawrence...	Cosmopolitans and Locals: Some Differential Correlations Between Leader Behavior, Organizatio...	1969	Academy of Management Proceedings
	1	0.02	12	Kae H. Chung	Theoretical and Empirical Bases of A Markov Chain Model of Human Needs.	1969	Academy of Management Proceedings
	1	0.02	14	Stephen J. Carroll, Henry L...	The Relation of Characteristics of the Review Process as Moderated By Personality and Situation...	1969	Academy of Management Proceedings

Search terms	Source	Papers	Cites	Cites/year	h	g	hi,norm	hi,annual	hA	acc10	Search date	Cache date
ISSN 0065-0668 from 1970 to 1970	Crossref	47	40	0.75	3	4	3	0.06	0	0	29/07/2023	29/07/2023
✓ ISSN 0065-0668 from 1969 to 1969	Crossref	31	40	0.74	2	5	2	0.04	0	0	29/07/2023	29/07/2023

Crossref search

Authors: Years: 1970 - 1970

Affiliations: Search Direct

Publication name: ISSN: 0065-0668 Clear All

Title words: Revert

Keywords: New

Cites		Per year	Rank	Authors	Title	Year	Publication
h	7	0.13	19	André L. Delbecq, Andy Va...	NOMINAL GROUP TECHNIQUES FOR INVOLVING CLIENTS AND RESOURCE EXPERTS IN PROGR...	1970	Academy of Management Proceedings
h	6	0.11	9	Bernard H. Baum, Peter F....	CONTEMPORARY STUDENT ATTITUDES AND THE FUTURE OF MANAGEMENT.	1970	Academy of Management Proceedings
h	4	0.08	43	Harold Lazarus	CHANGING SOCIAL VALUES AND THEIR IMPACT ON FUTURE MANAGEMENT ORGANIZATION A...	1970	Academy of Management Proceedings
	3	0.06	25	Craig C. Lundberg, Francis...	CHANGING EXECUTIVE STYLE: A MODEL FOR PROFESSIONAL DEVELOPMENT.	1970	Academy of Management Proceedings
	3	0.06	28	Dewey E. Johnson	THE MILITARY PERSPECTIVE.	1970	Academy of Management Proceedings
	2	0.04	4	Barry Richman	STATUS OF INTERNATIONAL MANAGEMENT OFFERINGS.	1970	Academy of Management Proceedings
	2	0.04	31	Joseph W. McGuire	THE PRESENT RESPONSIBILITY FOR BUSINESS.	1970	Academy of Management Proceedings
	2	0.04	33	Bernard M. Bass	THE UNIVERSITY RESEARCHER SPEAKS.	1970	Academy of Management Proceedings
	1	0.02	1	A. J. Grimes, S. M. Klein	THE TECHNOLOGICAL IMPERATIVE: THE RELATIVE IMPACT OF TASK UNIT, MODAL TECHNOLO...	1970	Academy of Management Proceedings
	1	0.02	6	Joseph A. Litterer	MANAGEMENT AS A THIRD CULTURE.	1970	Academy of Management Proceedings
	1	0.02	11	Frederick H. Good	A CONSULTANT'S VIEW.	1970	Academy of Management Proceedings
	1	0.02	12	J. N. Cetenich	MODELING FOR THE WHAT-IF-ER: COMMENTS.	1970	Academy of Management Proceedings
	1	0.02	14	Hans A. Ries	THE CHIEF EXECUTIVE'S VIEWPOINT.	1970	Academy of Management Proceedings
	1	0.02	15	James B. Boulden	INTERACTIVE DECISION SIMULATION: A REVOLUTION IN MANAGEMENT.	1970	Academy of Management Proceedings
	1	0.02	20	Jean Boddewyn	'How Can Practicing Executives Better Use Comparative Management Theory and Research?'.	1970	Academy of Management Proceedings

This allows for a whole host of observations:

1. The complete absence of female academics in the proceedings (and presumably at the conference).
2. The presence of quite a few academics that would later play a big role in the field of International Business (my own discipline): Howard Perlmutter, Barry Richman, and Jean Boddewyn.
3. The presence of consultants and managers at the conference and the interest in the research/praxis nexus.
4. The interest in educational aspects, such as course offerings and student attitudes.

5. The usage of terms that later have taken on different meanings, such as cosmopolitans and review process.
6. The frequent reference to technology and simulation models.

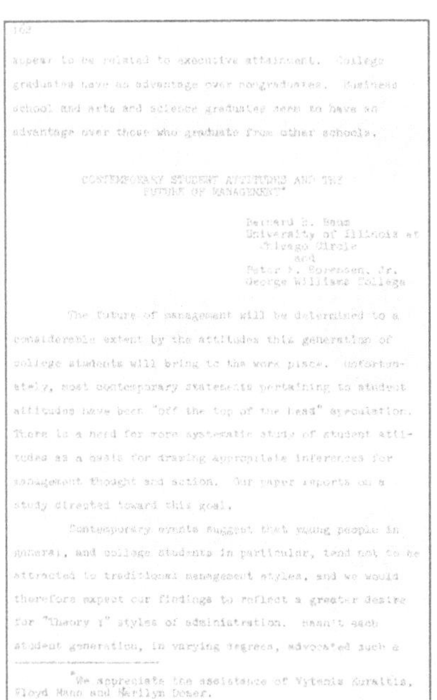

162

appear to be related to executive attainment. College graduates have an advantage over nongraduates. Business school and arts and science graduates seem to have an advantage over those who graduate from other schools.

CONTEMPORARY STUDENT ATTITUDES AND THE
FUTURE OF MANAGEMENT*

Bernard H. Baum
University of Illinois at
Chicago Circle
and
Peter B. Sorensen, Jr.
George Williams College

The future of management will be determined to a considerable extent by the attitudes this generation of college students will bring to the work place. Unfortunately, most contemporary statements pertaining to student attitudes have been "off the top of the head" speculation. There is a need for more systematic study of student attitudes as a basis for drawing appropriate inferences for management thought and action. Our paper reports on a study directed toward this goal.

Contemporary events suggest that young people in general, and college students in particular, tend not to be attracted to traditional management styles, and we would therefore expect our findings to reflect a greater desire for "Theory Y" styles of administration. Hasn't each student generation, in varying degrees, advocated such a

*We appreciate the assistance of Vytenis Kuraitis, Floyd Mann and Marilyn Doner.

103

change in authority systems? The answer, of course, is yes. However, business is being staffed more by college educated young people. Thus, even though the basic condition is historically repetitive, it is one that will be of greater magnitude in the future.

In addition, there is every reason to believe that the mores and folkways of today "unsack" less of the protestant ethic mandate that "the boss is the boss!" The concept of what constitutes Weber's classical "legitimate authority" has, although still constituting a basic premise of organization, been considerably modified. Bankers, for example, were able at one time to require employees not to live in certain neighborhoods. The area in which authority is perceived to be "legitimate" has been considerably narrowed.

The parallel observation on campus is the demise of the in loco parentis concept, as evidenced by new dormitory rules and arrangements. As a result of this changing environment, what can we predict regarding acceptance of authority in business organizations?

Other examples of the "handwriting on the wall" are the orientations of (1) the Black and (2) the changing orientation of women. There appears little doubt that the nature of the cultural conditioning and consequent orientations of blacks and women will comprise an ever-increasing element in the future of management. We suggest that their range of acceptance of what has traditionally been called

Above and below, I also present two results that I found of particular historical interest. First, a 1970 paper on student attitudes, a particularly important topic after 1968, the year of student revolutions across the world. Second, a very early mention of social responsibility and a suggestion of refocusing the Academy's official domain.

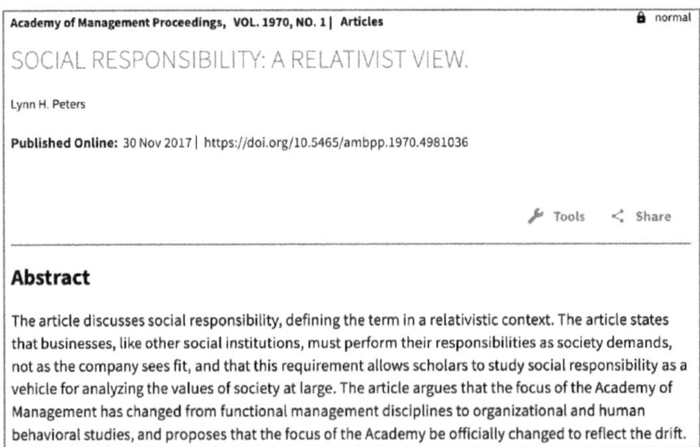

Academy of Management Proceedings, VOL. 1970, NO. 1 | Articles 🔒 normal

SOCIAL RESPONSIBILITY: A RELATIVIST VIEW.

Lynn H. Peters

Published Online: 30 Nov 2017 | https://doi.org/10.5465/ambpp.1970.4981036

🔧 Tools ≪ Share

Abstract

The article discusses social responsibility, defining the term in a relativistic context. The article states that businesses, like other social institutions, must perform their responsibilities as society demands, not as the company sees fit, and that this requirement allows scholars to study social responsibility as a vehicle for analyzing the values of society at large. The article argues that the focus of the Academy of Management has changed from functional management disciplines to organizational and human behavioral studies, and proposes that the focus of the Academy be officially changed to reflect the drift.

Bibliometric research for research topics

In addition to doing research on authors and journals, you can also conduct bibliometrics analyses on research topics. Many academics have used Publish or Perish to write up articles on the development of a particular research field. The simplest of these analyses just list the top-100/50/25 most cited articles published in a field, providing some cursory reflections.

Other articles present a more involved analysis of the longitudinal development of a field, its most popular journals, and the authors most frequently publishing in it. Yet more extensive analyses might include a thematic analysis based on an export of article abstracts or a visual representation of the research field using a programme such as VOSviewer that can import Publish or Perish data.

However, each of these analyses will start with a collection of the most cited articles in a particular field. PoP can help with this task by doing a search that uses either the **Title words** field or the **Keywords** field. The former will obviously result in a smaller subset of publications than the latter, especially in Google Scholar where search terms in the Keywords field are matched in the entire article. Below is a Google Scholar search for the relatively new topic of "green finance" in the Keywords field, with the first six results shown.

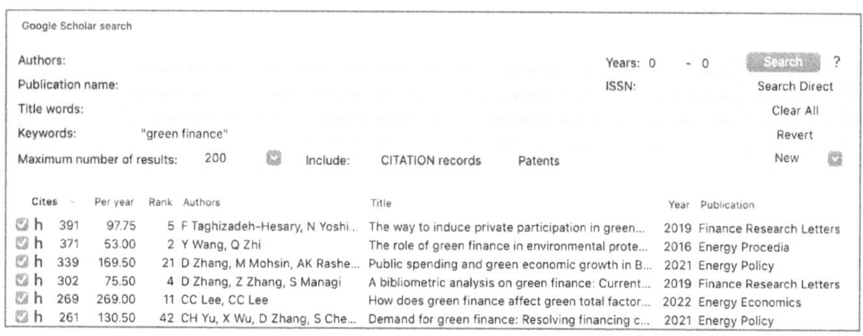

Cites	Per year	Rank	Authors	Title	Year	Publication
h 391	97.75	5	F Taghizadeh-Hesary, N Yoshi...	The way to induce private participation in green...	2019	Finance Research Letters
h 371	53.00	2	Y Wang, Q Zhi	The role of green finance in environmental prote...	2016	Energy Procedia
h 339	169.50	21	D Zhang, M Mohsin, AK Rashe...	Public spending and green economic growth in B...	2021	Energy Policy
h 302	75.50	4	D Zhang, Z Zhang, S Managi	A bibliometric analysis on green finance: Current...	2019	Finance Research Letters
h 269	269.00	11	CC Lee, CC Lee	How does green finance affect green total factor...	2022	Energy Economics
h 261	130.50	42	CH Yu, X Wu, D Zhang, S Che...	Demand for green finance: Resolving financing c...	2021	Energy Policy

Note that I included quotes around the two keywords to ensure they appear together. Otherwise, your results might include highly cited publications that include the words green and finance separately, but are unrelated to green finance as such.

I also excluded patents and CITATION records. First, it is unlikely that there are any patents for this search. Second, excluding CITATION records ensures a cleaner result as many CITATION records are stray citations (see Chapter 5). However, note that this will also exclude any books and other publications for which Google Scholar can find citations but not the publication itself.

Alternative data sources

As Google Scholar matches keywords *anywhere* in the article, you might end up with some highly cited articles that simply list your keywords in the body of the article or even in the references. Hence, you may also want to try some of the other data sources that Publish or Perish interfaces with to double-check your results. Below are the results for OpenAlex. As you can see it shows the same six articles though in a slightly different order.

OpenAlex

Cites	Per year	Rank	Authors	Title	Year	Publication
h 298	74.50	1	Farhad Taghizadeh-Hesary, N...	The way to induce private participation in green...	2019	Finance Research Letters
h 264	132.00	2	Dong-Yang Zhang, Muhamma...	Public spending and green economic growth in B...	2021	Energy Policy
h 242	242.00	3	Chien-Chiang Lee, Chien-Chi...	How does green finance affect green total factor...	2022	Energy Economics
h 231	115.50	4	Chin-Hsien Yu, Xiuqin Wu, Da...	Demand for green finance: Resolving financing c...	2021	Energy Policy
h 224	32.00	5	Yao Wang, Qiang Zhi	The Role of Green Finance in Environmental Prot...	2016	Energy Procedia
h 222	55.50	6	Dayong Zhang, Zhiwei Zhang,...	A bibliometric analysis on green finance: Current...	2019	Finance Research Letters

The advantage of OpenAlex is that – like Google Scholar, but unlike most of the other data sources – it provides 1,000 results. It can also export full abstracts, making it possible to conduct content analysis. However, if you prefer to stick with the traditional data sources, you can also do the same search in Scopus and the Web of the Science. The results are below.

Scopus

Cites	Per year	Rank	Authors	Title	Year	Publication
h 293	73.25	1	F. Taghizadeh-Hesary	The way to induce private participation in green...	2019	Finance Research Letters
h 292	146.00	2	D. Zhang	Public spending and green economic growth in B...	2021	Energy Policy
h 246	246.00	3	C.C. Lee	How does green finance affect green total factor...	2022	Energy Economics
h 229	114.50	4	C.H. Yu	Demand for green finance: Resolving financing c...	2021	Energy Policy
h 199	49.75	5	D. Zhang	A bibliometric analysis on green finance: Current...	2019	Finance Research Letters
h 197	28.14	6	Y. Wang	The Role of Green Finance in Environmental Prot...	2016	Energy Procedia

Web of Science

	Cites ∨	Per year	Rank	Authors	Title	Year	Publication
☑ h	259	129.50	1	Dongyang Zhang, Muhamma...	Public spending and green economic growth in B...	2021	Energy Policy
☑ h	255	63.75	2	Farhad Taghizadeh-Hesary, N...	The way to induce private participation in green...	2019	Finance Research Letters
☑ h	219	219.00	3	Chi-Chuan Lee, Chien-Chiang...	How does green finance affect green total factor...	2022	Energy Economics
☑ h	211	105.50	4	Chin-Hsien Yu, Xiuqin Wu, Da...	Demand for green finance: Resolving financing c...	2021	Energy Policy
☑ h	179	44.75	5	Dayong Zhang, Zhiwei Zhang,...	A bibliometric analysis on green finance: Current...	2019	Finance Research Letters
☑ h	172	24.57	6	Yao Wang, Qiang Zhi	The role of green finance in environmental prote...	2016	Clean Energy For Clean City

In this case, all four data sources provide the same six results, though in a slightly different order and with different overall citation counts. However, this will not always be the case. Hence, triangulation by running your search in different data sources is always a good idea. This also allows you to pick up highly cited publications that – for one reason or another – are not covered in a particular data source.

Publish or Perish makes it easy to do this. Simply select the search and click on the downward arrow next to the **New** button (see below). Select the data source in which you want to run the search. PoP will now automatically populate the relevant fields. Do remember though that different data sources might have different search syntaxes. An overview for topic searches can be found in Chapter 9.

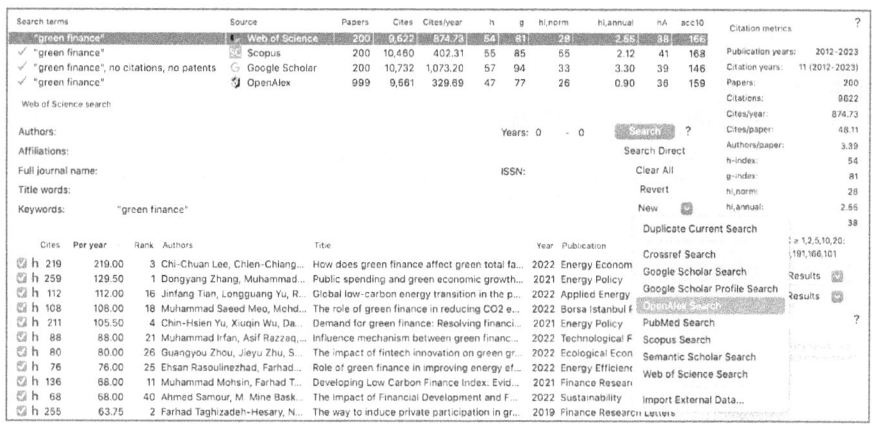

Visualisation: longitudinal development

After exporting the full results of your search to Excel or another spreadsheet programme, you can easily create a graph of the growth of the number of articles on a specific research topic over the years.

Below is a graph of the number of articles in Green Finance over the years. Interest in this topic has clearly exploded in the last five years.

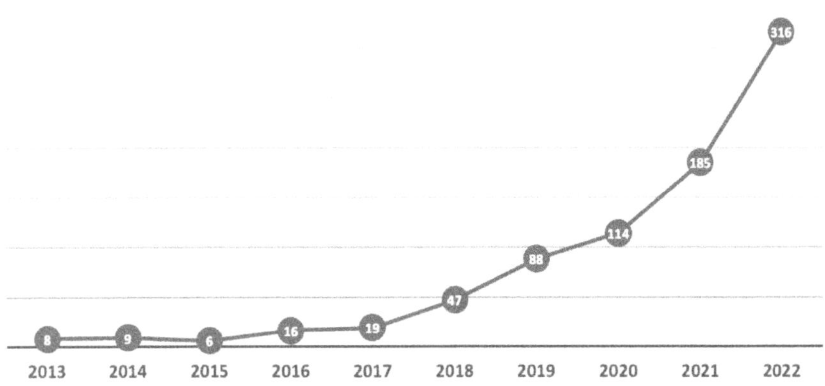

However, all data sources are limited in the number of results they return, showing only the top 200 to 1,000 results by relevance and/or citations. This means that although the above graph gives an *indication* of the tendency of growth, it does not provide fully accurate number of the number of articles published by year.

To get a more accurate result of the number of articles per year, you will need to partition your results by year. This is easily done in PoP by duplicating the search and changing the year range. The screenshot below shows how the results for the green finance search.

Search terms	Source	Papers
"green finance" from 2018 to 2018	OpenAlex	71
"green finance" from 2019 to 2019	OpenAlex	125
"green finance" from 2020 to 2020	OpenAlex	150
"green finance" from 2021 to 2021	OpenAlex	222
"green finance" from 2022 to 2022	OpenAlex	451

As expected, the correct number of articles published each year is higher than was found for a search for all years combined. Especially the number of publications in recent years will be underestimated as they are generally not yet highly cited. However, the conclusion of a strong increase in publications over the years doesn't change.

Visualisation: analysis of themes

A quick-and-dirty visualisation can easily be done by exporting the abstracts and using a free Word cloud generator. It literally took me only a minute to export the OpenAlex results, copy the abstracts and create the word cloud below. Whilst not sufficient for an academic it is a very easy way to get a quick overview of a research topic.

Bibliometric research for institutions

Finally, you can also use Publish or Perish to do bibliometric research on institutions. One obvious application would be to create rankings of universities. The detailed example below is such an application. However, it could also be used to analyse for instance:

- the development of publications for a single institution over the years to assess its increasing (or decreasing) research power,
- the themes covered by a group of universities, after exporting either titles or abstracts for further analyses,
- the number of publications in a specific journal or a group of journals for a group of universities

Given the flexibility of the Publish or Perish interface the opportunities are literally endless. Below I provide an example of university rankings as well as a comparison of publications across universities for a set of journals. Before conducting your analyses, please refer to Chapter 9 for details on affiliation searches across data sources.

University rankings: Do metrics match peer review?

In 2017 I conducted a study that aimed at establishing whether the results of the 2014 Research Excellence Framework (REF) exercise, could be replaced by a simple bibliometric analysis. The study – entitled *Running the REF on a rainy Sunday afternoon* – was also presented at the Science and Technology Indicators conference in 2018.

I used the Publish or Perish software to source citation data from the – now unfortunately defunct – Microsoft Academic. This allowed me to create a citation-based ranking of British universities which showed a very strong (0.97) correlation with the REF power ranking. After defining the searches in PoP, the whole process took me less than two hours of data collection and less than two hours of analysis.

Search terms	Source	Papers	Cites	Cites/year	h	g	hl,norm	hl,annual
University of Oxford OR Said Business School...	Microsoft Academic	1,000	1,054,892	117,210.22	504	1,000	195	21.67
University of Cambridge from 2008 to 2013	Microsoft Academic	1,000	828,449	92,049.89	490	892	174	19.33
Imperial College London OR Imperial College...	Microsoft Academic	1,000	697,991	77,554.56	438	805	150	16.67
University College London from 2008 to 2013	Microsoft Academic	1,000	690,023	76,669.22	446	796	160	17.78
University of Edinburgh from 2008 to 2013	Microsoft Academic	1,000	578,266	64,251.78	383	720	137	15.22
University of Glasgow from 2008 to 2013	Microsoft Academic	1,000	518,096	57,566.22	324	681	122	13.56
University of Manchester OR Manchester Bus...	Microsoft Academic	1,000	516,914	57,434.89	354	674	133	14.78
University of Birmingham OR Birmingham Bus...	Microsoft Academic	1,000	467,076	51,897.33	311	639	114	12.67
Kings College London from 2008 to 2013	Microsoft Academic	1,000	452,559	50,284.33	349	609	122	13.56
University of Sheffield from 2008 to 2013	Microsoft Academic	1,000	421,776	46,864.00	296	602	119	13.22

Above you can see part of the search results with the ten top-ranked universities for the total number of citations. This mirrors most other institutional rankings, with Oxford, Cambridge, Imperial and UCL topping the list. All universities ranked in the top-10 by citations ranked in the top-15 on the REF power ranking. The most notable divergence was Birmingham University, which ranked 8 in the citation ranking, but only scored 15 in the REF ranking. As we will see below this was largely caused by its involvement in highly cited mega-authored publications.

The metrics for the full search results were subsequently exported and a further analysis was conducted using Excel. The figure below shows the regression plot for the correlation between the REF Power Rank and the MA Citation Rank. Most universities cluster around the regression line and the average difference in rank is only 6.8 (for a ranking of 118 universities).

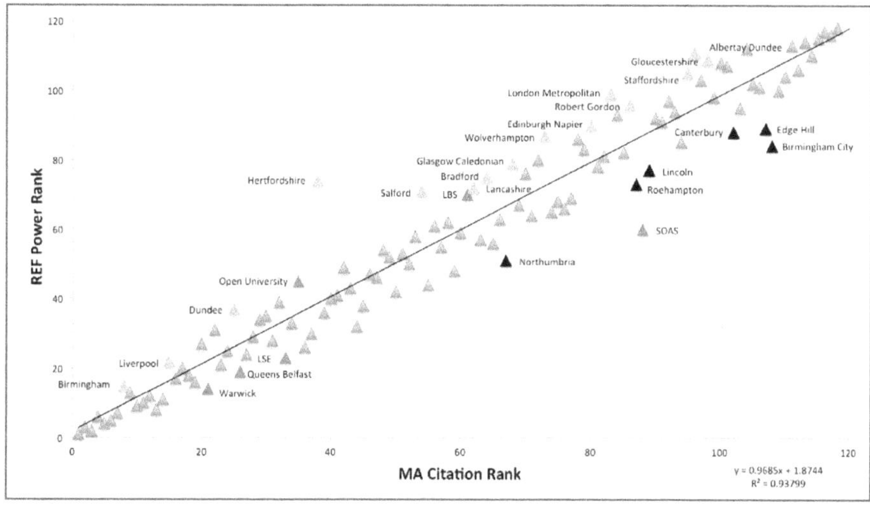

Although most universities clustered around the regression line, there were some notable deviations. However, we should realise that publications only counted for 65% of the REF power score. So, the first discrepancy might simply arise from the one third of the REF power score made up of societal impact and research environment (the two other criteria). Universities below the regression line are ranked higher in the REF than on citations. These universities might simply have had better scores for societal impact and/or research environment. The most significant deviations are marked in black.

Possible problems with bibliometric analysis

From a bibliometric perspective, these deviations from the regression line could be largely explained by three issues: data source problems, disciplinary differences, and the small numbers problem. These three issues are common to most bibliometric analyses. Hence, they are worth discussing in some detail.

First, there was a specific problem with the Microsoft Academic data for two universities (coloured red in the figure). Queens University (Belfast) saw part of their publications usurped by its Canadian namesake. In contrast, the Open University saw its number of publications boosted by its affiliates in the Netherlands and Israel. Running the same analyses with several data sources – something which is easy to do with Publish or Perish – could allow for triangulation. Each data source has its own flaws, and many have problems with affiliation and author disambiguation. However, collectively they are likely to provide a more accurate picture.

Second, several institutions (coloured orange in the figure) saw their citation levels boosted by having one, or a small group of, academics participating in large consortia doing research in for instance particle physics or gene technology. Publications from these collaborations might have over a thousand authors, as well as a huge number of citations as every author will cite these publications in their other work. These mega-authored articles are thus likely to represent a disproportionate share of citations, especially for smaller institutions. A solution might be to remove these papers from the comparison.

A related more general problem is that citation practices differ by discipline. Citation levels are therefore much higher in the Sciences and Medicine than in the Social Sciences and Humanities, with Engineering between these two extremes. Thus, universities that have a heavy concentration in the Sciences and Medicine (coloured orange) are likely to outperform universities with a strong presence in the Social Sciences and Humanities (coloured purple) in citations. The use of metrics that correct for disciplinary differences such as the various individual h-indexes could be solution for this problem.

Third, in smaller institutions, individual highly cited papers or a small number of very productive academics might have an outsized impact. The former could be addressed by using h-index type indicators, rather than total citation levels. The latter might necessitate a restriction of the number of papers considered for a single academic (as is done in the REF itself). This small numbers problem is particularly important for the former polytechnic institutions that became universities in 1992, as they typically have fewer active researchers. The universities market green in the above figure are some of the most important proponents of this problem.

Conclusion

Although the bibliometric analysis was by no means flawless, it did lead to a ranking of universities that was very similar to the ranking that occupied the productive time of thousands of academics for a substantial part of the 7-year period. By using metrics, we could win back the time wasted on evaluating publications for REF submission, a soul-destroying activity in the first place. Instead, we could spend our "evaluation time" where it really matters, i.e., in reading papers and funding applications of our (junior) colleagues *before* their submission, and in reading their cases for tenure and promotion.

Academics that were part of the REF panels would win back even more time. Imagine if those 1,000 scholars, rather than spending all of their time evaluating the end products of their colleagues' research activity, would use that time to mentor their junior colleagues. Wouldn't that create a far more positive as well as more productive research culture?

University publications in a set of journals

Bibliometric research doesn't always have to involve large-scale data collection and publication of the results. You may have narrowly framed questions that can be answered by collecting data on a small group of institutions.

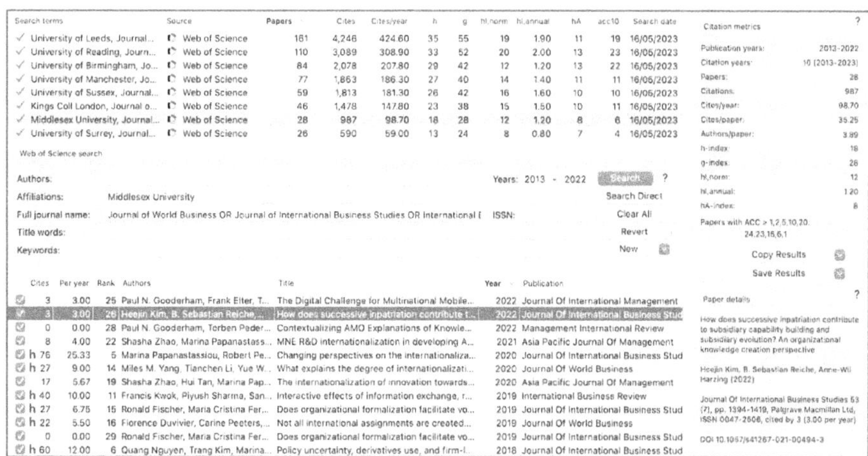

Search terms	Source	Papers	Cites	Cites/year	h	g	hI,norm	hI,annual	hA	acc10	Search date
✓ University of Leeds, Journal...	Web of Science	161	4,246	424.60	35	55	19	1.90	11	19	16/05/2023
✓ University of Reading, Journ...	Web of Science	110	3,089	308.90	33	52	20	2.00	13	23	16/05/2023
✓ University of Birmingham, Jo...	Web of Science	84	2,078	207.80	29	42	12	1.20	13	22	16/05/2023
✓ University of Manchester, Jo...	Web of Science	77	1,863	186.30	27	40	14	1.40	11	11	16/05/2023
✓ University of Sussex, Journal...	Web of Science	59	1,813	181.30	26	42	16	1.60	10	10	16/05/2023
✓ Kings Coll London, Journal o...	Web of Science	46	1,478	147.80	23	38	15	1.50	10	11	16/05/2023
✓ Middlesex University, Journal...	Web of Science	28	987	98.70	18	28	12	1.20	8	6	16/05/2023
✓ University of Surrey, Journal...	Web of Science	26	590	59.00	13	24	8	0.80	7	4	16/05/2023

Web of Science search

Authors:		Years: 2013 - 2022	Search ?
Affiliations:	Middlesex University		Search Direct
Full journal name:	Journal of World Business OR Journal of International Business Studies OR International E ISSN:		Clear All
Title words:			Revert
Keywords:			New

Citation metrics

Publication years:	2013-2022
Citation years:	10 (2013-2023)
Papers:	28
Citations:	987
Cites/year:	98.70
Cites/paper:	35.25
Authors/paper:	3.89
h-index:	18
g-index:	28
hI,norm:	12
hI,annual:	1.20
hA-index:	8

Papers with ACC ≥ 1,2,5,10,20:
24,23,16,6,1

Copy Results

Save Results

Cites	Per year	Rank	Authors	Title	Year	Publication
3	3.00	25	Paul N. Gooderham, Frank Elter, T...	The Digital Challenge for Multinational Mobile...	2022	Journal Of International Management
3	3.00	26	Heejin Kim, B. Sebastian Reiche, ...	How does successive inpatriation contribute t...	2022	Journal Of International Business Stud
0	0.00	28	Paul N. Gooderham, Torben Peder...	Contextualizing AMO Explanations of Knowle...	2022	Management International Review
8	4.00	22	Shasha Zhao, Marina Papanastass...	MNE R&D internationalization in developing A...	2021	Asia Pacific Journal Of Management
h 76	25.33	5	Marina Papanastassiou, Robert Pe...	Changing perspectives on the internationaliza...	2020	Journal Of International Business Stud
h 27	9.00	14	Miles M. Yang, Tianchen Li, Yue W...	What explains the degree of internationalizati...	2020	Journal Of World Business
17	5.67	19	Shasha Zhao, Hui Tan, Marina Pap...	The internationalization of innovation towards...	2020	Asia Pacific Journal Of Management
h 40	10.00	11	Francis Kwok, Piyush Sharma, San...	Interactive effects of information exchange, r...	2019	International Business Review
h 27	6.75	15	Ronald Fischer, Maria Cristina Fer...	Does organizational formalization facilitate vo...	2019	Journal Of International Business Stud
h 22	5.50	16	Florence Duvivier, Carine Peeters,...	Not all international assignments are created...	2019	Journal Of World Business
0	0.00	29	Ronald Fischer, Maria Cristina Fer...	Does organizational formalization facilitate vo...	2019	Journal Of International Business Stud
h 60	12.00	6	Quang Nguyen, Trang Kim, Marina...	Policy uncertainty, derivatives use, and firm-l...	2018	Journal Of International Business Stud

Paper details

How does successive inpatriation contribute to subsidiary capability building and subsidiary evolution? An organizational knowledge creation perspective

Heejin Kim, B. Sebastian Reiche, Anne-Wil Harzing (2022)

Journal Of International Business Studies 53 (7), pp. 1394-1419, Palgrave Macmillan Ltd, ISSN 0047-2506, cited by 3 (3.00 per year)

DOI 10.1067/s41267-021-00494-3

Above is an analysis of publications in a set of seven key International Business journals for eight UK institutions. I selected six institutions that are well-known for their focus on IB research. I then added my own institution (Middlesex University) as well as another institution where one of my mentees had applied for a job.

This allowed me to assess the relative standing of these institutions in the field of International Business. Information like this might be useful for job applicants or PhD students looking for an institution in a specific field. It may also help in preparing an institution's research environment statement for the national research evaluation or funding applications.

This analysis allowed me to compare not only the institutions' productivity in the field, but also their citation impact. For instance, I noticed that although Middlesex University was not one of the most productive universities in terms of the number of *publications*, it did have a higher number of *citations* per paper. It was also striking that institutions differed far less in their hA (which looks at citations per year) than in their h-index.

In sum

Publish or Perish can be a very useful tool for bibliometric analysis. You can use it for large-scale publishable studies, analysing research topics, investigating co-authorship patterns, or creating rankings of individuals, journals, or institutions.

However, you can also use it for smaller scale investigations that answer more narrowly focused questions. PoP's flexibility to combine searches in a wide range of fields means that "the sky is the limit" in terms of analyses that can be conducted.

In the next and final chapter, we will look at how the usage of Publish or Perish has developed over the years, looking at where, why, when and by whom it has been used.

Chapter 15: Development of PoP over the years

For Publish or Perish's 15th anniversary in 2021, I looked back to where, why, when, and by whom it had been used over the years, and what they would have used if PoP hadn't been around.

There has been quite a bit of change over the years. However, the PoP features that users like most have remained quite stable. In addition to the ability to search for and export data on authors, articles, papers, publications, journals, citations, and metrics – in particular the h-index – PoP's most important selling point is its ease of use and the fact that it is so quick.

One of the key reasons why I like PoP myself is that I can avoid using the web interfaces of other services. They are often confusing and frequently load so slowly that I give up after only a few searches. A growing number of academics and students seem to agree. Over the years PoP usage has increased to well over a million individuals.

Where? From Anglo/Western to world-wide

I don't have systematic data on where PoP was used in the first ten years. However, my web analytics service does allow me to compare visits to my website – two thirds of which are directly or indirectly related to Publish or Perish – between 2016 and 2020.

In both years my website drew visitors from more than 200 different countries and territories. In 2016, the most exotic countries on the list were Vatican City and Palau, in 2020 they included Greenland and Antartica. However, in both years nearly 75% of the visitors came from the top-20 countries represented below.

Top-20 countries in 2016				Top-20 countries in 2020			
United States	17.0%	Netherlands	2.4%	United States	14.0%	Turkey	2.2%
Australia	8.6%	China	1.7%	Indonesia	10.3%	Poland	2.1%
Great Britain (UK)	6.9%	Spain	1.6%	Great Britain (UK)	6.2%	Malaysia	1.9%
India	4.9%	Malaysia	1.6%	India	5.8%	Netherlands	1.7%
Germany	4.7%	Iran	1.5%	Germany	5.2%	Colombia	1.7%
Poland	4.2%	Colombia	1.5%	Brazil	4.4%	China	1.6%
Italy	4.2%	Philippines	1.4%	Italy	2.8%	South Africa	1.6%
France	3.4%	Greece	1.4%	Australia	2.6%	Philippines	1.6%
Canada	2.7%	Russian Federation	1.2%	France	2.6%	Spain	1.5%
Brazil	2.4%	Turkey	1.2%	Canada	2.4%	Mexico	1.4%

Although we see many of the same countries represented in the top-20 in both years, the dominance of both Anglophone countries and European countries has decreased quite significantly. In 2016 more than 35% of the visitors in the top-20 came from the USA, Australia, Great Britain, or Canada; in 2020 this had dropped to 25%. In 2016, 22% of the visitors in the top-20 came from continental European countries, whereas in 2020 this had shrunk to nearly 16%.

Back in 2016, India was the only non-Western country that was significantly represented with nearly 5% of total visitors. Brazil, China, Malaysia, Iran, Colombia, the Philippines, Russia, and Turkey were all represented in much smaller numbers for a total of 17.4%.

In 2020, three non-Western countries featured in the top-6 - Indonesia, India, and Brazil - which combined represented 20.5% of total visitors. With Turkey, Malaysia, Colombia, China, South Africa, the Philippines and Mexico, non-Western countries now make up 32.5%, i.e., nearly double their proportion in 2016. PoP clearly fulfils a strong need in these countries as is evidenced by this user response.

> *I live in a very poor country [Venezuela]. It not possible for me to pay WOS or any other bibliographic service. In that sense, PoP has been a huge help and relief. I really thank you for this extraordinary program. You are making our academic lives in economically depressed countries much easier.*

Why? From h-index calculator to literature reviews

Since 2015 I have been running a PoP user survey. To date nearly 10,000 users have responded. One question in the survey asks users how long they have been using the software. In 2015, two thirds of the respondents indicated that they had been using the software for either more than 5 years, or 3-5 years. Hence, the 2015 responses also give us a good picture of earlier usage.

As is evident below, PoP started out as a h-index calculator. In 2015 more than four in five users used it to check their own h-index or citations. Given that the first version of PoP launched a year after the h-index had been introduced, this is not entirely surprising. It was also used to look up other academics, either out of curiosity (by nearly two thirds of the users), or to evaluate them for promotion, tenure, job, or funding applications (by nearly half of the users).

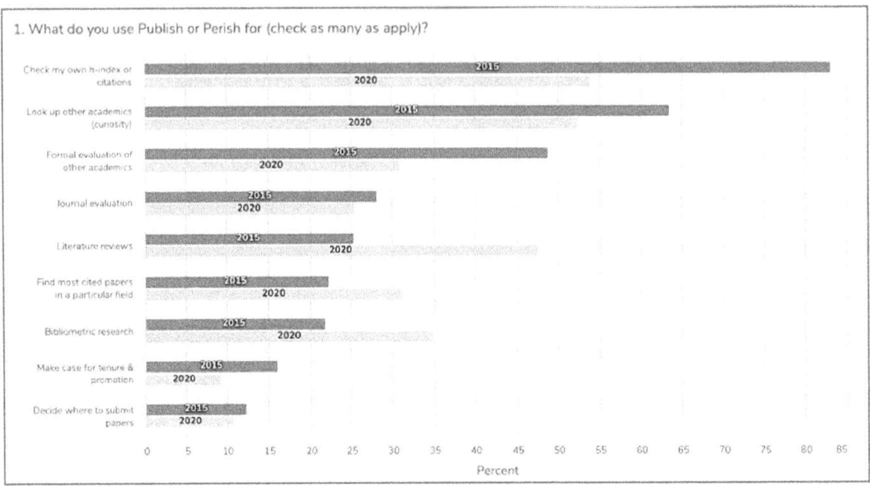

In addition, however, PoP was also used quite frequently to evaluate journals (28% of the respondents), do literature reviews (25%) or simply to find the most cited papers in a particular field (22%). More specialised use cases were used by a smaller number of respondents: bibliometric research (21%), tenure and promotion applications (16%), and deciding where to submit papers (12%).

In 2020, the most common PoP usage remained looking up one's own h-index or citation record or looking up other academics. However, the proportion of survey respondents citing this as one of their use cases had now declined to just over half. Formal evaluation of other academics had also declined in importance with less than a third of the survey respondents using it for this purpose. This was matched by a decline in using it to make your case for tenure or promotion.

Usage for journal evaluation, either more generally or in deciding where to submit papers declined marginally. However, usage for research purposes, whether for literature reviews (from 25% to 43%), to find the most cited papers (from 22% to 32%) or for bibliometric research (from 21% to 35%) had increased quite dramatically between 2015 and 2020.

This trend has continued since 2020. The figure below shows the outcome of a Google Scholar search for "Harzing Publish or Perish" to establish the number of academic articles referring to the software, with 2023 estimated based on results to date.

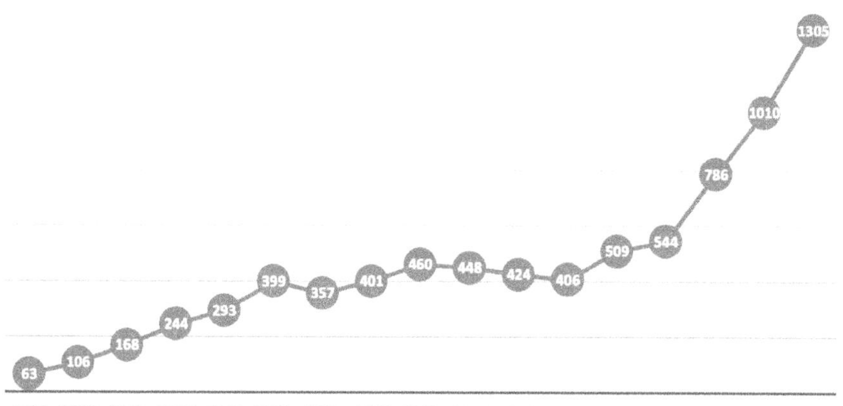

Especially since the Covid-19 pandemic struck in 2020, making field-based data collection more difficult, a lot of academics appear to be using Publish or Perish to do desk-based research. In the past seven years, we have further facilitated this type of usage by introducing six new data sources in 2016 (Microsoft Academic), 2017 (Google Scholar Citation Profiles, Crossref, Scopus, and Web of Science) 2020 (PubMed), 2021 (Semantic Scholar), and 2022 (OpenAlex).

We also added the option to export full abstracts in 2020, creating a more flexible keyword search, and making it easier to replicate searches across data sources by pre-filling the searches form with identical search terms. I can't think of a better way to summarise the advantages of using PoP than these two recent user survey responses.

Searching for publications through internet portals is a pain as they are typically quite slow, all have different interfaces that aren't particularly intuitive and don't help at all to keep track of the searches you have already done. PoP solves all the issues above; it is both easier and faster to use than web portal alternatives. With PoP I feel much more confident that I can perform a systematic review of available literature on a topic. I also really like how the results from a search are displayed; it is easy to rank them and/or filter them by a wide variety of criteria and this is really helpful.

My current research project included 44 unique keyword & author searches with 14 citing work retrievals. I did a similar project last year using only Google Scholar and an EBSCO search interface; it took me several weeks to get to the same point. Using PoP cut the time by 60-80% and I have the search results stored - I can look back over the results history. PoP is extremely powerful for this kind of research project.

When? Increasingly frequently...

Changing usage also led users to use PoP more frequently. You don't look up your own h-index or citations every day (although some users do confide that they find PoP addictive and check their citation counts several times a week). However, if literature reviews are your key reason for using PoP, you are likely to use it quite often.

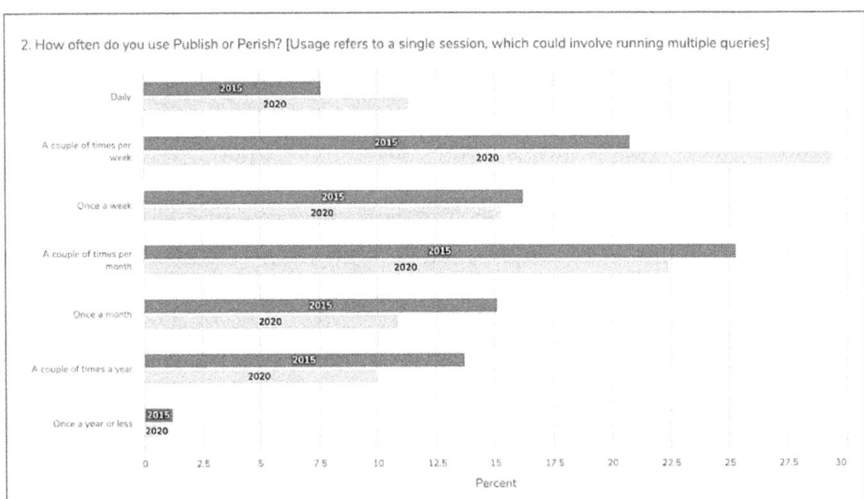

The proportion of survey respondents using the software either daily or several times a week has increased from just over a quarter to more than 40%, whereas the proportion using PoP only once a month or less has declined from 16.5% to less than 10%. In 2015 the largest number of respondents used the software a couple of times a month, whereas in 2020 the largest number of respondents used PoP a couple of times a week.

What alternatives? Free services dominate

Although a few years ago we opened up the possibility to provide donations, Publish or Perish has always been free. Many of the survey respondents let us know in the open answer questions how much they appreciate this. It is therefore not surprising that, both in 2015 and in 2020, the most frequently used alternative services are the free Google Scholar and Google Scholar Profiles.

However, none of the other free data sources are very suitable for literature reviews or bibliometric research on their own. So, it is not surprising that the proportion of survey users saying PoP is the only service that suits their needs has doubled over the last five years. Nearly a quarter of the respondents now choose this option.

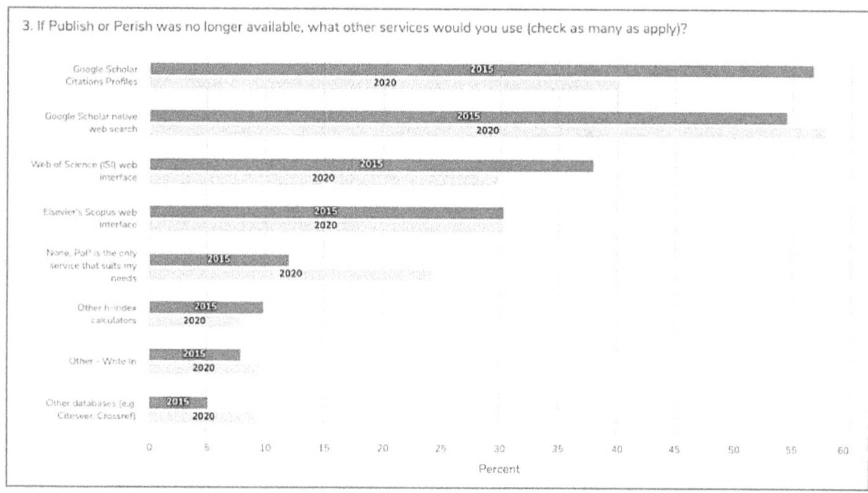

In addition, the open answer option includes many pleas to keep PoP forever. Below I listed the most funny and heart-warming answers to the question: If Publish or Perish was no longer available, what other services would you use?

Beverage serving services to drown my sorrow, really happy for this program.

For me after use PorP I don't want to use any other.

I have no idea. Then I have to find replacement. So, do not punish me. PP is perfect for my needs.

I would cry.

If publish and perish was no longer available it would be a great loss to the scientific community, it has taught researchers to evaluate publication worth alongside volume.

It will be catastrophic! please don't do that.

Need Publish or Perish because it is more user friendly and easy to use.

None, you are unique and very important.

Oh no please.

Please do not leave us without this tool, there is nothing like it ever.

Please do not stop Publish or Perish. If need be, I can pay from my own pocket to be able to use this tool.

Using google scholar without PoP is painful, so I would probably end up having to write something in R or python to scrape and it would never be the same!!

What? There's software which can replace POP???

Wha- why would you do that to us???

Who? From professors to students

Publish or Perish was first developed in 2006 to help me make my own case for citation impact in my second application for promotion to full Professor at the University of Melbourne. In the early days, its users seem to have mainly been similar academics in traditional research career trajectories. More than a third of the users in 2015 were full professors, with another 30% Associate or Assistant Professor and more than 10% Research Fellow or Postdoc.

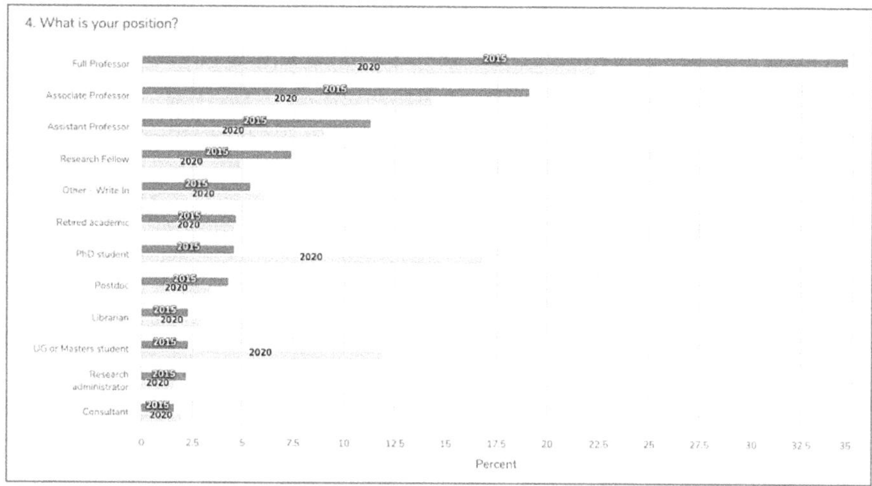

Student usage was fairly limited in 2015. More retired academics were using the survey than PhD students. With 2.3% of the survey respondents the proportion of UG and Masters students using the software was very low indeed. Usage by librarians, research administrators, consultants, and government officials (not shown in the graph) was similarly limited.

The 2020 survey responses, however, illustrated that PoP users had diversified significantly. Although with 22% full professors are still the largest group of users, all professorial categories declined in importance. Only 45% of the 2020 respondents have a regular assistant, associate, or full professorial job, compared with 65% in 2015. The proportion of research fellows, postdocs and retired academics also declined slightly, from 16.3% to 12.6%.

The biggest increase in users came from students. The proportion of PhD students more than tripled from 4.6% to 16.6%. The proportion of Masters and UG students increased even more than five-fold, from 2.3% to 11.8%. The proportion of smaller use groups such as librarians, consultants and government officials also increased. The "other" category also evidenced increasingly diversified use not just by independent, freelance, and unemployed researchers, but also by medical practitioners, industry researchers, publishers, and NGOs.

There is likely to be a relationship between the changing use cases as reported above, the diversification in PoP users and the increasing use frequency. Students are likely to use the software frequently for research purposes such as literature reviews, finding highly cited articles, and bibliometric research. Professors are more likely to use the software a bit less frequently in order to look up their own records or evaluate other academics.

That said, even university professors have significantly increased their use of Publish or Perish for research purposes, whereas their usage for research evaluation purposes declined. They are also using it more frequently than they did in the past, and in 2020 are twice as likely to say that they see no alternatives for Publish or Perish than they did in 2015.

Publish or Perish technical support

With new audiences come new challenges. Publish or Perish needs to meet the needs of 75+ year old retired academics who have spent much of their careers without a computer; 55+ year olds like me who only started to use computers after their initial studies and can still remember a working life without email and the Internet; but also 18-25 year old students who grew up with smartphones and don't understand that Publish or Perish is a desktop software program, not an app or a website. So, whenever we introduce new features to the software or create support materials, we need to keep *all* these users in mind and make sure the software works for all of them.

We happily do this, but if you do write to us for technical support, please have the courtesy to be polite and realise that I am providing a **free service to you** in my spare time. Every week I receive many emails about Publish or Perish. Very rarely (maybe once a year), the email is a kind thank-you, expressing gratitude and encouragement and nothing more. A bit more frequently the email starts out with a brief thank-you before launching into a request for help.

95% of the questions asked are covered in the Publish or Perish FAQs or Publish or Perish manual; 99.9% of the questions are covered in the Publish or Perish Book, the Publish or Perish tutorial, or this guide. So usually, my responses are a brief referral to the relevant sections of these sources. But I **always** respond. Unfortunately, some of the emails I receive are of one of the following types:

- Cryptic emails such as: "It doesn't work" or "I have problems with Harzing" *[I even have to guess they are referring to Publish or Perish]*, "your programme has serious bugs" *[usually meaning that the user hasn't bothered the help resources and is searching incorrectly]*

- Angry emails: "We are all going on strike tomorrow because CNRS applies the Harzing index" *[I presume they meant Hirsch's h-index :-)]*

- Direct orders "Here's my CV, you should enter my publications in the Harzing database now! You are damaging my career because my publications are not in your system." A variant blames me for incorrect data without realising that PoP simply draws on data from Google Scholar or other data sources. *[I am sometimes tempted to reply: If you are foolish enough to think that I sit up there at night entering millions of academic publications in a database you really shouldn't be an academic.]*

- Offensive emails suggesting that I intentionally exclude publications from certain countries or languages because I discriminate against them. *[The simple reason that even comprehensive data sources such as Google Scholar don't cover every single publication is that not all publications are available online. And even if they are sometimes the publisher has not structured their website in a standard way, so Google Scholar cannot parse it.]*

- Stroppy email exchanges where the recipient [invariably male] keeps implying they know better how Google Scholar and PoP works than I do, even though they seem to have been using it for 10 minutes and I have been using it every day for 17 years :-). *[Sometimes I cannot help wondering: would they react the same way if my website picture had shown a guy in a suit?]*

So again, if you do need help using the software, feel free to write to me, but realise that I am taking time out of my busy day to help you. You can help me by providing enough details about the problem you are experiencing. Remember, I can't look into your computer or read your mind. Finally, when I do send you a response and it has helped you, a short thank-you would be appreciated. It is quite disconcerting – as well as demotivating – to not hear anything back to 80% of the technical support emails I send.

It costs money to keep software free

These days software and apps are often free. However, free software doesn't materialise out of thin air. *Someone* needs to create, maintain, and support it. That costs money. This might not an issue for commercial giants with deep pockets such as Google and Meta, but it is for individuals like me. Therefore, your contribution toward our costs of hosting, bandwidth, and software development is appreciated. If you find the Publish or Perish software useful, then this is your chance to say "thank you" to the developers. There are several ways in which you can support us:

1. If you have borrowed this guide from someone else, consider buying your own copy.
2. If you have already bought this guide, consider suggesting it to someone else. Maybe you even want to suggest to your library or Research Dean that they buy multiple copies?
3. Buy other books in my "Crafting your career in academia" series: *Publishing in academic journals, Writing successful promotion applications, Creating social media profiles,* and *Measuring and improving research impact.* They only cost £5.95 (Kindle) or £9.95 (pbk).
4. Suggest your (Research) Dean they buy a stack of these books to distribute to academics for free. They make perfect presents to accompany a push for academics to become more effective in any of these areas.
5. Honour us with a (small) donation. For details see: https://harzing.com/resources/publish-or-perish/donation.

In sum

This chapter discussed the development of Publish or Perish over the years. I hope you enjoyed this little peek into the history of a software product that will reaching its adulthood in 2024. I have enjoyed providing this service to the academic community.

I hope this guide has given you a good overview of the many things that you can use the Publish or Perish software for. If the software has helped you, I would love to hear from you at anne@harzing.com.

Conclusion

In this guide I have provided a detailed and comprehensive overview of how to get the best out of the Publish or Perish software. This guide was composed of four sections. The first section presented the PoP user interface (Chapter 1) and its Multi-searches centre (Chapter 2). The second section explained PoP's metrics (Chapter 3) and data sources (Chapter 4), including detailed analyses of the two most widely used data sources, Google Scholar (Chapter 5) and Google Scholar Profiles (Chapter 6). A third section showed you how to do basic author searches (Chapter 7), journal searches (Chapter 8), and topic searches (Chapter 9).

The fourth section provided detailed guidance for some of the more specialised tasks that you can use the software for: presenting your case for tenure/promotion (Chapter 10), evaluating other academics (Chapter 11), doing a literature review (Chapter 12), deciding where to submit your paper (Chapter 13), and doing bibliometric research (Chapter 14). The final chapter of the book (Chapter 15) reviewed how usage of Publish or Perish has developed over the years.

Over the last 17 years, Publish or Perish has evolved from a h-index calculator interfacing with Google Scholar only, to a Swiss army knife providing you with support for a very wide range of scenarios you will encounter in your academic career. It now interfaces with no less than eight data sources and is used by a very wide variety of users all over the world.

I hope this guide has helped you to improve your own usage of the software and has inspired you to use for a wider range of purposes. I also hope you enjoyed reading it and will be applying its content to good use. I would be delighted to hear about your usage of Publish or Perish for future editions of the book. Feel free to get in touch with me at anne@harzing.com.

www.ingramcontent.com/pod-product-compliance
Lightning Source LLC
Chambersburg PA
CBHW051434050726
47593CB00005B/1784